This is a true story. All names and places are real and did exist in New York City at the time of the telling (1980s and 90s). Any errors in documentation are accidental.

New York City Bum is presented as an odyssey, as well as a historical record, delineating the underground counterculture of urban street life, with emphasis on the crack culture, the homeless and their associations, including a few aberrant personalities.

This chronicle unfolds at a time when such taboo cultural symbiosis witnesses the decline of an era, and would be preserved by a writer of the age.

A New York Story

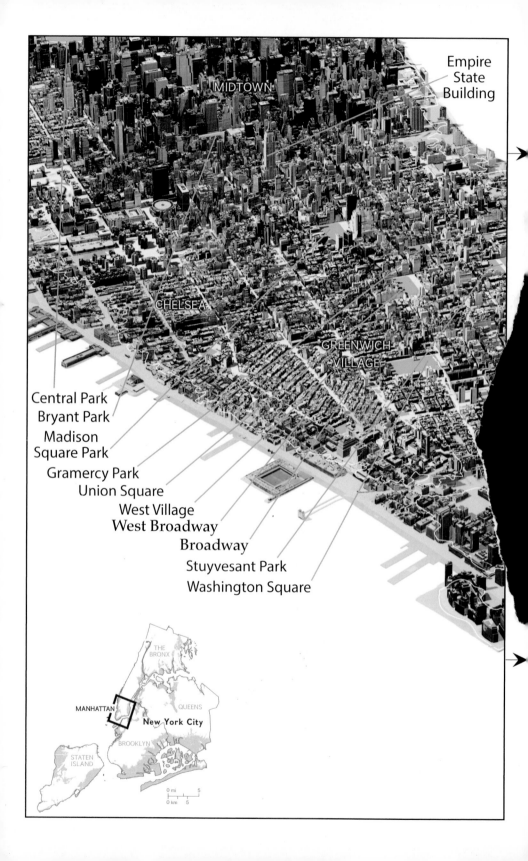

Empire
State
Building

MIDTOWN

CHELSEA

GREENWICH
VILLAGE

Central Park
Bryant Park
Madison
Square Park
Gramercy Park
Union Square
West Village
West Broadway
Broadway
Stuyvesant Park
Washington Square

THE
BRONX

QUEENS

MANHATTAN

New York City

BROOKLYN

STATEN
ISLAND

0 mi   5
0 km   5

Manhattan Locations

Stuyvesant Park
Lafayette St.
Little Italy
East Village
Tompkins Square
Delancey St.
14th Street
Houston St.
East River Park
Sara D. Roosevelt Park
Seward Park
Essex St. &
E. Broadway

ALPHABET CITY

SOHO

CHINATOWN

Allen St.
Second Ave.
Bowery
Canal St.

TRIBECA

City Hall

FINANCIAL
DISTRICT

E
N ✴ S
W SW

World
Financial
Center

World Trade Center

Battery   South Ferry

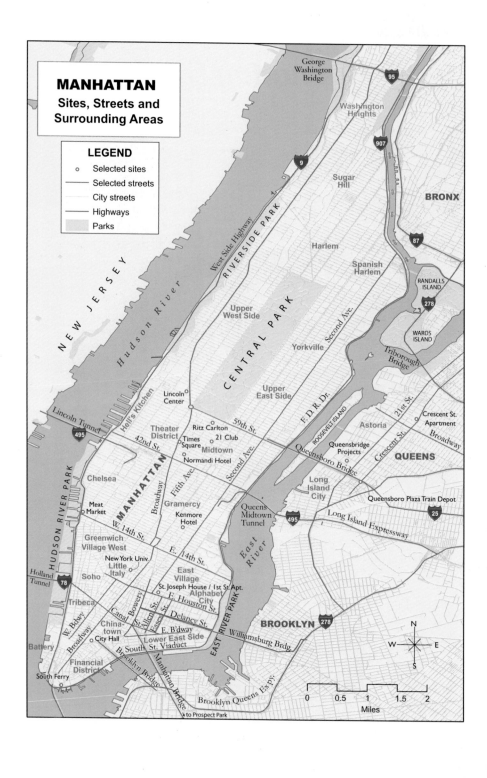

MANHATTAN
Sites, Streets and Surrounding Areas

LEGEND
- ○ Selected sites
- ── Selected streets
- ── City streets
- ── Highways
- ▨ Parks

George Washington Bridge

Washington Heights

BRONX

Sugar Hill

Harlem

Spanish Harlem

RANDALLS ISLAND

WARDS ISLAND

Upper West Side

CENTRAL PARK

Yorkville

Triborough Bridge

West Side Highway

RIVERSIDE PARK

Hudson River

NEW JERSEY

Lincoln Center

Upper East Side

F. D. R. Dr.

21st St.

Crescent St. Apartment

Broadway

Lincoln Tunnel

Hell's Kitchen

59th St.

Second Ave.

ROOSEVELT ISLAND

Astoria

Crescent St.

Theater District

Ritz Carlton

Times Square

21 Club

Midtown

42nd St.

Normandi Hotel

Queensboro Bridge

Queensbridge Projects

QUEENS

Chelsea

Broadway

Fifth Ave.

Second Ave.

Long Island City

Queensboro Plaza Train Depot

Meat Market

Gramercy

Kenmore Hotel

Queens Midtown Tunnel

Long Island Expressway

25

HUDSON RIVER PARK

W. 14th St.

Greenwich Village West

E. 14th St.

East River

New York Univ.

Little Italy

East Village

Holland Tunnel

Soho

St. Joseph House / 1st St. Apt.

Alphabet City

E. Houston St.

Tribeca

W. B'dway

Bowery

Delancy St.

Canal St.

Allen St.

Essex St.

China-town

Broadway

E. B'way

EAST RIVER PARK

Battery

City Hall

Lower East Side

South St. Viaduct

Williamsburg Brdg.

BROOKLYN

278

Financial District

South Ferry

Brooklyn Bridge

Manhattan Bridge

Brooklyn Queens Exp'y

to Prospect Park

MANHATTAN

0   0.5   1   1.5   2
Miles

N
W ✦ E
S

I have given up long ago, saw it as useless, I could not please others. I tried, failed. I tried again, failed, and a few times more and that was it. My lifetime as a member of the Establishment. I gave up pleasing them and thereby discovered, I believe, my true soul. Genius? Contemptible hack? At least I am my own.

Joyce Carol Oates, *The Assassins*, paraphrase

Also by David Boglioli

Canapés That Work

Wolf Pack

Detour

NEW YORK CITY BUM

DAVID BOGLIOLI

A MIDWAY BOOK

NEW YORK

New York City Bum
Copyright © 2017 by David Boglioli

Midway Books
36 East First Street
New York, NY 10003
Phone: 800 773-7782
Blog: davidboglioli.wordpress.com
To contact the author: David.Boglioli@yahoo.com

Cover and book design by the author
Illustrations for Parts One, Two, and Four also by the author.
Part One inspired by Alden Spillman and William Shepard;
Part Three art direction by the author, drawn by Nancie McLean;
Inhabited initials by the author;
Author portrait by Tony Gorman, 1989
Three-dimensional map of Manhattan reproduced with permission, Ryan, Morris/National Geographic Creative.
Cartographic direction by the author, map preparation by Rixanne Wehren

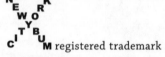 registered trademark

Even this do-it-yourself book had help behind the scenes.
The author thanks Cynthia Frank at Cypress House

Publisher's Cataloging-in-Publication Data

Names: Boglioli, David, author.

Title: New York City Bum / David Boglioli.

Description: First edition. | New York : Midway Books, [2017]

Identifiers: ISBN: 978-0-9860476-0-2 | LCCN: 2016913504

Subjects: LCSH: Boglioli, David. | Homeless persons--New York (State)--New York--Biography. | Homeless persons--Drug use--New York (State)--New York--Personal narratives. | Homeless persons--New York (State)--New York--Social aspects. | Criminals--New York (State)--New York--Biography. | Tramps--New York (State)--New York--Biography. | New York (N.Y.)-- Biography. | Autonomy (Psychology)--Case studies. | LCGFT: Autobiographies. | BISAC: BIOGRAPHY & AUTOBIOGRAPHY / Criminals & Outlaws. | SOCIAL SCIENCE / Poverty & Homelessness. | HISTORY / Social History.

Classification: LCC: HV4506.N6 B64 2017 | DDC: 305.5/6920927471--dc23

Printed in the United States of America
First edition

FOR
WOOLLY AND POLLY

bum 1: LOAF

     2: to spend time unemployed and often wandering:
to obtain by asking or begging: CADGE

bum 1: one who sponges off others and avoids work

     2: VAGRANT, TRAMP

on the bum: with no settled residence or means of support

vagrant: 1: a person who has no job and wanders from place
to place

     2: following no fixed course: RANDOM, CAPRICIOUS

tramp: 1: a foot traveler

     2: a begging or thieving vagrant

     3: an immoral woman: esp: PROSTITUTE

*The
Merriam-Webster
Dictionary*

PART ONE

he amazing thing about New York City is that you can get lost in it, in the space of a city block you can disappear. It's simply the number of people crammed into that small space, ten million[1] on any given day. And there is the contributing factor, the survival instinct of native New Yorkers to mind their own business. It's not so much they don't notice things as that things go in one eye and out the other. I have been hit while crossing the street and nearly run over by a fire truck that had its siren screaming and horn blaring merely because I was immune to, or chose to ignore such mundane sounds. Likewise is the case when stickups, muggings and robberies occur that the savvy New Yorker turns away. Self-preservation is the issue wherein to try to help is to become involved which often as not makes the Samaritan a victim. I have been accused of robbery when I turned in a found purse to the front desk of a hotel. I have had to plead guilty to assault when the person who assaulted me turned around and said I started it and produced a paid witness to corroborate his charge. Take it from a native New Yorker, it doesn't pay to get involved.

There are, however, those certain New Yorkers who see and hear all, ones who must do so for their very survival. Resourceful opportunists, living on the edge, whose interest in their surroundings span from idle curiosity to a matter of putting food in their bellies or starving. Ones whose very existence depends on their ability to note and interpret the sounds, smells, the ever so gradual or swift shifts of the mood swings of the city. For those ignoble souls are the bums of the city, outcasts who by circumstance or choice are a formidable and integral part of the city's millions, living on the fringe of decent society.

Vagrants, hobos and tramps have now, by way of city style, become the homeless; winos, drunks and dope fiends become substance

---

1 8.3 million registered residents, .5+ million undocumented immigrants, .5+ million homeless, 608,000 commuters

abusers with a disease; masochistic prostitutes and heterodox practitioners become oppressed minorities—all victims of their own game. Industry has been developed to accommodate this vast segment of society and it is of this industry and slice of society that I speak.

I never aspired to be a bum. In all my affluent upbringing, bums were viewed to be worthless, shiftless scum who wouldn't help themselves by working or caring about nutrition, hygiene, love and compassion, who would relinquish all pretex at decency. I never, in my youth, could comprehend one who did not have faith and hope in tomorrow. Leave it to time and the city to hammer it into my head.

When I was a kid, Bowery bum meant staggering or passed out alcoholic, dressed in rags, dirty, smelly, face a stubble of whiskers, black-eyed, cracked lipped, with feet and ankles red and swollen from dropsy. They were all over the Bowery[1] sidewalks, could barely stand up, panhandling spare change or cigarettes. My earliest recollections are of Sunday mornings, riding with my parents in the big De Soto, going to Orchard Street and its carnival atmosphere to buy me a suede or leather jacket for school; and the bums brazenly or blindly approaching my mom for a handout and Daddy chasing them off with an imprecation. I would look at those woesome creatures in uncomprehending fascination and, had I a crystal ball, would still not believe that in twenty-five short years I too would be a Bowery bum, riven with crack and the slum as if I were born to it.

---

1 New York City's skid row

I was brought up sheltered from life's sub-rosa taboos which I knew were out there and I wanted in on. Things happening around me of which I was denied and things within me which I feared to acknowledge or express. This may be a child's universal lot but how was I, as a child, to know that? I cannot blame those responsible for nurturing me during my formative years that I sought those interdictive answers and expressions in forbidden and sinister schoolrooms, sometimes of my own invention. My earliest discoveries and analogies could be quite crude. I spit out tobacco, it comes out of my lips not smooth and neat but splattered. Splattered things in life going all out crazy than where you wanted them to.

When I was only around five or six years old, my dad gave me a birthday card covered with black and white line drawings of a crowd of people in overcoats and top hats with, in their midst, a naked child colored in flesh pink for contrast, with the caption, "You'd stand out in any crowd." Inside it said, "Happy Birthday to a nonconformist." All the adults in my family tittered and winked while I stood there, the straight man, perplexed and uncomprehending. And embarrassed. What was the big joke? What did they mean? It didn't take long, however, as the years unfolded, for the light to go on.

My life has been and remains a rugged terrain of not fitting in, even during episodes of conformity, being somehow tainted, drifting off somewhere on the periphery of mainstream society. And so, my story begins at one such point of departure when New York City's daily headlines screamed COP SHOT and a new epidemic held the city in its grip and crack and homeless were coined as buzzwords.

––––––––––

I started copping crack in 1985, shortly after its American intro-duction (basuco from Columbia), on Eighth Avenue at Forty-Sixth Street—a strip of cheap honky-tonk bars, grubby candy stores, rundown hotels, ethnic grocery souks, noisome pizzerias and catch-all delis—a dingy, gloomy neighborhood for all its commerce and tinny glitter, in the heart of New York City's Hell's Kitchen. For those first few summer months I was cold-copping (buying from strangers) on the street, ten dollar capsules (the only quantity sold in those early days), using prostitutes as a go-between until I became familiar with the street workers and developed my own connections. The crack trade at that time, in Hell's Kitchen, was controlled by Dominicans, the material was potent, the counts were healthy, and the street action, for me, under that early influence was in itself addictive—hot, fast, and heady. With crack an entire alternative universe opened for me, mutable, unencumbered by the mores and strictures of society, a savage blossoming of emotions and passions too long held in check. A door through which crack was the ticket to pass, a metamorphosis.

I had tried following a green path by which emotive and fiscal fulfillment were attainable, a spiritual and material freeway of modern Americanism, achievement, the dream realized. Yet, for me, thirty-five years later, I was unfulfilled, the dream found wanting, never reached that big payday, my hopes and aspira-tions proved hollow. My friends and family had turned on me, my profession only a whore. Filled with umbrage, I found myself suddenly paid and turned out, bewildered, disheartened. And crack was there waiting. The pandemic outbreak of crack, wait-ing like an augur to parse my unwonted, malleable future; crack, the magic bullet to solve my dilemma; crack, which rang through the country like a siren's song—anodyne for ills the flesh is heir to. With crack all my prurient dreams came to the fore. Into the red-hot embrace of desire and the subversive world of sex, celebrity and vice.

Crack began to break down, to abrogate the rules and guidelines by which I lived, my resistance to unwholesome temptations were eroded so that previously forbidden attractions were suddenly fair play. I was seeking to penetrate, to enjoin the meretricious world of the street yet was afraid of giving up the security of a weekly paycheck, a safe and comfortable home, for the ostracizing of an outcast, the degradation, addiction, disease and insanity that such a draconian lifestyle carried. I was to enter a place of no return, to recast my life, my outlook, as a tramp, a weirdo, because all drug aficionados are weirdoes. So, at the beginning, I was holding back, seeing myself but afraid to be seen, shocked at what I had become yet thrilled by the shock, my surrender, horrified yet powerless to stop the transformation, the proslytization, the feverish anathema of the street. Enfin, an odyssey was beginning to unfold.

To begin with, just going into the neighborhood of Hell's Kitchen was a dicey endeavor for one not used to that type of native heath, especially looking to cold-cop, you stand out like a sore thumb, open to every con man, trimmer and beat artist. And that was some of the allure, the buzz and tingle of the street, the danger, walking the gauntlet of city blocks alive with every scapegrace and odious malefactor, blacklegs, dealers, pimps, vamps, dips, buncos, fakirs and grifters of every stripe. What a thrill, what a difference from a sane, conventional lifestyle. Hell's Kitchen, where the rawness of scandal and vice were laid bare like porno in a display window. Prostitutes and transexuals crowd the sidewalks to offer themselves for sale, crack dealers rushing you to ask, "How many?" Every dinky candy store selling all the illegal paraphernalia you need, needles on sale right on the sidewalk. And the more dangerous and spooky the streets become the farther west you go,

Tenth, Eleventh, Twelfth Avenue. Deep in the asphalt jungle of illusion and sin where the stakes are your life. Desperate. Hype. Exciting. At night, slashings are as common as rats in a trashcan. Your senses are screwed as tight as an alley cat's. Heart rate up a few notches, pulse a beat or two faster. Those daily and nightly forays into the slums for vice were my earliest infatuation and come-on of the street. I was drawn like a moth to a flame, flying directly in to singe my wings, winking at death, my world that was soon going to have to be immolated.

I had created a prison for myself in the structured discipline of my life. My days and nights were filled with military-type precision, even down to my daily escape with drugs and alcohol. My only real fulfillment was through my distinguished flourishing at my job, my work. In that I strove inveterately as I needed to bolster my (imagined) inadequacy with plaudits, and it was occasionally enough to carry me through the remainder of the ordered routine of my daily existence. Alone in my lifeboat of swelled ego, floating on a hostile ocean of envy and greed, a merciless arena in which I functioned automatically on a warped if preordained plane of mental and physical dysphoria. My keen zeal was fed by my career in consummate, niggardly decrements. It was a stifling and hopeless paradigm, like an endless Escher staircase, from which I needed to break out. But break out into what? The ocean depths? Siberia? The moon? Society had me in its grip perforce surrounded by our culture. Yet beneath my very nose was a sub-culture, the flexuous netherworld of the street. Unpredictable. Delusive. Scary. The street was the gutter, the very bottom of the barrel, always a trek through new terrain where experience, caution, and instinct are one's only guide and where competition with those born to it was deadly. A long way from anyplace with places that might not even exist. Such was my challenge; my catharsis. My escape.

I had little time to feel sorry for myself, things were moving too swiftly for that. I wanted to hurry up and morph into whatever it was that I was becoming, an Argonaut, to cross my Rubicon; I felt it had been foretold and I averred that I could do it. I was shy to just let go yet, at the same time, kept forcing my own hand. It was crazy. That was actually my better judgment holding me back and my crack persona egging me onward. With crack I had merely dipped my foot in the fateful slough whose "unsounded depths, though perilous, was not without its charm; such as the Indian perhaps feels when he slips over the rapids in his canoe."[1] An exciting time, a sensuous time. A time of fruition and wealth in the jive of the street. I would bring prostitutes home with me, specimens lured into my lair for close inspection and study. They would either laugh at me or feel sorry for me. I was especially attracted to transexuals, weird exotic crazies who gave all for sex with their implants and hormones and surgery. Indelible freaks which is exactly what I, peradventure, was becoming, or wished to be. Avatars of my wildest dreams.

Apart from my profession, my home had been the seat of my life. My heart and soul were rooted deep in the fecund soil of salubrious domesticity. All of my resources were devoted towards creating a comfortable habitat for myself and, over time, I had achieved the epitome of Nirvana. I did all of the work myself. I

---

1 Charlotte Brontë, *Jane Eyre*

painted, papered, paneled, tiled. I enjoyed every prodigal meed that money could buy: copper cookware, cable TV, AC, quadraphonic sound, antique furnishings—heavy, plush and rich, Oriental rug, floppy leather couch, macrame wall hangings, satin bedsheets. I had six twenty gallon aquariums, from a peaceful tropical tank to aggressive African cichlids, and a fifty-five gallon terrarium with a quaternary of tiny green tree frogs living in a jungle, plus a pair of reformed alley cats, and a couple of diamondback terrapins (rescued from the cooking pot), with a spicy yellow señorita to share my lascivious proclivities. In the evening, with only the aquarium lights for illumination and a single candle burning, a slight waft of incense and soft peripheral music, it was possible to drift through a fifth dimension where the mundane concerns that tack onto space and time[1] are suspended; or to perceive ourselves submerged underwater with curious aquatic creatures surrounding us goggle-eyed.

I would cook for my cats nightly: chicken liver, calves liver, fillet of grey or lemon sole. They'd be on the kitchen counter meowing plagently, practically jumping into the pan. And fresh raw sole daily for my terrapins who would eagerly snap the tip of my finger if I was careless. The tree frogs ate crickets, which I raised, and the insects' nocturnal chirr was an added vehicle to transport us into the twilit sphere of Neverland.

Yet, somehow, the cohesive element that cemented all this together was bound up with my work. Once my job contentment and security began to fracture, my ambition and identity and sense of purpose began to falter and tremble, affecting the entire equilibrium and tenor of my life, its priorities and values. And, hence, did the screw turn.

---

1 C. Day Lewis, *Desire is a Witch*, some words and ideas

My professional as well as my private life had become jaundiced by crack, though I would transpose my conundrum into an extrusion whereby crack would become my liberation as well as a sort of Rosetta stone, allowing me to explore new horizons and find purpose if not contentment on the trail of a prospector. There was no terrible sense of loss, because there was none, only breaking free, only the present, for my life had devolved as a halting, perennial erosion which had brought me to this climactic, tangential impasse. I did suffer intermittent pangs of mild regret, after all, unable to ignore the abnegating, the forsaking and sundering of a lifestyle to which I'd devoted so much of my kinetic vigor. But crack was always there encouraging me, making me realize how useless it was to waste time in repining, in crying over spilt milk, for my life had become insipid, vapid, jejune. The day of reckoning was upon me and I had to gather myself in order to be ready, for this was the decisive struggle, the test of my will, to choose where my heart lay. Would I trust my soul to some perpetual quotidian stasis or did I have faith in my own courage and initiative, enough to freewheel and to pioneer my fortune, my fabric, my fate on some exigent quixotic venture, some unknown bourne, and expect to not only survive but to prosper. I doubt if I was cognizant of such clever sophistry or casuistry at the time, such noumenon, as drug addiction does not lend itself to rational deliberations. I believe I acted more on impulse and the stochastic influence of crack in all its stultifying affectation. But the workings of my mind in mulling over those Pyrrhic strategies transpired over a period of at least one year so the choice, the decision had been reached long before my departure, my rending from one world familiar into a strange and foreign land which, through my anomy, was to be my deliverance. A move from the rumble seat of my dreams into the reinsman's seat of determination, letting go to discover my destiny instead of trying to design my doom and doctor it.

———————

It seemed to me, in moments of pensive clarity, that we are a culture based on hypocrisy. Everybody has an angle. Religion, politics and science preach sentetious humanitarianism yet amass great wealth and power for themselves at the expense of the poor and defenseless. Nature and species of lower intellect are continually abused and eradicated in the name of progress. Even the average working stiff looks for every opportunity to get over, union sinecures continually demanding more for doing less.

Luridness, propaganda and repugnance in the media, education that teaches apocryphal history and ethical flummery, shysters that twist and exploit the law, industry that poisons and abuses the public, a mendacious government that compiles secret dossiers on its constituents, a justice system that is biased and corrupt; plutocratic/hegemonic egalitarianism—the modern American dream.

It's just a matter of knowing how to manipulate the system, heh heh, wink wink, while the affluent go along their merry way, each driving their own polluting automobile, wearing jewelry that was mined by slave labor, watching contrived newscasts that are geared towards catchpenny charlatanry, eating meat and dressing in leather and fur, complaining about the price of oil while their taxes pay for more sophisticated weapons and spy satellites, space exploration, and animal, genetic and mind control experiments. This great American civilization, so smart that they can't live without overbreeding, planned obsolescence and Imperialism (The White Man's Burden)[1]—we must civilize those poor heathens, bring Christianity to the infidels, and stuff women's lib and designer independence and Burger King down their throats—while the worthless junk piles up, sewers are flushed into the sea, radioac-

———————

1 Rudyard Kipling

tive waste produced and dumped, the atmosphere, the oceans, the rainforests being polluted and hacked down so that the few who can afford it can have it all now. And the clincher is that the duped mediocrity want to be exactly like the rich. A warmongering consumer nation purchasing our technology from abroad, selling out to foreign investors while handing out billions of dollars in foreign aid. As America celebrates the millennium, one needn't look at the falling stock and real estate prices to gauge our national well being, that index is reflected on the streets of our urban cities in the swelling homeless population that, through no machinations of their own, won't be ignored.

I don't purport to have the answers, but damn if I'm going to keep feeding into that bugbear. I'll smoke crack and drop out and take whatever lot comes my way. I am the quintessential anomaly who finally says, "Screw it," and vanishes into the void. I had given my best shot at one game, but there was another game in town and I was still going strong. I had to run away from it all, but where to go? Anywhere reasonable offered just more of the same gestalt. Plus, I'm a New Yorker to the bone, born and bred. My morale was high despite my labile crack-induced mood swings. The obvious option was looking me in the face, the essential terrain that ten million people navigate every day, though few notice the abstruse, recondite underground who dwell there. It seemed as though homelessness were a corollary of crack abuse, the Tweedledum and Tweedledee of the street, to wit, the gutters were literally crawling with crack addicts. The timing was right, the coast was clear. Hi-ho Silver, away!

And so the urban streets become the promised land, the home of the homeless in America[1] , a contemporary trace coterminous with the influx of immigrants who flocked to this country ("Mother

---

1 Peter Lawler, *Homeless and at Home in America: Evidence for the Dignity of the Human Soul in Our Time and Place*: paraphrase

of Exiles")[1] to avoid persecution and find freedom and follow their dreams. "Send these, the homeless, tempest-tost to me..."[2] Wagon's ho!

It's been one hundred twenty-three years since fifteen year old Annie Moore stepped onto Ellis Island, the first of over twelve million immigrants to register at that federal immigration station, the foundation of America—men, women, and children filled with dreams of a new life.[3] The America of 1892 was truly the land of opportunity where, for the most part, hard work resulted in earning a living for oneself; one hundred twenty-three short years since which have witnessed such consequential advancements in science and technology, the growth of the largest city in the world, where immigrants still flock with dreams of a new life—with dreams of a free ride.

The America of today is still the land of opportunity. However, Americans today do not have to work. Immigrants unable to even speak English sign up for welfare right off the boat (interpreters are waiting), tipping the welfare scales at 109,631,000, of which 610,042 are homeless. Today's America boasts not only the highest worldwide welfare rolls, but the largest prison system, the most illicit drugs, the most crack, and gay regulations that are some of the most relaxed in the world.

Welcome to America, sign up and party, where cocaine can be had on the street for twenty dollars per gram and civil unions can adopt orphans thereby boosting their welfare payments to more than $10,000 per month. And if that doesn't work out, collect

---

1,2 Emma Lazarus, *The New Colossus*
3 Christopher Winn, *I Never Knew That About New York*

alimony like legitimate divorcees of yore. Love, marriage, boy, girl, it's all for one and one for all in today's America.

The world of crack is a lonely life, solitary in many respects, where companionship is select because of the strained intensity the addiction carries. The crack society is hostile, unlike the psychedelic camaraderie of the (1960s) hippie era. The crack territory is a violent landscape full of acrimony, betrayal and deceit. It's impossible, in mixed company, to put your head back and enjoy euphoria, you must have one eye open at all times for the looming surprisal, for the knife in the back. With each conventicle of crackheads in action, the sessions take on all the reverence and mystique of a séance whereby spiritual communications are passed and interpreted with diagnostic callidity by all teched attendees whose radar, with each puff of the elixir, zero in and fine-tune the cerebral broadcasts, invoking their sympathetic sorcery. A weird scene. Pabulum for mind games. Yet, with nothing to lose, I found prostitutes to be the best companionship for hard drug usage. They were all hard addicts themselves and, being tired of sex, would usually make agreeable company for socializing. And they were crazy. Sick wackos one and all, hookers, and drag queens some of the craziest. Witch doctors to treat my malady.

Sunday morning, the sun is shining through a tristful, canescent haze peculiar to all urban sprawl, I ride the Ⓡ train from Astoria into the city, the subway cars are empty. I alone disembark at Forty-Seventh Street and Broadway (Duffy Square) and walk crosstown to Eighth Avenue, the streets and sidewalks are empty, the only sound carillon-like tintinnabulation of church bells through the early morning stillness, a few scattered taxis are the only traffic on the avenues. I'm dressed in casual clothes from Barney's, the only wardrobe I have, a yuppie out on a lark. I'm an easy mark for the area I enter, Hell's Kitchen, seemingly deserted but not deserted, never deserted, even early Sunday morning, for vice and desire do not take a day off, they never rest.

I find distaff life on the front steps of a soot-blackened tenement, a few of the building's tenants sitting outside with some neighbors, chatting, scanning the sidewalk, already looking for business. They welcome my approach. "We only smoke pot and drink beer. And smoke crack." A transexual pushes forward, "You want come upstairs? Look, feel (cupping her breasts), soff." Smiling. I'm tempted but that's not why I've come there. I have to supply a can of beer (blue laws notwithstanding in the ghetto). Cigarettes are passed around. One of the girls runs around the corner and comes back with a greasy dealer. "How many?" I walk a little away from the crowd with the Dominican and make my score. The doxy who ran for the dealer is watching expectantly. A ten dollar cap is too much to pay, I open one of the vials and take out a single rock. I hand it over and she smiles her thanks. It is enough. I turn and walk quickly away, heading back to my remand house and moribund existence.

It was Autumn when I began copping crack at the Normandi Hotel, my favorite season, when there is a clean clear bite to the air, brisk and refulgent, sidewalk traffic moves a little quicker and there's a bit of expectancy and determination that's far removed from its preceding summer torpor. Death in the life cycle, yet also behaving as though a rebirth were at hand, a springtime resurgence of awakening and purpose as if the approaching winter season held no mortal grip over its dissipative nature. For me, it was more than a symbolic death in my own life orbit, a birthing change of mores and values, a shedding of the sheath of restraint that had previously controlled me. A brighter more vibrant self emerging into the perverse nativity of the life cycle's death and dissolution quarters that would conversely climax under a sub-terranean, subsuming world of vice. And, to this day I am moved every Autumn by a phantom hand nudging me gently, heightening my senses, and reminding my memory of a time when every care was shrugged off and I was thirty-five years young and my legs bore me at a run and the taste of crack is in my nose and on my tongue and I am shaken to my roots by temptation once more.

My first winter with crack. Single digit temperatures and ven-turi winds. Blood pounding in my ears, I was feeling a thousand different things at once. Everyday. Taking off work. By then I was copping at the Normandi Hotel on Forty-Fifth Street between Sixth and Seventh Avenues, riding the train back and forth to the city. Snow whirled and flurried in a parody of my fragmented thoughts; stained and grimy buildings dusted with white mim-icked a blurry past frosted with fresh spellbinding possibility; frozen sidewalks of denuded reality back-swept in a skidding black camera-eye, an external ambiguity to supplement my own endogenous supply. Pressing pedestrians bent and brittle, shifting fiches severe and grimaced with cold. I the louche, invisible man moving through fuming, oily, exhaust-choked traffic, dodging like a crooked arrow, some demented worm, quick to my score, my destination, single-minded and implacable. Euphoric in my new freedom, shrugging off sanity and control in a kaleidoscope of chaos, throbbing with the pulse of the city, the beat of the street. Crazy. Smoking crack right on my job. Drinking. I was coming apart at the seams. Only insofar as I struggled with crack and the street could I lay claim to my place in things. Into the city from Astoria, my overcoat in tatters, the lining ripped out, long rents in the light corduroy all the way down past my knees. I looked like a ragpicker. An obvious maniac, a crazed, strung-out look to my face. I would wrap my coat around me tightly, then cross my arms to keep it closed. No buttons. Riding the train in a daze, the few passengers staring at me. Standing up to my self-abuse. Courageously criminal. The ichor of dissidence already flowing through my veins. I was developing a street sense that would serve me well in my upcoming homelessness.

One of my favorite things about the city was being able to vanish in it, to become completely invisible. This was meat-and-potatoes in regard to my crack usage, insofar as the paranoia concurrent with crack—the inability to disguise being under its influence—forced me to shank's mare double-quick through the accusing eyes of the crowded masses, thankful for the anonymity afforded by the city's bustling congestion and indifference of many New Yorkers.

The wintry early morning trade at the Normandi Hotel was nil. With a container of coffee I would stand in the tiny lobby for fifteen minutes while I thawed. The desk clerk, a kindly older man, would allow me to get some feeling back in my nose and fingers. I had no gloves. Then, I'd cop my ten caps of crack and use the squalid lavatory for a quick hit. That would bring a roaring heat rush that would carry me all the way home.

There was a crowded candy store that sold tobacco and magazines, on Forty-Seventh Street at Broadway, where I'd buy my crack accessories. Disposable lighters, glass stems, pipe screens, glass bowls and butane torches. Such contraband was kept out of sight, behind the counter, and the oleaginous Sikh would secretly bag my order before handing it over. This one more shady deal helped to enhance the overall illicit atmosphere of my lubricious and incorrigible act. The furtive looks, the concealed handover, the quick exit, they all added to that febrile, nebulous scene and in so doing provided my name, a self-worth, a distinction that at once gave me a right to be where I was, a poignant and caustic part of the city. The drug scene. Said candy store was conveniently situated directly across from the subway, the Forty-Seventh Street Ⓡ train from which I traversed between the city and Astoria and, after copping at the Normandi, before descending the stairs for home and my snowbound madness, I would stop and lean right against the stairway's retaining wall, on the sideline of hurried sidewalk traffic and, with my head back, stem to my lips, lighter flaming above, and a whole dime cap in the demo, I brazenly slam-dunked that humungous hit that all but knocked me over, swooning and dizzy I'd stagger, seeing triple, down the steps to the train platform. Now the people take notice, the same New Yorkers who a moment ago, above ground, paid no attention as they passed me by, are suddenly alert to all their surroundings, being subterranean and confined. Trapped. Waiting victims of the next ravaging lunatic who will run rampant swinging a hatchet, or spraying bullets from his handgun.

I am spotted and clocked for the maniac that I am, unable and unwilling to conceal the face of crack in all its gory glory, sometimes the hit still coming on and taking hold as I flow with it and my fellow commuters are mesmerized with witnessing this spectacle, while the train doors close and we are together, alone in a small space, as I unfurl and blossom before the astonished eyes of the city. Welcome to New York.

Some days I'd make it to work, late, skating on thin ice there, union or not. The boss hated me so much (everyone knew I was a crack fiend), but I always managed to slip through his claws. I would grab a morning taxi at rush hour, stopping at the Normandi Hotel along the way to cop. I'd obtain a printed meter receipt from the driver, to show the boss, and claim heavy traffic after I couldn't use the-train-was-late excuse anymore. Always late. Leaving on time when I was needed to stay overtime. Hitting the bottle. I had my own liquor supply. As head of a department, I dispensed spirits to my subordinates for cooking purposes. And requisitioned whatever I wanted from the liquor room (usque-baugh included). I kept a veritable stock of brandy and wine in my supply cabinet. Smoking crack in the locker room, in the walk-in freezers and refrigerators as though it were a bagatelle. It became a game with the staff to try and catch me in the act. Sometimes they succeeded. I would disappear and sleep for hours. Somehow, I managed to perform while I was there. Cut my hand good opening oysters, coked to the gills, had to go to the hospital.

I used to steal food. One evening, the owner of the hotel was having a private party and ordered a pound of the finest beluga caviar from Petrossian, the USSR's sole authorized purveyor. An hour before the party, the caviar took a powder from a specially locked refrigerator (someone having lifted the key from the executive chef's office), and it was sold to a waiter, for his wife, at a fraction of its value. The hotel administration was pulling their hair out trying to replace the caviar in time for the party. I was laughing my grass off. The audacity of the caper was the talk amongst the hotel staff for long after the fact. When I was fired from the hotel, a year hence, I left owing that same waiter (one of my shylocks) two hundred dollars, which he never collected. So, he finally paid for the caviar after all. My Parthian shot.

Whenever I entered the hotel laundry for linen, the ladies all kept one eye on me and the other eye on their handbags. I was the big joke in the hotel. Mamma Lucca. Employees took bets on when I'd be fired. It happened, finally, when I was drunk and lay hands on a Japanese girl in my department. Lucky to have gotten off without the police getting involved. Attended the formal hearing the next day drunk. Left my tools there for two weeks before going back to collect them, smashed on crack. What a scene. I was so far gone, I didn't even file for unemployment to which (as part of the settlement) I was entitled. Lived off severance pay until I got broke and then hit the street. Beginning of my homelessness.

I hated my job at the Ritz and all that it symbolized, its constraints and regimentation, its snobbishness. It's admirable I lasted as long as I did, holding on out of fear, habit, pure inertia. My salary. I would slink up to the pastry shop (to which I had a key) in the night and drink my fill of creme anglaise, made fresh daily by the gallon for the Floating Islands, often my sole nourishment for the day, contending with the resulting diarrhea which all that cream mixed with my daily consumption of alcohol would produce. The only solid food I managed was a matutinal bacon and egg sandwich if I was lucky enough to catch the breakfast chef before he clocked out for the day. I had long abandoned lingering after my shift to have the dinner line prepare a plate for me as if I were ordering off the menu in the dining room.

My inimical attitude towards society militated against my effectiveness in both my professional and personal relations. I had become the kitchen boogey man, a consummate crack fiend (having lost thirty-five pounds), and staffers regarded me as if I were an exotic and dangerous zoo animal. Similarly, my aversion to and renunciation of those nouveau gentrified yuppies was absolute and I couldn't abide their phony piety and cant in that charade of an occupation which I persited in pantomiming. Thus, my quick exits, both after or before my duties were fulfilled, replaced my prior extroverted indulgence in the workplace and became a spoliating affront to an organization which had come to rely on me and to which I'd contracted and now reneged.

I would serenade the laundresses when I worked alone into the night in my subterranean production suite that I shared with the butchery, opposite the laundry, flying on crack, delivering "Rough and Ready Man" in a most soulful, threnodic dirge. Those wise washerwomen must have been cracking up, I literally was. Occasionally, the executive chef (the most recent hire in a long line of succession) would put in a vesperal appearance and scrutinize me as I performed some highly specialized feat—like heating naturally colored aspic and isinglass in a water bath to precipitate the air bubbles to the surface, or laminating melted tallow onto a ramose tree limb with a pastry brush, or creating any number of fustian phenomena in food decoration or canapés for which I was esteemed—studying my technique, jealous and astounded that I could function thus while so obviously blasted, as I smugly sniggered to myself, conceited in the fact that I was light years ahead of that guy in garde-manger and he was too proud to query me and maybe learn something. But they were all quick to collect accolades for my work while grudging in their attribution of my facility. What a bunch of emulous, denigrating tinhorns which I was glad to soon leave behind me.

But everything comes and goes in its own time and I think I enjoyed squeezing every last drop of experience out of a way of life, however la di da, that I knew intuitively would never come my way again. It was a time, rather than a place, of adventure and marvelous daring, and of revelry, building within me, moving in a frenzy as though bidden by Bacchus, blasphemed by the burning bush, and a torrent of attitude that was uncompromising, veracious as well as voracious in all its conjured cunning, my novel and venerated ritual of glorious triumphant sorrow.

I was denouncing and leaving behind a life that I'd grown into and revered for dire, execrable horizons. I had reached a crossroads, a point of departure, or more accurately a point of no return. I'd lost heart for the continual battle of my profession, having reached the pinnacle and fallen, my vocation having sufflated into a cancerous thing, gnawing away at my inner Hygeia, my cathexis, forcing me to take stock and, in the end, alter the course of my dual nature. My social life was a shambles. The material world had lost its charm. It was a sad, dolorous state of affairs and crack had me in its vise-like grip, an octopus pulling me downward into the murky, crepuscular depths of its protean, concupiscent embrace, deep into the pernicious, flinty currents of Styx, boiling up to climax, promising Valhalla, though I knew the cauldron would one day, eventually, self-destruct.

That first year with crack was such a melancholy time—I was more alone than ever, stepping away from a world, a walk of life that I had known and was part of, to the wandering blindly in a limbo-land with which I was unfamiliar, passing through once wont and friendly byways that were suddenly foreign and strange. Venturing into new and extraneous corners of the city in a kind of equivocal cognitive dissonance, lonely and lost, surrendering my identity to that of an estranger, vertiginous and weltering, away and away from all that surrounded me. That period stands out most poignantly because it was a liminal stage in my sojourn, highly emotional and I felt its impact keenly. An all pervading sense of kithlessness, forlorn and at sea, as I drifted towards the greatest adventure of my life.

There was only the one avenue open to me, one course to choose if I would indeed follow my heart, and that adventitious pathway was a career as a bum, the situs of the street whence I would extemporize my faculty and reman myself. I didn't feel suicidal, I was ever optimistic in my elan, but I held no illusions as to the nature of my endeavor. This was serious, desperate business and no mistake, though I was unblenched at the challenge. Did I think the street held answers that I couldn't find from any other walk of life? Not really. But it was what I was doing for now.

Of course I always had my art; that is what drove me, tortured me. I was then but changing mediums, abandoning my career and allowing my passions to run rampant—dissolving—and who knew what Promethean magic might emerge? Only that, for certain, the creative force which dwelled within me would flocculate and take shape—I had no fear. For all my frustration and pain I accepted as inescapable. I would be brave.

On the street, dissevered and bereft in my banishment, amidst all the misery and gloom there burgeoned a joy and a happiness that I had heretofore pursued but was not to be found, and for which I would endure long tumultuous hardships before I tripped over it. For all that it were some durable mystery, "happiness is to be dissolved into something complete and great."[1] Thus, as I became absorbed in the city, blended with the rhythm of the street at its most basic, gut level, I became whole and integrated and infused with a indefatigable optimism. And able to love. Moreover, happiness became an internal perspective to be carried around all over the city—my philosopher's stone.

I remember confiding to a bouncer at the Normandi Hotel one evening that I was losing my apartment due to nonpayment of rent and he advised me to find a cheaper pad, a furnished room. Hell, I was living in a studio already and knew I'd never find a cheaper dark corner. Fact was, I couldn't afford *any* rent as long as I kept on with the cacodemon, the cacoëthes of crack.

---

1 Willa Cather, *My Antonia*

And as long as I had a hidey-hole I'd keep right on using. Hitting the street wasn't simply a means of sobering up, it was an alternative to, a hegira from the deeper problem of which crack was merely a symptom. I had to do something with my life to shock it back into some meaningful orbit and the street was my ignis fatuus.

Life had become too boring, too easy; perhaps all I needed was a little hardship on which my life depended—a bold new challenge. An emprise both profligate and arduous. For as my life abated, became palsied and I lapsed restive and dissipated, it was easy to fool myself, crack has that way about it, insidious and conniving in its anfractuous effect. And though I would survive the street for ten years and live to tell the tale, it wouldn't be easy. Not by a long shot. My aberrant, manumitting gris-gris.

The current executive chef at that time at the Ritz Carlton Hotel, the fourth in two years, despised me with a passion and had suspended me for three days, prior to Thanksgiving, for taking excessive days off from work. I was to be reinstated on Thanksgiving Day, there being a full complement of reservations for the Jockey Club, and was to report to the hotel early in the morning, only to have overslept in my drunken stupor and missed my scheduled reveille by five hours. Upon phoning up the job well after lunch was underway, my choleric tormentor was having paroxysms and reviled me with the threat of knocking me out for a couple more days.

I remember going to the Sanford coffee shop, near my home in Astoria, later that day, all but flat broke, to beg some food, managing to cadge no more than a cup of coffee, as I sat at the counter forlorn and wondering what was to become of me and watched the other patrons scoff a full turkey dinner with all the trimmings. By that phase in my demise, I was selling off my furniture, jumping the subway turnstiles, spending every last nickel on crack.

My return to work lasted only until Christmas by which time my adversary had contrived to dissemble my job, parcelling out my responsibilities to minor subordinates, thereby eliminating my position and terminating my employment. As I was passing by the security booth in my departure that fateful day, I was called in and informed of my new status, or ex-status as it were. The executive chef and his sycophants were standing by for this coup de grace, grinning and sneering as they witnessed my perdition at last. But the game was far from over. I went straight to the Hotel and Restaurant Workers Union headquarters where I enlisted the aid of the hotel's delegate and he forthwith notified the hotel's Personnel Director that it was in violation of their contract to abolish my position as none other than a certified Garde-Manger could perform the tasks which ... etcetera, etcetera. Ha ha ha. But the biggest yuck came when my ribald Cro-Magnon commander himself was sacked a few days later. Oh, he who laughs last laughs hardest.

An unexpected fillip came a few months after the fact when, as I was approaching the employee entrance of the hotel, I spotted the fallen cretin loitering on the sidewalk, visiting with some of his friends, and our eyes collided and I felt his malvolence, though I never broke stride, while I casually entered the portal of my employ, a premises no longer open to that deflated prophylactic. Sorry Charlie, only the best tuna for the Ritz.

I recall with crystal clarity the marvelous day I learned the wonderful news of the latest kitchen general to bite the dust at the famed Ritz Carlton Hotel, 50 Central Park South, New York City. I had gone to civil court in Queensborough county, following that ominous day of my discharge, to contest my eviction from my Astoria apartment. An eleventh hour gambit, I had borrowed one thousand dollars from my dear old dad (bless his soul) in the hopes of requiting my rent arrears and salvaging my residence. And so I had walked from Astoria to Kew Gardens, a ten-mile trek along Queens Boulevard, in the lashing December wind biting me to the bone, suffering all the privations of an arctic expedition explorer—cold, hunger, thirst, windburn, dehydration, fatigue—a kind of hell. No hat or gloves nor even buttons on my overcoat, tramping along gamely, the bottoms of my frost-numbed feet burning from the friction of the rucked up sidewalk through holes in the soles of my brown shoes and corroded socks. I stopped again and again to fit folded pieces of scavenged paper, then cardboard into the shoes, only to have those wear through in another mile, vowing to jump the Ⓕ train at Union Turnpike on the way back and risk the consequences. I was still waiting for the final decision from the Ritz concerning the propitious revival of my job and was to phone in that afternoon to learn if I had been restored to the roster; my desire to spite my enemy competing with my lust for recovering my income which translated into my crack supply, never factoring in the rent which I was on my way to attempt to rectify.

I was expending my energy exponentially in a variety of conflicting directions yet was unfazed, such was my hubris, vitality and sangfroid, my moxie, especially when under pressure; that my sole motivation was to persevere, to battle onward, with no cogitation of defeat, despite my professional laches. I was pushing forty yet felt like a teenager, in the prime of life and peak physical and mental prowess. My maxim was simple if base: I would not surrender; "Come and get me ya bastids, I'll take as many sonsabitches with me as I can."

After what seemed like an entire morning of bushwacking my way through the suburban fetches of no-man's-land, that which belongs entirely to the road, I finally arrived at the opressive halls of justice which determine the fate and future of all who dare to challenge the almighty system (and get caught). In the landlord/ tenant theater, amidst the officious rigamarole of plaintiffs, defendants, witnesses, lawyers, clerks, and police, I located the attorneys (two, no less) who represented my building's owners. During a brief caucus in which I assured them that I had in my possession all of the four months' back rent in its entirety, and inquired if I would be permitted to continue to hold the lease for the premises, they (a little too quickly) avouched that once I settled the arrears, then we could renew the current lease (wink wink to each other) while I gaped dolefully up at them. As I hung back to await our docket to be called, I overheard the two shysters barracking between them that I had less than a dog's chance once they collected their money and, "We'll get rid of that guy"—I listened no more as I made a mad dash for the door and, before exiting the building, turned to look one look at the two who were casting about for me, side by side, swiveling their heads back and forth, for all the world like a pair of vaudevillian burlesquers. Well, too little too late for those legal eagles. At least, then, I had some lolly in my poke.

I pegged pell-mell across Queens Boulevard to a shoddy pay phone whose receiver was sticky with the grime of desperation from countless court victims, anxious to learn my dubitable destiny on the next spin of the wheel, and called the Ritz. Bingo. I not only had my old position back but my nemesis had gotten the boot as icing on the cake. They told me I'd have to work the GM station on New Year's Eve though, to which I chirruped, "I'll play the whole piano single handed," I was so elated. Yet, New Year's Eve found me on duty guzzling beer like a fish and running across to Central Park to smoke joints... Ah, well, you can't change a leopard's spots. Twelve-month that spring I would be homeless on the streets of New York City.

My inroads smoking crack, both in public and private, were filled with insanity. I'd leave the Ritz with a Friday crowd of employees at lunchtime, en route to cash our hebdomadal paychecks at a check cash on Forty-Fifth Street, a fifteen block walk each way from Central Park South, and I'd shoot two long blocks over to the Normandi Hotel to score. Ducking into doorways on the way back to work, slam dunking whole dime caps at a time, hiding behind a column in front of the New York Hilton on Avenue of the Americas, beaming up; I'd get so blasted that I'd lose my sense of direction, cutting down blind alleys and through parking lots, careening and caroming around the city in a daze.

One day after work, rushing on crack, I had a great idea for a tallow pièce montée and went into *Woolworth's* and bought a chunk of *Styrofoam*, glue, skewers, and whatnot, and by the time I reached home I'd forgotten what it was that I'd dreamed up. I'd often purchase items impulsively on the street for some project and they'd lie ignored and forgotten at home as I spaced out with the crack. I would go into a toilet stall in some busy whiskey bar and get so carried away smoking crack that the patrons, and occasionally the bartender, would be banging on the door to roust me out. Many places of business were wise to addicts using the facilities to get high and, as my appearance deteriorated, it became more and more difficult to evade alert personnel. I was once followed into and bounced from a lavatory in T.G.I. Fridays by a trio of gung ho middle managers who'd clocked me as soon as I entered the premises. I'd seek and find abandoned buildings, construction sites, alleyways, porticos, tunnels in which to beam up. And often would contend with the irresistible urge to destroy something or to search around uncontrollably whilst in the grip of an overwhelming rush, as if possessed by some arcane afreet. Everything was possible with crack and nothing ever came of it except the irrepressible urge to have another blast.

For a year before hitting the street I had already become a bum, drifting through crowds on sidewalks and subways as removed and apart as a ghost. I could view myself and my future from above, watching me go through the motions of blending into the crowd, the masses, being reshaped like a drifting cloud, as my mind was screaming with revolt. It was a period that I knew could not last, the rigors and principles which had one time sanctioned my resolve could no longer sustain me, that containment of my repressed self was nigh to bursting and the urgent need to unleash my freedom was gathering itself. No tie held me to human society; I had no relative to importune save for the heartless, man-made city—slaughterer of souls.

The Normandi was a welfare hotel-cum-crack house, gone to seed, a haven for street mavens and cognoscente of low-level rackets. Like similar infestations that would intimidate me later on, the Normandi held me cowed and awed by its permanence, its concentration of vice, its visibility. This was no dark alley doorway. The whores and pimps outside were its flashing lights, the parade of crack trade its billing. There was a little vestibule between the street door and that of the lobby, a sally port, whose inner door was manned by a seasoned bouncer. At night, the Normandi's front desk was staffed by a pair of heavy bruisers, Animal and Streetfighter. If too much time passed without any trouble, those two would start some. The Normandi did a brisk trade at night, selling up to three thousand dime capsules per. The Afro-American owner, Jimmy, carried a .45 calber revolver whose rounds were topped off with a drop of nitroglycerin. One of those slugs would blow a hole right through a bulletproof vest and the local cops knew it. Jimmy's Normandi was the only crack hotel in the area not to get popped.

Life at the Normandi was my maiden (and thus the most touching) entry into a foreign culture that (contrary to my past) was, curiously, both fraternal and familiar. I entered a den of career thieves, hustlers and hoodwinks and was quickly, however reservedly, admitted. My approach, my heart in hand, my entire life force was so pure, so open, so desperate, there was little doubt of my authenticity, my intentions. When I stopped in Ritchie and Ray Ray's room for my daily beam up, I entered flush with a yard's worth of crack, a bottle of sweet wine (Manischewitz Cream Red Concord) that I handed around, immediately paid the house (one dime cap), and used the house pipe whose residue was a further contribution to my hosts. I was a gentleman, I was respectful, I was considerate. I was there to get high and nothing else was hidden on my agenda. I was always generous. And, I was protected by my hosts from encroaching predators. If some jungle buzzard asked me for a hit, Ray Ray interceded with, "Don't squeeze the customer." It was Ritchie who enlightened me of the appellation "Scotty" as an irony for the taxon of crack. "As long as you've got Scotty, you've always got a friend," Ritchie allegorized. I bandied friend with crutch in my thoughts. Though, for all its enslaving manifestation, the appeal and radiant charm of crack could not be gainsaid. For the most part, I was usually the only white-bread in that wholly black crowd. Ritchie's was a harbor for ferine street sharks who all smoked crack. Almost no one knew that I worked a straight job. I was a mystery man, coming and going like an apparition.

I met many real and interesting people in Ritchie's room, such as one Mercedes (ex-stripper). I recall how Mercedes was so excited, so proud that she was being trained for assistant manager in a shoe store where she was employed. Feeling that this was the big break for her; she had an opportunity to better herself, and get out of the sickening skin trade. She was a very cute eighteen-year old, the whole world opening up for her. So sincere. Ready and

31

willing to sell out for this one chance, to work herself to death, with not a penny increase in her salary. The ego blast of being entrusted with such grave responsibility, the keys to the store, combination to the safe. Anxious to prove herself, to burn out for nothing more than a pat on the head. I knew the sad reality of having blazed the same trail and gone down in an honorable hero-death, in the same war, being fought endlessly since the coming of the white man. I felt such compassion, such empathy for this beautiful creature who was being sent forth to the front line, a pawn being played by her higher powers. Glad for her chance to escape the inhuman skin trade, for the all too human power trade of capitalism.

One time, in Ritchie and Ray Ray's room, serried about with every type of predatory scoundrel in the ranks, all black, as I was genially conversing with Mercedes, a facile nymph who had worked the peep shows on Forty-Second Street, one slashed and surly tough valiantly asked me, "What's your hustle, Pig?" to which I replied glibly, "I work a straight job." Half the room turned to stare at me as though I were Saint Elmo's Fire. Mercedes gave a sprightful simper and batted her eyelashes. I couldn't have provided a more incongruous occupation if I had said I was a cop. The seeming backhand tag was of my own choosing.

In junior high school, my nickname was Pig because I was fat. In high school, I used Pig as a cognomen for my clandestine marijuana connection when James Bond was in vogue. By the time I was copping crack at the Normandi Hotel, and wallowing in my own squalor, Pig seemed a natural sobriquet to adapt. "All the qualities that made up the animal to which I was akin now struggled with human personality and point of view. What, after all, did I owe society? What had they done for me? Even in the old days, as one of them, I'd felt apart, different, an odd element that felt itself somehow superior to, alien to the normal people around me. They hadn't done much for me, only a lot to me. In turn, I had used them, as one would use a tool in completing a task. I had been among them, but not of them, always, for as long as I could remember. They had made me an animal; very well. I would be one. A very smart pig to be sure, but a pig just the same. The competing elements inside my mind stopped their warfare. A pig I was and would always be, and it was alright."[1] I so much wanted to belong yet, at the same time, was afraid of those people and the life they represented. But I was already caught in the undertow and was being pulled out to sea with the ebb tide.

A dam of emotions inside me broke. All my pent up hopes and dreams poured out, engulfing my senses, flooding my judgment with awareness. I was losing the battle of control over my ardor—I didn't care. I had no pride left when it came to crack; it was zero hour and overdue to acknowledge my carnal impulses and allow my lustful fires to blaze with passion. I would deny myself no longer. It was time and past time to experience all the well of libidinous fervor and frenzy that raged within me; to surrender my fearless heart to crack and its satyric polymorphous perversity.

There was a confidence, a fullness, a puissance at that time, my entire life caught up in a supreme and significant act. Estranged from a society that had ruled me through conditioning, apart from the fear and guilt and shame of not measuring up, beyond the enmity and domination of the ruling class who make our laws and decide the fate of the beset populace, while all the while manipulating those laws themselves and fleering at the pretzel-plight of the victimized masses who run around in a maze of their own unsuspecting faith while paying tribute to the muckety-mucks who govern them, impost and tax them, own them. I wanted out, away from all that oppressive civic control, the censorship and propaganda, the cupidity and rat race of being better than the Joneses, away from the haunting need to stand out while

---

1 Jack L. Chalker, *Quest for the Well of Souls*

all the while conforming, of being a member of the hoi polloi, the herd. What to do? Where to go? To escape society's rigid constraints, the pressure and influence of civilization's mores, myths and canons, the buzzwords, the fashions, the styles of the day; the maddening headlong plunge into blind obedience, of a convention over whose control we have no say, no choice. I was a round peg in a square hole.

I would follow my heart, a victim of my own hopeless hope, faithless faith, where something real was waiting deep down within me. With every step I paused—I could turn around and go back at any point, it wasn't too late. But there was nowhere left to go back to, no answers awaited me in the past. I was stranded, could only move forward into the unknown, into the mystery and darkness of abandon and privation to grapple with the amorphous firmament that is the street, a deracination of all I had heretofore known, the antipodes of my previous existence. I was now on a journey in which all events were perilous, where no acts were meaningless; a very abatis of treacheries to harpoon the unwary. I was on a course where the slightest undertaking might alter fate and shift the balance of power and of doom, for I was going towards a place where light and darkness meet and those who so travel make no choice carelessly, to their peril. Thus was my quest, street life, the compass for my destiny, the jumping-off point, an explorer in the guise of a bum, a minnow, albeit defenseless, too quick to be caught. In relationship to my previous life, the street was at once my expiatory theater as well as a Renaissance that would shape my future life. Though a very worrisome prospect, an enlivening time, a shock to knock me to my senses, an awakening, a challenge, yet one that would be extremely taxing to my body, my spirit, my soul. New York City, the gutters, the shadows, the alleys, the tunnels, the border zone: the edge.

———————

It was a short hop from Hell's Kitchen to the Normandi Hotel, west side to midtown. The idea of a permanent building, as opposed to the street, appealed to me. The Normandi product was first rate. And there was a resident cabal that was magnetic. I was dying to hook up with just such an in-group. Prior to the Normandi, I had been scoring and running home to smoke alone, breaking down my previous identity, my calyx, and emerging as a chrysalis, anxious to bloom with my brethren. And so, providentially, I fell in with the hackneyed crowd at the Normandi Hotel and developed a persona that would serve me well in my forthcoming street life as a full-fledged bum, a rebel existence of corruption and vice, and also of purity and truth. A whirlwind of confusion and determination, sacrifice and redemption, retribution and resurrection. Gloria in Excelsis.

I had assorted crack connections (which I maintained for a year) in between Hell's Kitchen and during my association with the Normandi Hotel. The Strand Hotel on Forty-Eighth Street at Broadway where one phoned up to the crack dispensary from the lobby and the dealer brought down your order. Next, a pair of Hispanic hombres who loitered on Forty-Seventh Street between Sixth and Seventh Avenues (Jewelry Row)—"I am here lay" (late)—sipping from their half-pint of whiskey. And a lone Hispanic who roved about Forty-Sixth Street between Sixth and Seventh Avenues like a wraith—"If I not be here, You beeper me." Both Hispanic connections were excellent—reliable, ace product, healthy counts.

The mid-Forties between Avenue of the Americas and where Broadway crosses Seventh Avenue on the diagonal is a busy, active business area—the diamond district—with (at the time) new skyscrapers being erected on almost every block. A madhouse of knotted pedestrian traffic, construction confusion and snarled vehicular logjams, those crack dealers were easily rendered invisible in that impelling deluge of earthlings. How I came to make the acquaintance of so many crack sources in so short a span of time was invariably through prostitutes. Beautiful slutty whores who'll do anything for thirty pieces of silver. Who, like all transgressors, would do anything underhanded just for the sake of it. My crack life mentors. My left-hand companions. Infallible in their devilry.

The Normandi Hotel was a privy as well as intrinsic entryway into the maze of the street, a stepping-stone for a tyro such as myself, a convert who would transpose into a mendicant under the pious tutelage of the grand viziers and scions of the underworld. For seasoned veterans love rookies to take under their wings, to teach and guide, to show the ropes, to be revered by. And to use.

Withal this was genuine, actual, hard-boiled noir, the sensation and seduction of pulp magazines come to real life, sinister, sleazy and sublime. To what does one owe such concupiscence towards those tawdry stimuli and pleasures as would consume one's soul, like so much fuel, for its ephemeral, fugitive blaze. But love and lust and desire know no boundaries so mundane as rational constraints or guidelines or conscience, do not conform to reason. Thus did I enter the netherworld of the street, a living penny dreadful, where all of my fantasies and horrors beckoned, like a Pied Piper, and I, the willful child, blithely followed.

The action going on inside the Normandi Hotel frightened me. The first time I snagged a moll outside there, to join me getting high, she suggested renting a room at the Normandi. She had just gone in to cop for us, I wasn't even known then at the desk. Waiting outside on the sidewalk, it never occurred to me in those naif days that the mab might run with the money or the drugs, as they sometimes do. I was so trusting, so needy, so willing that many of the dolls (and guys) treated me fairly and gently, and those were sensuous moments, intervals of compassion and trust in an otherwise cold and suspicious world. So, my date comes out with the crack as I was peering in through the open doorway of the Normandi at the bedlam and ruckus within. Coaxingly she warbled, "I can get a glass bowl and a torch thrown in if we go in there for a room." At that moment, a crazed mongol with no shirt on jumped from the floor up onto the front desk and screamed. I said, "I'm not going in there with those maniacs." So we proceeded two doors over to the Saint James Hotel. Up in our schoolroom, the drab showed me how to melt down the residue from the coated glass stem, using a lighter, and mixing just a little (a cherry) of fresh crack with the slightly cooled brown goo to make a high octane rocket fuel. After we're done, playmate litters the room with the empty vials and I'm shocked. I run around collecting them to pack out with us, the while admonishing her for leaving evidence. The jade finds all this amusing. Later on in my journeying, I would surpass that jezebel's mild act of defiance by destroying the premises after I'd finished beaming up or boosting.

Places I frequented to smoke crack were irresistible targets for depredation and destruction, such as public lavatories that I used regularly. One such was in a restaurant whose ladies' room I employed almost every time I copped at the Normandi. The toilet had a water closet and after my first blast on the crack pipe, I was in that water tank bending the wire of the float mechanism, breaking the chain, removing the rubber ball so the water would constantly run. This ruinous behavior was uncontrollable. I would try to restrain myself because I had to keep reusing the same restroom everyday and, forsooth, didn't want to undermine my fortuity, but I couldn't control myself, could not resist the temptation to sabotage something that worked properly. Another comfort station I used was in a coffee shop in Astoria where I disembarked from the Ⓡ train. There, a roller type cloth towel dispenser was my target and I'd pull and pull and pull the entire roll out, usually so fast that the retracting mechanism couldn't keep up with the speed of my pulling, so that the length of towel would pile up on the floor. Such crazed insane behavior. I just could not refrain from vandalism. As the drug took hold and did with me its violent transformation, took my willpower and control from my personal command and fettered it in its own, and I slavishly obeyed.

Forty-Fifth Street, between Sixth Avenue and Broadway, at the time of this story, was going through major renovation. Two new skyscrapers were being erected and both the Normandi and the Saint James Hotels were slated for demolition. The street was a stroll, taken over by crack dealers, whores and bird dogs touting their wares, where spent trey bag hookers clung to the final vestiges of their trade. There was an episode I recall from the Normandi Hotel which occurred one afternoon that I'd taken off from work. I had travelled from my Astoria apartment to the Normandi to score, and planned on abducting a likely slattern who would, for sure, be on duty there and I had some bizarre fantasies in mind so I brought along a pair of handcuffs (from my mojo gear). Upon reaching the dowdy dosshouse, I first copped ten caps of rock at the desk (a nugget's worth), then picked up a handy NDE[1] (one of Ray Ray's turned-out girlfriends—a junkie), as vicious and nasty a piece of work as will be found on any stroll. She had once done a pat down on me (when I was a tenderfoot) after the constabulary raided Ritchie and Ray Ray's room (six buttons with drawn sidearms ready to drop the hook on us), and she claimed to have lost a readhead. She had me open my mouth, in which was a cap, and she exclaimed, "Holdin' out, huh?" And I laughed in her face, like I would share my drugs with a parasite like her? Anyhow, I thought I'd enjoy tying up that piece of rat poison and, thus, we hired a room. We undressed to our underwear. We're smoking crack and the meretrix is looking in her handbag for a straw (but was really searching my pant's pockets) and I caught out her legerity so, as a distraction, she insisted on performing some unnatural act, which I didn't want (I knew she had AIDS) when, finally, she

---

1 near-death experience

had to go to the loo so the paphian dresses and leaves the room and I hurriedly check my pockets and the crack was all there but my money was gone. I dashed into the hallway, only to find that the slick chippie has left the building, vanished; the desk clerk was shaking his head as I ran out into the street, searching high and low, but I never spotted the slyboots. She took me good and proper but I was thankful that she hadn't stolen the crack. You can't beat those floozies at their own game. They're magicians. Yet, the strange thing is that those pickups subconsciously want to get caught and beat up so that they can officially become victims. Like the foolish johns who really want to be ripped off. Who, me?

The Normandi Hotel on West Forty-Fifth Street—across from where once stood the Peppermint Lounge (of the early 1960s "Peppermint Twist" renown), whose house band Joey Dee and the Starliters once regaled the Beat Generation over the driving syncopated rhythm of one of rock's greatest drummers, Dino Danelli, who later lent his genius to the 1960s chartbusters, The Young Rascals—was a small flyblown building, narrow and deep, five floors, a single tiny elevator and dim narrow stairs. Only a few residents occupied the premises. There were empty rooms on the top floor that were trashed to the rafters and were absolute heaven for ghostbusting, tweaking and searching around while buzzing on a blast of crack; digging through the foliated landscape of garbage and junk that could have been an ideogram of paradise for crack addicts. The front desk sported no proper lobby, only a cramped barren foyer that allowed crack customers to come and go unimpeded. A dilapidated, bleak and desperate hovel, at once recognizable for what it was—a straw front.

My initial observation of the Normandi Hotel came prior to my crack or street years during a period of assays at trying to bolster my life with benevolence and good deeds. I was a volunteer in the Our Neighbors mission of Saint Patrick's Cathedral on

Fifth Avenue, and had been sent to Forty-Fifth Street to visit a homebound World War Two veteran in the withering Saint James Hotel, a mere couple of doors over from the even more rundown Normandi Hotel. The onetime glamorous Saint James was sorely decrepit and had become a welfare hotel and single-room occupancy (SRO), renting out rooms by the half hour to prostitutes. The recipient of my brotherly visits was horrified by the goings-on in his residence and filled me in on many of the deprecations and gory details. Meanwhile, in my dropping by that dwelling place, I waded through a whole mob of trollops and their contingent bloodsuckers overflowing from the Normandi next door. The hookers were dreary and worn-out, yet still young, with the occasional not quite burned-out specimen smiling and beaming amongst the droll chaff. Trash. Loathly. Diseased. Yet, at the same time, attractive and eager with promise and taboo. I was simultaneously becharmed and revulsed.

"At night I fared forth on strange journeys through the mazes of an invisible city, into forbidden dwellings for erasing the memory of day when a vicious caprice aroused by crack took me to secret apartments where personal identity was left at the door."[1] By the time of my ripening into the crack culture, I would saunter out from the Normandi Hotel at one, two, three o'clock in the morning so totally blasted, I was floating. Everything around me was sharp, crisp, defined, the very air hummed, sounds were magnified. I had eyes all around my head, my senses were fine tuned, my third eye roving. I spotted every hooligan and mack daddy in a street full of shadows, a dozen if there was one, lurking silently like bad luck, dark energy simmering, only their eyes moving as they read my sign. I developed a walk I had picked up at the gym from muscle-bound jocks that was a sort of lanky Texas strut, with torso leaned slightly back, not unlike those old Italian *paisanos*

---

1 Alejo Carpentier, *The Lost Steps*, paraphrase

from the other side, an almost careless rolling gait. It projected a laid-back macho confidence, or at least that's what I assumed, arms swinging, head bobbing, as I passed through the gauntlet unmolested, never once was accosted. Plenty of worry on those lonely and vulnerable walks.

At other times, zooming on crack, roving the lurid night-world of Times Square, the huge flashing signs, blazing cascades of white light, the Fourth of July colors, the pornographic decay of the dirty litter-blown sidewalks and sleazy sex shops, the omnifarious hustlers pandering to every degeneracy; and I at one with them in my loneliness and willingness to debase myself to satisfy some incessant, lecherous desire, though fearful and aloof as I slip through the minefield of fascination and sin that tauntingly evulgate my future and my doom.[1]

"Venturing forth on foot, attired in my raggedy clothes, an object marked out for observation, through the midst of the nocturnal pedestrians, such base passions raged within me like a tempest. Walking fast, hunted by my fears, skulking through the less frequented thoroughfares, imagining with every glance a target for my assaults."[2] Such was my early seasoning.

I sold a twenty-gauge shotgun (childhood relic) at the Normandi Hotel late one night. Strung out at home, looking for something to pawn or barter, I broke down and packed that entire shotgun inside a fifty-five gallon aquarium hood with light fixture, removed the fluorescent bulb and taped in the gun barrel and, held under my arm, with the remaining stock and forearm packed in a shopping bag amongst assorted aquarium apparatus. Devil-may-care and feckless at three o'clock in the morning, I paraded right through Times Square carrying a shotgun, surrounded by

---

1 John Rechy, *City of Night*, inspiration; Donna Tartt, *The Goldfinch*, inspiration
2 Robert Lewis Stevenson, *The Strange Case of Dr. Jekyll and Mr. Hyde*

police in every guise—every cab driver, bum, transient was a cop (the city guards' limpid surveillance). I was so bold and confident, such brio, right under the noses of New York's finest (the worst). At the Normandi, I traded the weapon for some coke, some crack, a hooker and a room. Once inside our chamber, the tart advised me (upon viewing the burn marks on my legs), "You really should stop burning yourself." This from a vagrant degenerate slattern, a track-scarred heroin addict and crack addict, counseling me on how to comport myself. Just what I needed. And Streetfighter ruined the piece when he sawed down the barrel so short that he cut into the forestock, rending the gun useless. But the sale of the shotgun enhanced my image at the Normandi, so it worked out well for me.

Working the door (as a guard) at the Normandi Hotel was a vital, consequential responsibility, relegated only to those individuals who had the faculty, the street smarts to screen the would-be buyers seeking entry from the outside. Such competence preempted the security and confidence of the front desk dealers and demanded, in addition to alertness, snap judgment as the commerce was lively in the night trade, often having to contend with six simultaneous customers cramming the sally port at once. Thus it was with some astonishment I heard Streetfighter call out one evening, upon my exiting the privy, "Pig, take the door." I was flying, having just beamed up, and I fell to like a veteran Cerberus. Announcing to the desk my take on each patron as they approached the sheenless plate glass entrance: "Spanish guy, kinda skanky, looks alright; Black guy, hustler, looks alright; Hooker, I'm lettin' her by; Spanish guy, strung out, looks alright; Tough guy, black, looks alright; Spanish guy, hyped-up, could be trouble; Hooker, strung out; Black guy, set up, looks alright…" The desk jockeys were laughing at my frank delivery. I was inspired. During a lull in the traffic, I managed to stuff a rock in the end of a cigarette and fired up right there in the lobby. Streetfighter was on the case pronto, "I smell crack!" As I stood there smoking, the dummy, I concurred, "I smell it too," puff puff. What a bust.

When I first began smoking crack I was always quitting after a hard run. I used to buy a new glass bowl (resembled a miniature glass hookah) with each score and, ignorant of compressing the screen or melting down the thick white residue from the sides of the bowl, like delicate inflorescence (thereby forfeiting half the product), I would throw away all that paraphernalia after the crack was gone, not wanting to have any evidence or reminders of my fell deed around to haunt me. One time, after consuming twenty caps of crack (a deuce of dirty dancers), I was so horrified that I went to an AA meeting -- a midnight meeting in Astoria --wherein all the fellowship look like they had their last drink right before coming in. There, I poured my heart out like a recalcitrant penitent, seeking sympathy and self-aggrandizement. On another occasion, after a two-day run, upon preparing to embark to the city to re-up, I looked down at my naked torso and noticed my palpitating heart practically bouncing out of my chest. I became so panicky that I went out and bought something to eat instead. Then, sitting around my apartment wondering if my onerous behavior was going to give me a heart attack.

In the heat of a run, I would shave my body and reindue my bewitching erotic mojo gear then, when I came down, would fold and pack away all the gear in a box stashed in my closet, too smitten to even contemplate what I'd done. Like Jekyll renouncing Hyde, "locking the door to his cabinet and grinding the key under his heel."[1] I was learning because I was changing through reckless,

---

1 Robert Lewis Stevenson, *The Strange Case of Dr. Jekyll and Mr. Hyde*

flagrant experiment. With each foray into the dome world did I resuscitate the diablerie of my duplexity.

My first experience at getting clipped buying crack occurred one New Year's Eve. I rode the Ⓡ train into the city around eleven p.m. and disembarked at Forty-Seventh Street to be greeted by a mob of over one million pedestrians packed into every square inch of space on the streets and sidewalks for blocks surrounding Times Square, with every bluecoat in the city on duty blocking off egress to every side street off Broadway. The perimeter was jam-up and jelly tight with shoulder-to-shoulder coppers. It was a nightmare. What could have possessed all those human sheep to brave the subzero Hebrides and stand around squashed like glaciating sardines for hours, in order to watch a pagan device descend from the top of the Times Tower at midnight? I had to weasel my way through that claustrophobic press along Seventh Avenue all the way to Fiftieth Street before I could slip between the barricades and lines of fuzz to make my way to Sixth Avenue, then to double back to Forty-Fifth Street. Only to find that the Normandi Hotel was dry for the night. They were not selling on New Year's Eve amidst all that concentrated law enforcement and celebratory melee. Frantic, I made my way to the neighboring Saint James Hotel in whose lobby were a group of grotty black grifters. There I purchased two caps, my last twenty lettuce leaves in the whole world—the vials even had green tops just like the caps from the Normandi. In the middle of the block I stopped for a quick hit. The bottles were filled with chunks of soap. Back to the Saint James, I couldn't identify the wily coyote I'd let mulct me on the dummies. I was so devastated that, in a sudden spate of remorse, I smashed my glass stem on the sidewalk and threw away my lighter and determined, then and there, that I would forever renounce smoking crack. I made my way back through the scrum and entered the subway station, there to find that the token booth was closed and the turnstiles were set to work without requiring a token. The subway was free for the night, a breakaway amenity in New York City, a New Year's blessing by some New Age urban Hecate. I had one token left to my name (tokens then cost seventy-five cents). So I went up to a delicatessen and purchased a can of beer, my sole get-high on New Year's Eve. My newly vowed abstinence from crack lasted until I acquired some more green.

As I got going with crack, my apartment seemed to be too white-bready to enjoy, did not enhance my new crack culture, thus I began to dismantle and trash it. Framed photographic studies on the wall, Castro davenport, teakwood stereo cabinet were all covered with bedsheets. The Oriental carpet was rolled up. Garbage began to accumulate all over. I wrote on the ceiling, wrote on my Italian leather couch. I ruined the rush caning on a pair of Hitchcock chairs. Electricity and telephone were disconnected. My apartment reflected a past that I wanted no more of, no part of, material representations of the man I had been, of a life that fell short of dividends returned for devotion rendered. Money I still had yes, it could not buy contentment.

All throughout my adult life I'd dallied with divergent coteries whose unconventional lifestyles were proof of alternative paths outside of the box that were bright and enticing. Yet, I'd continued to pin my faith on the one tried and true-blue formula around which American myth seemed to be chiseled. Until crack. Until now. Now all of my blind faith and blind obedience were shattered and a new dawn was breaking on the horizon.

One time I brought home to Astoria a wily fox of a transexual and we smoked together for a couple of hours until the crack was

45

all gone and then she was about to leave. I checked in my closet where I'd hidden my paycheck from work and found it missing. So I confronted the queen and she consented to a body search. Nothing. She didn't have it. But I hadn't looked under her wig. She refused to remove the wig. I insisted. We began to scuffle and then to fight in earnest; we were wrecking the place, lamps and tables were smashing, screaming, a racket when, finally, one of my neighbors called the police. The fuzz showed up and, for once, I'm glad to see them. They made the hermaphrodite remove her wig and there was no check. After my guest leaves, I'm baffled. I search and search the closet and, eventually, unearth the elusive check, hidden where I'd put it and forgot, falsely accusing the poor kid who never committed the slightest perfidy. Embarrassing. Evidence of the insidiousness of the disease of a doper. That wouldn't be the only time I falsely accused someone of plundering me when I'd forgotten where I'd secreted my cabbage. Terrible flaw in my character over which I had no control. Part and parcel of the paranoia that coincides with addictedness.

My irruptions with crack led me farther and farther away from a life for which I had little desire to return. An underground route to my destiny beckoned, irresistably, stronger, and I had no induration to sustain me. Like Jesus at Gethsemane, I concentrated my new resolve with a fixedness that I would be equal to the rigors and agonies awaiting me. I had sold-out to a future so random and illusory that my very survival became an immediate stimulus. I had become morose and left out in a time-honored society as it rushed past me while I stood an observer as if watching a film.

My social participation had fallen flat with the cessation of my job at the Twenty-One Club, 21 West Fifty-Second (Swing) Street, New York City, which was prevenient to my induction at the Ritz Carlton Hotel. "21" was my pride, my identification, my aspiration, the highlight of my career. "21" was a rare institution that, for all its lugs and high-hat arrogance, was ever loyal to their personnel. Since the club's inception during Prohibition, they had never laid off a single member of their legion ranks. Personal loans were extended to employees and every accommodation was endowed and vested to insure their welfare. Every staff member was afforded equal respect from potwashers to chefs, from bread boys to captains, from runners to bartenders. No position was insignificant and all workhands were inspired with a pride and team spirit, resulting in a harmony and devotion which enabled them to cope with any situation, any problem, any order that came through the door. An invincible workforce that ticked with the precision of a Swiss clock. Yet when the original family of owners sold out (for 21 million dollars), that long tradition of loyalty and devotion went with them and the entire complexion of the club shifted and realigned into just another corporate clone with no more concern for their staff than a fast-food chain. And thence, from that apex of my career, did I traipse through the cream of New York's hotel and catering foundations (settling at the Ritz), losing heart, step by step, in not only my profession but in society, our culture, the Establishment as a whole. The ubiquity of my work in my life had produced a kind of tunnel vision where job-related incidents filled the landscape to an abnormal extent, taking on exaggerated importance and innuendos, above which I found it difficult to transcend and detach.

If I had to put my finger on one single reason that my life's disenchantment came to a head, it was the situation at "21" when that landmark club was sold and closed for renovation, (staff) loyalties predicated on prejudice, everyone laid off. For me, it was all downhill from then on. My job, my work, that was the aspect of my life which filled in the blanks of all that was missing. Once that all-important component was removed, my will to go on, to endure, went with it. The jobs that followed "21" did not fill the gaps adequately. Unmindful at the time of the full significance of its impact, little did I realize that a gospel creed had been violated which unalterably lay waste forever my faith in my fellow man, rendering my stock and store in our folkways, its ideology and ancient wisdom null and void.

My coworkers at "21," who had become over the years my extended family and compadres, turned their backs on me as a unified body when the club was sold and a new breed of innovative young chefs were hired with whom I became friendly. For my new friends were of a WASP persuasion withal I was identified and my Hispanic frater, in their ignorant fear, showed their true face and feelings at last—a fidelity, esteem and regard for me which had never been there, whose illusion had meant so much to me—everything in fact—false values upon which I had scaled my very worth. All a sham. "It seemed they had always harbored hostility towards me, though they had dared not show it openly, because I was not of their race; they saw me as a friend to the fresh feather of American interlopers who threatened to usurp their place in the time-honored hierarchy of royal favor."[1]

As if the betrayal of my coworkers wasn't bad enough, I felt an equal Judas kiss from the club's new owner who had hired a firm to conduct exit interviews with all "21"'s employees prior to closing their doors. The interviews were videotaped, which I opposed, requiring the interviewer to take hand notes which included my demands for bonus pay for ice sculptures (which I had priorly done at my hourly union scale wage). Plus all the years of managery and administrative responsibility I'd shouldered out of pride and loyalty, the mounds of uncompensated overtime—I expected in future to be paid for. I wasn't surprised when they declined to reinstate me. But that was all right. I went on to make much more money at the Ritz, and not liking it very much.

---

1 Barry Unsworth, *The Ruby in Her Navel*, paraphrase

Though I knew I wouldn't like it anymore at the new "21", not for any amount of money.

Ergo, I felt cheated and shamed at having been duped for following a chimera. I embosomed only rebellion, a need of vindication, and a desire to reclaim something that had been lost, stolen, my faith, my innocuous heart, my unwavering fealty, my innocence. And there was something more, a shifting facet of my personality going from green to gold, a reallocating of values, priorities, a grabbing for something long denied, taboo, an erotic, a scatological edge to things once mundane. I so desperately needed something to fill the void in my heart, in my soul, and crack was willing and able. With crack "all had a sweeping amplitude of array that seemed to magnify its effect on my surroundings as a mist magnifies a moor. I joined, and had acute pleasure in joining, a poignant pleasure like what the thirst-perishing man might feel who knows the well to which he has crept is poisoned, yet stoops and drinks divine draughts nevertheless."[1] Such was my design. A blanket conversion. Once the big decision had been reached, once I was finally on the street, I was unbelievably light-headed. Nothing mattered.

Cities are so sullied to begin with, there's nothing natural about them save some transplanted, contrived topiary all carefully augmented and arranged; tortured, tormented, achromatic landscapes like some twisted creation by a depraved science fiction byline, offering no naturalistic Lebensraum (space for life) for its inhabitants. One of the most depressing views I ever laid eyes on was the panoramic vista from the top of the Empire State skyscraper.

---

1 Charlotte Brontë, *Jane Eyre*

Everywhere I looked, as far as the eye could see, was a dull bruised grey, washed in grime and suspended pollution, right down to the leaden East River. This was the greatest city on earth in all its glory! Even the soothing comfort and reassurance of the sun couldn't penetrate the blanketing layers of contamination. Add to the mix underground tunnels with deafening cattle car trains, manslaughtering taxis, choking noxious buses, topped off with living in strata, subliminal media, abnormal working environments, and whiskey or drugs available on every corner and it's no wonder that sexual expression takes on some unusual twists. Humanity has mutated, become alien to its own nature. One can either yield to the swelling ranks of Sodom or deny the vacillating fears of Lot's wife. As for myself, I chose the best of both worlds: back to basics in the primal jungle of the street, and partaking of the most refined elixirs modern pharmacology have to offer.

What was I thinking by jumping into the matrix of humanity's monstrosity; searching for beauty amongst the vile, ugly man-made monuments of materialism. The entire American commonwealth, "the whole national and human consciousness hammering out the fact of material prosperity above all things."[1] It made me sick. Sick, disgusted and disheartened. "The human soul needs actual beauty even more than bread, and not the base competition of mere acquisition, a great scrabble for ugly pettiness."[2]

On the street there was no materialism, no acquisition. Homeless people, and I for one, found and created beauty from junk. Crack offered beauty, inchoatively unleashing one's repressed potential and latent ability, to emerge from the constraints of conditioning and, (though not a psychedelic) like LSD, allow the mind to expand and appreciate the natural or symbolic beauty of otherwise

---

[1,2] D.H. Lawrence, *Nottingham and the Mining Countryside,* from *Phoenix: The Posthumous Papers of D.H. Lawrence* (Viking Press, NY 1936) essay

mundane phenomenon. Regretfully, that infatuation was an ill-freighted silver hook yet at least it was something—something pure and of value for the coin.

I began to adopt a Gnostic attitude regarding our culture and, with crack serving as both catalyst and aperture through which to defect, it seemed, as new theories and canons gestated and filtered through the alembic of my mind, only natural that the epitome, the quintessence of my new rout, my chosen métier should be at the apogee, the farthest point from civilization... I was never one for half measures. How much further could one distance oneself from organized society than to be a homeless tramp, a bum in the gutter.

I wonder if (m)any city bums expend as much thought to their plight as I did. Beginning with my crack usage during my pre-street years, I laid the groundwork for my side tripping, my homeless-ness, consciously, carefully, lovingly, deliberately. Crack opened the floodgate. I willingly allowed it to consume me. Like Timothy Leary with LSD, I worshiped crack with divine unction. During my final years of employment (at the Ritz), alone in my apart-ment in Astoria, with twisted and sedulous care I converted my lifestyle and my life. I was experiencing crack in all its newness, its power and majesty, its evincible welkin, its total control over my life, the speed of its sledgehammer blows, the uniqueness of its makeup and appearance, the special pipe with which to smoke it, its aphrodisiac aroma and piquant flavor, the manner of its concentrating residue, the crackling of it as it burns (from whence comes its name), the hallucinogenic effect of snowflaking where one's vision is blurred and clouded with white snowflakes as though a blizzard were blowing into your eyes, the ease with which it is used, disguised, hidden, transported, consumed, its mysticism. A heretofore unknown heavenly spice and nostrum that I was rapidly acquiring a taste for; some occult prodigy of irresistible magnetism and promise—the holy grail. All that I ever wanted in a palliative, in a get-high and more. Initially, it seemed "the drug had no discriminating action; it was both diabolical and divine; it shook the doors of the prison house of my disposition and, like the captives of Philippi, that which stood within ran forth."[1]

Crack spoke to me in a most tender and equivocal guise, offering a pastiche of salacious and sensual pleasures of which she teased me with an exciting, saltatory birl of samples; leading me on with Jesuitical temptations and titillating vistas until I was swimming in a terminal river of wanton lust, irretrievable in the serpentine current of dark intrigue and dazzling possibility; mesmerized by the flaming fire of my transposed, wayward soul and a burning desire to ratify my ignominious, proscriptive role.

Well, hell, it wasn't my first experience with such hanky-panky dalliance. The novelty was in the coming out solely on my own without a support system in place, a cadre from which to draw guidance, assistance and encouragement. But I had crack on which to lean and to help lead me astray into the ruined dreams of our own manufacture, crack, always crack upon which to rely for subliminal seduction and outrageous, maniacal blasting of my own contemptible compunction.

Ah, praise the chthonic deity crack as I follow its twinkling, scintillating fascination, spiraling down the drain in a vortex of voluble, voluptuary visions: Venus staked out at the whipping post; Snow White beset by the seven deadly sins; my own crafty crucifixion crossing the threshold of Dante's Inferno. With every puff, enthralling, amorphous, synecdochial crack drawing forth through its benison the juggernaut of enormous potential that it represents, from the elixir of my emancipation to the virulent incarnation of Mr. Hyde.

I erected an awful fane with an altar (atop my stereo cabinet) covered with a satin bedsheet, a tilting vanity mirror (like

---

1 Robert Lewis Stevenson, *The Strange Case of Dr. Jekyll and Mr. Hyde*

a diminutive cheval glass) on its surface, candles to either side, red mat like a runway advancing forward from its center. Vials of crack were lined up on the altar in front of the mirror, extending out to each wing, like miniature cromlechs—icons, building blocks, the body and blood of life. I would kneel and bow in supplication to my pagan idol, my Apollyon, enshrined within my adytum and offer myself up as sacrifice in deranged oblation. I rewrote the twelve-steps so as to extol crack's virtues in liturgical orison and would recite this mantra while enrobed in mock barristerial splendor, receiving holy Benediction and Communion with crack. The glass crack pipe was the monstrous monstrance. I became mesmerized, hypnotized, glamorized with crack to the exclusion of all else. I jeered the top hotels—my livelihood—called in sick all week then went in on Friday to collect my pay. Blatant, outrageous, spit in your face behavior.

There was branding, bloodletting, scarification. I went so far in my self-modification as to conscientiously perform ordinary tasks left-handed. For instance, when dressing, the alternate leg went into the pants first than was my usual habit, same with putting on my shoes, threading my belt through the loops, buttoning my shirt. Whatever was in my power, to reverse my every idiosyncrasy, was my intention in order to awaken my new resolve and enhance my new occupation—cultivated, hybridized insanity. With each of those irrevocable occurrences—trashing my apartment, pagan idolatry, left hand practice—"this reversal of my previous experience seemed like the Babylonian finger on the wall to be spelling out the letters of my judgment."[1] Such was my relish for entropy, for dissonance and disorder that I would sometimes tune in my radio between two discordant stations thereby receiving a conflicting mixture of both overlapping broadcasts or, better

---

1 Robert Lewis Stevenson, *The Strange Case of Dr. Jekyll and Mr. Hyde*

yet, tuning into a reception of pure unadulterated static for an intrusive, amplified, head-jamming white noise. Zap!

There was an assiduous, systematic breaking down of self and values until no job remained, every stick of furniture had been sold or lost, my apartment forfeit. The last bit of fear at being homeless vanquished. Until I couldn't wait to hit the street and have done with all that had previously mattered, that had comprised my past life. Where, at the end of those days, holding out in a barren apartment, no utilities, no furniture, no food, hating it, wondering what the hell I was doing there until the last possible moment. Having long stopped smoking crack, not having any more money, the lasting effects of the drug lingering, knowing I couldn't do that crap on the street anyway. I had hammered myself into a base substance that was to be recast into a most primitive conscription. A call to unadorned, unpretentious, uninspired existence, experience, exegesis. I was as prepared for the street as like I could read tea leaves. My bum's attitude, outlook, resignation in place. In such wise was my valediction to my (past) straight life. The *mis-en-place* of a lunatic.

I likened what I was then embarking on as the grand scale, the main event, the real McCoy of what I went through in school. Rejection of the offered curriculum with its bogus republican adjuration; research and development of my own agenda—"a chemism of dreams;"[1] enlistment in a sociocultural microcosm. The streets of the city drew me like a magnet, like a suction, the incessant buzzing of down to earth life, down and dirty city life, cold and hard and hot, life on fire. A dream world, a living nightmare, a fervid, fiendish, febrile task waiting to be done, to tackle and complete. A crazy man's empyrean dream of construction, of destruction, heedless and wanton and holy. A humble man's desire for redemption, resurrection. The street drew me into its

---

1 Theodore Dreiser, *An American Tragedy*

bowels, I became its very blood, pumping through the heart of the metro. I was the needle plunging into the city's soul, cold as ice and burning with passion and resolve, with blind faith and a fierce will did I enjoin the hardship, enlightenment, the desecration and rebirth of my soul as the Phoenix rising from the advent of the street, pulled beyond my intrinsic elasticity never to resume my original form.

Mostly, at first, I wallowed in the gutter, in a vacuum, a void. But I was where I wanted to be, in the eternal vastness of the street, on the wild frontier. The hard part had been in letting go. Giving up the security and sanity of the Establishment for the knife-edge and lunacy of street life. Why would I do such a crazy thing? For the same reasons that people have always taken risks: for liberty and deliverance; for glory or gain; for adventure; for vengeance; for knowledge; for divination; for immortality. Why do speculators play the stock market, pilots fly hundreds of miles per hour, sailors go to sea, soldiers lust for war? Why the steeplejack, the sandhog, the rodeo rider? Why do people sit glued to the boob tube and watch assaults and explosions while listening to clamor and screaming? Are any of those activities more reasonable, more easily understood than pioneering and prospecting the urban streets to experience the reality which passes for life therein. *Suum cuique.*

There's no excuse for me to have been forced onto the street, to have lost my apartment for nonpayment of rent. The monthly rent ($250) was so low to begin with, being a rent-controlled building, the annual increase negligible. And the landlord, a huge conglomerate, was so tolerant of missed and late rent payments that it took almost a year of not paying my rent to be evicted.

The selling or auctioning of my furniture was a depressingly painful experience, though not enough to deter me. I began with a Louis XVI style tilting vanity mirror that had a little drawer underneath it, made out of cherry wood, with a high lacquer finish. It was manufactured by Stickley and turned out to be quite a valuable piece. I brought it to ABC Carpet Showroom on Broadway near Fourteenth Street. They snatched it up instantly for a fat price. I owned a matching three-drawer lowboy, also by Stickley, and the buyer at ABC told me to bring it in. I did so and it was purchased without qualm. The agent then told me to bring in photographs of anything else I wanted to sell. However, I next brought in a schoolmarm's chair, an Early American piece of heritage by Ethan Allen. By then the shill knew me for what I was, a desperate drug addict, and he mourned that I should have come in with a photo, the piece was fairly common, they already had a few on hand, etcetera, etcetera, and he clinched it for peanuts. He knew I wasn't going to schlep back home with that unwieldy item and so I let it go for a fraction of its worth. I really liked that chair too, it had a spindle back, contoured seat, attached desk top with a couple of drawers, and it was a grand old piece of joinery. I was so addicted, so desperate for more crack, and I was still working at the time, making big money at the Ritz Carlton. It didn't matter, no amount of money was enough, I was spending more than a benny—one hundred dollars a day on crack alone. I knew conclusively that I couldn't go back to ABC Carpet Showroom to put any more furniture on the block.

I then looked up the location of a Long Island City antique storehouse in the Yellow Pages and walked there carrying a consulate-style jewelry box reproduction that my dad had made for me. It had four velvet lined, compartmentalized drawers, the whole covered in gold and silver leaf, with dainty French porcelain drawer knobs. It was a unique handcrafted item easily worth five hundred dollars (or double that figure). By the time I arrived (five miles later) at the warehouse, my arms and shoulders were screaming from carrying the better than thirty pound piece—it weighed. Well, the emptor there read me immediately (druggy that I was) and told me he didn't want the piece, it wasn't worth anything, there was no market for it, he had one himself, and so on. I ended up practically giving the treasure to the jackal just to be rid of it. In exhibiting the cabinet, I discovered a hidden message written to me from my dad on the bottom of one of the drawers. It said, "One of the last things I made in my shop." I was almost in tears. But hey, let's not lose sight of what we are and why we're here. I had to rid myself of every last vestige of my life that had made up my past, to face what I had become. The price I sold that superlative item for bought me a flask of gin and a bag of weed.

I sold my pots and pans, tableware and most of my books at my hometown subway station. Solid Revereware, Wedgwood china, Weller pottery and Delftware, along with beautiful hand-tooled, leather-bound volumes—all went for best offer. I sold a couple of German beer tankards made of crockery, with hinged filigree leaden tops and hunting scenes in relief around the outside—I brought them into a whiskey bar to fence. I would have felt better if I had destroyed the goods rather than to cheapen myself in flaunting the despicable wastrel that I had become by pandering my pathetic addiction in public. Now I knew how dirty a prostitute feels when she's finally forced to abandon her pride, self-respect and dignity to the lusts and perversions of strangers in order to survive. Gone the dream, America, lost in the profligate junkie vortex of perdition, derision, and government mind control.

By the time I had sold what I easily could of my furniture and possessions, when my utilities were disconnected and I was expecting the sheriff to come by any day to padlock the premises, I hired a moving company to evacuate my remaining property to a local storage facility. In fierce denial, passed out drunk the night before, when the movers woke me up the following morning they found nothing packed, pictures still hanging on the walls, clothes hung in the closets, water in the otherwise empty aquariums. One look and they were ready to turn around and leave. However, I jumped up like a jack-in-the-box, effusive and at my most persuasive, I started directing the compliant fellows to take this, take that, while I frantically kept feeding them tables, chairs, lamps, piles of clothes still on hangers, boxes of records, dishware, hollow ware, I was throwing stuff at the movers as I jam packed bags, boxes, it was comic if not preposterous. An hour later the truck was loaded, the apartment empty.

Big Yellow ministorage in Astoria is a (not so mini) twenty-story edifice comprised of individual wire enclosed units whose safety and security are practically nonexistent. The freight elevators in the rear and the miles of corridors are open to the four winds and the public at large. Each individual unit is fastened by a measly padlock, provided by the tenant—that is one's sole protection. Having brought no lock of my own, the management supplied a temporary loaner until I could replace it with my own crimp. Needless to say, I never returned with my own padlock and so, a month later, when I put back to the facility to claim my property, I found the lock missing, the cage door open, and half of my possessions missing as well. I gave away most of the remaining goods and chattels.

Only a few items have survived the cataclysm of my ten year sojourn on the streets of New York City: my (work) knives, my drums, and my dictionary and thesaurus. Unbelievable. All those four items, like their owner, bear the scars and foxing of having weathered the flood. It's a wonder that I never pawned the first two and, as for the last two, I'm inclined to think we'd be better off going, "Ugh, ugh, Booga, booga." Like, how many frigging words do we need? I am continually astounded at the number of English words, many of which mean the same thing, and the minutiae of investigation, classification and explanation in which

Homo sapiens deems necessary to indulge, leaving no room for a filament of mystery or allowing one iota to escape his interference. But alas, "the root function of language is to control the universe by describing it."[1] (Another clever tool of the white man). What does it mean? What does it mean? Never content to allow for a single interpretation or disambiguation lest it be dissected, mutilated and "held up to the fire to reveal its hidden significance."[2] For "humanity's deepest desire, its goal, is nothing less than a complete description of the universe we live in."[3] What an arrogant, unworthy race is humanity, deserving to lose the natural beauty with which we were endowed and to wallow in the filth which we alone create.

I have heard, time and again, the comment by street urchins, that they could write a book. And it's true, every homeless bum has a story to tell. If my story is at times offensive then the better for it because the street is offensive, crack is offensive, and it's high time some of the myths were shattered. For, to stretch a point, "American history is built upon a fictive foundation of cultural myth, that of American innocence which breeds American democracy as the social utopia."[4] As though Americans were the intrinsic noble savage. Yet (minorities notwithstanding) "the incorporation and institutionalization of America has abused and perverted these myths in order to legitimize a lust for power (such as the upsurge in government employee unions) and a materialism in a society believed devoid of traditional (European) culture and moral values."[5] Hence, the contours of American History have obstinately repudiated the homeless as if they didn't exist. "America's homeless as a segment of society have always been ignored by historians,

---

1 James Baldwin, *Notes of a Native Son, Stranger in the Village*
2 Van Wyck Brooks, *America's Coming of Age*
3 Stephen Hawking, *A Brief History of Time*
4 William Carlos Williams, *In the American Grain*
5 Vera M. Kutzinski, *Against the American Grain* (parenthesis by the author)

resulting in an incomplete view of the evolution of the American social order over the last two centuries, doubtless because the homeless represent alienation and failure in a society that has long worshipped upward mobility and success. Nonetheless, the tramps and beggars are an important part of the American experience."[1] Heretofore mine is a contribution to a latter-day New World landscape, an effort to define and document a piece of the mysterious encystment of our current American heritage (heaven help us) despite my polemic on American myths.

Crack is the convenient patsy or proxy for allowing rent money to be so readily consumed, a bottomless pit of an addiction as far as monetary cost goes. In like manner, such effect extends to ideology and philosophy, a superfluity of corruption where crack is concerned. Yet my whole attitude, my outlook towards society, the government in particular, my assessment of my life and its prospects, my depression, were all in place well before crack came along. Yet I lacked the nerve to just throw in the towel on it all and become homeless. I couldn't have brought myself to sell my furniture, my antiques, would never have behaved so reprehensibly in my work, to desecrate my good name, had it not been for crack. What a crock my values turned out to be, the mystic ontological values I ascribed to my blind faith, blind allegiance, blind obedience seemed less convincing now, meaningless in all that they stood for, as worthless as the ego they kept pumped. I needed only the slightest nudge to push me over the edge, so disenchanted was I with my life, my job, my motivation. A malcontent waiting for something just like crack to enable me to take the plunge, is why I embraced it so once discovered, and just as easily abandoned once

1 Leonard C. Feldman, *Citizens Without Shelter*

it served its purpose. Not that it had lost its appeal, only that I knew I wouldn't be able to handle crack newly turned out on the street, that once homeless my hands would be full with survival. Did I ever once think that homelessness was an answer? Never. But, like anarachy, when a situation becomes intolerable, that was how I saw my life, my miserable, dilatory life which, though upscale, gave me no satisfaction. So I became a bum.

Being homeless is itself hard work—New Age urban hunter gatherers, foraging for survival, eluding attack, roaming, watching, maybe making the rounds of social services and soup kitchens, trying to protect what little property they have, starting over from nothing when their possessions (medications, identities) are stolen by compatriots or the police. The city, to such displaced persons, is a wilderness, entropic, a war zone. Some feel they cannot leave their shelters (boxes, tents) for even short lengths of time, for fear of losing their belongings. Others suffer from sleep deprivation, since they can find no safe place to rest.[1] You are here; you are gone.

I was gladdened when, after a good six months of copping crack in New York City, I was able to ferret my way into the dome world at Queensbridge projects. It was closer to home, only a twenty minute walk down Twenty-First Street from my Astoria flat, and saved me the hassle of traveling back and forth to Manhattan. I was already well enough acquainted with the crack vending in the city so that those connections were comfortingly nearby if

---

1 Rebecca Solnit, *Harpers Magazine*, October 2016, paraphrase.

required. Moreover, I had, at that early stage in my new career, a premonition that I'd wind up on the streets of Gotham eventually—there was no rush to urbanize. So it was with relief and eager optimism that I entered the Negroid crack community at Queensbridge projects and Debbie's, my home away from home for the year before crack took me to the streets of the Big Apple.

An alternate route between my Astoria flat and Queensbridge projects ran parallel to the main thoroughfare of Twenty-First Street, an industrial strip along Twenty-Second Street of untenanted black-and-blue brick factories with steel doors and barred, turbid windows, blasted sidewalks and trapped, windblown litter; the cobbled street sparsely trafficked and lonely, a strip of recurring infamies for which that district was of mark, embracing the Queensbridge stroll where shifting shadows create sinister portents and forebodings, while the silence whispers tomes of warning. Where, at night, the darkness looms and trembles with fear and malison. An immutable eyesore, soiled and seedy and dangerous, an antonymic backdrop for the sexy slags who stroll its squalid course, a path I ranged through with pleasure and often.

Having had long acquaintance with that dismal excrescence as my local marijuana connection, I knew Queensbridge projects as a indurated crucible whose inhabitants' sylvatic ideal of themselves was bound up with existentialism and narcissism and whose economy was built upon welfare and vice. It didn't take much effort to hook up with Debbie, a resident Gen-X pleasure-lover, who was my ingress into that reeking, impenetrable casbah world, a thanatological nadir of bellicose scoundrels as heathen and full of menace as they come—furtive and skulking and frightening. Thusly, my forays into their numinous crack houses were fraught with peril.

Queensbridge projects, a low-income public housing development, is an object lesson in the conditions and mentality of just such a degenerate living environment. A sprawling complex of eight story, pleasingly coarse surfaced cocoa-colored brick apartment buildings, arranged in a perplexing labyrinth of obtuse angles, meandering pathways, greensward commons, and intricate lanes, sprinkled with sand-filled playgrounds and cozy nests of grocery stores and convenience eateries, dotted with old fashioned lampposts and outdoor phone kiosks, the grounds resembled a modern version of an Ivy League college campus, complete with the attendant landscape of dense shrubbery, hedge selvage and towering shade trees. Or such was its inceptive intention.

Pan to the bricks' inhabitants. All of the residents are on relief of one sort or another and most have their rent paid directly to the housing office. All of the endemic population are of a cultural minority, predominately people of color. And many of the extended households include no less than four natal generations of recipients, none of whom have ever worked a legitimate job save for pushing dope, turning tricks, boosting property, or muggings and stickups. Children run wild and unchaperoned in packs like feral dogs. Parents sit on benches lining the commons drinking Night Train and passing joints while they gossip and ridicule their neighbors and neighborhood. Dope dealing is blatantly conducted out in the open while prostitutes solicit johns right on the sidewalk. Rap music blares from open windows through which garbage is casually tossed without warning. Hedgerows and fairways have been trampled, every streetlamp has been smashed, playgrounds are littered with broken glass and trash, and a working telephone is rare—the whole having been transformed into some stylized lunar wasteland.

The storefronts have been covered with graffiti and stripped abandoned cars line the streets. Most of the apartment buildings' entryways have had their locks broken, vestibule mailboxes have been pried, bent and jimmied. The hallways reek of urine and no one uses the elevators for the lave of dejecta that smirch their decks and walls. Refuse litters the stairwells and hallways and every surface has a sticky adhesion to it as if having been sprayed with soda. Stairwell landings are hangouts for loitering adolescents and crack smoking, while rooftops are always occupied by junkies shooting up and nodding, and juvenile crews practicing with their handguns and machine pistols: pop, pow, rat-tat-tat in the darkness.

And while the middle generation of resident miscreants bitch and moan over their detestable standard of living, their jackanapes are having a ball running harum-scarum or are crouched, petrified in a locked closet while the grandmothers tremble in timorous trepidation deep within their cocoons, straining to keep a clean house and to place a square meal on the table for their nearly lost grandchildren, playing at some semblance of order and normalcy and faith and hope, being surrounded by the crumbling reality of their American dream.

I've had the pleasure and honor of making the acquaintance of a couple of those veteran, matron troopers and they are some of the sweetest, most noble and compassionate persons I have ever met. I even brought one of the ladies a box of chocolates once who, after eating one piece, gave the remainder to her brood of observing, hopeful, salivating grandchildren, carrying on profusely over such a nice gift. Meanwhile, her daughter, mother of the litter, was boosting the week's supply of meat from the refrigerator (which Grandma had stocked) to sell for money for dope. Fortunately, that once, me and Debbie intercepted the swag and returned it to Grandma who graciously accepted the recovered bounty and, sagacious of her progeny's shenanigans, asked no questions: *à bon chat, bon rat*.

Debbie was my refuge and referral in that totally black world, but her protection went only so far and there were a lot of eyes on me at all times, hostile eyes biding their time. I got whacked there a few times, and always managed to walk away in one piece but my nine lives were getting used up too fast for comfort. Over time, I made new contacts at Queensbridge projects and that didn't sit too well with Debbie. Because I was in those environs for one reason only (drugs) and I was always generous.

At once, of a harrowing occasion, I grasped it all like an eidetic remembrance from a dream, a living nightmare, as rats overcrowded in a sewer, climbing over one another in their confinement, the noise at such a high decibel level so as to drown out or distract other sensations from focusing on their own intolerance. Habitations designed for poverty inhabitants that made Robert Moses' projects enviable by comparison; efficiency units that could by no stretch of the imagination be regarded as apartments. Cribs no larger than a small kitchen complete with sink, toilet, and bunks, the resemblance more like a prison cell than any other facsimile. Built to answer no need other than to cover the requirements of those whose job it is to house welfare recipients. Breeding grounds for fodder for society's prisons (to feed an industry that is a major cornerstone of our economy). This is what I was drawn into, a one-way trip for black or white alike.

It was between dusk and dark and I was being chased, being run down by at least a five-man crew on their home turf and I was out of tricks, no place to run, no place to hide. It was a matter of minutes before they had me. Running through fractal arteries between palisades of buildings with which I was unfamiliar, having run and run just to keep ahead of them, deeper and deeper into a cat's cradle of unknown territory—I could have been circling right back into their waiting meat-hooks, I didn't know. I only knew that this time it was over for me. And suddenly, from heaven or hell, I don't know which, there was Brenda reaching from the shadows to grab my arm as I fled past and pulled me through a doorway I never could have opened and I was assaulted with Bullioki, Bullioki, Bullioki, loud, deafening, pulsating gansta rap. I was in a hallway packed with white eyeballs in the darkness, relieved only by hazy outlines of black faces and pulled aside by

Brenda, into the first room to our left even before those eyes could register what they thought they might have just seen. And we were inside a crib and the door slammed behind us, shutting out the faces with their eyeballs but not in the slightest the beat, Bullioki, Bullioki pounding its way throughout the building as if there were no doors, no walls. And the room was hot, one hundred degrees, and three naked young black girls were bending over an equally buff gerontic woman on her back, on the floor, wedged between toilet and wall, grey hair on her head and mons, hands and arms crossed over her flat, sagged breasts as if in modesty, eyes closed, cracked lips smiling even in death.

And the girls bending closer to her face saying, "Grandma, Grandma? Is she dead?" And I can see death more plainly than can the children who haven't yet faced the fact that they are left alone now, rudderless, and Grandma who has been overdosing daily for the past ten years has found peace at last. And one child is faster than the others to inspect me, always at the ready to be infiltrated by the police, feeling along the seams of my slacks, the soles of my shoes for something hidden, and she had my wallet (I still carried) and was looking at a picture she found of an ofay clan seated at a Thanksgiving Day table laden with bounty, a baby in full swaddling regalia being fussed over, and she's fixated on a platter of sliced Italian bread piled high and she kept pointing at the bread saying over and over, "Look at dat," for which I was relieved because the nipper was me.

Brenda had extracted some silver dollars from her shoe and was secreting them inside her miniskirt as she chirped to me, "Come on," while I was gazing at a tray made for keeping flatware separated, overflowing with spoons, forks, spatulas onto the floor, but no visible hotplate or pots, and I was drawn back to the present and the impossibleness of it all as Brenda yanks the door open, pulling me along with her, and we push our way out into the packed hallway, shoving our way through the undulating mass of humanity, making our quick way on boldness alone, the only language understood there, Bullioki pulsing us along through another door and a laundry room, unattended save for a mumbling juvenile high on glue or Carbona from the smell of it, and out of the building where could be seen the lights and traffic of Twenty-First Street. And Brenda motions with her chin, giving me a little shove in that direction and says in parting, "Go on, now." And I go.

She'll get a crack smile slashed into that pretty cheek of hers for helping me, by the ones chasing me, if they ever catch on. Bless her brave soul. That was but only the first time Brenda risked her neck for me; payback big-time as I was only ever nice to Brenda. As I was always only nice to all the black girls who deserved no less, being nice themselves underneath it all and treated like crap by the scummy black guys surrounding them. And, boy, did those black cats hate me. I was white, I always seemed to have money for drugs, and I had refuge and affection from their chicks. I insulted them just by being on their turf. And I was only there for drugs, not like I had anything to learn from the blacks, they just lived like anyone else. And were defensive like everyone else. I knew I was trespassing and so I always tread lightly. And when I let myself get ripped off I had to walk away just as lightly. And still it was a toss-up, a lottery. The only gambling I ever did, what made it so irresistible, the stakes were not for money but my life.

One late night as I was leaving Debbie's, having just descended the stairs of her building's entryway, I was confronted by a three-alarm black hoodlum who made some reference to my frequent comings and goings at that location and he shook me down for a fin, which I fortunately had, lest he might have extracted payment in flesh. I consider myself lucky to have never encountered more of the same contumely, irregardless that I was always as alert as a fox in those suburbs.

Debbie's pad was often filled with a half-dozen dopers, smoking crack, shooting up, hanging out, arguing, conniving, being pests. There was always a radio playing pop songs, tuned in as cover noise, as if the neighbors didn't know what was going on, that Debbie's was a crack house. Debbie was forever running out to purchase supplies—crack, needles, beer, dope—and she ruled her roost with an iron hand, letting things get rowdy and then bringing the hammer down amidst yells, hollers and shrieks. An out-and-out zoo. A broad mix of patrons trafficked with Debbie, mostly her friends, for Debbie's was a private club and always (as at the Normandi Hotel) I was the only paleface amidst that black crowd; flappers from the stroll stopped in, local dealers, gangbangers, loose canons of a wide variety. Sometimes hot merchandise was harbored at Debbie's between fencing.

Debbie lived alone but her flat was provided for her three by-blows, thus a two-bedroom crib with large living room, full bath, modern kitchen and dinette, all rent free supplied by (welfare) the taxpayers. There were so many similar situations there at Queensbridge projects (welfare city) where single moms farmed out their kids to Grams and led a desultory life of drugs, sex and violence, often supporting the sires (the bums) of their love chiles, whose absentee function was only to enable mammy to enroll on relief. What a system. Food stamps turned into cash and spent on drugs. There was a welfare office right at Queensbridge that was so rife with drugs and violence that the forces of law and order had a command post right inside the precincts. I've been in there when New York's finest have busted a dude for smoking crack right in the waiting room and then cracking wise. Too much!

Debbie was a maniac in a number of small ways. Part of her dominance stemmed from her being a little crazier than anyone else. For example, the glass crack pipe (a Pyrex-type glass tube the diameter of and a little shorter than a common lead pencil) had to have a pipe screen (a circular brass screen the size of a dime) that was rolled into a cylinder and inserted into one end of the glass tube to hold the crack while you sucked from the other end. Many people preferred to compress the cylindrical screen by pushing a new pencil or chopstick through the glass stem against the screen and flattening it somewhat. Some users would place a bed of cigarette ashes between the crack and the screen to fill in air gaps. Debbie would insert her pencil into the prepared stem and, while holding the stem upright upon a tabletop with one hand, would bang the projecting end of the pencil with a hammer, BANG! BANG! BANG! And, yes, sometimes the stem would shatter and Debbie's hand would be shredded with shards of glass, blood, and we'd all stare... She was crazy.

Debbie was a matriarch who didn't take crap from anyone. She was one tough cookie. I was at Debbie's when some bum came in with a box of cereal and a packet of powdered milk. He told Debbie to wash a bowl from her overflowing sink, mix up the milk, and serve him his cereal. "What?! I'm not serving you! You're not my man! Nobody eats here," (turns to me) "Did you ever see me eat? You can get out of here right now with your box and your milk, I never hear nothin' like that in my life!"

And I'm one of the few who has seen Debbie eat. Hamburgers I bring her early mornings knowing she's starved. I'd slip into her crib and find her in the bedroom, curled up on her queen-size bed, staring at her television tuned into a white family scene of mummy with sonny and sissy, all garbed so smart in their comfortably furnished hearth, bantering some harmonious triviality—the contrast between that trim charade and Debbie's true situation, the juxtaposition of heaven and hell—I'd see Debbie transfixed by the absurdity of such disparity, somehow simultaneously contravening and confirming her own misery by that one tableau, while I pitied her not for her condition, but for her masochism. When Debbie receives her welfare check she's buying Häagen-Dazs ice cream,

Pepperridge Farm cookies and bananas—the bananas being the only wholesome item on the menu. Amazing how we keep going on a cup of coffee and a bag of potato chips. Youth burning hot hot. Burning out on the street.

I had a few girlfriends at Queensbridge projects although amorous liaisons were not my primary reason for being there. Drugs were number one, refuge number two and companionship number three. I never thought any of the girls there would go for me as most of them worked the local stroll and I was never a paying customer. But friends I had several, amongst which Brenda and Debbie numbered. Margaret, however, was different and I fell for her immediately. She obviously had the kink like mine.

I had quit Debbie's for Buddha's, one of the biggest crack houses at Queensbridge projects. Buddha was a sage and wizened old black man, rail thin and carious with a balding grey pate, rheumy eyes in a sere basset hound face complete with flews, who ran his apartment for two groups of black-a-vised crack suppliers. He was always encircled by a leash of slick young beauties, Buddha sitting at the head of his cheap Formica-topped kitchen table, the room filled with the fragrance of chicken soup simmering on the stove, the sheilas surrounding him, leaning against the walls or sitting on the floor because you had to pay to sit at the table. Buddha would repose, ensconced on his rickety aluminum dinette chair, gnarled hands gripping his glass stem and lighter, and pontificate in an orotund tone to the assembled riffraff: "This here's a five dollar table. You got to pay five dollars to sit in that chair." While the girls would call me "the newspaper," a tag I didn't comprehend. Only later, in sobriety (in writing this book) did I voyeuristically utilize those lives upon which I had intruded. And appreciate their perception.

And Margaret was Buddha's daughter, not that she was entitled to any preferential treatment. She was always more ragtag
than the skulk of vixens who used to taunt her: "Margaret, stop
pulling your hair; Margaret, get up off the floor; I seen you out
there (the stroll) in your short skirt and high heels, don't pretend
you don't." And Margaret (asthenic, reticent, in situ on the floor)
wouldn't meet their gaze as she would try to sneak in a pull at
her hair. She wore a wig because she was half bald from pulling
out her hair (a sign of psychological distress) and I loved her for
that. I used to burn myself with the hot crack pipe or hot lighter,
so I understood. I was working at the time in an all-night deli
and Buddha's was my diurnal stop on the way home. The other
girls would tease Margaret while they waited for me to show:
"Is your boyfriend coming today, Margaret?" And I would bring
Margaret presents, a pack of cigarettes, a disposable lighter, a
vitamin drink like Nutriment vanilla shake or Snapple vitamin
supreme, and cough drops. And Margaret would berate me later
for giving her those things in front of everyone else, though she
was secretly pleased to show off the attention she received. "Why'd
you give me the cigarettes so everybody could see? Now they
knew I had them and they all bummed from me." So I'd say, "Who
gives a shit, I'll get you another pack," but Margaret refused to
be mollified.

I'd buy a bunch of crack and we'd split Buddha's for my Astoria pad,
a twenty minute walk up Twenty-First Street, stopping first at the
Sanford coffee shop where I'd order a hamburger deluxe to go, often
on credit, having spent all my money on crack, and me and Margaret
would share the meal later after polishing off the crack, passing the
burger back and forth and Margaret would allow for her bleeding
gums saying, "I got pyorrhea." Sometimes Margaret would spend the
night, other times I'd accompany her back to the stroll, where I'd
stand by in deep-freeze for an hour while she would work a little so
we could score more crack, and she'd give me the slip (crafty scamp

that she was) so she wouldn't have to share her hard-earned cake. Well, that romance fizzled out pretty quick though I did enjoy being with Margaret.

I recall one time getting high with Margaret when she told me, "You're running with a thoroughbred." And I just looked at that scrofulous wreck of a human being, emaciated, gums rotted, hair pulled out, careworn and weather-beaten right down to her rough, chapped hands (a trademark of crack abuse) and marvelled that, for all that detriment, here was a hard, fierce defiance and determination, astute enough to recognize the vast gulf that separated us, she who had been born to the life and I who stood on the outside looking in. Well, it didn't take Dick Tracy to pin me as a greenhorn, nor could a man conceal his lustful desires from a pro who earned her daily bread by servicing such pernicious peccadillos. It only served to remind me that I was miles from where I wanted to be and would discover, once I arrived there, that it was no place for a vegete or longevous future, if only I could get out alive.

When I first started going to Buddha's, after being frisked by the door guards (two) for a rod or a wire, I learned the drill, chapter and verse, from Buddha himself. Five dollars gratuity (cash or crack) to the house for every five bottles (caps/vials) purchased. A hit to Buddha from every bottle if you sat at the table. You placed your currency on a little tray (provided) and slipped it under the (sealed) bedroom door (with a sign hanging that stated: NO SHORTS) and, in a flash, out came the tray with your purchase on it. Five dollar bottles only. Anything accidentally dropped stayed dropped. If you brought anything to drink (I always had a quart of Miller High Life), you had to share it with Buddha. Much more ordered than Debbie's free-for-all with her grousing about throwing her fits like a crusty old bat (though I knew that as largely an act). Buddha's crib was neat and orderly and the bathroom, like Debbie's, was spotless—remarkable, especially considering the heavy traffic. Well, it didn't take Debbie long to track me down at Buddha's and she came flying in one day (I was sitting at Buddha's table) and demanded to know what did I think I was doing there? She had come to take me home. Everyone present was enjoying that scene immensely except for me and Debbie. Regular Peyton Place. Bad boy is caught truant by schoolmarm.

I had been going to Debbie's exclusively for a year; I'd walk to the side of her building and yell up to her fourth floor window and she'd lean out and throw down her keys to me. I'd let myself into the apartment house, being watched by old man Higgins, the local vigilante, who would patrol the structure looking for crack smokers on the stairwell landings and, when he discovered an offender, would blow a whistle he carried, loud and continuous, until the culprit ran away. I'm surprised no one ever clobbered him on the noggin. He would watch me like a hawk, making sure I used a key and not a jimmy. Then, once inside Debbie's, I would give her palm oil and she would make the run to cop. She always came back to me, waiting in her chambers, and invariably skimmed a little extra off the top before she returned. I knew that and would tip her anyway; she was good company and would make me laugh, and her nest was always warm and comfortable. We became easy with each other and she would occasionally try to shag me, but really wanted to be taken by me though, mostly, I couldn't be bothered because if I wanted action at all it was much heavier than that, reflecting the torturous lifestyle we each lived, manifesting such suffering through symbolic expressions sexual; though it was easier to pass over this heteroclite embodiment with a friend where normal lovey-dovey fornication would be more appropriate, saving the weird stuff for less personable acquaintances and strangers. As such, idiocratic sex is too fey to introduce between sound-minded (?) friends, at least with crack added to the mix (or so I persuaded myself), though Debbie probably would have complied, but I was usually too out of control on crack to make any moves; it would have been entirely for Debbie to initiate.

Sex, for me then, was a theater in which I expressed all the symbolic emotions that comprised my life through carnal translations. Sensations such as pain, anger, frustration took on erogenic manifestations and, as such (displaced sexual aggressions), comprised my perverse passions. And my interests in sharing those indiscretions were restricted to like-minded enthusiasts. I didn't wish to ramify mine and Debbie's friendship with such business (whips and chains) nor to feign some corny romance for which I had no desire. And so I refrained from any sexual involvement with friends like Debbie, not willing to risk complicating a relationship that had developed without sex. I was too green with crack, too shy to feel confident enough to expose those fetishes with a potentially straight participant. Thus my reticence to come out of the closet with Debbie. Even though, I should have known that, as a junkie, Debbie harbored such secret tendencies herself. My experience with crack then was still in the foundling stage. Actually, had I been more untimid or less embarrassed, Debbie could have been the perfect teacher for me, my ideal dominatrix. I missed a golden opportunity there because my macho imago stood in the way.

Finally, in exasperation, Debbie sent a limp-wrist she knew into her bedroom with me to find out if I was a nance. I remember the poof coming out of the room and shouting at Debbie, "He like queen!" But Debbie could get me hot just by wearing her tight, red latex hip huggers and a tight top. She had very long legs, a wide mouth indicative of a capacious well, eminent headlights with provocatively erect papillae and, naturally, she would have balled like a nigger. All in all, a pretty nice package. Yet, somehow, it never happened between us when it really should have. One of my small regrets.

When I got underway on my urban walkabout and irresolute future, I left a large suitcase of belongings stashed at Debbie's that she was still going through as I left her apartment. Buddha wound up in jail, his hot spot having finally gotten popped, door battered down and all.

There were homeless bums living on the top landings of some of the stairwells in Queensbridge projects, the first close look I ever had at the like. One of those fellows was friends with most of the girls I knew there and I became acquainted with him. His *nom de guerre* was Cowboy, a tall, handsome, magnetic cat, he belonged to a popular rap group that had a current hit album out. They had a unique style, original at the time, of blending female background singers into the chorus of the song's melody, a descant to the main theme, very effective in breaking up the repetitive rap and homogenizing it into contemporary rhythms, rendering the rap more melodious and palatable to the status quo. They had a current hit single at the time with the refrain, "I need a roundabout girl/Someone like you." I liked their music and I liked Cowboy. His Mom ran a flash house from her crib in one of the project's apartment buildings and I had been in her home aplenty (where local girls were allowed to hang out), sitting at her table, or even in her bedroom, smoking crack.

It was to Mom's kitchen I went one time when Brenda endeavored to cop for me and was hustled for (my) ten smackers. She was so peeved at the local dirtbags because they ripped her only because it was for (me) a honky. So Brenda summoned a flatfoot on the beat and recovered the sawbuck. Meanwhile, she knew she had payback coming big-time, possibly even a crack smile for ratting to the bulls and she had her head down on Mom's table and was crying and Mom came over and said to Brenda (completely overlooking the tears), "Come on now and sit up, you know you can't sleep at my table." And I felt so terrible for the poor kid for sticking her neck out for me like that. And Brenda was a fox too. Most all of the girls on the block there were gorgeous young vixens and the creepy neighborhood jokers all gave them flak and ripped them off and it is telling how Brenda stood up for me, a white boy, because I was always kind and respectful and solid with those girls.

That incident with Brenda was only one instance of the jackals taking me off at the Queensbridge projects. On another occasion, I negotiated with a loitering black street hoser for a clip (ten five dollar vials taped in a row like a cartridge belt)—fifty dollars worth of crack. As I was waiting for him to produce the material for my inspection, his associate came running over exclaiming, "Five-0, five-0, Come on!" Meaning the police were approaching, no doubt in a prowl car. So the dealer, picking up on the urgency, blurts out to me, "Hurry up, hurry up, Five-0," at which I (swallowing the hook) hurriedly concluded the deal and vanished into the ether. I later had to concede that those mechanics were smooth as I examined the clip of ten dummies.

Another episode occurred right between Debbie's and Buddha's buildings, on the open sidewalk where I was hanging out with Margaret. A slick darkie accepted from me three Jacksons to go cop. When he returned it was with only two Jacksons worth of product. He claimed that one of the greenbacks was counterfeit and that the dealer wouldn't accept it. When I asked for the return of the questionable bill, the beat artist claimed that the dealer kept it. As though I were conducting business with a bank. At least Margaret had the grace and acumen to proclaim to the runner, "Don't sweat it, there's plenty more where that came from." The point, if there is one, of these three illustrations of treachery is that it always pays to deal with an established crack house or bodega rather than trusting to the unpredictable vagaries of cold-copping.

At Queensbridge projects I had found camaraderie with other outcasts from society, identification, acceptance, fraternity amongst the persecuted. My brethren, fellow victims, the needy, unwanted, drug abusers and pariahs because of their profession (hustling), their race (a minority), their class (poverty). Amongst this procacious group of people I shared their separation from the median masses, felt no need to explain myself, to perform, to compete. I finally felt at ease. I wasn't lonely anymore. I fit in. Although, for the most part, such latitude applied predominantly towards the females, though I did make a few male acquaintances. For I was Caucasian and, as such, it was doubly hard to gain acceptance with the Afro-American bucks, to be trusted. Therefore, the few male confreres I made at Queensbridge projects were unique and rated amongst the treasured female associations for which that era of my life is of note and so fondly remembered. And it played a vital role in my development as a streetwise vagrant and tramp whose time was imminent.

Cowboy seemed to have it all. He was good-looking, long, lean and athletic. He had charisma, the girls flocked to him like bees to honey. He was a pop rapper whose group had a hit album and a video on MTV. He was popular, he knew everybody. Yet he was estranged from his mother and lived as a bum on a projects' stairwell landing, feeding his crack addiction as though stoking a furnace. At the same time, people regarded me as though I were of rank. Of a green-eyed profession, education, social standing, address. And yet, we each, Cowboy and myself, one black, one white, could not fit the pieces together and, sadly, stuffed the empty spaces with drugs and alcohol, becoming mired ever deeper in the morass, the limbo of an outcast.

My Korean boss at the all-night deli where I worked on First Avenue used to call me a bum. And I'd say to him, "I work twelve hours a day (7 p.m. to 7 a.m.), how can I be a bum?" But he was wiser than I, and able to see much of what I didn't keep hidden. He would remark, as he handed me my twenty dollar advance each morning, "You doing something; I don't know what, but you doing something." And deep down I knew that he had me pegged, but we both also knew I was good for him, and thus my job surety was iced. As I ran off to Buddha's, stopping at the liquor store along the way (liquor stores being open at 7 a.m.—this is New York).

To be free in the middle of the bustling city with hard money in my pocket, the whole world unfolding before me, was the greatest feeling. I was Marco Polo bringing tea and spices back from the Far East. I was Genghis Khan marauding across the great plains of China. I was Dr. David Livingston embarking unto darkest Africa on the cusp of the Gilded Age, heading up the White Nile in a dugout. A dream world? A fantasy world? It was real enough, I can attest. A dream come true, though, like a successful union, something that had to be worked at day by day.

One very late, hibernal night, after departing from work at the First Avenue deli, I entered the Union Square subway station to be assailed by blasting rock music. In an almost deserted underground corridor, I found two young disheveled Mexican kids playing amplified electric bass and guitar in a frenzy worthy of

Jimi Hendrix. I stood agog and listened, captivated by the energy and the sound, swigging from my pint of gin, tossing coins into the open guitar case. The guitarist had three foot pedals covered with his jacket—fuzz box, echo chamber, and wah-wah pedal—all of which he employed with proficient abandon. I noticed, too, that the bass player played with his fingers, sans pick. Those guys were awesome. All they needed was a drummer. Finally, at the end of a set, I approached them (they were all smiles) and told them, "I'm your drummer." This they accepted with cavalier graciousness, fellow caitiff that I was, and I invited them home with me to Astoria, where I was still in possession of those premises, for to play together as our newly formed trio, Xeno. Thus we happily made our way into the night, the two lugging their enormous *Marshall* amplifier and guitars, all the while palavering like a pail of wasps.

The Mexicans were brothers, the guitarist being the elder and leader, the bassist having callous fingers split and raw and corrupted from playing bare-handed in the icy grip of winter's tooth, the which he regarded as a badge of honor. They were wandering minstrels, homeless, and we quickly bonded. On the train ride to Astoria, elder brother (who was the spokesman) asked me, "Do you know where we could get some crack?" The magic word. So we disembarked at Queensboro Plaza and proceeded to the Queensbridge projects and Debbie's. Upon insinuating into Debbie's with my newfound friends, introducing them as my new band (the guitarist proclaiming, "He's our drummer"), Debbie regarded me with derision. "How could you bring complete strangers up here?!" To which I assured her soothingly that they were cool, "Just look at them." So the guitarist dug out from the back of the amplifier fifty simoleons and gave it over for Debbie to go out to cop with. Upon her return and handing over the crack to the Mexicans, they proceeded to enter into a la-la land of their own, so engrossed with the embrace of the drug, oblivious to all else and, regarding this, Debbie gave me a glower that said, Look at those two novices, Why do you vex me so? At which I only shrugged. Certainly two Mexican neatherds couldn't come between me and Debbie.

Finally, the band left the projects and, at length, we arrived at my redoubt whereupon (typically) the guitarist announced that he wanted to return to Debbie's and purchase more crack. I shook my head and told him flat out, "No." His brother was flipping out that the guy was spending all their hard earned mazuma. Elder cautions that if I won't accompany him back to Debbie's, he'll truck there alone. I explain that even if he were to locate Debbie's flat again she would never serve him. But he is in the grip of crack fever, having a crack attack and it takes me awhile to convince him of his folly. At last, we settle down on the floor to rest (it was, like, three a.m.). Upon removing their decrepit sneakers, the kids informed me, "Our feet really stink." And did they ever. So much so that I rolled up the carpet so as not to have them despoil the pile with their rotten stench.

Come morning, we went out to a deli where I bought a container of coffee and the kids copped a dozen eggs, which they brought back to my pad and broke into a glass and drank raw, *a la* Rocky Balboa. Amazing. Thus nourished, we attempted to play together, our maiden voyage. Well, never, I think, did an acid rock group have their finest moment first thing in the morning, especially with the drummer hungover and everyone trying to impress the other. Ours was no doubt the most short-lived rock band in history, nothing of worth coming from our efforts, the resonance of the drums and the *Marshall* amplifier quaking the building and, by mutual consent, we packed it in. Xeno, just another pipe dream gone up in smoke.

My experience with public assistance, hereafter referred to as welfare, began (as a crack addict) with the cessation of my professional career in the formal food service industry and the onset of my sporadic interment into the peculiar, covert society of coffee shops and delis as temporary, casual labor. Coming at a time of unwillingness or inability to work, with no unemployment benefits or any other form of income, and urged on by my new friends in the dome world, welfare was the logical next step for me.

I began my welfare involvement from the Queensbridge offices in Long Island City, while I still retained my apartment in that same township, though I graduated to the Fourteenth Street offices in New York City when I became homeless in Manhattan. For the sake of simplicity, my description of the typical welfare experience, in signing up and remaining signed up, shall be a summation of my overall participation with welfare, combining numerous locations in both Queens and Manhattan, covering a period of ten years.

My comprehensive impression of the average, overcrowded welfare office is of a brightly lit, sterile (if only it were clean), utilitarian space of Kafkaesque quality, such as huge waiting rooms where one might sit for days unnoticed; tedious interviews by idiot savants of whom the closer you looked, the less of them you saw; and of rote processes of whose design "puzzling" would seem generous.

Step one: Go early in the morning and bring your own pen and a bag lunch and cigarettes and something to read. You will probably be there all day. You will need to produce a birth certificate, a state motor vehicle ID, and a SS card. Bring a green card if applicable.

Step two: Do not attend intoxicated or under the influence. You will not be served.

Step three: Have your story rehearsed. Do not wing it. Those interviewers can tell if you're inventing your story on the spot. They do this all day. If you're a mother, bring the kids. It will help if you already applied for unemployment and were denied.

Bring proof. Somewhere along the line, you will have to register with the state employment office unless you can prove that you can't work; i.e., disabled or a mother with an infant. If you're losing your residence, bring an eviction notice.

Step four: You must have an address. If you are homeless on the street, have someone or a shelter allow you to use their address. You may be living in a shelter or a rehab.

Step five: Be polite. Those interviewers are the ones who will help you or not. Your application must be approved by the first person you see. Do not alienate them by abusing them. Find out what they want and give it to them. You will probably have to return more than once.

Step six: Be needy. Do not admit to having any assets. You won't receive welfare if you own a car or present yourself in a designer outfit and a hairdo. Remember, you are desperate, that's why you are there.

Step seven: If you admit to having a substance abuse problem, you'll have to enroll in a treatment program. This can work to your advantage if you're willing to participate. It can be superfluously simple, i.e., some counseling you attend for thirty minutes or an hour once a week. Check your Yellow Pages for a treatment center near you.

Step eight: Be firm in your answers, yet brief. Do not prevaricate. Be consistent, do not change course midstream. If you don't drink, you never have even one beer. If you're hungry, you don't have even one egg in the refrigerator. When asked about your finances, say that you are flat broke. How did you travel to the welfare office? You walked. You do not have a bank account. Bills, when you can afford it, are paid by money order procured at the post office. If asked how often you clean your residence, the answer is everyday, including the bathroom. You can not have any legitimate job, on the books, using your real SS number. Do not lie. They automatically check, irregardless. Becoming emotional rarely helps. Those interviewers are immune, they've seen it all. Just make certain that you are desperate, but in control, that's why you have come to apply for welfare.

Step nine: Try to obtain emergency relief immediately—cash, food stamps, subway tokens. Those resources are available.

Step ten: Once you receive your welfare card (after the eternal longueurs of waiting at a disjunct location to be photographed, and at another location for finger imaging) you will be on the payroll. Your benefits will be available from any check cash location regularly. Also, you'll be eligible for medical treatment at many clinics and select private practitioners. Your welfare card will be the only ID required for most citywide purposes as the requirements for obtaining one preclude any additional ID.

Step eleven: Your benefits have to be renewed regularly. Do not ever miss a recertification appointment or any scheduled appointment. You will be terminated immediately if you are even late. Then it's back to square one.

Step twelve: Welfare will pay your rent direct to your landlord if you live in an approved housing unit, like a resident hotel or public housing projects. This relieves the temptation of spending the rent money. There is a program called One-Shot Rent where welfare will pay your arrears to stop an eviction. This can only be utilized once. You need an eviction notice to qualify.

Step thirteen: Selling Food Stamps—Usually, most check cash concerns attract a hustler outside buying food stamps for cash; something like six or eight dollars green for ten dollars value in food stamps. Also, many Spanish bodegas will sell beer and cigarettes for food stamps. May the force be with you.

Medical treatment, as a welfare recipient, generally leaves a lot to be desired. In my experience, attending public assistance clinics, like the Stuyvesant Polyclinic on Second Avenue in the East Village, was an endlessly futile repetition of return visits that rarely provided satisfactory treatment. Instead, I felt like a pawn being manipulated in a scam to milk welfare, billing Medicaid in a bureaucratic cycle of fraud.

Appointments for from fifty to one hundred charity cases are all scheduled for nine o'clock a.m., a cattle call where you can wait until late afternoon to be seen by a provider. Then you are referred for some test, an X-ray, blood work, consult with a specialist, all at different locations, which could take weeks, then back to square one where you are given a placebo by the resident mountebank. I've received the runaround on numerous occasions until I've finally given up the struggle. Psychoanalysis, which is available, that I felt might be of some benefit to me, was repeatedly denied on the grounds that I achieve something like one year of sobriety first. I felt that my substance abuse was merely symptomatic of a deeper problem. I mean, does the obese patient need to lose one hundred pounds in order to qualify? Or the nymphomaniac abstain from fornicating before being treated?

Another adventure was dental treatment. Welfare, as a rule, will pay only for extractions. One event took place in a dental college where the student was preparing to perform an extraction without having first taken an X-ray. Upon being intercepted by her instructor on this oversight, it was also noted that she (the student) was reusing a hypodermic syringe which she had laid down without capping the needle. "No problem," the foreigner remarked, as she sheathed the contaminated nib. On a separate occasion, at another hospital, as I was undergoing an extraction, the assistant (a mean, evil-hearted distaff of color), whose role was to suction my salvia, used her sharp-edged tubular metal tool to gouge my gums, whose pressure I was able to discern and purpose to intuit, so that I communicated those suspicions to the dentist, who confirmed the vile, hateful deed and dismissed the malevolent felon forthwith. Afterwards, I was able to see (in a mirror) the damage that showed my gums sliced to ribbons. Payback to whitey for a miserable black lifetime of persecution.

Nevertheless, I have enjoyed some competent, expedient and pleasant treatment as a Medicaid recipient, one such instance of which I will relate and for which I wrote a letter of appreciation that found its way to the bulletin board of the appropriate department. I had a sebaceous cyst on my shoulder that required removal, whose procedure was performed in the ambulatory clinic at Beth Israel Hospital. The entire process went so smoothly and painlessly, with every effort made for my accommodation and comfort, the staff being so pleasant, right down to soft music in the operating room. I was totally unprepared for such royal treatment, afforded every courtesy (I'm just a bum), that I told all my friends and sent a letter of gratitude to the hospital. Six months later, I was back at the same ambulatory clinic for some new treatment and recalled to the personnel my prior pleasure there when a couple of the nurses exclaimed, "You're the one who wrote the nice letter." In my limited experience of Manhattan hospitals—midtown, downtown, east side, and west side—I rate Beth Israel the all-around best.

At one point, well into my homeless career, I determined to attempt to enlist on the SSDI program. My monthly welfare cash allotment was $120, whereas Social Security benefits paid up to $1,000 for the same installment. So many bums who I knew of were reaping those rewards, qualifying by being either substance abusers, psychotic, or meeting any number of other equally absurd eligibility requirements. With the assistance of an alcoholism counselor, I submitted my application. Denied—a new ruling whereby alcoholics no longer qualified, one must be a full-blown heroin addict to fill the bill. More than a couple of local bums of my acquaintance met the requirements by being clinically diagnosed as manic-depressive, schizophrenic, or subject to seizures. All one needed was the right swami. Up to the mental health office at Stuyvesant Polyclinic, I enlisted the aid of a psychiatrist and resubmitted my SSDI application as a certified psycho. Denied. I was crestfallen. My program counselor, however, encouraged me to try again, claiming that everyone is denied on the first attempt. "You'll get it on the appeal," he urged. But I'd had it by then and quit in discouragement. Years later, I would succeed, though it required two additional applications, with my enrollment in a psychiatric treatment program and a year's worth of vegetating from the massive doses of psychotropic medication. If you weren't crazy before the treatment, you were gaga after those boffins were through with you.

There was a Catholic organization, run by ordained sisters, a shelter or halfway house of sorts, deep in the bowels of Long Island City, behind the Queensbridge projects, an hour's walk from my home in Astoria. To this charity was I directed when I was broke and starving in the vernal days of my fledgling career as a bum. There, the kindly sisters handed out foodstuffs, on the first Wednesday of every month, to needy walk-ins. Thus did I present myself, where I was required to wait (the sole applicant at the moment) in a well-appointed sitting room for thirty minutes. During my period on standby, there arrived an odd couple of slovenly hobos, practically blind drunk, the crass one of the two going on about how they'll just catch a free box of eats and,

"Ain't we a couple of city slickers, haw haw." I was eventually summoned into a large pantry room, a small warehouse stocked to the ceiling with packed shelves of boxed and canned goods. This was my first acquaintance with such staples as powdered milk, powdered eggs, cheapo boxes of macaroni and cheese whose powdered cheese sauce mix called for the addition of butter and whole milk (duh?), freeze dried pouches of questionable (product of Venezuela) meat, and instant potatoes and cereal products. Also included were packages of macaroni, dry legumes, cornmeal and rice, cans of tomato sauce, kernel corn, beans, carrots, peas, a veritable treasure trove of complimentary, filling nutrition. And, which weighed a ton when carried, in a cumbrous box, three miles home on foot. As I was exiting the premises with my donated parcel, I happened to pass by the besotted po' crackers who were being turned out empty-handed by a reproving sister, irregardless of the crass one's mitigation that, "Well, I had a couple of beers with lunch," (neglecting to add that his lunch consisted of a pint of Jack Daniels).

Being a bum is not easy. If you want to survive, and eat, and rest, then you need all your wits about you. The ones who always let their guard down simply vanish. It takes practice, like anything else, to be a successful bum, and time on the street as a bum gives you that practice pdq.

What I found on the street was real in a sense that all pretext was stripped away and what was revealed was pure, immediate, urgent. This, to me, was a relief from behaving according to codes, canons, a conventional prescribed system where everything seemed contrived, bogus, non-genuine, caught up in the rat race of conforming to a mold, judged and persecuted by sane, civilized men, "to submit myself to the criticisms of an obtuse middle class which entrusts its morality to policemen and its fine arts to impresarios."[1] I never want to follow the leader, there is no rational frontier other than the street. To be a bum everything is vital and true unto itself, everything is up-front. To be a bum is to separate yourself from civilization, to escape into the anonymity of the street, one of the only recourses left for autonomy. Meanwhile, the sacrifices of the homeless are greater than of those living in the material world, yet a worthy price for freedom, or at least the illusion of freedom because the contemporary urban bum relies heavily upon the society from whose strictures he's escaping, a quasi-wild state, tamed only as the city's mice and sparrows are tamed in their dependence upon whatever the city discards.

The mind-set of the homeless is as varied as in any other walk of life. There are the perennial victims, the proud aggressors, the sly and cunning, the ambitious, the fatalists and the prosaic; there are cold-blooded killers for hire and those who kill for lust. Personally, I maintained a minimalist approach towards self-preservation, obtaining only what I absolutely needed when I desperately needed it; I never sought to stock up on supplies or to steal something just because it was there for the taking. I mixed with all types of characters in situations where it was unavoidable but I preferred to be alone. Virtually no bums are social animals, though I've seen various pairs buddy up, a tag team where one is always awake and on guard. The only real friends I ever had on the street were prostitutes and those I loved, respected and admired (*aux aguets*)[2]. The only social bums I ever knew were long-term residents in flophouses or welfare hotels but,

---

1 James Joyce, *A Painful Case* (*Dubliners*)
2 on one's guard

for the most part, the urban bum is a solitary being, living and dying alone.

When I turned to crack, I did so with a vengeance. I had been cheated and abused in my profession which had been the lynchpin of my life. I was hurt, frustrated and vindictive. Twenty years of devotion kaput. I had no interest in starting over. At the end of a career I had nothing to show—some fine furniture, a marketable trade, an erstwhile spread in an opulent (*Town & Country*) leisure magazine—a memoried stela to my quondam pride. No family, no friends, no life insurance policy. No ambition. I'll drop out of this miserable existence and be a bum. Cast my fate to the winds and the dogs. What was left of my fervent, fabled and failed career wasn't worth rousing myself to salvage. Pandering my talents to some ostentatious, unremunerative pimp, my fraudulent act of the zealous, dutiful servant—of this work I resign. I'll never be a company man again. Never pledge allegiance. *Res publica* doesn't need me. I've become an outlaw, expatriate, misanthrope. My devolution was the street and the life of a bum, to go native, savage, wild. Surrounded by a vogue, sophisticated, technological culture I must go underground to flower out. Into an uncharted frontier, across a boundary, out of the known into the unknown; an indivisible desideratum, a rite of passage, something raw, unwonted, challenging; a recrudescence. A place that remains alien even to its own inhabitants, the street, the netherworld right beneath our very noses, that dark unknown region around back where civilized culture doesn't reach, the deserted zone that's haunted after the sun goes down, the ragged edge, beyond the pale, the barren and twisting stretches of asphalt jungle where dangerous animals lurk in every shadow, around every corner and Red Indians stalk your defenseless wake. Thus is the street, the wilderness into which every homeless vagrant enters and where exits, when they exist, are either closed or in deep camouflage.

As a bum, oppression is all around you. Any establishment you enter you are watched openly, be it a Korean deli, a supermarket, or drugstore. Restrooms are denied you from coffee shops to whiskey bars. People don't sit next to you on subway trains and you are given a wide berth in any crowd. You are an outcast, a freak. No one wants to be near you. You feel this even in places that minister to your ilk: welfare offices, hospitals, soup lines and free clinics. Even in public terminals you are shunned by your own kind. You are a pariah. Police often harass you on sight. You are driven into the deepest corners of the city, out of sight, underground where the water rats compete with you for space.

You are a lowlife, you are withdrawn, forced into yourself. Not an introspection but a receding of sense and sensation, a pathos, a dulling of enthusiasm and faith, a blocking out of stimulus so that you are rendered defenseless and vulnerable. Prey. Days wandering knee-deep in pea soup, slogging along, keeping your eye on the sparrow, beating the drum, waving the flag. I could not say precisely what I sought in the city—excitement and composure both? A purposefulness, a blossoming of my true nature? All I knew was, at that strategic point in my life the city felt right.

I was frightened all right. And hinky. Dropping out from an existence, an environment in which I wasn't making it into a cesspit, the anonymous abyss of the street. I try to glamorize it, romanticize it, and in many respects it was glamorous and romantic. Avant-garde. I looked for and created those qualities. But let's face it, street life is desperate business and there is little enjoyment to be had without a secure spot, some room or space you can call your own. The raw street—the parks and sidewalks and alleyways, the waterfront and subway tunnels and abandoned buildings—are all snares to trap the human game that tread there. A maze through quicksand and deadfalls that I miraculously navigated for nearly ten years. A country boy, a college boy, jumping into the snake pit of depravity, psychosis and death. I was never haughty. Always wary. Forever blessed. I tell my story with the deepest humility. And not a small sense of satisfaction. I loved the street but I never lost my fear, my respect of what the street can do. The big bad street. I didn't beat the street but I survived it.

And suddenly there is capture in the moment and the future is now and it is good and there is no past nor regrets, only impetuous *joi de vivre* at being footloose and fancy-free and happening in the metropolis, the sap and marrow and jive of the days and nighttime traffic and action in a ever happening presence; hip, hot, cool, singing "Pea Soup," "Chee Poo Pa," bouncing, as happy as can be; grinning, laughing, shouting, "Yahoo!" Not having a care in the world, no responsibilities, no bills, no rent, meals were all handouts, clothes from charity, cash from welfare or hustling. Most bums, if they last for years on the street, have developed a formula, a system for survival that includes complacency, harmony and acceptance with their surroundings. A *laissez-passer.* They enjoy being a bum, looking like a bum and, often, being regarded as a bum. They say, "Drop dead," right back at their persecutors, they are mean and they are proud. They are simple people, animal lovers, humanitarians, liberals, as well as being broadly tolerant. We enjoy playing our character to the hilt, in the big picture, being a part of it all—to capture the moment.

A convenient asset of the urban bum is variety in his otherwise boring routine of daily life as he watches the world pass him by. For many bums, laziness is paramount in their own often limited activities, a sameness to their days of passivity. And so people-watching provides a variation to the otherwise monotony of daily subsistence and it comes by of its own accord, a perpetual parade of characters to entertain and inform the stationary bum. There's nothing like the city streets to dish up an endless array of people, especially in polyglot residential areas like the Lower East Side or Hell's Kitchen or Harlem or Washington Heights. Areas that lend themselves to bums rather than the cookie-cutter, rubber stamp areas like Wall Street and City Hall or the Upper East Side and Midtown. Only the city can offer such an omnium-gatherum of peculiar characters: livid, eccentric, surreal, prosaic, ineffable, intellectual, homophobic, homosexual, vegetarian, macrobiotic, perspicacious, chary, religious, symbiotic, natty, tatty—a wordbook full, the city's got 'em all.

My first months on the street were filled with uncertainty, suspicion and angst, the adjustment akin to arriving in China. My days and nights were consumed with survival: food, shelter, safety. There was no room at that time for enjoying my liberation, for following the cockles of my heart. My very naiveté made me a rube, a ben, a target for street predators, for the police. Yet for all that hardship and hazard never once did I have even a rind of regret for choosing the street and the life of a bum. I had precious little acumen, aptitude, animus to consider that this skein of existence might one day improve, that I stood a chance to develop the didactic street skills, the edifying elixir, the sweet arcana to not simply endure, but to prosper in my new sovereignty. It was a time of discovery and of plenitude in sensation, extremes, a maximum experience. I was enmeshed on a battlefield and my sole concern was victory. I would eventually suffer from battle fatigue, shell shock, schizophrenic paranoia, but that would come later. For now, in the beginning of my new occupation, the manifold lessons came in lively succession from that stern, remorseless taskmaster, the street.

There I was, "having cast my bread upon the waters, doing exactly what I had promised myself what seemed like so long ago,"[1] undertaking a voyage upon the dark, uncharted streets of New York City. "And there was music of a kind, barbaric though it might be, crude and mournful and my spirits revived as I emerged to face a whole new life,"[2] though, perhaps, no better than a child, a naif seduced by the riddle of terra incognita, that which would destinate my sweet by-and-by.

I had joined the ranks of the exiled, the damaged, the walking wounded who could not, for some reason, function within the confines of organized society. This had become my manifest destiny, the future expansion of myself. Yet, weren't some of those walking wounded simply wearing their defects on the outside? Wasn't our culture, as a whole, defective in its approach to the surrounding environment, the spoliation of our planet and its various life forms, being abused, pillaged and polluted by a superior intelligence that must prove its dominion by anatomizing and reordering what providence or the heavens granted us in all its natural beauty and wonder? Are our concrete cities better than the forests which have been cleared to make way for snarling traffic jams? Do we need to go faster in order to achieve happiness sooner? Must we increase and extend our species until the planet can no longer sustain us? These are questions for which I have no satisfactory answer, only that I knew I needed to withdraw from it all, to extricate myself from the demands and intricacies which with society had me bound. I had been wrapped in a web that, for me, was no longer working, and I could see this syndrome in my fellow man all the more clearly as I stepped back, hoping, perhaps, for some new insight or some turn of events that would, for me, finally make sense.

For now, I was no longer living against the barriers and constraints imposed upon me by a society, an ideology rigid in its theory yet amoral in its practice. I was released into the wilderness

---

1,2 John Brunner, *The Great Steamboat Race*

of the street, a primal jungle where values were met head-on and every consequence was immediate. I was free to follow my inclinations and impulses wherever they might lead with no concern for recriminations or reprisals that had heretofore inhibited my choices and plagued my resolve.

Much of my wandering, vagabond homelessness were times of trouble and travail, having no security against the ever constant threat of street predators which wore down my emotional reserves to neurosis. Also, periodic episodes of working incompatible (temporary) straight jobs inculcated me into bouts of deep disquietude and depression. I recall one such period during which I sought refuge in the little brown jug, mindlessly drinking myself senseless daily, whence I was propped in a stupor against a storefront, sitting splaylegged on a afternoon rush hour sidewalk, nearby to an AA conclave which I had previously patronized, when an AA acquaintance passed by and paused upon noticing me and our eyes locked in *entre nous* recognition and that personage remarked, "Well, you're happy." Embarrassing, because I was the farthest thing at that moment from being happy. I had yet to discover my personal formula for peace and happiness amidst the confusing distractions of urban culture in which I bounced around like a yo-yo. For me, it took a miracle to find my true path, my telos, an uncustomary phenomenon for a misbegotten derelict.

The bum is treated as the lowest of the low, he is beneath the criminal; often perceived as something subhuman or, at best, uncivilized. He, the bum, is reminded of this inferior status repeatedly in his day-to-day living, does not become calloused to it, the rebuffs, the jibes, having to bypass restroom facilities and eateries because they are not open to him. Each new reminder strikes the raw spot and deepens the wound until the bum despises the society upon which he depends, despises himself for being dependent upon those who despise him in return. A dignity so trampled upon that it is all but recognizable.[1] Bums are the eternal strangers, outsiders in a Waspy, capitalist culture who are beneath racial/anti-Semitic prejudices, on a level with vermin, like roaches swarming on the garbage heap of our great civilization. This was a popular sentiment as prefigured in 1895 when the New York Conference of Charities urged NYC officials to underwrite a "Tramp and Beggar Farm," where vagabonds who remained unregenerate would face segregation for life.[2]

Bums lie dying in doorways, on sidewalks, in tunnels as Manhattanites pass them by, day after day, even as they turn into corpses, no one will offer assistance in the slightest. The dying bum is resented as a detraction to the illusion that all is well; how dare they display their suffering so, reminding us of the human misery in our midst and of our own heartlessness and unyielding self-centeredness, disrupting our fantasy of plenitude, forcing us to face the boundaries we've constructed between our image and our humanity; refusing to share the intimacy of connecting with a fellow shattered life.

To describe the bum, in his doggerel praxis, is to describe a species whose individuals are as varied as the idiosyncrasies they possess. The sour perfume of sweat, rot and ordure; gaze of eyes stark and wary; posture and ethos heedless and indifferent; movement reserved; garments of rags incongruous; laughter real; hearing acute; perception of smell keen; third eye and sixth sense developed; purpose enduring; airs aristocratic; heart and soul beset. The bum by all accounts is rancorous and not one to cross paths with, a resigned life force fueled by animosity, a self-contained

1 John Howard Griffin, *Black Like Me,* some words and ideas
2 Kenneth L. Kusmer, *Down and Out, On the Road: The Homeless in American History*

vessel of sorrow. However, though this generalization may fit the majority of street bums, there exists a vast number of bums who take much better care of themselves and have outgoing attitudes, working bums and full-time guests of flophouses, shelters and resident hotels, well-groomed prostitutes and a significant segment of bums who want to be noticed, who go to great lengths with their appearance, with the cut of their jib. I never did laundry during my years on the street. I would wear clothes until they were too dirty and then throw them away and obtain fresh apparel from the Catholic Worker or the Salvation Army or some other charity. I'd go through half a dozen pair of socks a week, twice that (wearing triple layers) during winter. All in all, the bum, the street, is an existence that defies understanding in lieu of experience. *Je ne sais quoi.*

The homeless do not carry wallets, backpacks, fanny packs, handbags, or other such carry contrivances. They use shopping bags or wheeled canvas hampers, sometimes a thirty-gallon plastic trash bag slung over the shoulder or, less often, wheeled grocery wagons. (Some prostitutes will carry a clutch.) Like a majority of street people, I carried my necessary lose papers (welfare card, Social Security card, and phone numbers) in a plastic Baggie folded into a neat little rectangle and often rubber banded. Paper money (unless on a drug run) was broken into small denominations and dispersed about my person. Drug paraphernalia and cigarettes were readily accessible. And I have never seen a homeless person wearing a watch. The average bum wears nothing of value on his person—no jewelry, no rings or necklaces, no designer labels. In fact, the average bum won't even have a pack of cigarettes visible in a shirt pocket. Nothing to attract attention or to make themselves likely targets for a stickup.

Bums want the feelings that other, ordinary people want. Surety—that something, somewhere belongs to them, is their own. Safety and well-being—shelter, warmth, comfort, a good meal. Reassurance—a friend, a pet, a nurse, a priest, a counselor or caseworker. Satisfaction (from something accomplished or well-done)—a bountiful harvest from the day's foraging, some rewarding work, a hobby, making someone happy, earning the approval of a paragon. These things come from different sources and with varying regularity: shelters, hospitals, detoxes, rehabs, flophouses, churches, jobs, 12-step meeting rooms, chance encounters. Bums don't want the responsibility, the constraints of the straight world, of society, they don't want to act, perform, or behave according to rules, codes, laws. Bums are rebels, nonconformists, misanthropes, retards, psychos, sociopaths, addicts, nut jobs, outcasts of every description, most of whom execrate the city that provides them with a plausible means of support which they'd be hard pressed to duplicate in a rural environment.

Like every Manhattanite, I had observed bums in my daily travels, in parks, on sidewalks, and camped out underground around subway token booths. Sometimes I donated spare change, most times I passed them by ignored, and once drew up a mock eviction notice (shared with a coworker) to heckle one young lady who had taken up residence in the Forty-Seventh Street ® train station at Broadway where she gradually established a regular household in which she seemed thoroughly content. She even had regular suitors approach her evenings when my friend and I awaited our train back home to Astoria.

Another young woman had been encamped on a lower level at Grand Central Terminal, opposite the Oyster Bar, surrounded on the cold concrete floor by a litter of glossy magazines—*Seventeen, Harper's Bazaar, Variety*—smiling mischievously at the milling press of commuters. And I, in my crescent disdain, would pity those unfortunate creatures, never once considering that such downtrod thrall might be content, at peace with their circumstances, aspiring to none of the commiserating, condescending sentiments of the mainstream masses.

Only years later could I, in retrospect, see that I had been the piteous one, rushing through my ingenuous majority always drunk, with no more glistering goal than to inflate my own ego and satisfy my narcissistic urges, concerned with appearances and philandering and scoring the best dope; going in circles, the relentless distractions, the years of devastating loneliness. Just another modern American dogging the dream. While the decades mounted with dozens of false starts, caught up in chasing happiness while never slowing down to find and enjoy it. "What was it all about? Once I thought I knew. But now I'm not so sure. You know, the Hungarians have a saying—Before you have a chance to look around, the picnic is over. It has all gone by so fast. Like a dream. How is it the days crawl by and yet the years fly? I begin to wonder, is it the way we live that matters? Or is it what we accomplish that's really important?"[1]

I came to the earth-shattering illumination, whence I drew an unhappy end to my professional career, approaching midlife (with the profit of crack), that I would do the unthinkable and drop out from society, foreswearing all its impedimenta, and hit the road with no more evident planning than the bums whom I'd passed by for so many years. And with no more expectation of happiness than I had heretofore experienced, yet determined to at least forgo that beau ideal, which had latterly proved to be but an elusive rainbow. And mayhap it was nothing more than that change of attitude which allowed me to find happiness or to accept happiness when it found me.

I was possibly experiencing a kind of mid-life crisis where I wished for one last fling, perhaps nothing more than a desire to shake things up a bit, for I was surely embarking on a kooky new course. The forties are funny that way, strange things occur to

---

1 Laurence Sanders, *The Anderson Tapes*

people in their forties.[1] A longing for juvenescence, for a departure from habit, routine, the very yoke of civilization. Many things in my life had been tossed on the rocks at that time. "21" had closed their doors and I was unhappy in my new situation at the Ritz—my career often being the only stability in my deviable existence. I had split up with a girlfriend of long acquaintanceship, had lost some of my pets, was bereft of family and friendless. I had fallen into a funk from which I fervently despaired to rouse myself yet couldn't seem to take any initiative. Meanwhile, the daily newspapers were plastered with reports of (crack) a new scourge upon the city—just the ticket, perhaps, to give a kick to my laconical, forty year old life. And thus it was with eager anticipation that I ventured forth to seek my imminence in vaporous spirals sublime, in the womb of a fourth dimension, a lotusland which would prove to be a black hole that eventually sucked all my energy, spirit and goodness into its quenchless abyss, the Challenger Deep of urbanization.

City congestion breeds personal withdrawal as a defense reaction, a psychotaxis (automatic reflex), a self-centering isolation that cocoons oneself from one's neighboring surroundings, sort of a protective coating. Subways are a good example of such congestion wherein riders try to not touch one another and refrain from eye contact, which often can be interpreted as a challenge. Bums, who are shunned in the best of circumstances, become adept at psychotaxis while simultaneously, as if by osmosis, they interpret through extrasensory perception their surrounding stimuli and environs. This sixth sense is useful in both avoiding potential hazards and optimizing positive reinforcement, an added sensibility that the

---

1 Valerie W. Wesley, *Ain't Nobody's Business If I Do,* some words and ideas

bum hones to razor edge as part and parcel of his survival gear. A stranger's glance, a slight shift in posture, a reflex are enough for the bum to read between the lines. To get the message. He is not wanted. And so the bum moves through the sea of humanity looking for that single aberration, the compassionate heart that is open to, who feels sorry for his predicament. The deli where a coffee and roll will be forthcoming, the pizza parlor for a slice on the house, the hot dog wagon for a free bowwow. Often, retail markets will succumb to the bum's plight just to get rid of the guy, the busy establishment that doesn't want a bum outside dissuading away their business. The bum must be in tune with all of these facets in order to survive, in order to eat, in order to avoid a bashing. There is no greater target for abuse than the bum and he knows this all too well as he trawls the city for his provender. Foraging like a mouse or a sparrow all around the trampling horde, always a butt for the displaced vagaries of the straight world. Br'er Rabbit in the cabbage patch.

I once witnessed the police stop an old bum on the street who was pushing a large canvas clothes hamper in which were piled all his earthly possessions. At that moment, a garbage truck was making its rounds past the aforesaid confrontation and the police stopped the truck and proceeded to empty the poor bum's hamper into the hydraulic maw of the rolling sanitation receptacle, the fuzz laughing as the poor old soul watched all of his property vanish forever before his bewildered eyes. New York's finest in action when they could have been pursuing real criminals instead of amusing themselves by harassing a poor bum, making his miserable life more miserable. This specific sort of harassment became more prevalent with the city's new criminalization of the homeless and concurrent (1990s) sweep of the city streets.

There is something profound at work in society that is all but invisible yet whose force is fierce, will not be diminished, irregardless of the denial, the whitewashing, the counterfeit face put upon it. That is the disingenuous duplicity that is upon almost every facet of normal everyday life. To be civilized. And it is that deceit—mimicry of honest American ideals, artful integrity, very falsity—that all but assigned me to the street, driven into a confused, lugubrious travesty as a mutant of American gentry.

I was entertaining a new self of forbidden desires unleashed, flagrant, unchecked. Fueled by vengeance at a life that had failed me, or that I had failed and now must be abandoned forever, severed like an umbilical cord, the past, aborted, could not serve me any longer. So many different emotions merging, precipitating, mixing, separating, a mishmash of old and new, buried and surfaced, good and bad, yin and yang. I was becoming the center of my universe. I was experiencing Zen. Neither ideology or dogma held any boundaries for me. I had emptied myself of the past and would fill myself with the present, devoid of any future, a trip with the urgency of an endgame.

I was entering the world of the streetwalker who so blatantly reveal their bent. Though I was not selling myself as a sex object, I was selling out to a subculture whose values were erotic, importunate and exponentially induced. I entered a life of drugs, sex and violence with my latent image already poking through the thin veneer of convention I'd so easily assumed up to that point. My desire now was to tear away the conservative façade of sanity and to don the attire of hunger, savagery and sin. In all my unrestrained license I would make a statement, a living work of art, the product of bondage and discipline unfettered to burn unchecked to the universal, the anthropological ictus of our age, our culture, our modern attire. Thus, then and there, I gave my life, a reflection of all that's gone wrong with civilization, the inherent desire to subvert and augment nature, a passionate expression of ego and eros, the id overriding the superego in a valiant conflagration of lust. *Sartor Resartus* in twentieth-century America, my personal philosophy on clothes, the tailor retailored, represented on the backdrop, the canvas of our modern times. A fantasy world where people are called tag names and infantile regression is the norm, a game where repercussions are ill considered and justice may be circumvented. A shadow world where the Grim Reaper intrinsically stalks your every step.

Whatever made me give up a preordained life of affluence, vocation, primogeniture, to become a worthless piece of flotsam? I'm not sure I can accurately answer that. Or not want to. Laziness? Drug addiction? Insecurity? Shame? Those are the negative responses. But there are also in equal measure courage to cross a frontier. Pluck to face the street and its questionable moira. Faith to forfeit the status of my lineage for the concept of liberty. Lust for vice and its trappings. Disgust with a thankless profession. Betrayal by a political and cultural system that is a farce. Loneliness, sexual frustration, isolation. I was stuck in a morass that held me fast.

An added drawback was my work schedule. It always seemed to me, after a near lifetime of working nights, that night work was somewhat abnormal, a breaking of the natural rhythm and order of things, becoming largely a nocturnal being, sleeping during the day and denied the sharing of and immersion in average sociology. A freak, part of the night world, an alien to generic life cycles and their strictures. Apart from my job, I conceded little to the conventions which regulate civic life. The few dissipations in my down-home, night-clad existence quickly grew stale. There were clubs and bars open to me, both very costly; or cruising in my ride with a joint and a bottle—equally rewarding. There was cable television. There were silent projects on paper at the kitchen table so as not to disturb the neighbors, quiet hobbies, reading. And there were the blackouts—drunken episodes of incorrigible recklessness. And the denial.

Too, there was a larger, nagging sadness that served to harden my new resolve, being that ours is a culture of vultures, sadists and ghouls. We rape and defile our country leaving a trail of unconscionable filth in our wake. We have no respect for the dead or the living, excavating tombs and raising the Titanic to profane corpses and performing abominable autopsies on our own deceased in the most vulgar, obscene, irreverent manner, not to mention atrocious, profit-geared drug experiments upon innocent, unsuspecting humanoids and Third World peoples by big pharmaceutical companies and the United States Army, all in the name of science. We have thermonuclear devices developed to indiscriminately obliterate our own planet, having advanced over the past century from annihilating our own indigenous population (twelve million American Indians) and stealing their land, to the eradicating of entire cities of civilians across the board (Hiroshima and Nagasaki, not to mention razing Hamburg and Dresden)—all this mass genocide from a fastuous nation that coined the buzzword and leads the tribunals on war crimes. Abortion has become standard procedure, ripping out sentient fetuses from the worthless wombs of barbaric breeders who then have the audacity to call themselves Christian or Jewish or other pro-life religion. And not least is the cruel vivisection inflicted upon beautiful, defenseless, innocent creatures to test superfluous cosmetics and cleansers and other inane otioseness. This is a sick, pharisaical, blasphemous society from which I'm relieved to disengage myself.

Towards the end of my having a job and an apartment I used to walk home from work, the Fifty-Ninth Street Bridge over the East River to Astoria (London to Southwark), and the small patch of park at the city end of the bridge was always, in its garden-like splendor, littered with bums. Lining the benches, setting up house with their cardboard, a little hobo jungle. Naturally, from a romantic's eye view, this all looked very appealing, peaceful, part of nature in the city, carefree, autonomous. Naturally as well not to notice the small print to the program. Because once you're in the game the small print becomes the big print and the peaceful and carefree illusion disappear. But naturally we knew all that, it was merely a classic matter of displacement, of misdirected sexual aggressions. Well, what can I say.

Prior to my hitting the street, still entrenched in my soon to be ex-apartment in Astoria, I had become a pariah to my family. Those living in California told me not to phone anymore. My sister on Long Island said the same, didn't want to speak to me, wouldn't allow me to come to her home. "Don't come near my babies you maniac." Her husband, the only family I have by inheritance, would invite me out, meet me at the train station, we'd ride around in his car while he listened to my tales of woe, gave me encouragement, and always a twenty dollar bill. That was one friend who stood by me through thick and thin.

In spite of my own sister's disavowal of me, my brother-in-law managed to find and set up a furnished room for me to call my own, with a private bathroom stocked with toiletries and like amenities, complete with a made-up bed. He even drove me around to prospective job sites. Bending over backwards to help me. He just couldn't comprehend how I wanted shut from all that domestic and commercial commitment at that time. I had a job and apartment all along and was giving it up, packing it in for the ungoverned war zone of the street. Just the look of that constraining room and the thought of working in some orderly place of business was repulsive, stifling, claustrophobic. My relative was being so good and couldn't understand my aversion to something so basic that I just had to distance myself from. Moreover, he was suggesting that I move out to Long Island, away from the genesis of the city which is what drew me. My brother-in-law's abhorrence being dead against the very congested thrall and pollution of the city; we were two opposing forces clashing. I couldn't bring myself to even give his proposal a chance, feeling so bad to turn down his good will, and he being baffled at my determination to seemingly self-destruct. I was irrefragable in my iconoclasm, my tergiversation, in my resolution to cast off all remnants of a faith in the dogma, philosophy and ethics of a lifestyle, a belief in which I'd become maudlin.

There were a couple of weeks during which my young nephew from California was flying to New York for a short holiday, staying over at my sister and brother-in-law's home on Long Island, and it was expected that I'd meet him either there or in the city for a reunion. I hadn't seen him in a coon's age and this trip had been scheduled years in advance. At the point in time of the event (a good year into my homelessness), I was enrolled in Manhattan's Bowery detox and remembered, in my sobriety, the appointed rendezvous with haunting clarity. So I phoned my Long Island sister and told her I was in the hospital and wouldn't be able to meet with our nephew after all. She completely blew me off with such obloquy for my insurrection, charging me, "Well, that was to be expected of someone who was, after all, just a bum," with not a drop of concern as to why I was in the hospital or any related inquiries. Boy, how quick we are to forget our roots (both sis and hubby being cut from the same black cloth).

I see it still to this day, if one doesn't conform to the mold of one's own family's politics, or if one suddenly becomes an infidel, they're not wanted, they're an embarrassment, they're disowned. And so desperate am I for familial love and acceptance, for their approval, I forget all that condemnation in a heartbeat and come running at the first smile. Pathetic. Why, in all my alleged insensitivity and self-indulgence, am I always the sorry guy, the one to propitiate the breach, to tender the calumet.

All throughout my years on the street, I was in and out of touch with my heritage, my past, bringing the straight world—normalcy, the Establishment, society, family life, the work world—back in line with my new occupation only to be slapped in the face again and again, let down and kicked in the arse once more, ripped off in emotion and loyalty and speci, reminded over and over lest I forget that society does not take care of their own, the straight life is a backstabber, an arse bugger, a heartbreaker. Don't forget why you packed it in once, twice, don't forget a third time you idiot, because although the street will let you down, it never pledged allegiance to begin with.

It is not my intention to lampoon or disparage my family no matter how equitably I could shred their fidelity, probity and rectitude. It is enough to debunk and blast the mechanics of our culture in general to make my point, which is to delineate the myriad dissatisfactions and disenchantments which combined to lead me to crack and, subsequently, to the street. Once I was on the street I seldom attempted to contact anyone who remained from my previous life. I was on my own, wouldn't tumble to dragging anyone down with me. I hit the street not so much with wrath as with humility.

At all events, to deny the irresistible power of crack to tip the balance, to take control of my life, my willpower, is to misinterpret the facts. Let's face it, I never would have become a bum, homeless, on the street, were it not for crack. I saw it time and again the more embroiled in the crack and bum culture I became. That I so readily gave into crack's domination is meaningless, it would have gotten me anyway. Once you enjoy that mouthwatering flavor, take flight with crack, once you get a taste for all crack has to offer in one teeny-weeny puff—the euphoria, the endless possibilities—then you are hooked, line and sinker. That's why crack is so popular, the big epidemic. What you don't grasp until it's too late is you're a crazed addict. Turned me inside out. The city never saw so many cop killers, assaults, stickups. Only thing is, my stickups were a disaster—

I got a vic up against a fence one night in Astoria, me left paw coverin' 'is gob while I's pushin' a pigsticker against 'is gullet. I squeeze 'im fer 'is cake. The jay bites me mitt, what I pulls away from 'is chops, an' 'e screams bloody murder. I coulda either ice 'im in the gizzard or RUN! I weren't gonna get pinched bendin' over a bleedin' stiff, blood all over the place... I was shakin' like a leaf and I didn't even do it. Such is the criminal madness, the terror inherent in crack. Its power of eversion.

One of the side effects of crack, and I have seen it time after time, is violence in all its myriad faces. This may be likened to a sort of yohimbine challenge[1] for one with post-traumatic stress disorder, induced by crack, whereby the user dissembles into a fugue state and experiences the dissociation and helpless violent rage related to PTS as a result of the psychochemical alteration (alpha-adrenergic antagonist) that is the hallmark of crack toxicology. This is only a hypothesis, but whatever the scientific explanation, the actual effect is horrific and very real. And then there are varying degrees and manifestations of this tendency. I have experienced this phenomenon and witnessed myself go from a docile, gentle person into a destructive maniac in the space of a breath, an inhalation. My need and desire to destroy my surroundings, to trash my environment became overwhelming, irresistible as the effects of crack took hold of me. I was no longer comfortable in clean, orderly settings, I required squalor and chaos to appease and salve my emotions. I would cover my furniture with bedsheets (in my Astoria apartment) because it was too decorative and dignified to look at. I desired murkiness and severe, bare confines. I would fantasize having a duplex domicile, a stark and smutty remand cell for erotic crack sessions with newsprint

---

1 Scott Turow, *Unnatural Death*, idea

sheets masking taped over the windows, the only furniture tor-
ture devices—(unbeknownst to me then, I would create such an
environment in my future journey through the infernal regions
of crack addiction). And, by contrast, a neat, plush chambers as
a sober retreat. But alas crack would never allow or vouchsafe
the necessary discipline for such duplicity.

I also stopped bathing and began to stink, my feet went months
without being washed and would reek when I removed my shoes
(like my Mexican band brothers). I no longer took haircuts. I no
longer attended to laundry. It became embarrassing at work because
I knew I smelled rank and was unshaven and looked scruffy, even
in uniform. And, *cri de coeur*, I was the head of a top department
in a fancy hotel. As my superiors and subordinates began to dis-
approve of me, I began to lose my effectiveness as a leader. With
each notch lower on the ladder of respectability I descended, the
more my spite and malice increased. I took pleasure in sabotag-
ing the organization, the food production, the mechanics of the
hotel. I would allow important items to run out, like mayonnaise
(this was made by my department). I would fail to prepare, the
night before, items needed first thing in the early morning for a
breakfast meeting or the Sunday brunch buffet. I would walk out
on time when a last minute order came in for some GM specialty
work. Or I would call in sick on a day when cold canapés were
needed for one hundred fifty guests. Anything to discommode
the hotel staff and their clientele. I didn't give a damn. The
union protected me. I was borrowing money from the waiters,
buying cocaine from a porter, smoking crack right on the job. I
was stealing food and selling it to the waiters to take home. I was
the hotel subversive, in the teeth of my authority.

Part and parcel of violence in its many manifestations is larceny, a black corner of the soul whose depths are plumbed by drug
addiction and most notably by crack. I have fallen under this spell
at times, this hex, a spontaneous, irresistible lure to not only feed

my own selfish needs, but to violate some chivalrous boundary whose roots somehow belong to the sober or well-heeled.

My old friend Ernesto (whose home on West Forty-Seventh Street, only a block from the once famed Grapevine, which was at one time a matrix of transexual high life in a pre-crack era that was more honor bound and less invidious than the current crack-crazed climate), had the misfortune of falling under the magical glamour of crack and its concurrent dark side. Our reunion—long lost friends coming together to catch up on old times—predictably focused on crack, whence we required a supply of that nuclear particle (magical rock), where in the old days we'd chat over a drink or a joint. Thus, Ernesto gave me four Hamiltons with which to score while he awaited my return across the street. Needless to say I ran in the other direction as soon as I had my hands on the gelt. Who needed to share the drugs? Sad, sad, when Ernesto was a kind soul whom I liked. Lost, a friendship; lost, a rosy life, all for the fleeting, solitary wonder of crack.

By the time I was evicted from my Astoria apartment, I had trashed it beyond belief. I had priorly covered the walls in knotty cedar planks and now began pulling the planks off, leaving nail holes in the plaster walls. I had laid down imitation slate floor tiles and began ripping them up, requiring the remainder of the floor to be removed and new flooring installed after my eviction. Garbage was strewn so thickly that the entire floor was obscured. I had stripped the premises of all my property and was living in the barren apartment, sleeping on the floor in a bundle of blankets, sans electricity. I would steal rice from a supermarket and eat that, boiled, mixed with appropriated salad dressing. I had exhausted every coffee shop, pizza parlor and diner in the area for food on credit and was existing on my rice, food scraps purloined from trash cans and stale donuts discarded by Dunkin Donuts. Crack had left me demented and destitute.

On a Sunday, I would sit outside Most Precious Blood RC church in Astoria and beg spare change from parishioners exiting mass. I would even attend mass so as to be seen by the congregation, thereby evoking some sympathy (I hoped) for a fellow secular. And the cash thus panhandled was spent on beer and cigarettes, commodities I found hard to steal. There were a couple of local all night gas stations that sold cigarettes from a sliding drawer, like a drive-up bank window, and I would order a couple of packs of coffin nails while reaching for my wallet and usually the smokes would be passed through the drawer before the dough was put in and I would grab the fags and bolt, knowing that the lone attendant wouldn't leave the station to chase me. I pulled the same stunt in liquor stores where I'd order a pint of geneva and reach for my wallet and as soon as the booze was placed on the counter I'd grab it and tear out the door, knowing the cashier wouldn't leave the store to pursue me. Typical bum method of shopping. Eventually, my appearance became so slovenly and decrepit that I looked like a derelict even though I was working and sleeping in an apartment. For in fact I had become a bum in my mind and heart and soul. When I finally hit the street, my overall externals improved because I had stopped smoking crack for awhile and kept myself groomed and clean, and had even begun bodybuilding again. How incongruous could one get? Living on the street yet working out in a gym daily and holding a steady (part-time) job in a health food restaurant (description forthcoming).

But with crack came violence and my residences in Astoria and later in Manhattan at both First Street and the Kenmore Hotel were reflections of that tendency, creating and living in a pigsty (figuratively speaking since pigs are the cleanest of barnyard animals). Often, during a run of using crack, I would burn and lacerate myself to such extremes that to this day I carry lasting scars. It is to crack use also that I owe my heavy tattooing. Although I always admired tattoos, I don't think I would have covered most of my body if it weren't for crack. I have also witnessed, at least twice, crack-crazed maniacs tearing doors and doorframes apart from their rooms in a fit and frenzy of destruction that was so violent, scary and dangerous that to be nearby was to risk injury. I wonder if such behavior were a subconscious, symbolic act of breaching an opening or an escape image.

Similarly, I've seen slavering crack lunatics tearing up the slatted wooden seats of park benches in an uncontrollable rage of vehement destruction that caused me, on two occasions, to move to a different vicinity to escape their proximity. Another time, I watched a deranged maniac, in only shirtsleeves, sweating profusely, outdoors in the dead of arctic winter, clearly in the throes of a crack rush, tearing apart the metal security gate protecting the showcase window of a liquor store in the black hours of the night. To look upon his ravaged face was to gaze into the nightmare depths of insanity. There is no question as to the violent spirit of crack. Never has there been the degree, the level of stickups, muggings and murders before crack came along. Nor has there been the high number of policemen gunned down, all attributed to the name and nature of crack. I have witnessed copious masochistic behavior with crack, people hurting themselves (myself included) just for the fun of it. That is why prostitutes love crack; it enables them to totally demean, humiliate and harm themselves by performing fellatio, being maltreated and abused, and open to disease. They just love feeling like a piece of crap. "Mmm, dirty, dirty. Put it in my back pussy. Harder. Harder!"

There is also an obsession customary to crack fiends that involves the uncontrollable searching, the endless quest for something that will never be found, the ever-elusive illusion that lurks in the periphery of the crack addicts' imagination. Often looking for a piece of crack that's been dropped, lost or hidden (this activity sometimes known as ghostbusting), but usually it's just abstract searching as the crack causes synapses in the brain to shut down alpha-receptors which decrease the production of L-dopa which reduces the higher human intelligence to a lower form of monkey-type behavior (*i.e.*, searching for bugs), and produces uncontrollable tremors, shaking palsy, rigidity, impaired balance, and other chronic, progressive neurological disorders (associated with anti-dopaminergic symptoms of Parkinson's disease); looking through debris on the floor or a pile of clobber or a jacket pocket, hours, even days can be passed in this manner, as long as the effects of the drug last. Crackhead behavior. Cluck heads. Thus is the suchness of crack.

One time, between my termination from the Ritz and my hitting the streets of New York City, I worked in a fast-food emporium in Manhattan's downtown area. My sole job was to set up their cold salad bar where self-serve items were sold by the pound, everything was the same price, so one could mix-up their take-out tray with any combination of items. Many Korean delis offer that style of food service. In this store, the salad bar was a popular attraction yielding high sales daily. My selections were copious and my presentation was a key marketing strategy which included flowers and animals carved out of fruits and vegetables. This added touch became very popular amongst the routine courthouse clientele who came to look forward to the daily displays, and my Jewish bosses would ask me each morning, "What kind of animal are you going to make today?" For it was rare indeed to find that type of fancy work in low-level hash houses like delicatessens and coffee shops that never utilized even a tomato rose.

In the rear kitchen area where my workstation was located, was also the concern's cash safe. Of all places, the coffer was right next to my worktable. It was too irresistible, the proximity of the money was so close that I began to test the lock regularly by turning the combination dial clockwise slowly while exerting pressure on the handle. This was to determine if the combination had been left on daylock, a practice that is taboo and against policy and procedure in large corporations, whereby the combination of an open safe is turned to zero after the door has been closed so that one need only turn the combination to the final number for the door to open. It is used to save time in dialing through the entire combination on a safe that is opened and closed frequently, the door is locked at first try but quickly opened by dialing to the last number of the combination. Day after day, (patience, patience) trial after trial, I tested that lock knowing those lazy bums would sooner or later leave the safe door on daylock. I used to watch the bosses, out of the corner of my eye, going to the money chest and I could tell by how long it took them to open the door if they dialed through the entire combination. At busy times they'd have to run back for rolled change or packs of singles and it was much faster to leave the combination on daylock for in those places speed was of the essence. But I had to time my strike for when not only was I alone in the back of the house (which was a fully staffed kitchen) but during busy periods out front when the bosses would most likely not come back. Finally, one day, all of the pieces were in place and "click," the safe door responded like Open Sesame.

There were two metallic cash boxes inside the vault. The top box contained rolled change only. The bottom box contained banded packs of greenbacks. Some packs were singles and one pack looked like a mixed bundle of larger bills so I took that one only. Almost immediately after I closed the safe door and stood up, one of the bosses came back and opened the armored depository for change. My heart was in my throat. But he had no reason to suspect any monkey business so he took what he had come for and rushed back out to the front. I hurriedly ran downstairs to the storage area and hid the plunder deep in the bowels of the paper storeroom where it would never be searched out. I then proceeded to conclude my workday which, fortunately, was all but over anyhow since lunch had already started and my spread was out. That salad bar was my sole responsibility. All during cleanup time and while I was changing my clothes I was shaking like a leaf. All I wanted to do was to get out of there. If I were caught, the boss might have shot me, he kept a handgun under the counter. As I left the establishment, wampum stuffed into my sneakers so that I felt like I was on stilts, I asked for my usual twenty dollar advance so as not to arouse suspicion (I would be forfeiting my pitiful wages for the week as it was). I had to walk out leaving behind one of my favorite knives also, which really tore at my heart.

Waiting for the subway train was the longest wait I could ever remember, watching the stairway for the boss to come running down. The mean green, crammed in my uptown Cadillacs, made it impossible and painful to walk normally but I should have raced down the street anyhow to get as far away from that crime scene as fast as I could. I went straight back to my pad in Astoria where I counted the swag. An even grand. One thousand dollars. My heart was palpitating wildly. This was truly the end of the rainbow. (Although as long as I worked anywhere ever after, I had to worry about that Yid spotting me.) I immediately returned to the city and contacted my current crack connection on the street (he carried a beeper). I bought a yard worth of product from him (ten caps), all he had left. I ordered forty more caps so he doubled back to the Bronx to re-up while I waited on the street, smoking in doorways and alleys. Ninety minutes later I called my contact's beeper and met him to complete the transaction with another four hundred dollars, my largest crack purchase ever, a five hundred dollar score of fifty ten dollar capsules. (And yes, my man threw in a few extra.)

God, what a feeling, walking around holding that much crack, like the bagman from the latest Brinks heist, stealing and sidling around the city through crowds with every dick and dolly looking for me. I was beside myself with paranoia and ecstasy, an endless rush of mixed emotions clashing within my body and brain, freaking me out. One thing I learned regarding myself long ago is my inability to act cool when I'm hot. My only hope was to keep moving. Fast.

I stopped at my paraphernalia candy store and bought a dozen stems with screens, twenty-four disposable lighters and went home. That night I succeeded in setting fire to my Castro couch, blacked out underneath the sofa bed, seized up while holding the flaming lighter up against the mattress. It was the first real occasion whereby I would cloy myself to satiation (and oblivion) with a surfeit of crack. The excess residue in the stems kept me high all the next day. Debbie, whom I was seeing during that period, was quick to hone in on my windfall. She showed up at my apartment building the following day for the first time—somehow they can smell money and drugs.

I was dumbfounded when I answered the intercom to ascertain that Debbie had tracked me to my lair. I had her wait downstairs in the lobby, a provincial scandal as there were no blacks in my 250-unit building (nor in all Astoria for that matter, Archie Bunker town that it was). Debbie, with all the instinct of a wild animal, was quick to perceive her conspicuousness and intuit that I didn't want her there. I was still, at that time, straddling the fence between two cultures, two worlds. (Chip, chip at the bias of my self-image.) Not one to overlook an opportunity for leverage, Debbie would bring up such contrariety, feigning indignation over the fact that she made me welcome in her home all the time.

How could I respond to that? I think that Debbie just caught me at an awkward moment since I heartily welcomed her into my harborage thereafter.

For all the horrid, torturous workdays throughout my occupation as a New York City bum in those foul delis and coffee shops (detail forthcoming), there are a few days that shine as spectacularly satisfying. And those, like the thousand dollar day salad bar, remain comfortingly memorable as proof that every dog has his day. On another occasion, I had gone to work for the day as a (tempo) counterman in a Korean deli. The business turned out to be slow so the work was easy. I spent much time discoursing with the line supervisor, a Mr. Charlie my own age who varnished his superior status and magnanimity by allowing me to relax and loaf around. At day's end, that foreman bolstered his own ego further by fetching my pay from the cashier and handing it to me himself, a parting *beau geste*. As I was leaving, one of the Korean secretaries came down from the upstairs office and handed me my pay envelope. I took that pay packet and lit out lickety-split, running down the sidewalk as fast as my knavish legs could carry me. It was Friday with a three-day holiday weekend pending. That double pay could not have come at a better time. When I finally went back to the employment agency the following week, the dispatcher asked me, "Did they pay you twice over there last week?" And I replied, "Are you joking me? I should be so lucky." And he concurred, "That's what I told them, those Koreans would never make that kind of mistake."

Of another occurrence, a fellow agency extra was about to enter a deli with a ticket to work for the day when a courier pulled up on a motorcycle, hopped off, and ran into the shop to deliver a package, leaving the key in his bike. The agency extra leaped onto the motorcycle and took off, heading downtown where he sold the bike on Avenue D for fifty bucks. Everybody at the agency had a good boff when we heard that story. That was the same dude who, when a Korean *ouma* threw his pay at him, threw a full can of soda back at her and hit her square in the chest.

At Show Time coffee shop on Twenty-Sixth Street opposite Madison Square Park, I was backing up the griddle man (a junkie) when one of the packers (a crackhead) was discharged for setting his coworker's locker afire in retaliation over a dispute. Hence, I was promoted to packer. The take-out orders for the packers (in that godforsaken Pago Pago) were scribbled on small scraps of cardboard in tiny cribbed hieroglyphics by the gynic Korean refugees who answered the phones. Often, there were cross-outs and add-ons written sideways and upside-down and on the reverse side with lines and arrows drawn in so that the order resembled a maze of chutes and ladders, a delphic imbrication of undecipherable confusion. With regards to one such order I was given to both fill and deliver: upon presenting the customer in his office with his sandwich, it seemed I had overlooked the soda. I dashed back to the coffee shop, grabbed the soda, and fast-tracked it back to the customer. Nope, wrong again, he wanted diet soda. Back to the coffee shop, exchange the soda for diet, back to the office. By then, the poor guy was about finished eating his sandwich, I felt so sorry for him. But that was it for me at that coffee shop. I was cashiered and offhandedly bounced out of the place. No matter that it would have taken a master SIS cryptographer at London's MI-6 to interpret the order card. There is just no margin for error in the fast-food rat race.

In the beginning when I first hit the street, I knew nothing about soup kitchens(spoiled richie that I was). I would literally starve for days, never having enough to eat. I ate donuts for weeks, going to the Dunkin Donuts *Dumpster* in Astoria where they cleared the shelves every twelve hours. Sometimes I'd hit the Kentucky Fried

Chicken *Dumpster*, usually chained and locked, pawing my way through mashed potatoes with cigarette butts stuck in them and cole slaw mixed with burnt matches or used *Band-Aids*, chicken frames already picked clean but I would crunch the bones anyway. There were floor sweepings thrown in, slimy tissues, soiled napkins. Once in a blue moon I would get lucky. A passing motorist saw me rummaging through a *Dumpster* and pulled over to ask me what I was doing. I answered, "Looking for something to eat," and the driver handed over a wrapped hero sandwich, breaded fried chicken breast, still warm, his wife probably just made it for his lunch as he was going to work. Another time, I was sleeping on a subway station bench and when I awoke, there was next to me a Styrofoam take-out tray from an Italian restaurant and inside, pristine and steaming, was a pasta concoction with garlic and olives and a touch of the Mediterranean.

One fine sunny Sunday, I seized on the flukiness to eat lunch at the Ritz Carlton as I found myself at Central Park South during brunch time and, knowing the hotel's security would be lax, I walked right in the employee entrance with authority, grabbed a random time card from the rack and punched it in the time clock and with my head slightly bowed, face slightly turned away from the security booth, I scampered down the stairs to where the employee cafeteria was waiting for me. The staff dining room was nearly empty yet there was, behooving like a recurrent bad dream, the logy employee attendant, Ramone, who managed to clock in forty hours a week wiping tables. "Mamma Lucca, what are you doing?" "I came to visit," I replied, "And to have some lunch." "You're not supposed to be doing that, I think." (That pusillanimous insect, ever ready to crawl over a dead body, was going to get stepped on in another second.) But I was already done making my boodle swag and a nice one it was, a roll of aluminum foil conveniently provided for the self-service steam table that was a veritable beggar's banquet. I made a neat exit like the insouciant little imp that I was, a fading aphelion memory gone like the ghost of Christmas past.

A similar instance occurred one seven o'clock morning at LOLA on West Twenty-Second Street, my roving that desolate area of Chelsea like a starving dog and, knowing, from having worked at that three-star restaurant when it was young, that a couple of Mexican porters would have the front door unlocked while they cleared up the aftermath of last night's festivities. And knowing that in one of the service kitchen's coolers would be cheesecake and bourbon pecan pie, I walked in as bold as brass (as I had a hundred times past), and helped myself to a healthy slice of this and that, wrapping the booty in aluminum foil, when a little Mexican appeared and questioned my obvious larceny. When I ignored him, he vanished and reappeared with an anabolic version of himself who informed me, "I call the police." At which point I bolted empty-handed—who knew how close the black-and-white might have been?

And finally, I did not neglect dropping in upon "21" one day at shift change, stopping first at the White Rose Bar on Forty-Ninth Street at Broadway where many of the waiters (and cooks on Fridays) drank, graciously accepting a beer (at two dollars per bottle), then let out my hellos at the time clock at "21" as former fellow coworkers took in my street togs and honest tale of misfortune. I pocketed nearly one hundred cool clams from those benevolent souls (many of whom would have caught hell from their wives for such generosity).

Finding out about soup kitchens took a lot of the stress out of living on the street. During all of my street life, one of the most outstanding needs was finding food. I would eat out of garbage cans, *Dumpsters*, any place refuse was tossed. Yet despite this degradation there is an overall search for and maintenance of dignity amongst the homeless, so incongruous to living on the street. And it's all over the mean neighborhoods of the city.

There is a home made of cardboard, not even worthy enough to be called a shack, inside of which is an orderliness, a neatness and cleanliness that belies its outside surroundings of garbage, excrement and vermin that is general city filth. Inside this dwelling that would not withstand even a moderate storm is a pallet of cardboard, elevated off the ground, complete with pillow and coverings made of charity fabrics, a modular chest or wardrobe made of cinder blocks and boxes, toilet articles and books on top, a chair made of vegetable crates, and a shelf made of planks and milk cases, complete with candles and bric-a-brac. Spare clothes in the chest, even drawings on the inside walls. There is a curtain hanging over the entry and the structure is tall enough to stand up in. The inhabitant doesn't entertain there nor is he proud, but is fiercely protective. He spends his days foraging and manages a hot meal and a shower almost daily from charity organizations. He has an independence and a dignity denied him in any other walk of life because of his afflictions and, equally important, he has freedom from the suffocating constraints of society. There are thousands of such homeless on the streets of New York City of which I became one.

PART TWO

The Street

came to the city across a burning bridge, abandoning community, willing to spelunk the darker removes of the urban puzzle, a single-minded departure from a stymied and unsatisfying life towards a new one fraught with endless possibilities—or such had become my unregenerate *idee fixe* as foretold in the providential ashes of a crack pipe. Less towards any tenuous or tenebrous dream than as a fugitive from whole people, on the run, desperate, monkey-wrenching and bankrupt. Though optimistic for all that. Like the first day at summer camp—uncertain yet eager.

With crack as enabler, I moved between worlds with glib dispatch, my transition effortless, chameleon-like—though not without its emotional toll. My hope, burnished by an ocean of heartbreak, still banged away with a passion, often, it seemed, my sole virtue. But the city had yet to play its hand and despair would one day spread the toils for me. And that would be a sticky wicket indeed. This would be the final cadenza before I slumped into retirement mode, my last opportunity prior to having neither the fortitude or the thirst for such a long shot, the lunacy that such folly called for.

In those first days on the street I didn't see myself in much the same way that domiciled citizens don't see bums; people don't want to notice things that make them feel uncomfortable and so their eyes slide over and around bums without conscious recognition. For myself, as one who had normally paid careful attention to appearance, my falling into the bum aspect was a signal turn indicative of a shift in outlook on and approach to life (at least in the very beginning), I didn't care what I looked like. This helped me blend into the shadows, the background—I didn't want to be noticed. Also, in the beginning, I couldn't be bothered noticing myself too much as everything was so unfamiliar, the old city (reflecting my fungible predicament) wasn't the same. My entire situation—concerned with survival, safety, being broke—consumed me. It was like being in a strange new land, not the old New York of my prior life, for I had never seen this town through

123

the desperate, needy eyes of a full-fledged bum. I had to learn fast and change fast in order to not only bear up and cheat death, but to ripen and flourish. For life on the street is anything but stagnant and old ideals die hard, always lurking about, ready to revive in another wise. And although my approach had changed, I was still the same old DP[1] underneath it all, outlandish and willful for all my caution, striking out (as of yesteryear) on my own and making my mark.

My first night out as a bum. I had chosen Grand Central Terminal to bed down, the largest railway station in the world, as quintessential a New York landmark as the Empire State skyscraper, one of the greatest enclosed public spaces ever erected. Built at a time when cost and effort were secondary considerations, a terminal through which I passed daily for years as part of my city commute, whose wonder never flagged. On this historic fall of day, as if in keeping with my new bottom, I chose the lowest concourse, three floors below street level, all the way at the end of a train platform where commuters to and from New Jersey would board and depart, a secluded spot. It was midnight. I laid out my cardboard sheeting on the floor, against a cinderblock wall; the platform was concrete as were the supporting columns and ceiling. With the steel railroad tracks shimmering in the bottom of the trackbed pit, reeking of loneliness and misfortune. I had two double-bagged shopping bags stuffed with all my portable possessions beside me and, dressed in triple layers of clothes, I went to sleep.

It couldn't have been more than an hour later when I was roused by the city guard who evidently patrolled such remote regions on off-hours and forced to pack up and vacate the terminal or face

---

1 Displaced person

arrest, all my possessions confiscated, never to be returned. It struck me then of the wisdom of the vagrant pair I'd noticed earlier passing me by on the end of the platform and continuing down onto the tracks and blinking out of sight into the blackness of the tunnel. As the guards ran me out, I envied that vagrant pair safe and sound for the night in whatever niche they had found for themselves.

The only people loitering about the vicinity of Grand Central Terminal at that time of night are nighthawks, solitary creatures whose motives are suspect simply for being on the street at that hour. I do not hesitate or falter as I pass through their midst in my exit at Park Avenue and Forty-Second Street, cringing in my *bêtise*, my flimsy vulnerability, with my shopping bags, rousted already in my opening move on that hideous gameboard on which I have recklessly bet the farm.

There I was at two a.m., tired, with no prospects, that this-was-not-working-out-as-planned made its first impact, the realization that my new undertaking was not going to be easy. I might have gone to Pennsylvania Station to doss but I knew that place was battened down as tight as Grand Central so, as the night thickened, I headed to South Ferry (Whitehall Terminal) at 4 South Street. I didn't guess then that South Ferry would be my sleeping camp for the next month.

It was a difficult time adjusting to living on the street. It was an unrestful night for me that first night, and for many more nights thereafter. In fact, it was the very matter of not being able to rest, the wearing down of my nerves to a frazzle, which finally drove me off the street, through the shelter system, and back into society.

During the semi-warm days of that spring of my maiden bum voyage in New York City, it rained every day for a month, a nonstop cataract. I was completely waterlogged. My nights in Whitehall Terminal were not adequate to dry out, to exsiccate my soaked shoes, pants; everything I wore or carried with me remained wet. My feet began to rot. During a rare moment of sunshine I would sprawl on a bench in Battery Park and toast my sodden dogs in the sun for as many hours as it shone in combat against jungle rot.

Evenings at South Ferry were rarely smooth. To begin with, the terminal was the crash pad for, and full-time home of, a phalanx of bums. The large waiting room (a 19,000 square foot arena surrounded by ferry boarding slips) is lined with slatted wooden benches. There are oscillating fans high up on the walls that blow down onto the benches and it was the manner of preference to secure an entire bench for oneself for the night. To do this you had to either be living on the bench full-time or arrive there before rush hour, meaning by three o'clock in the afternoon. There was one particular bench that was always last to be occupied and this was because the stationary fan on the wall blew directly onto that bench and it became quite cold in the evening dank. I have more than a few times tried to unplug that fan by jumping up from the bench and attempting to grab the plug wire in mid-flight—it was a dangerous stunt and I, being unsuccessful, soon tired of it. And so, usually, I slept in that spot having to be bundled up as if I were out of doors to keep from freezing in my sleep.

South Ferry on the Hudson River, under the watchful eyes of Liberty Enlightening the World (Statue of Liberty), is situated at Battery Park, which boasts tourist boats as well as ferries to Staten Island (the best free ride in the world since 1997, prior to which the fare was twenty-five cents charged only on the New York side, always New York's best value), a half dozen ferries operating during rush hours—departing and docking every ten minutes—a busy spot, some twenty million passengers moving through there annually (or 55,000 pilgrims per day), the five miles between Staten Island and lower Manhattan. And it was basically un-policed inside the terminal waiting area. Bums could lie about all over the benches and floor and be left unmolested by the law. It was a dry, sheltered, mostly safe place to bum out in, all sorts of hot dog, pizza, and candy counters, coffee bars and fruiterer lined the walls and if you had twenty-five cents you could buy something.

It would take me nearly a year as a bum on the Lower East Side of New York City before I ever heard of the Catholic Worker, Bowery Mission, or any number of other charities for free meals and succor for transient bums: that is, of their location and ready accessibility, so solitary and introspective was my advertence in those cub days. Up until that point, I ate from garbage cans, handouts, theft, and free lunch at my part-time job. For my first four or five months on the street, I not only had a lunch job as a waiter but belonged to a gym as well. I still had, at the time of my eviction from my Astoria apartment, a good third of a year left on my membership at Better Bodies in Chelsea. I would sleep at South Ferry on benches in the waiting room, empty of commuters through the night but packed like sardines with homeless. As the early ferries began to run in the morning it was mobilization time to mooch a coffee from one of the many vendors at nearby Peter Minuit Plaza, and then, before the first crush of straphangers overtook Manhattan, to find a momentarily private spot for the all-important morning necessary. This daily function must be performed quickly and on demand for once the daytime traffic ensued all such opportunity was vanished. No rest rooms are open to bums. One must keep a ready supply of paper napkins handy at all times and have no compunction about paying a call in the lee of someone's doorway.

By seven a.m. it was off to the gym where, on an empty stomach, I would bodybuild for three hours. The locker room attendant allowed me to keep shopping bags of clothes on top of the lockers. After my workout I'd shower, beginning with washing my clothes and, afterward, put them back on wet to quickly dry in the hot outdoors. Thus, freshly laundered, combed and shaved, with a dab of Canoe, I'd head for work at Naturally Tasty on Fifth

Avenue at Twenty-Fifth Street (the wholesale toy district), right across from Madison Square Park. That was where I scarfed my good feed of the day. Fresh squeezed juice, pitas stuffed with sprouts and shredded raw veggies topped with a garlicky yogurt dressing, deluxe burgers.

My job at Naturally Tasty ended on a discord but by that time I was rolling with the punches like an old sea dog. I'd already found that as a working bum I was far from unique. "According to a 1997 report by the National Coalition for the Homeless, nearly one-fifth of all homeless people (in twenty-nine cities nationwide) are employed in full or part-time jobs."[1] In fact, two bums other than myself were employed at Naturally Tasty. One was the griddle man who would later move into Trinity Lutheran shelter on my referral, and another homeless employee was a temporary wait-ress whom I used to observe living at South Ferry terminal when I myself was crashing there. On one occasion, Trinity Lutheran shelter's headman, Charley, came into the restaurant and sat in my section, placing a small order. On his way out, he forewarned me that the aforementioned waitress was lurking suspiciously about the booth where I'd just served him and that he had left a two dollar tip. Upon bussing the table, I found no gravy. When I confronted the misguided ganef she was all blubbering apologies and readily surrendered the fish. Although I empathized with the poor kid, who was feeling sorry for me?

Well, it was Harry, the original Korean owner of Naturally Tasty, who felt sorry for me. Beautiful Harry who was compassionate, sensitive to my quandary and initially hired me, giving me a chance to stand on my own two feet without restrictions that a less casual employer might insist upon; Harry, who let me stash a couple of valises of clothes in his basement, who bent over backwards to help me when I was roving the streets homeless. But eventually

---

1 Barbara Ehrenreich, *Nickel and Dimed, On (Not) Getting By in America*

beautiful Harry sold out to a new owner—black-hearted Grace—and that's when the countdown to my termination began.

The quartet of Korean youngbloods Grace had imported to help out at the restaurant somehow intuitively perceived that I was homeless and allowed me no respite in their cutting barbs and charades. "Hey Dave, how'd you go about finding your apartment? I'm thinking of moving into the city and was wondering what the best way is of finding a place." Yet I kept my aplomb as best I could, not being drawn into playing their game and ignoring their insulting japery. But my situation reflected poorly on my visibility in a point of sale position as a representative of Grace's spanking new eatery.

Another black mark against me was when, after Grace returned from having taken the NYC Department of Health exam for her Food Protection Certificate, I asked our Asian leader what grade she had received. She told me, "Ninety-four," to which I snidely replied that I had scored ninety-eight. Grace just gave me the cold basilisk stare. For the life of me, I just could not kiss the nates of people I didn't like. The final debacle unfolded as follows.

My Janus-faced coworker (waitress), Darleen, and I shared the two dozen booths at the rear of the restaurant that I dubbed "the forgotten land" and "another country." After I caught Darleen stealing some of my tips one day (distinct from the homeless waitress incident), she launched a covert campaign to have me fired. Darleen began chumming up to Grace, told her I drank on the job everyday and sexually harassed her. Grace (a recent emigré) took my reference to "the forgotten land" as malevolence ("Forgotten land, Dave?"), and mistook the scent of my cologne for whiskey aroma. The ludicrousness of it all was that I was cold sober, having gone back to AA, was ascetic in my adherence to the program, daily meetings, sponsor and all. So when the two females ganged up on me, I threw my little black apron in their faces and walked out. I was about to be fired anyway. And Grace hollering after me, "Drinking everyday!" If I hadn't been sober I might have gone back at night and done something nasty to that store, like putting Krazy Glue in their locks.

Around the point in time of my employ at Naturally Tasty, during my vernal unhoused roving of the Lower East Side, I happened across a middle-aged suffragette one afternoon near Tompkins Square Park who showed the kindness of offering me shelter in her tenement for that evening. She lived on Fifth Street between Avenues B and C, an area which was outside my (then) current familiarity. "You'll have a roof over your head tonight," pledged my new friend. She told me to find her in Tompkins Square Park that evening where she'd be "visible." Well, it was dark by the time I located her (scavenging on the street) whence she barely remembered her earlier offer. Up to the top (fifth) floor of her wreckful, semi-barren squatter's walk-away where half the roof and one wall was burnt assunder... "Oh, there was a fire." There was a five-gallon (full) plastic vessel for use as a "pee pot," with a good inch of crystalized white crust surrounding its opening. And there was a dog. A mangy, feral-looking Shepherd that dispelled any notions of snuggly encounters. She conjured up some sort of food, which I artfully declined. And she prattled on and on of her litigating for the rights of the squatters therein, her friend the judge, z-z-z. I spotted her about a year thereafter, sitting in Saint Joe's soup kitchen at the Catholic Worker, dog and all.

In the early days of my homelessness I was completely sober, afraid to be intoxicated while vulnerable on the street. Besides, everything was such a new experience to me and, what with my pair of shopping bags, I was an open book. Bums attract negativity, are deemed defenseless and weak. My only edge was my physique, my aura and my moxie. If I so much as appeared lax for a second would be to invite calamity. As soon as I lay down and closed my eyes the sharks were circling and eyeing me, inching closer. If I was nodding on a park bench, the hyenas were moving in stealthily and steadily. And when I was passed out drunk, I always awoke with my pants' pockets slit open. So initially, I was cold sober and sharp as a razor as I roved the city sidewalks, walking hard and ever mindful of my surroundings; not being aggressive or even assertive, but leery and alert, not hugging buildings and avoiding lonely recesses and parks. Crowds offered safety, especially for sleeping, yet crowds were suffocating and claustrophobic, annoying and wearing on the nerves. Nonetheless, acclimatization came fast and soon I was drinking until I dropped. I became one of those drunken bums passed out on the sidewalk that everyone would step over.

Yet in the beginning, after lunch work, with the day's tips in my pocket and a shopping bag in each hand I would walk, the jolly swagman. Nonstop pedestrianizing over the southern half of Manhattan, always taking different routes, exploring different neighborhoods, looking in stores, examining architecture, visiting churches, voyeuring. Blending in with the crushing sea of humanity, as indistinguishable as a discarded tabloid scandal sheet. Careless and free, part of civilization's modern day urban wilderness.

I often didn't pay attention to where I was, heading towards some destination or merely just aimless rambling, I'd gaze at the sights all around me without actually placing them on the map, so to speak. This approach lent a sort of marvelment to an already marvelous city, like traveling through Oz. How many times I've passed (and even patronized) unique shops only to knock my head against a wall when trying to remember where they were so as to return. The city always had and never lost its captivation, its enchantment, its rapture whereby I could so easily lose myself in its fascination. Like a carnival midway, I passed through the spectrum of New York City's allurements, its cajolery, always amazed and in admiration, fortunate to be part of so fantastic a place.

My tramping days blurred together into a stream of broken and random images and impressions, a montage of alarums and excursions, a reification of my quest as though a diorama—jostling crowded sidewalks, choking slaughtering traffic, diapasons of sonance, rank street corner trash baskets, gliding unctuous storefronts, the frowsy odor of wet clothing, congested public terminals that were like the inside of some great circus tent, days and nights intertwined with both trepidation and wonder.[1] I wasn't cognizant of all that was transpiring within and around me but I was sanguine in my vicissitude, joined now with the city in something enormous, woven into a profound and inordinate part of its essence and, no matter what happened, always would be so joined. For this was my city and I belonged to it, as inseparable as a grain of sand from a glass tumbler, my future as shifting and fertile as an alluvial delta.

Back at South Ferry (a misnomer since lower Manhattan points Southwest and the Battery faces West) which stands next to the Battery Maritime Building, the last surviving example of Structural Expressionism (for which the Eiffel Tower was created), there was one sweet old granny who of an evening would share her bench with me. And there were a covey of missioners who showed up each day handing out quite substantial bag lunches for the bums during which time I was out working. My dear old bench-mate would collect one extra bag lunch for me and save it until my return that night. Now, that same dear woman who was reduced to living in a public terminal but, upon my arrival (not even having a bench on which to sleep or the bag lunch to have for dinner, yet might offer some semblance of security), she was

---

1 Kim Edwards, *The Memory Keeper's Daughter,* some words and ideas

suddenly elevated in status. This was a comedy not lost on either of us as my new friend shared her meager possessions with one who was more poor. We could, in all our misery, laugh at not only ourselves but at the commuters, of whom a proportion would one day emulate our circumstances.

Some of those bag ladies you see, face peeping out from a bundle of rags, shopping bags stuffed with newspapers, shuffling down a sidewalk or huddled in a doorway are carrying thousands of dollars in cold cash. One such woman, found dead in her room at the Kenmore Hotel, was rumored to have had forty thousand smackers stashed in her shopping bags. A decade's worth of welfare checks cashed and never spent. Afraid, every one of them, to show that they have any money for fear of it being stolen.

One woman would shamble into a coffee shop where I worked every single morning, wrapped in rags and lugging her shopping bags; she would sit at the counter and order an elaborate breakfast platter, complete with a large chocolate milk, finalizing the whole with a huge bowl of rice pudding—easily a ten dollar spread. I figured that to be her solitary feedbag of the day, bless her soul. She was so secretive in extracting her cash from a small change purse that she withdrew from the folds of her clothing. And not for nothing her worry. I wasn't the only one clocking her.

I eventually abandoned South Ferry terminal after an altercation with the resident bully. I was sleeping on a crowded dais near the front turnstiles, the only available spot off the floor, when I was awakened by someone squeezing my big toe. I opened my eyes to see some deranged goon leering wolfishly down at me and I said, "Don't do that," and curled up a little tighter and closed my eyes again only to have the toe squeezing repeated, a bit harder if that were possible. Then I was kneeling, facing the thug, and he grabbed my drumsticks from my waistband and turned and jumped to the floor and started to hobnob around the somnolent press waving the sticks. I was fit to be tied though still in control so

I rushed out and fetched a shamus who returned with me to the scene of the crime, the drumsticks were returned to their rightful and loving owner (me) who had to prudently vacate the premises henceforth or risk a bashing next time I was alone. Well, what the hey. After that episode the weather cleared so I began to camp in the little park at the foot of the Fifty-Ninth Street Bridge. That was pretty good for awhile.

The ramp onto the Queensborough (aka Fifty-Ninth Street) Bridge intersects with Third Avenue, opposite where East Fifty-Ninth Street terminates, and my little park abuts the stone wall (ramp supports) between Third and Second Avenues (on the south face), the ramp roadbed already soaring at that point. By the time the bridge roadway leaves Manhattan Island, crossing over First and York Avenues and the FDR Drive, it has reached its height as it spans the East River and Welfare (Roosevelt) Island, debouching into Queens Boulevard in Long Island City, borough of Queens.

Bedding down within that naturalistic bunker on a wood-slatted bench, fully bundled up right down to my shoes for both warmth and antitheft, with my shopping bags beneath my head, I'd savor my slumber. There was even a small covered bandstand at one end of the little flower-bound park that provided shelter on rainy nights or as a hideout for smoking a doobie. Kind of ratty (literally) for sleeping, though. When I was driven from that lovely spot by an influx of nocturnal crack maniacs, I began keeping on the move during the night. Walking downtown's maze of skyscrapers, carrying my shopping bags wherever I roamed, there was never a shortage of benches in front of those mammoth office buildings; little plazas for secretaries and clerks on lunch break. I would lie down on a bench practically right on the sidewalk, wake up an hour later and move to an identical bench on the next block, same routine three or more times per night. It didn't pay to settle in or get too comfortable, better to keep moving, taking evenly spaced naps like a rabbit.

I even camped for one night in the small oasis across from the United Nations building (Mitchell Place). Although not a proper park, it is one of the many refuging commons which lend metropolitan New York the appellation, "City of Parks." A lovely spot, facing east on First Avenue at Forty-Ninth Street, it usually (predictably) has no vacancy for the homeless crowding out its benches. Yet that retreat still maintains a host of gorgeous towering horse chestnuts and a thick ground cover of Boston ivy, which conceals some soft, secretive, nocturnal metropolitans.

Parks in general were not good camping spots, even those given over entirely to shantytowns, ramadas and rickety cot-shelters unless you had a little group in which to band together for strength and post guards around-the-clock—commemorative of card-carrying pioneers. Parks, usually, are a haven for junkies, dope dealers, beat artists, stickup men and carousing bad boys. If you want to get mugged, just hang around a park at night. This is why all the beautiful old city parks have been elided and modernized with no bushes, no rambling pathways through shaggy old growth, no snuggly havens of nature and refuge from a wasteland of asphalt, concrete, glass and brick. Showcase parks that took a century to mature and develop: Bryant Park, Union Square, Madison Square, Washington Square, Tompkins Square, all gone, never to be gazed at, experienced, enjoyed ever again; the last drop of nurture for wildlife blotted out forever in the city's vengeance to sterilize itself against crime and normal, natural life. It would have been more frugal to erect an iron fence and lock it at night or pay a few watchmen to patrol the pleasure ground, rather than the millions of dollars to rip them all up and replace the sacred preserves with open, roped off lawns. (Or was there a more sinister motive involved in awarding the contracts to the crooked corporations who performed the renewal). Ah, the modern bureaucratic mentality is a vacuous thing, light years from the vision of the city's founders.

Gramercy Park, a miniature holdout lovingly tended—the only private park in New York City—tall old oak, elm, maple and beech trees, as well as dogwood and apple, thick hedges, gramineous glades, pachysandra, azalea, rhododendron, hydrangea, lupine, winding gravel walks bordered by Queen Anne's lace, flower beds of peony, pansy, primrose and snapdragon, black-eyed Susan, forget-me-not, nasturtium, narcissus, hyacinth and gladiolus, bird baths, iron benches, and scores of house sparrows. Surrounded by its namesake townhouses and mansions (Gramercy Park), whose tenants are the sole patrons and caretakers, the garden is enclosed by an unassailable fence of wrought iron spears whose gate is perpetually locked, the park tenants being the exclusive keyholders, one must key themselves both in and out. I would weasel my way into that splendid Shangri-la on the heels of some sweet, trusting member and, after being inadvertently locked in one night, I would regularly seek my summer evening solace, safe and sound, shut within the unsullied boundaries of Gramercy Park.

At last are the community gardens of the Lower East Side ranging in size from a small tenement plot to hundred-foot frontages with a depth the width of the block spanning, say, Fifth Street to Sixth Street. Tracts where apartment buildings have been torn down and razed to the earth, sealed with chain-link or avant-garde iron work or a hodgepodge of wooden boards, locked or not, those lots are easily accessible. Usually laid out in some sort of grid, each section or bed belonging to one resident of the neighborhood to cultivate as they choose—flowers, vegetables, vines, sculpture—by midsummer those parcels are veritable jungles, dense, teeming with life, vegetable, animal, mineral, snakes, spiders, bees, even fish in manmade ponds; and ladybugs by the thousand (New York's official insect), imported from nurseries to offset the summer aphid explosion. Those neighborhood gardens have the most charm, character, personality, vibrancy, color, soul. I spent an entire summer in one such garden—the Sixth Street and Avenue B Community Garden (founded 1983)—with my leg in a cast, hobbling around on crutches, reading or sleeping at a redwood picnic table, jotting down the germinal drafts of *New York City Bum*, grilling my lunch on the garden barbeque, smoking fags, drinking beer, talking with the nonage of a woman who'd work there all day. It was easy enough to get lost in one of those overgrown plantations for the night though the tenant contingency often worked on after taps under spotlights. In some fields deep in Alphabet City, the locals would drink all night, jarring and squabbling until they passed out drunk.

However, my most affectionate predilection for the neighborhood gardens was in watching the house sparrows hopping about in such playful, joyous abandon, safe within their pastoral pale, wild and free and natural, with such a limitless proclivity for seizing the moment, hearts as big as a house—if only I could emulate their outlook.

The community gardens took hold when, in 1974, the city approved a one-dollar lease to create the Bowery Houston Community Farm and Garden, the city's first official community garden, which today boasts a pond stocked with side-neck turtles, rare plants, the tallest dawn redwood tree in Manhattan, weeping birch trees, sixty vegetable beds and hundreds of different flowering perennials.[1] Over 600 community gardens now exist throughout the city, all open to the public, such as my old hangout at Sixth Street and Avenue B, where 200 registered members tend 110 plots.[2]

---

1 Jeryl Brunner, *My City, My New York*
2 Peter De Jonge, *Buried on Avenue B*, statistic

To backpedal a bit, in preparation for hitting the street I knew I'd need an act. There would be no getting high, smoking crack, acting out. Something that would both give me an acceptable front and that would generate income as well. Without giving a passing thought to the likelihood of being ripped off, I chose to do a sidewalk drum act, playing along on my drum set to a boom box. While still castellated at my Astoria safehold, I started practicing on my drums at ten o'clock in the morning when I returned home from my all-night deli job, much to the consternation of my neighbors. Buzzing on crack and swigging gin, I was in the perfect mood to play. I had seen an act once, outdoors, a guy on a drum set playing along to records on a sound system. Sounded like a live band. I knew that such an act would endow me the necessary respect of the street people and also provide adequate income to get by on. (This false premise was based on the misapprehension that street people would respect one another.)

In the beginning of my homelessness, during my early days on the street (my drums in storage), I used to play on a practice pad along to tapes or the radio on my newly acquired boom box. Light FM, the Rippingtons, the Crusaders, sounds to stimulate yet not offend. I played at Grand Central Terminal, Fifth Avenue New York Public Library, South Street Seaport, Battery Park, Bryant Park, Union Square, Washington Square, and subway trains and stations throughout the city. And was sent packing by the city fuzz from every one of them. I should have been left alone, I was providing a non-offensive service, supplying color to the landscape. An evident bum keeping out of trouble. Yet those creepy rozzers would harass me. That is how they flex and posture, always looking for an easy target while the real criminals go unmolested. But then I thought that I might be able to obtain a permit from the city (only $50) to perform my drum act in one of the terminals, like Pennsylvania Station or Grand Central Terminal, or even in the subway stations like so many entertainers do, small ensembles or solo acts, regaling the commuters as well as earning a cash return for their efforts. However, that didn't pan out as the drum business thus unfolded.

I concentrated on bringing my drums into the city from storage on Long Island. I posted notices on the bulletin boards at the local gym, laundromat, supermarket and library for a situation wherein to stable the drums. I eventually hooked up with a young cat at the gym who, coincidentally, was himself a drummer. He agreed to let me dock the drums in his room if I would permit him to play them. An Italian kid from South America who spoke Spanish. New York is truly the melting pot. We became pals.

I trucked the drums into the city on the Long Island Railroad, trap case on wheels containing the snare drum, bass drum foot pedal, cymbals, hi-hat, sticks and stands; with the bass drum, floor tom and two tom-toms piled on top—a rolling pyramid of drums. Having to leave the bulk of the passel at the bottom of stairways as I ran drum by drum up to the top, afraid someone would snatch something left unattended, running back and forth like a madman. Trundling the drums by subway from Pennsylvania Station, rolling them along the sidewalks, pushing a mountain of drums, I finally made it.

My new friend, Gustavo, lived in a room in an apartment complex in the Essex Street projects, south of Delancey Street, where he apartment-sat and walked the dogs in exchange for his room rent. I wound up walking the dogs as my drum warehousing gratuity. One fateful day when I had the dogs off their leashes, the vicious one, Bandit, jumped up on a woman holding a baby and the beast tore a chunk right out of the baby's arm. What a disaster, a total fiasco. Lady and baby screaming, mongrel terrier barking, blood, a goodly gobbet missing from the baby's chubby bicep. The mortified apartment leaseholder who owned the dogs threw my friend and me and the drums the hell out of there. My friend, who had to move, came to land uptown in Spanish Harlem and, mercifully, took my drums with him. I finally recovered the drums, months later, whence they went back into storage on Long Island again. I never realized my drum act on the street. I hadn't grasped the impracticality of it all, dragging around an entire drum set, especially when I would have been drinking. I could just envision myself passed out drunk alongside the drums on the sidewalk or trying to protect them from a crew of young delinquents high on crack. In the end, I couldn't even protect my boom box when I was sober. That's how bad the street is. Ah well, live and learn.

This friend of mine, Gus, who saved my drum set, he told me he was also a cook in a restaurant and worked at the South Street Seaport. I was impressed. I arranged to go meet him there one afternoon and asked him the name of the eatery in which he worked. He told me, "French Fries." I thought, well, some trendy nouvelle tourist trap, no doubt nobby and trig. When I arrived at the seaport and made my way up to the third story deck and at last located "French Fries," it turned out to be a tiny French fry stand selling nothing but French fried potatoes, a greasy fast-food concession manned by red and white candy stripe shirted teens wearing those paper soda jerk caps. And there was my friend, up to his elbows in grease, giving me a worried look as I approached, his boss moving in to admonish him with "No talking," and to me, "You there, what do you want?" And so away I went, shaking my head in dismay, wondering how on earth that kid could consider himself a cook and in a restaurant no less. It turned out that Gus came from Argentina where they evidently are at a variance with American standards.

It jogged my memory that the South Street Seaport had their fair share of rejects when a coworker from the Ritz Carlton came to mind. This cook, a roundsman elevated to one of the sous-chefs, once asked me, upon noticing a cake in one of the glass vitrines (which makes them so attractive), "How do they get it so shiny?" I told him, "Royal Icing," (a snide deception—Royal Icing is matte), to which he replied (as if he had just remembered) "Oh yeah, Royal Icing." I could have truthfully told him it was Sugarpaste (rolled fondant) and mentioned other tricky techniques for brightening a cake finish, such as adding glucose, corn syrup or honey to the icing. Or glazing with couverature.[1] But why should I enlighten that jerk? He was supposed to be my boss. I sometime later ran into the tinker copping grass at Saint Mark's Place in the East Village where he appropinquated upon me a rodomontade of how he was now a self-styled chef at some restaurant at the South Street Seaport where he had full reign to deploy his own menus, blah blah blah. He was with his tiny Japanese wife, who spoke no English, and he inundated me with a diatribe on how, "When water boils it's because of the enzymes moving back and forth." Christ!

Getting back to drumming; I'd be walking down the street with my hair flying wild, my shirt open, carrying the boom box, blasting the *OJ's Greatest Hits* on 10—"Backstabbers," "Money," "She Used to be My Girl"—drumsticks stuck in my front waistband, everyone on the street looking at me. I'd go into a crowded subway car, sit down, and blast the boom box, OJ's always, playing along on top of the box with my sticks, the entire car gripped by this *tableau vivant*. I'd gad about the streets of Loesida and, when I saw a likely trash can, I'd stop and play, loud, with the backs of the sticks on top of the trash can cover along to the OJ's, people looking out of their windows at me; or play along to music blaring out of open windows, which was normal, life in the ghetto spilling out into the streets, from fire escapes, from rooftops (tar beach), alleyways, stoops and stairways. I was wild in the street.

In the cool of the evening, if I passed by a road crew working on the pavement with jackhammers (which was not uncommon),

---

1 Finishing cocoa butter

I'd stop and play fast rolls along with the jackhammer tattoo for practice. For a half an hour straight, rat-tat-tat-tat, nonstop, as fast as I could go. On subways, twirling my sticks constantly for practice, a street performer putting on a show. I looked like an ape-man, a skell dressed incongruously in raggedy flash gear, withy, fearless and importunate. Sometimes people would clap, yell, "Go man, yeah!" It was crazy. I was free, recusant and gay.

In the early mornings, when I'd leave Trinity Lutheran shelter (detail forthcoming), before going to the gym, I'd go over to East River Park, between Franklin Delano Roosevelt Drive and the East River (opposite the Avenue D projects), and sit on a bench along the long jogging track, looking out over the channel, and practice for an hour straight along to tapes or a successive ictus of rataplan—(paradiddle, paradiddle). I gave up my shopping bags (as a shelter dweller) and carried the boom box wherever I went, always blasting the music, setting the New York City streets on fire.

Once, when I'd just bought my second box, (they were big twenty-five pound units with double six-inch speakers) I was blasting my way along Fourteenth Street when a squad of police stopped me and almost confiscated the boom box for noise pollution. When I refused to lower the volume they offered to arrest me and appropriate the portable sound system and I couldn't believe those creeps when the street traffic was deafening with horns honking and sirens screaming and beep beep backup signals and whoop whoop car alarms and slamming doors and backfires and you name it all competing against the music. The bulls chased me wherever I set up, in train stations, Grand Central, the Battery, parks, South Street Seaport, where every con artist plied their trade, the mounted pigs would zero in on and run me off, playing for the crowds of tourists with my cup out, rat-a-tat-tat along to the OJ's /Money, Money Money. I never let it dampen my enthusiasm. I just moved along on my resolute way, me against the world. Me and my boom box. Drinking beer and smoking joints I played everywhere I went; I was preeminent, invincible, omnipotent. I was in top form. Bodybuilding daily. Eating fresh foods and drinking fresh squeezed juices faithfully. I wasn't smoking crack at all during that period. I was high on my trip, defying the greatest city in the world, New York City, and I was part of it all, making my mark on the pages of history. Nobody and nothing could hinder my resolve nor enervate my spirit. I was unstoppable.

I was making good money at my waiter job in the health food restaurant, enough to save and stay high. My room and board were handouts from Trinity Lutheran shelter. My future was boundless. I roamed the Lower East Side stews as an integral part, like I'd been born to it; the city, like the crowds before Christ on Palm Sunday, parted for me as I passed through, surrounded me, engulfed me. I was a cornerstone in the structure, in the building blocks of ghetto life, a gunner in the ranks, a flag bearer, a drummer boy.

After only about three months on the street, I started to purchase a few outfits from the second hand shops, a couple of vintage open back vests, a pair of beige stretch lace pants, a pair of red stretch Ban Lon pants, a pair of navy blue canvas moccasins. It was high summer, blistering hot. I was gaining confidence fast on the street, I was Courageous Cat, hale and spanking. I had an act. Sometimes I would change clothes at work after my lunch gig was over for the day and charge out into the street like a firework exploding and as colorful. I was coming into my own, my fruition, and I was gung ho. Nothing could stop me. This was what I wanted to do, where I wanted to be, and I was at once a natural. My tomorrow was open-ended, the horizon. I was euphoric, wired up and tuned-in. My heart swelled, my soul expanded, my open road stretched untrammelled before me. This was privilege, liberty and opportunity—America hot out of the oven.

My street life career was an opportunity for me to amalgamate my latent erotic desires into my overall persona without fear of recriminations or any concern over my projected image. I bring this out to provide a little explanatory background as this singularity crops up throughout my story and thus this clarification may preclude any wild presaging, lest such occur, that is, more wild than this true case history of a madcap fetch or alter ego that spelled out its integument of salacity.

My exploration into the world of fetishism went hand in hand with my pansexuality, seeking and finding alternative avenues to increase and satisfy my carnal urges. Incorporating material elements feminine into my sexual proclivities served to enhance the normal course of nature and, thusly, the conventional apparel (especially intimate) enjoyed by women themselves became a fixation for me. I found that by wearing racy attire I could achieve extra mileage from the natural acts of foreplay and coitus. My role and participation were always masculine, I never desired to surrender my manhood like so many transexuals. But the symbolism involved through the fetishes themselves offered an expansion of coital activities mundane and commonplace. And likewise allowed my partner to experience additional magnitude and zest to those routine heterosexual acts. Like an aphrodisiac, the fetishes characteristically became utile and, in some cases, necessary.

Thus my progression into the world of cross-dressing as a gratifying means to an end in itself, an adumbrating alternative to the act of fornication. So, I came to know and rely on such sexual peccadilloes as an integral part of the makeup of my sexual preferences. Always maintaining my performance as a male yet including the accouterments of a female. As a coke and crack addict (which was my street drug of choice), the fetishes acted as an attraction for gamines who, likewise, sought added dimensions to their prosy sexual activities and boring lovemaking. So, ultimately, this aversion for transvestism assisted me in luring otherwise uninterested molls to experiment and experience sexual liaisons which otherwise may not have been forthcoming. The best of both worlds.

By the time I was on the street, I had a world of experience behind me. I had come out of the press long ago, gender-bending, while I maintained my macho role working a straight job during the week. It was a compartmentalizing of my life into a manageable, doable structure that worked and was fulfilling. So I could change at will into a role, side tripping, to fit my impulses. All I needed to work out was some gear. Mojo gear. On the street, whenever I could, I always had a supply of mojo gear at hand on which to draw, to side trip at will, and change roles like a quick-change artist. In an hour or two I was able to transform myself into a hot transvestite, often passable as a real girl, at least at casual observation. This was an impersonation I loved to perform but was usually restricted to acting out amongst friends and acquaintances since to be so attired was to be vulnerable and safety was always a concern when my male persona was modified or in remission. There is no more convenient scapegoat, no easier target for abuse from uptight morons than an apparent queer. Once I stepped into that characterization, as a sex object, I became subject to projected fears and insecurities by every frustrated, half-baked jerk looking for release. So, as a street urchin, I had to combine my roles as a macho man and a sexualized freak, decked out in drag yet able and ready to defend myself. It was a stimulating role to play and enjoyed with some regularity.

What I actually accomplished on the street was a blending of roles that was both freakish and alluring without giving up my dominant male personality. Being a street performer, as a drummer, afforded me license to be more casual in my projected image, my appearance became part of my act and so granted me more freedom in how I presented myself, allowing me the benefit of the doubt, enabling me to carry on as a weirdo yet wholly, unmistakably male. It was my aura, my effulgence that defined me in spite of my attire. And so I reveled in this new freedom, the aggregation of my selves, my animus and anima, a complete whole of various parts working together to embody the pure spirit and soul of myself. This is what I feel I achieved on the street. A coming together of fragmented impulses and passions and dreams.

I recall my First Street super, Mattie, once telling me, "You're my kind of image." He was so frustrated and jealous, envious of anyone who could make a success out of failure. The way we saw it, a failure to succeed within the boundaries of the Establishment, outcasts trying to function within their limited restrictions. It wasn't easy. It took courage, perseverance and know-how. And a lot of luck. There was a point in time when, for me, I seemed to have it all. A fortuitous occurrence that somehow just seems to happen on its own irregardless of all one's planning and hoping and scheming. A truly miraculous unfoldment, like a weed flourishing through a crack in a busy sidewalk. Life in spite of all the odds against it. I had it and played it for all it was worth.

Transvestism is part of my story if only in its abatement. During my time on the street and in my First Street apartment when it was open as a crack house, admitting complete strangers, I couldn't allow myself to be regarded as a wuss. I had to defend not only myself but my habitat. Thus a consistent macho exterior was essential in order not to be misinterpreted. That's why, when living with Robin at First Street, I didn't engage in any open cross-dressing. It would have invited muggings and rip-offs so only my most intimate acquaintances were even aware of my propensity for that fetish. Some who did know, like my friend Mattie, pestered me continually for sexual sessions in which I had no interest. When I went out on parade into the city proper, dressed to the nines, it was to flash and show off. I never worked the stroll or the meat market, never picked up guys. I wasn't a hustler in that respect, don't have the temperament for it, nor the penchant. For in extremis though I may have been, I never subjected myself to the world of numbers, to the sexual skewnesses of male scores for money. Mine was an altogether different carrot, different scene.

I did go with queens on occasion but my sexual activity in mojo gear, as it were, was carried out in my own pad, either at First Street or the Kenmore Hotel, with acquaintances from the stroll or girlfriends, like Wanda, who actually worked the stroll. I could never allow myself to let down my guard with strangers, to be submissive and vincible with some demented nut who was going to give me what he or she thought I deserved. I didn't want to get hurt. I may have sometimes enjoyed pain, but in a controlled, consenting situation. I was wild and crazy but out for a good time and fun. I never worked a sexual con or scam (except with Robin) and wasn't suicidal enough to wittingly expose myself to danger. Once you let someone own you that way they never let go and your free will is compromised. I was always my own man, in charge and wary. And so I learned to tailor my fetishistic urges to fit in with my lifestyle and, to a greater or lesser extent, control the danger to myself when engaged in cross-dressing activity.

When, on occasion, I was out and about in wig and makeup and tight skirt and high heels with my legs shaved, believe me, desirable though I was to some I was never futzed with. Usually, I was flying so high on coke and crack that it was a lose-lose situation to mess with me. I never challenged anyone. I moved too swiftly to be caught. Mainly, I guess, I was lucky. But you have to create your own luck a lot of times. Many of the girls on the stroll disappear, are murdered, kidnapped, chopped up by berserk lunatics who are all over the place out there on the street just looking for an easy target, a pregnable mark to satisfy their mad, sadistic impulses. So I played my transvestite cards very cagey, canny and cutesy-poo, always on guard for dangerous misdirected sexual aggressions from my surrounding environment. This, as well, added extra stimulus to my fetishized exploits, an increased excitement to the venture of allure and illusion, of dreams blent with verity. Ah, well, those were the days.

On the street it's a young person's game. The old and feeble are too vulnerable and become instant victims. That's why most of the aged homeless are invisible, part of the shadow world, living out their existence in secret, as far away from being noticed as they can get. I ran on the street until I was almost fifty years old, a long stretch for an active gamin engaged in the drug culture and offbeat lifestyle of the fetishist. Dreams that sometimes come true and are fleeting.

Sexual activity amongst the homeless took place around any corner or in any shadow. I once spotted a dastardly black punk masturbating behind a wall on a subway platform while kissing provocative photos of smutty white chicks in a *Penthouse* magazine. I once passed a fully loaded six-foot-high *Dumpster* on the street with a heterodox couple fornicating right on top of the garbage. I once saw a decadent white doll-baby ardently performing fellatio on a dandy black dude in a begrimed parking lot. And once I heard the unmistakable sounds of a couple copulating in a toilet stall in a public lavatory. When the spirit moves you, the urge will not be repressed. And then, some people just like to boff in the dirt.

Many of the bums I've observed and come to know on the street, as well as people in straight society, struggle to come to grips with their sexuality. Karen (character coming up) who proclaims in a bluff and boastful manner to a roomful of cairds, in front of her sons, "I'm bisexual," and then was frigid when finally alone with a partner. Mattie (First Street super) who asserts to the street at large in his booming, overcompensating growl, "I'm a stud, I go with anybody," yet couldn't seem to make it with his own wife. Robin (persona forthcoming) who walks around with a mattress strapped to her back yet has to be zonked on doojee to do the nasty. So many whores become lesbians, not able to tolerate the touch of a man any longer for the wretched reality of their daily bread. Latent homosexuals who censure sodomy then sneak off to the trucks under cover of darkness. Everyday working society clones who cruise the stroll in their shiny cars looking for masochistic harlots or rough trade, only to be bamboozled and left flat by the bewitching magicians who snare them in their beguiling webs. And insecure guttersnipes with no self-identity who need to beat a woman black and blue in order to achieve an erection and, equally pathetic, their willing, passive, perpetual victims.

Is it an urban phenomenon or a societal result of the binding disciplines one must function within that engenders such perverse sexuality, further nurtured by fashion, psychological exponents and pornography? I am not referring to conventional "straight" transgressions—the goodman who stops off for a quick BJ on the way home from work or the married secretary who has an impetuous liaison with her boss. I speak of a more devious, twisted sexuality that seems, to me, born and bred of excursive human organization. For I observe in nature birds of a feather flocking together and zoic conspecific species joining for procreation. I never notice homosexuality amongst wild animals nor the intentional changing of appearance in any other creature than deranged humans. Or are we just an aberrative race who keep scientists busy in their laboratories and psychologists occupied in their think tanks formulating new hypotheses that it is inherent

in us to stray from the basics, our foundation, and keep inventing new ways of being unnatural. And I am a product of this
great society. Ole!

Crack was great for sex—a philter—but it was always a tease. I
would almost never climax with it. Always foreplay and negation
until you're down to your last cap, your last rock, your last little
hit and then you missed it, the big ejaculation, and frustration and
new schemes send you scrambling around for more crack, you'll
make it this time, and the next bijou is the same old merry-go-
round. It's too good to stop, just a little more tease, bearding the
lion until you're out of crack once more and compulsion and duress
drive you hither for another score. It's never enough, you're out
of control, in the grip of the power, fervor, splendor and euphoria,
the dementia that is the hallmark of crack addiction. And hence
you become inured to the struggle and persist with the habit for
whatever you can get out of it for, in the end (*faute de mieux*) it's
better than nothing and the monkey is all you have left.

There is so much intra-violence amongst the homeless that, as
far as I can see, the police resent having to deal with it. Of course,
the NYC police (slobs that they are), the largest police force in the
world, resent having to do their job, period, unless it's harassing
some poor, honest taxpayer. A young Latino I knew, Hector, had
his throat slit on Ludlow Street, not a skip and a jump from my
First Street apartment and the Catholic Worker. I'd seen him the
day before in Saint Joe's soup kitchen, his face red and swollen
like he was on Antabuse and drank. Rapid breathing. He must
have done something stupid over on his home turf for him to end
up like that, or so I'd like to think, trusting that he wasn't just an
unlucky victim of a stickup. But then, dead is dead. Probably this
is as much eulogy as he will pull down. City refuse where life is

cheap. You never read about such crimes in the newspaper, the yellow press; too common, too plentiful, too meaningless ever to be solved, insignificant deaths swept under the blotter of the police files. Hundreds of bodies scraped off the streets, many not even reported or heard of. The life cycle of the homeless.

There was a long, lean, blond and bearded chap I met early on in my homelessness, a denizen of Tompkins Square Park, who had offered me sanctuary in his ticky-tacky tenement nearby which, through some fortunate intuition, I turned down. He was a conspicuous figure, sporting a bantam gamecock that he carried around with him and was a sociable fellow, somewhat magnetic if not enigmatic. It became known some months later, after his confession to the police, that he'd killed at least three girls, one of whom he dismembered in his bathtub and boiled on his stove to make soup which he subsequently served to the homeless in Tompkins Square Park. The girl's bones were discovered in long-term storage at Grand Central Terminal. The local homeless population gave barely an eyeblink at this news since these things happen to any who are naive and unwary. The incident received only the briefest mention in the local newspapers. I recalled, after the fact, a scene I'd observed in Tompkins Square Park prior to the fiend's capture whence he was impressing upon two newly turned out all-American lads, who had evidently accepted his offer of sanctuary, certain rules of conduct which if violated, "I'll have to chop you up, cut out your liver..."

Those are some of the ugly, bleeding, raw ingredients of the street. It is a hard-hitting, depressing realization as a destitute bum in roaming the uphill, ice-cold canyons of the greatest city on earth, surrounded by skyscrapers of unimaginable wealth, to find not a single warm sheltered place to rest. There is no greater sense of disapprobation than to be shut out of everywhere, shunned by everyone, cast out to the elements and the wolves lest you possess the coin to pay.

Walking at midnight along downtown's warren of switchbacks, upper story sweatshops and godowns shut tight, dark, foreboding, the night-filled windows like mystic portals of ill will, the long street hard-edged and lethal as a henchman's axe. "I had never divined before that strange things hid themselves from men under pretense of being inanimate mounds of brick and steel; but now they came, moving shadow-silent, slipping out from their harmless covers to follow me and mock at my impotence, to make a monstrous kindred thing resolve to truer form, threatening and malefic."[1] This was the life I had chosen, from which there was no retreat.

Imagine your most secret, buried fears changing into ghosts and surfacing, meeting you at every turn, some anticipating paranormal vapor permeating every fiber of your life space, clinging, menacing and terrible. Plowing lumberously ever forward, ever hopeful for the next handout or libation, on to the next beckoning block, knowing within the deepest part of yourself that unseen eyes are on you, silently watching you weaken, waiting for you to falter, ready to pounce, when your will deserts you and you are rendered defenseless. And yet you persist blithely onward, despite your presentiment, bleary eyed, pushing into the pregnant shadows of the night, crossing over into the darkness and the lurking, indecent scavengers to whom you are prey; feeling courageous and venerable in your freedom, your autonomy, determined not to buckle under, to soldier onward in the face of insuperable odds and to prevail.[2] Hungry and exhausted, mechanically trudging ahead into uncharted wilderness, latent dread and misgivings looming immane out of the somber hush, despair is setting in because you know there is no place around you to rest for a few hours. This is the life of the street—no good times, only this. And yet—this is

---

1 Clemence Houseman, *The Were-Wolf*, paraphrase (Isaac Asimov, *Moons*)
2 Kevin Baker, *Paradise Alley*, some words and ideas

the street in all its beguiling allure and sorcery and fascination, casting its spell, its enchantment, its extraordinary invocation over the stricken, the wandering, the misled, the forsaken. This is the essence of the street stripped of all its brilliance, its glitter, its swagger and promise, the bottom line that it uses to eventually crush all those who dare to meddle in its murky business. The makeless street.

The city vans pull up to each target area well after midnight and out spring the bailiffs, armed and ready for resistance, they quickly and purposefully encircle the shapes huddled against the freezing cold and brutally grab and pull and shove and drag the vagrants, stiff with rigor and groggy with sleep, out from their flimsy, ramshackle shelters, away from their few pitiful possessions and into the waiting vans, readily dispensing blows with their batons as encouragement. Off to some brightly lit detention hall for the remainder of the night where no food or hot coffee are waiting. The city rescue service in full swing, the civilized welfare system saving the tramps from themselves.

Forced out into the streets again at daybreak with no breakfast or hot coffee or one-dollar bill, without even the few rags of extra clothing or scraps of food that were in their now vanished shopping bags, their worldly possessions, confiscated during the roundup the night before. Every single one of those bums would as soon be left alone to freeze to death, if that be their fate, rather than suffer the indignity of being forced, herded, by the very entity they despise most, the representatives of what inadvertently caused their being where they are in the first place, into the most repulsive environment that they detest, being kicked while they're down, taken out of their element and remanded into the stark, bright, fact-facing atmosphere of horror, punishment, the self-serving dark side of society, so the agency can show you proof on TV, can print the facts in the public press, that they are hard at work, doing their duty, saving the lives that they've already destroyed. The industry must continue.

Actually, the latter part of the 1980s was a good time to be homeless in New York City. It was a period that coincided with the backlash of earlier gay and communist witch hunts, all smack-dab in the middle of a resurgence of a age-old bum contingency that was correspondingly fixing its place in present-day society—visible, proud and unstoppable. For the crack culture lent an adaptability to the lifestyle of the urban street bum while vagrancy laws (which had been strict some two decades prior) were relaxed; that is until the 1990s witnessed the return of punitive measures for dealing with the homeless. Led by New York Mayor Rudolph Giuliani, New York City began to pass Dark Ages ordinances that allowed police to arrest homeless persons for trivial misdemeanors like panhandling and sleeping or sitting on the sidewalks.[1] A desper-ate, futile, Procrustean tactic for cleaning up the streets, akin to sweeping the dust under the carpet. For the homeless, like many heteroclite factions, are an embarrassing reminder that all is not well and economic growth does not benefit all and inequality in Our Great Society reigns supreme. And that Alternative Lifestyle is a folkloric American art whose (criminalized or tolerated) spirit will not be repressed or disclaimed.

During my freshman days as a bum on the New York City streets, to say I was very active would almost be an understatement. Except for the occasions when I would stop for a rest on a park bench to

---

1 Kenneth L. Kusmer, *Down and Out, On the Road: The Homeless in American History*, paraphrase

soak my soggy puppies in the sun (in defense against trench foot) I practically never stopped moving. There is safety in motion. I walked from one end of the city to the other, always taking different routes, exploring every street, every nook and cranny. Two trips back and forth over the Queensborough Bridge per day was not uncommon, making my daily weed run to the Queensbridge projects, carrying coals to Newcastle. It was peaceful up on the bridge and safe. I would often lean over the railing and watch the barges go by on the East River and gaze at the city skyline while smoking a joint, winsome, the bird's-eye view. And there were a couple of months that I worked on my cookbook, *Canapés That Work*, writing a recipe a day, knowing that if I didn't put it down soon it would be forgotten, what took me a career to develop and realize, something that, even in the hallowed archives of cookbooks, is still unique. That entire cookbook, nearly fifty recipes, was transcribed while roving the New York City streets. I'd buy a pint of cheap geneva and find a remote spot to be alone, a deserted stretch along East River Park in the early morning, or sometimes Union Square Park, or an abandoned building where I could write undisturbed, and pen one formula per diem while I'd quaff my four-gill potation. Recipes that reflect almost ten years of specialization in garde-manger in some of the finest restaurants and hotels in New York City (in the world). In fact, in later years, when I would endeavor to replicate some of the items, I'd have to refer back to my own book to refresh my memory. I knew that such a tendency to go stale and forget when ceasing to make canapés that I used to turn out daily by the hundred was inevitable. Especially after a period when my mind was no longer attuned to, was light years from, the high-production kitchens of haute and nouvelle cuisine. I typed out the final manuscript from a storefront rent-an-office (only in New York) where I rented, by the hour, the use of a typewriter. Need an office for a day or a few hours?

There are so many small things to love about New York City. There are still some delis (like Smiler's) that have the best kaiser rolls, big and crispy on the outside and like a cloud inside; and there are also the ironic things peculiar to New York. I have traveled wide and have yet to find anywhere that knows what a regular coffee is. And where else can you buy a freshly made bialy or handmade Danish or croissant? Or bagel with schmear. Neidick's famous orange drink and frankfurter at a stand-up counter. Papaya King for a foamy papaya drink and hot dog with more flavor than filet mignon (whose clientele can't even pronounce it). Nathan's Famous (Coney Island chicken). Katz's wurst factory for real beef navel pastrami with a Dr. Brown's cream soda. Chock Full O'Nuts for a crumbly corn muffin and coffee from a low stool at a low horseshoe counter. Grilled cheese, French fries, dill pickle spear and 7UP from *Woolworth's* lunch counter (only ten cents if you pop the lucky balloon). And who knows where the one and only surviving Automat is? (see glossary). Or the disappearing hot deli steam tables at select *McCann's* or *Blarney Stone* taverns, where you can still savor fresh brisket on a club roll. And a frankfurter on a Sabrette bun from the umbrella-topped dirty-man pushcart with mustard, sauerkraut and onions. Or a hot dog on the Staten Island Ferry. Roasted chestnuts, peanuts and (jumbo) soft pretzels from smoky sidewalk pushcarts. Sno-cones and water ices in the torrid summers. Shrafft's apple pie. Lindy's cheesecake. Ratner's chicken soup... New York comfort food that's somewhere between real food and a snack. Vestiges of olde New York hanging on with a death grip over the tar pits of malted milk, egg cream and lime rickey.

Somewhere in the deep recesses of my mind I knew that by living on the street I would be immersed in the total New York experience

(I loved the city so) and somewhere within me, I believe, that is what I secretly aspired to (such derring-do), in the thick of the didactic city, and if being a bum was the way I would have it then so be it. The adrenalin was flowing, I was ready. Never had I yet been afforded such a situation for close study and absorption in the very metaphysics of the city.

I had always wanted to live in Manhattan; every time my lease in Astoria expired I'd apartment hunt in the city only to strike out again and again, never finding anyplace suitable. Most of the situations that I found affordable were in the Lower East Side, an area which unnerved and put me off with its seedy squalor (hah!), exactly where I would eventually wind up, fit in and come to love. Being a bridge and tunnel commuter was never my cup of tea though it would be a far-flung, circuitous path that would eventually transplant me in the City That Never Sleeps, the Big Apple, City of Parks, Fun City, Sin City, Naked City, Gotham.

The contrast between the life of the street and what I'd been used to was so vast a chasm yet you could put out your arm and touch it. A frontier, a line of demarcation so to speak, beyond which a curtain drops: against the folds I push into the fabric of the unknown, my destiny, into fates both sinister and nefarious, amidst the shifting shoals of desire.

The only way to participate in the real nitty-gritty of the city stews, to be trusted by the dissolute renegades of the street, was to have absolutely nothing and, ideally, to be a full-blown addict. In choosing the capricious fate of an urban bum, thereby recanting normal society, I immediately cast myself as the genuine article and, as such, began to endure all the privations and prejudices such a baleful walk of life carries. Thus was my incipient insurrection into a mordant, outlandish, picaresque enterprise which only experience can gauge and apprehend. And attempt to describe. Parce que, "A pioneer needs imagination, able to enjoy the idea of things more than the things themselves."[1] "For, in the end, the journey itself is its destination."[2] And in this, I feel, I was able to manifest my ideals of freedom, enough to carry me through the grueling, endless tortures of street life for so many years, from my nascent gambit to my swan song. Many (too many) of the unimaginative homeless, however, feel trapped and of those the voracious, indiscriminate street devours.

To grasp the poetry of street life—there is no homelessness, for the city itself is home. All the institutions on which the bum relies are in his living room and backyard. As such, the bum is part of the street, they are conjoined.

There was a very kinky and fickle quandary I noticed on the street from day one that, at times, proved to be a matter of survival where I'd have to speak with my best (almost illiterate) stupid-from-Brooklyn affectation when in discourse with depraved, philistine unfortunates, invariably of a negritude state, who are stuck in the muck of privation and view an affluent person who has willfully chosen to be in the muck as a complete chump. They feel, if only they had the opportunity that guy had they'd make something of it. Touchy situation. I guess it's perplexing to comprehend how someone would voluntarily live as a bum whether they're pseudopatrician or cradled into the bondage of poverty. As to those ethnic New Jacks of the street, being chagrined wretches with no sense of purpose, no initiative, hiding behind a ribald, impudent façade with a gruff, macho manner that includes exaggerated gestures and a bastardized class dialect of Black English.

Every third word is nigga or some other obscenity: "Hey, yo! y'heard? Nigga sez, nigga sez ah dissed his ass. Ah ah ah say

---

1 Willa Cather, *O Pioneers*
2 Valerie Wilson Wesley, *Ain't Nobody's Business If I Do*

shee-it, dis nigga nevah woulda piss on yo, on yo worthless black ass, an' that's a fak (fact)! Yo! Nigga sez, nigga sez his hole be a witniss! Ah say, ah say shee-it, yo yo yo nigga pussy done dime yo sorry muthafuckin black ass to the po-lice, shee-it! Know what I'm sayin'?" (ipsissima verba) They are the antithesis of anything dignified, compassionate, benevolent or bright. It's their status symbol: po' black trash.

Are there no preventative measures for such sociopathic riffraff? Society is afraid to educate poverty-stricken minorities for fear of creating a truly intelligent revolutionary. Perhaps birth control might contribute a positive impact on this endemic dilemma and its collateral consequences, a Malthusian approach. Correctional institutions, which are nothing more than gigantic zoos, are a costly, defeatist answer to a problem that begs a viable solution. America can put men on the moon yet cannot seem to be able to deal with its own indigin countrymen.

I was just on the road. I had simple fun. I started watching the birds. For me it was the sparrows of the city that won my heart from out of the limited wildlife to choose. There were seagulls, massive and scary; pigeons by the million, docile and unwary; starlings were in profusion and so funny the way they walk; but the sparrows were the lively ones, assertive and feisty, demanding and errant in their taking of what the city has to offer. Funny and sweet, little, they were my dearest friends. I would spend half an hour or more, regularly, watching sparrows and they never once failed to pick up my spirits. And the fledglings, in the spring, in their fluffy, downy babyhood all over the sidewalks, so sweet and precious and vulnerable, only to be eaten by some foraging rat or stepped on by the tramping pedestrian horde, it's heartbreaking.

In addition to bird-watching, I also used to observe dogs' personalities which so clearly mirror the disposition of their owners.

Happy dog, happy owner. Timid or vicious dog, miserable owner. The open book of animal life versus the pathological unveracity of mankind whose premier achievement is the lie. We should expand the advocacy of spay and neuter your pet to include Homo sapiens, starting with hedonic Americans. Save the planet.

As a dissolute urban vagabond, there was no more heartrending misery than that suffered by my humble self in trying to effect a peaceful rest. A niggling pin that wouldn't fall into place causing the whole mechanism to overheat and break down. From the start of my tramping days I tried sleeping on the Staten Island ferry itself, beginning with my first night at Whitehall Terminal, having arrived there so late that all of the waiting room benches were occupied and, in my ignorance, I went for the ferryboat.

I recalled from long past when I used to ride the ferry to Staten Island occasionally: the lower bench deck is enclosed and the benches stretch continuously along each wall, uninterrupted in their length, and where the bench seat and backrest meet, the joint is coved into a parabola and slightly depressed to more comfortably accommodate one's buttocks. This was ideal for sleeping and stretching out as the curve naturally conformed to one's body and the depression prevented a recumbent form from being tossed out onto the floor as the ship rolled. But all that evidently was before the current homeless epidemic. What I discovered was an alteration to the benches that made lying down comfortably and sleeping all but impossible, the seats had been partitioned with raised slats of wood. Well, I spread out the extra clothes I had in my shopping bags, making a cushion over the slats, and lay down anyway, I was so tired. Next thing I knew, I was being rapped on the bottoms of my feet with a nightstick by a burly ferry employee who informed me that I'd have to disembark at the next docking or face arrest by the police. No wonder the ferry had been virtually empty at that time of night; easy for the patrolling watchman to take note of who was staying on for more than a one-way trip. So that was that.

I also tried, right at the commencement of my homelessness, sleeping on the subway trains. That too was met with equally disastrous results as the ferry. I'd wake up time after time with my pants' pockets slit open and anything I carried therein gone. Yet the most galling thing about that was the gaping slash in the pants to be carried around with me and waved like a flag that all but screamed, "Look at me (was impossible not to stare at), I'm a stupid bum who can't even keep the snapping dogs at bay." Embarrassing.

One evening, early on in my vagrant vocation, I awoke from my slumber in a moving subway car, empty whence I'd gone to sleep, to find I had been joined by four hoodlumish juvenile darkies, barely in their teens, one each of whom were guarding the end doors, the other two were frozen in their forward-bending close inspection of my prone form who, upon my eyes opening, quickly stepped back to the opposite side of the car and cooly met my gaze as they feigned nonchalance. Time momentarily checked, the air charged with menace, a mordent shift in a mordant atmosphere as though some cataclysmic disaster were about to unfold then, as quickly, dissipated. The crew could have successfully rushed me but I was, after all, no slouch, what with my daily weight training and active lifestyle I kept in fighting trim and, besides, they were cowards at heart, feeding off each other's bravado in classic mob mentality. As soon as one of their number falters, they all hesitate and dissolve into their component parts, their individual temperaments. Alas, the subway trains were a poor choice for a flop and I quickly grew weary of having to succumb to the role of benefactor for those deleterious poltroons that relentlessly roam the crepuscular underside of the nominal city, ruthlessly dogging my innocuous repose.

Irregardless (love that word), stubborn like a jackass, I persevered to suffer the subways for awhile as though it were my prerogative, I just changed tactics. I took to snatching a couple of hours sleep during early morning rush hour (seven o'clock to nine o'clock) on a platform bench closest to the turnstiles and token booth at a busy station. Trains screeched in and out, one behind the other, disgorging mobs of passengers which converged around and filed past my bench—too much traffic for a stealthy rip off. One had to be deliriously tired and imperiously jaded to sleep through that racket and bustle. Yet I adapted, or perhaps mutated is more accurate, as do all urban bums when on the horns of a dilemma, faced with risky situations where one choice is as bad as another, caught between the devil and the deep blue sea.

So I would win my rest but at what price? Always on edge even during sleep, like a high-strung Doberman pinscher, ready to go into action, to rumble at any instant, to survive. Nerves become frayed, response and reaction times slow down, vision and perception become blurred and distorted, you hear things, imagination plays hopscotch with reality, you are weary beyond recovery from lack of sleep, lack of proper nourishment, lack of positive reinforcement. Like the majority of bums, I was a loner who wouldn't trust anyone. Start to drink and drug and those problems become magnified a hundredfold until you're a basket case. Have a nervous breakdown and here comes a second and a third. AIDS is on your doorstep, anemia, hepatitis, tuberculosis, dyscrasia of the humors, OD's, VD, and suicide lurk around every corner. Food poisoning is on the menu daily as you go on eating garbage, dysentery, infections, ringworm, scabies and lice haunt your cold, hungry, fearful lifestyle. These are the prices, the cost of street life, the side no one sees save the bums themselves, the victims.

By my first July on the streets, a mere three months homeless, I was a bundle of shattered nerves. Waking up on benches in parks, in sidewalk alcoves and recesses, in Pennsylvania Station and Grand Central Terminal waiting rooms with strangers' hands in my pockets, on my crotch, circling me like wolves, inching closer to see if I was asleep, ready to smite me down, there was nowhere I could find to go to rest, to be safe, to be left alone. I was snapping from the strain, becoming psychotic and agoraphobic.

I started to leave the city in the pale dusk of the impending night[1], traveling back to Astoria where there are no bums, to sleep in the cab of a dump truck parked off Broadway at Thirty-First Street in front of a construction site and left unlocked. I would lock myself in and sleep on the front seat, safe until six o'clock in the morning. I even had clothes stashed under the seat. Building progress was slowed to a near standstill so I squeezed a good month out of that spot. On extra cold nights, as autumn waxed incipient, I would sneak back to my former apartment building on Crescent Street, to which I still retained a front door key, ten flights up the stairs to the top landing and spread out the contents of my shopping bags upon which I'd lie down, wondering, "What the hell am I doing back here?" By that point I was one third of the way back to reentering society for the first and final time.

But I still had so much to learn about the street. For one thing, I was still scrounging food from garbage cans and the like. I had yet to eat in a soup kitchen. I had not learned of drop-in centers or shelters or detoxes for a temporary respite from the street. I had not even heard of flophouses or resident hotels for cheap, if temporary, lodging (nor of abandoned subway tunnels—a refuge in which I never partook). Well, there was plenty of time to learn those things. Years. It took that initial big effort to take it on the lam—to get off the street, to pass through the shelter system, to reenter society and my profession, only to wind up back in the gutter some two years later—to etch indelibly on my mind that my capacity for civilized conformity and participation had been forever demolished. And, Our Lady speed, if I could just keep out

---

1 Longfellow

of the Big House. Society has little patience for nonconformists unless they're rich, then they're sentimentalized and validated as fancifully eccentric.

There are small things the city could do for the bums that would mean a great deal to the poor souls. For instance, vitamin B-12 shots and inoculations freely given out, especially during winter. Bums are living without adequate heat, or food even. They become sick, the flu or something, and have to keep going out to work or lose their jobs, they can barely stand up. To someone in such critical condition whose circumstances leave no room to wiggle, a B-12 injection could mean a lifesaving jump-start. I have been in just such a situation once and went to the emergency room at Beth Israel Hospital with the flu, unable to stand for twelve hours at my job in the deli next door that served the hospital staff all night; I mean, those people—doctors, nurses, technicians—all knew me, I made their sandwiches every evening. Yet I was refused the B-12 injection and consequently lost my place because I couldn't work and subsequently lost my apartment.

Now, those same people from the same institution operate a needle exchange program. Unmarked vans pull up to designated locations on designated days throughout Alphabet City and hand out, free of charge, brand new hypos and points, no questions asked. Theoretically you're supposed to exchange old works for new, set for set, yet the syringes are doled out indiscriminately since the whole point of the program is Clean Works to help stamp out the spread of AIDS through dirty diseased needles and syringes. For all its good intentions, everything about the program stinks to high heaven since it's a crime to possess a set of works, period. That they are being used to illegally inject narcotics by junkies is conveniently overlooked. Morally, society would rather let the addicts perish, but it's better business, better for the economy to keep the dopers dependent on the system, prolonging their suffering as alimentation for the insatiable Leviathan that is America.

The same hospital ministry (health care personnel) also conduct a Methadone clinic where druggies who are tired of the life are given synthetic dope to drink, free of charge, and walk around stoned all day on the Meth. Free abortions are performed on pregnant addicts by the same group of morality ministers who never once consult the fetus on whether or not it prefers to take a chance at life. This marvelous group of professionals also offer counseling for safe sex whereby sodomites who are waging warfare for equal rights are educated, free of charge, on alternative methods to coitus that involve the use of appliances for mutual masturbation. And those very same MDs refuse me, an artisian, a B-12 shot that would enable me to continue working, and needing a little less of the dole than otherwise, earning a living for myself, still a (working) bum but standing (or trying to stand) on my own two feet. Is there something wrong with this picture?

If those clinical not too good do-gooders wanted to be really effective about fighting AIDS, they would include a B-12 shot with each new clean set of works because the at-high-risk-of-AIDS group of addicts are the most run-down, their immune systems shot, resultant from their abusive, reckless lifestyles and the B-12 would, besides other good side effects, boost their immune systems thereby helping them to naturally resist such pathogens as could give them, say, pneumonia, the number one killer of AIDS victims. So give the poor bum a B-12 shot when he's on his knees and must be kept standing, give the bums influenza vaccine, give them pneumonia vaccine. Bums don't have, or wouldn't spend if they had, six or twelve or twenty-five dollars for boosters when it will cost the city in the end anyway for every inch downhill that bum slides until he's finally six feet under in potter's field at the city's expense. A lose-lose situation from the word go that in many cases could be avoided, or at least softened with just a little hand up from the city; a minimal underwriting to help the bum maintain a level of conditioning so he's employable, i.e., vaccinations, nutritional assistance, and provide vouchers for employment agencies so the bum can meet the fee for a day's work. Minor measures that in many cases would be enough to turn the tables into a win-win situation that allows the bum's dignity to remain intact by leaving the initiative to work up to the bum who then has a chance to earn cash each day.

There is an occurrence that I see all too often, young mothers who are addicts dragging their children around as props while they beg money to support their habit. Those whiffets who are raised thus and nurtured on depravity and neglect during their formative years will, as adults, get even with society and then society will have no choice but to deal with them. I have seen those malnourished saplings subjected to drop-in centers where drug abuse, sexual perversion and violence flourish. To help that child during his first ten years would save the city and state fifty subsequent years of prosecuting, incarcerating and rehabilitating in an endless cycle of futility for such progeny of the street. But, alas, the current age-old system is designed to keep minorities in their place and provide employment for millions of law enforcement and Department of Corrections personnel—bunker mentality minions doing their bit to help define America.

Although crack is the number one contributor of urban homelessness in this day and age, there is ample evidence that alcohol takes its toll, it's still there as of old and I see it on the street today. And while poverty alone may be the cause of copious homelessness, as it has been since cities evolved, in my personal experience (which is considerable), the homeless or street people (bums) soon succumb to the temptation of alcohol or other substance abuse if they have not done so before becoming homeless. It is a peril of the street. Hence they are then faced with a new major obstacle,

that is the monetary cost of alcohol or drugs which is often pro-
hibitive to someone in such dire straits.

Alternately, a mind-set is established amongst the homeless,
the bums, that mimics substance abusers with psychosis (delirium
tremens) and sociopathology which sets them apart from normal
society. It is the treatment and ostracizing by society, and the
bums' reaction to such treatment, and the fear and harshness
of the street that produces a neurotic mentality which is often
inseparable from that of an addict. "It is important to realize
that substance abuse and psychiatric problems are more often an
effect than a cause of homelessness. Given the sometimes hellish
nature of life on the street, it should come as no surprise that
many homeless persons become mentally disoriented or turn to
alcohol or drugs."[1] And so, sadly, the sober homeless as well as the
substance abuser all share a common psyche or psychasthenia[2] as
bums of the street who do not fit into or belong to normal society
yet live off that society as do the mice and the sparrows that, all
together, help form the reticular weft of the city, today's complex
New Age urban landscape.

Many of the homeless are victims of circumstance whereby
events just seemed to turn against them and they found themselves, somehow, with nowhere to go. Even substance abusers,
who are not necessarily defectors from society, could merely be
average everyday losers whose luck just ran out. It's no peccancy
to seek solace in a bottle or in a joint or a pill to relieve the ever
mounting pressures of everyday life. People give their future to
a system of institutions: a career, marriage, family, civilized society's organizations—they enter this maze of pathways with faith,
dedication, integrity, and determinately devote decades of their

---

1 Kenneth L. Kusmer, *Down and Out, On the Road: The Homeless in American
History*
2 phobia or compulsion

lives to following the prescribed routes that have been laid down for them historically, exponentially, anthropologically—taxpayers, parishioners, union fellows, political affiliates, Rotarians. And suddenly they find themselves with nothing to show for it. Their spouse has been unfaithful, their children use drugs or are lazy or promiscuous, they become unemployed through no fault of their own, can't meet the mortgage and face foreclosure, they become shunned by their neighbors for some obscure, embarrassing injustice. Any number of simple, mundane reasons can cause a normal, everyday citizen to become a substance abuser. Looking for a way out where no way exists. It is very easy to spiral downward from just such a predicament and find yourself suddenly with no place to go, the only help will entrench you deeper in the morass of indenture and obligation, of enslavement to a system that does not work for victims, does not care for its public, will only keep squeezing you until you're dry and used up. Your emotions and responsibilities count for nothing. Bureaucracies become the instruments that cause their own mechanisms to founder by abusing their privileges (such as with collective bargaining in a right-to-work state). A vicious cycle whose unbidden by-product adds to the growing homeless contagion on our streets—an additional strain on an already overburdened economy.

Many of the homeless try to make it somehow on their own. The average prostitute is not some sex-crazed maniac but a desperate pilgrim trying to survive. It is often the easiest thing for them to do, to close their eyes and lie back for fifteen minutes or open their mouth for five minutes in order to keep alive and avoid the binding, suffocating constraints of a straight job in an environment in which they cannot function. Do that two or three times and in a half hour they've earned as much as they would working eight hours for six or seven dollars per at some mind-numbing pink-collar labor. Not to mention that often those girls need upwards of $200 per day to cover their drug habits. So, their options are limited. Unpretentious, they are mostly what has happened to them, what the world has done to them. They cannot always make the choice.

People often begin pushing drugs only as a means to support their own habit. I knew a couple who operated a sex service, Paradise Lost, where sexually hung-up individuals (invariably men) paid for some weird fantasy to be acted out. The female of this duo was a bass guitar player in a rock band. Her boyfriend was a heroin addict who would do anything other than work. Together they offered their combined efforts to provide a service whereby they were able to supplement their income without joining society and its disciplines. Many bums engage in shadow work like collecting cast-off clothing and trinkets from various free sources (churches, trash, secondhand shops) and sell those items right on the sidewalk as if in some Far Eastern bazaar, reminiscent of the open air thieves' markets of the 1950s where jacklegs dealt in stolen goods. Other brummagem enterprisers sell bootleg watches, rings and handbags in parks, tee shirts and socks at sidewalk bridge tables; and ornamental calendars or batteries for a dollar on the subways. Or selling nothing at all but collecting for some alleged disability, handing out cards with the manual alphabet printed on them, placing these on the knees of riders sitting in subway cars, the most offensive dodge (to my sensibilities) of the hustling scam artists. And many bums do no more than collect empty beverage cans from the city's trash receptacles and redeem them at automated redemption machines usually located at chain supermarkets. All those people, street people, doing what they can to survive. Making the most of a bad situation. Finding a way to exist amidst a culture with which they cannot cope. Doing something, at least, to help themselves in the blind face of one of the richest civilizations the earth has ever known that cannot take care of their own despite a one-hundred-thirty-two billion dollar annual welfare price tag (food stamps and unemployment not included). If Americans would work for a reasonable wage, rather than demanding $50 an hour plus benefits, this country wouldn't need to import most manufactured goods and unemployment would be proportionately reduced. Only in America is it often more lucrative to collect welfare than to work, allowing illegal aliens (such as Mexicans) to fill the gaps in America's plummeting job market.

The average single welfare recipient collects sixty dollars in cash bimonthly and a hundred twenty dollars in food stamps per month and they are expected to survive, to live on this allotment. Incredible. If it weren't for soup kitchens, many bums would starve to death. It's no wonder that the jails are overflowing—the biggest hotel in America. I have been in prison and I can tell you that a majority of today's incarcerated inmates have been crack users, substance abusers, and street people of one stripe or another. The proportion of inmates in whose background crack has played a dominant role is staggering. Or should I say not surprising when considering the violent nature of crack.

Nonetheless, many minorities are incarcerated not for their (alleged) crime but for being undesirable by way of their class—poor and uneducated—or others simply because society needs culprits to balance out the scales for the victims whose assailants escape prosecution. These tactics have become our New Age pogroms, the clandestine rationale of a peremptory mandamus for whitewashing society and manipulating statistics to give the appearance, a fig leaf of respectability while boosting a failing economy with the largest prison system in the world. Ergo my captious assessment of American justice.

Prison is for many homeless or people from dysfunctional homes a place of refuge, structure and order where three square meals a day can be had along with a clean bed in which to sleep that is dry and warm and safe. Jail becomes a place where the homeless can take a break from the street and recover some of their reserves while receiving three hots and a cot. I've watched the same people returning to jail, time after time after time; some succumb every winter and revel in the security of the dayroom, playing cards and watching television, taking their meals with relish. You can tell by watching them that they haven't eaten as well in a long time, the young ones in their entire short lives. Many of those inmates talk freely of their experiences living on the street, of their hardships and the insanity of crack. Some receive long sentences as repeat offenders, people who just cannot make it in the outside world. I don't offer a solution—I wish I could. Many, not all, but most of today's inmates are from the lower classes. I believe there can be no hope for the middle and lower class as long as there is a class system. So the response of the city, the state, the Fed shall remain more prisons because more education alone is not enough of an answer. Hope may lie in the family unit, the very keystone of society, as many reprobates were neglected or abused as youngsters.[1] (According to one scientific study, more than half the homeless youngsters came from broken homes.)[2] (According to another source, the average age of a homeless person in the US today is nine years old.)[3] Yet the American family is disintegrating and will not be revived in a welfare/police state with Big Brother's nose up your arse, where individuality and divorce are at a premium and filial supervision is lax as dual working parents become the norm.

Being a bum today is more attractive than ever. It is chic, it is hip, it is avant-garde. As slumming has become fashionable with the adolescent affluent of our pop culture, it is rapidly being accepted to be decadent and to casually make sport of the unfortunate oppressed of our Great Society and to emulate their circumstances,

---

1 James Gilligan, MD, *Violence: Our Deadliest Epidemic*, statistics and ideas
2 Leonard C. Feldman, *Citizens without Shelter*
3 Atlanta Union Mission

if not in authenticity, then by caprice. The contemporary style of torn, raggedy bum attire and of baggy pants pulled down to below the buttocks and multiple oversize T-shirts, copied directly from prison uniforms, demonstrate how today's teenagers want to mimic felonious convicts or, more precisely, poor, ignorant, black convicts. Bums and prison inmates have become the New Age role models of today's youth, as representatives of defiance against the conventional values of the Establishment. Such negativity is foisted upon New York Fashion by "Japanese brand N. Hoolywood (that) debuted a clothing line inspired by homelessness,"[1] featuring sartorial incongruity and plastic sack-like tote bags. Tattoos have gained in popularity over the past ten years, especially Chicano black work that reflect prison tattoos. Rap music has reached new heights, patronized by misguided white youths who have discovered a new symbol of hatred, identifying with suppressed, uneducated blacks who at least have an etiology to fall back on, a heritage by way of excusing such anti-white-culture sentiments. Now American white trash have jumped on this bandwagon, brainwashing themselves with racial, anti-Semitic attitudes in place of anything positive which might accidentally identify them with or remind them of that which they lack—wholesome middle-class values. Street life may become the new Palm Springs weekend or "What I Did on My Summer Vacation" for the adventuresome.

Like the repressed discontents of Europe who came to America to found new homes,[2] our current civilization's discontents are to be found between the cracks of society on the streets, in the jails, in flophouses and resident hotels and shelters, and in the bizarre and offbeat and sinister occupations from prizefighters to circus performers, from hockey players to tattoo artists, from

---

1 *TIME* February 20, 2017, page 54 (photo)
2 Peter Lawler, *Homeless and At Home in America: Evidence for the Dignity of the Human Soul in Our Time and Place*

drug runners to race car drivers, from rock musicians to actresses and fashion models; these are our heroes, our role models, the antithesis of the status quo.

Today's bums—from the homeless vagrant to the street's three-card monte dealers to the skid row wino to the prostitute on the block, whether on a soup line or collecting cans—reflect an ever growing restiveness with current mores and values, with traditional myths and canons, in a welfare state which places such high standards on individuality, sexual freedom, civil unions, equal rights for gays and oppressed minorities, and daycare *in loco parentis*. Where the average working stiff is taxed to death for government over-expenditure that includes hi-tech weapons and anomalous experiments, more prisons and handouts to foreign nations, plus graft, graft and more graft.[1] While the government distracts taxpayers from relevant issues by focusing on and persecuting the homeless. The fat cats and robber barons are getting theirs at the expense of the planet, the ecology, their very own constituency in this (our) New Age of government employee unions—the modern version of Tammany Hall. Is it too onerous to edify the impoverished progeny of the street? Maybe we need another French or Russian revolution right here in the US of A or a good old-fashioned plague (like the Black Death of 1348) to decimate the earth's overpopulation and excoriate the world for its follies or, at the very least, some neo-Malthusianism across the board. In the meanwhile, register for unemployment, sign up for welfare, go on SSI, get what you can and do what you want, after all, "more than 50 percent of the American population now receive more from the government than they pay in."[2] Live for today, it's the American way and the New Age vagabond battle cry.

---

1 Mallory Factor, *Shadowbosses*,re, government employee union legislators
2 Mallory Factor, *Shadowbosses*

On the street everything was a swindle; everyone being out for themselves and looking for the slightest opportunity to get the upper hand. Especially where drugs were concerned. I was never like that which put me at a disadvantage but also worked in my favor sometimes. Again, for me it was all a side trip, observing and experiencing the lurid, scalding, dark escapades of a corrupt old city as if a voyeur in which I was also a participant as well as a victim, intertwined in a tangible and ethereal helix that was at once both real and a dream.

My early months on the New York City streets were largely fulfilling. Talk about an interesting study, this was one gigantic human zoo, an *olla podrida* of race, creed and culture and I was free to explore, at will, all the outward facets of it. There's so much to see on that small, twelve-mile island. My initial area of concentration was south of Central Park, orientating towards the East Side, mainly Fourteenth Street to Houston Street. Just north of Houston Street was my main living area which included Greenwich Village East, Tompkins Square Park and Alphabet City, as self-contained a microcosm as will be found, a plexiform area catering to the bum's every need including shelters, soup kitchens, thrift shops, pawn shops, drugs and alcohol, detoxes, rehabs, flop-houses, cheap hotels, employment agencies, parks, twelve-steps, check cash, churches and missions, hospitals and charities. Life at ground level—the crossroads, the power base, the taproot of the street. A network of institutions that were a spaghetti junction of communication amongst the homeless.

A tough demesne, the Ninth Precinct whose homicide rate is the highest in the city; during the period (1980s and 1990s) when New York City saw more than two thousand murders per year and the Zodiac Killer stalked Manhattan for six years running. And containing a disproportionately high number of stickup artists, whose very streets are alive with him, the most dangerous of the con men, the one most to be feared because he doesn't give a damn—the jack-roller.

Tompkins Square Park, at the time of my enlistment as a New York City bum, was given over somewhat to a homeless shantytown that grew over the next couple of years into quite an elaborate scrapheap settlement whose unwonted permanence may have contributed towards the city's later decision to remodel that eyesore into another one of the Big Apple's sterilized clones. For the homeless, in such situations, are never content to live in symmetry with their surroundings. Their shacky lifestyle spreads like a blight, encompassing all, the ground littered about with glassine dope bags and empty crack vials, like a scatter of deciduous New Age bracts and catkins upon the pining parkland. Loud music, unleashed dogs, unchaperoned children, public nudity, aggressive panhandling, open fires... Is it any wonder those bums are ousted from such squalid encampments to the outer fringes of the city.

My initial acquaintance with that area of the East Village and the bum element that inhabited it came about from a recommendation by a fellow coworker at Naturally Tasty (an aged black runner) who had advised me, "You need to be hanging out around Saint Mark's Place, that's where your kind of people be at." It was a good tip and steered me in the right direction for that was indeed where I not only found my bum brethren but where I would eventually make my own vagrant home as well. It's funny how, without a little guidance or experience, one can fare so completely astray in New York City. I sometime later on descried that same black cat rigged out in his glad rags painting the town on a Saturday night at Saint Mark's Place and Second Avenue and I was heartened to dekko the dude stripped of his workday cover in all his glory.

In the early days of my street life, I came across a homeless girl in Central Park who had a docile groundhog for a pet. She had somehow rescued and tamed a sick or injured groundhog (one of only a couple left in the bush of Central Park) and was nursing it back to health. She had the animal in the center of her rough, solitary encampment amidst a mound of assorted raw vegetables and lettuces of which the precious animal was intent on devouring. I was able to pet the creature and the girl produced a camera and had me click a snapshot of her embracing her pet. Touching. And fortunate for old (a large one) Mr./Ms. Groundhog to have found such a devout protectress.

It's curious how neighborhoods, areas of familiar regularity or sphere of activity, are confined to a few square blocks or sometimes less. Though I roamed a vast region of southern Manhattan, my immediate vicinity, my locale of concentration, my home turf was focused in and around a small territory of the East Village and Alphabet City, mainly First and Second Avenues from Houston Street to Saint Mark's Place (Eighth Street), Avenue B near Houston Street, and Allen Street (First Avenue below Houston Street) between Stanton and Rivington Streets (which was the stroll). This restricted terrain was smack-dab in the middle of the Lower East Side, the original city stews dating back three centuries to the founding of the city, the Ararat of the New World, as strained and squalid a geography as any this country has ever known, that segued from a locus of largely Jewish and Irish mediocrity (peppered with Italians and Germans), swarming with pushcarts, vermin and filth, to a radical and exotic matrix of bohemianism and starving artists, to the current depressed and desperate nadir of drugs and vice of which I became a part. A palimpsest of all that diasporic and extraneous ethnicity which merely ten years prior had scared the daylights out of me and, if truth be told, scared me still. Yet, for all its reduced circumstances and squalor, the precincts of the Lower East Side shared a spirited camaraderie that embraced life, an irrepressible optimism and sense of community that still pervades to this day. A harsh yet colorful and vibrant jurisdiction that I would come to know and love and call home, yet one of which I remained forever wary, though in which I was able to function and be free.

The Lower East Side: from Fourteenth Street south to City Hall, and from Broadway to the East River where, in Alphabet City, Avenue C's toponymic street signs read Loesida Avenue, recalling the historical, colloquial patois of lower-east-sider. Original tenements whose indoor rat holes are still to be found plugged with yellowed and brittle Yiddish newspapers, an agglomerative area whose origins are as old as the city itself, a patchwork quilt of simple, laboring immigrants of diverse European culture, the plurality of whom were homespun and honest, the majority of which were Russian and Polish Jews—refugees of pogroms staged in czarist Russia starting in the 1880s. By 1900 the Lower East Side was literally the most densely populated area on earth[1]; the Jewish ghetto housed 640,000 people per square mile—one half of New York City's entire population—the highest such density of humanity in world history.[2]

Of the abundant, tawdry trivia whose roots stem from the Loesida stews, comes the term "hookers," which trace back to Corlears Hook, the easternmost point of the Lower East Side, whose prostitutes of that area's shipyards and brothels lent their nickname to the trade's enduring infamy (*Ad rem*, from an etymological perspective, "stews or stewes was the term given to the brothels of Southwark which, from as early as the fourteenth century, were owned by the Bishops of Winchester who regulated prostitution in London.")[3]

Intrinsically teeming with pushcarts, it was always a ward of poverty radiating out from Five Points and Chatham Square where

1 Christopher Winn, *I Never Knew That About New York*
2 Kat Long, *The Forbidden Apple*
3 Kris & Nina Hollington, *Criminal London*

the first tattoo booths were in the back of panacean barber stalls where broken bones were set, teeth were extracted, lacerations stitched up, and could be obtained the catholicon of leeching. A scene which must have resembled a medieval market or bazaar—entropic, ever growing, ever more congested. The Lower East Side, where the city built its first Municipal Markets for fresh meat, fish and produce, vast enclosed structures that often included household notions and sundries, the precursor of the modern mall. And the city's first Public Baths erected when east side tenements had no running water—Public Baths and Municipal Markets still in operation today.

The Bowery[1] (Third Avenue south of Houston Street), the city's original theater district, where still some playhouses are lovingly in use, an area rife with nightlife, transients and novelty arcades, where the East Village spawned and blossomed into its own current Bohemian identity; an outgrowth of the pricier West Village. And as the rialto moved north to Fourteenth Street there stood, until this decade, the Jefferson Theater next to which Irving Klaw had his photography studio and earned infamy with his mail-order bondage photographs creating stardom for Midwestern model Bettie Page.

And as inexorably as the playhouses marched northward, so has urban renewal undermined the Lower East Side. As early as 1946 the New York Chamber of Commerce established the Bowery Improvement Committee (later renamed the Committee to Abolish Bowery Conditions) which pressured various agencies to rid the area of vagrants and peddlers. By 1980 skid row was no longer a significant part of our urban landscape. However, the demolition of skid row did not solve the homeless problem, only made them more visible as large numbers of ragged, displaced persons once

---

1 colonial Dutch for farm

more roamed the streets, emerging as the major societal enigma of America today.[1] And I had joined their ranks.

Yet, for all those remorseless efforts by the city at redemption, the Lower East Side remains a patulous area that holds to this day all the mystery and allure of yore and is one of the city's perpetual districts for drugs, poverty and bums. In those districts did I cut my swath, now humble, now bold—this is where I made my home, my friends, my serendipitous life during my decade as a bum on the streets of New York City. Once I'd set up housekeeping in the vicinity of Tompkins Square Park, my stomping grounds inched southward until I reached South Ferry at Battery Park (which includes the Irish Park, containing stone from every county in Ireland), spending time at City Hall while I worked there as a mail room messenger for welfare.

Being required to work for the city as a welfare recipient was a fairly new concept at that time, "part of the welfare reform of the 1990s—seeking to reintegrate welfare recipients into the sphere of productive labor."[2] Of the jobs offered (one was teacher's assistant in the public schools), I chose the municipal messenger because of its freedom to move around unsupervised, much of the time outdoors. And it turned out to be just that, with twice the time allowed to run errands than they should have taken. There was plenty of opportunity to stroll around, musing, window-shop, stop for coffee an', because there were plenty of messengers and the (sympathetic) boss used to be a messenger himself, and thus was lenient. I would sometimes be given subway tokens and sent all

1 Kenneth L. Kusmer, *Down and Out, On the Road: The Homeless in American History,* paraphrase and statistics
2 Leonard G. Feldman, *Citizens without Shelter*

over New York's conurbation, especially to Brooklyn, delivering manila envelopes to borough offices, running around the concatenate complexity of City Hall, to the courts, Municipal Building, Mayor's Office, different civic departments, Department of Education in the old Victorian "Tweed Courthouse," Motor Vehicles, Federal Building, Credit Union, over to the Department of Sanitation, collecting mail, delivering schedules and calendars, the air thick and heavy with curried city attar—diesel and gas fumes, roasting charcoal, cigarette smoke, cloying perfume and body odor, musty clothing, rotting garbage, hot tar and fried oil. All raddled with the resonant redolence of haste, anxiety, power and filthy lucre; the metastasizing ester of secrets and lust, desperate hope... But most of all, New York City reeks of arrogance—its sachet, its cachet.

I wore a photo ID pinned to my shirt, wandering around restricted areas uncontested. Those were territories of offices whose employees desks were covered with potted plants, framed photographs, children's drawings, greeting cards, stuffed animals, name plates, novelty coffee mugs, soda cans, pen caddies, desk clocks, ornamental calendars, vases of artificial flowers, jars of hard candy, pencil sharpeners, glazed figurines, Tensor lamps, fish bowls, open sandwich wrappers, in-out trays, index card boxes, Rolodexes, hole punchers, transistor radios, kitten or puppy motif desk blotters, handbags, curio paperweights... And everyone was always taking up a collection for someone else's birthday, anniversary, engagement, vacation, convalescence, christening, graduation, communion, confirmation, bat or bar mitzvah, wedding, sympathy, shower, retirement, you name it. How did those people ever get any work done?

I was living at Saint Joseph House of the Catholic Worker on First Street at Second Avenue at the time and would walk to and from work, six o'clock in the morning (the mailroom being the first department to get rolling at City Hall), tramping downtown, a different route each day, exploring the Lower East Side. SoHo (home of the largest collection of cast iron architecture in the world)[1] , Little Italy, Chinatown, the final vestiges of old Jewtown approaching East Broadway, opposite Seward Park. And on the way home in the afternoon, all the way over to the West Side, Hudson Street, West Broadway, Tribeca (with its cobblestone streets), the West Village, the Meat Market (with its baroque transexual trade), New York University, Chelsea. I really learned the downtown area during that period.

By the time I had been homeless for little more than a year, a veteran of the streets by then, felicity began to find me so completely unawares that it took someone (a fellow welfare messenger down at City Hall) to ask me, "You're a happy man, aren't you?" for me to realize that the only answer was, "Yes." And there I was, carrying interoffice memorandum around the city all day, having fallen into a sort of prelapsarian ovine bliss—The Happy Hooligan—earning two hundred forty dollars per month (food stamps included) and banking it, living in a run-down shelter, carving gourds (squash vases) up in my garret by night, cooking dinner for the shelter staff on Saturday afternoons, Sundays were devoted to religious duties (seven o'clock mass, choir, subservient priestcraft, ministry participation, pageant rehearsals or choir practice, and Julie), AA meetings around town, reading, writing and, always, studying the city. My weeks were full, through anesthetizingly frigid winters and burgeoning vital springs, weltering muggy summers and flush poignant autumns, filling myself up with the metropolis, functioning contentedly in what, at last, I felt to be my element. I had finally retired from the organized struggle, was living like a hermit in a faraway land, in the backwash of a prior universe, unknown and unloved, a mystery man. I had stopped ruminating on the logistics and survival quotient

---

1 Christopher Winn, *I Never Knew That About New York*

of the homeless, for in every ending is a beginning and this was my time and I had progressively taken hold. I had already experienced some of the worst that the street had to offer and had risen above in triumph; my fears, disappointments and anger having been transformed through some miraculous alchemy into something cathartic, beautiful and sustaining. I was liberated. And though the wheel would come round for me in future years, as the city still held new levels of allure, excitement and grief (to offer), I would, near the conclusion of my decade as a pejorative bum in the Big Apple, come to enrapture what would prove to be the best, most felicitous year of my life, perfectly feng shuied, in a tiny hotel room, pumping coffee in a bagel shop, at peace with my menagerie of pets, my books and my solitary life. My Camelot.

The Battery proper at Battery Park, at the lower tip of Manhattan, the actual cannon emplacement, a circular fortification built from solid quarry stone, is where the gun batteries of Fort Amsterdam stood in defense of the small Dutch trading post of New Amsterdam. Or so history tells us. However, contradictory evidence points to the Battery sitting out in the middle of the harbor, like one of the aquatic sentinels at Spithead, its own little island. Not only do early maps support this supposition, but the Battery itself has gun portals all the way around its perimeter, suggesting a 365-degree circumference of defense—unlikely if the fortification were landlocked, then the cannon would have aimed towards their own defenders. Yet, the truth is probably more prosaic: that Fort Amsterdam stood right beside the sea and that Castle Clinton (the Southwest Battery) is responsible for cartographic misconceptions as that fortress originally stood on a man-made island some 300 yards offshore. Over the years, landfill and the creation of Battery Park have extended the shoreline out into the bay, so that today the Battery joins firm shoreland, a considerable appreciation in New York real estate since its founding in 1625.

Museum by day, bum hostel by night. The central interior of this giant wheel is an open courtyard, as if to seat a huge axle, and the outer perimeter is like a giant gear between whose cogs are indentations, six feet deep by four feet by four feet, through which the cannon barrel would have protruded, though now artillery removed and interior side walled up, those recesses are made-to-order housing for the homeless. Facing southwest, the entire stone fortress is warmed on sunny days, the two-foot thick stones retaining the sun's heat most of the night; it was like sleeping in a little oven. Permanent residents would hang a blanket over the front opening rigged with pirate alarms, and with a mattress of cardboard on the floor, a box for a table and a candle or two, those digs had all the comfort and privacy a urban bum could ask for. However, during the night the stones would cool off and by morning you were lying in a refrigerator. Like a drawer in the morgue.

My favorite times walking the city were when I had it to myself. Three a.m. in the moist afterglow of Midtown on Third, Second, and First Avenues from Twenty-Third Street to Fifty-Ninth Street, the only traffic being taxis leaving the city and delivery trucks. Boulangeries working all night—are those bakeries state regulated as in France or can a New York boulangerie sell chopped liver? Kip's Bay, Murray Hill, Turtle Bay, Sutton Place. The Upper East Fifties dead-ends with little stiles up from each street's terminus, debouching into sandy rock gardens, concealed petite lawns, benches and barbeques, with wrought iron fences through which one can look right down onto and across the amphibolous East River.

Tranquil Sundays in New York, especially early mornings, the city is mine whether out copping around the East Village or Alphabet City at first blush or walking the West Village at Prime and finding an open café fully stocked with fresh pastries yet empty—I stop in for an espresso and sit for an hour, the only customer. How do those places make any money? Walking downtown on Sixth Avenue (Avenue of the Americas) from Fourteenth Street, an East End boy looking for West End girls...[1]

Snowstormy Sunday mornings on First and Second Avenues in the stilly maya of the East Village, the roads aren't plowed, vehicular traffic is nil, and here comes a guy in shorts, sliding over the street on cross-country skis, wraith-like, through a nebulous veil of white. Nobody loves the city like native New Yorkers, city dwellers, this is our town and we have license to say fuck you because to live here is to endure. And to love here is to cast your fate to the wind. For to perform in New York is to show the world and to fail in New York is just another day. And to succeed in New York is just another night. Welcome to New York; where's my wife?

I loved going out to cop in the thick nocturne void of Egyptian darkness or the wee hours of Scotch twilight, a foggy night on the Barbary Coast, cutting through the East Village projects to Avenue B or C, or scooting across Houston Street to Ludlow or Clinton Street, or tripping down Allen Street and the stroll—so many choices of spots, who has the best product tonight? It was an eerie, arcane occasion of quiescence, apprehension, solitude. In the misty world of curfew, while the proprietary city was asleep, the deserted streets belonged to the night owls and the underground moiety, emerging from their rookeries, from under their rocks, their burned-out buildings, their favellas, going about their devious monkey business, moving swiftly, surreptitious and secretive.

---

1 recording, The Pet Shop Boys, *West End Girls*

It was a time when the dream-lit city belonged to only me, with vaporous halos flickering round the streetlamps, the tarred tarmac smeared with fluid dewy phantasms awash and blurry and gleaming, eidolons and maggots of opalescent quicksilver motile and refluent—a surreal poem without words, now ethereal, now gouache—my solitary landscape, my blank canvas. I would lollop along the middle of the vacant streets singing "Pea Soup," I was Hiawatha, invincible and unstoppable, an escaped zebra lacking only a can of spray paint. There was a satisfying irony in being of the select to whom the coke or dope spots would serve, one of the chosen that the streets had claimed as their own, my heart and soul travesty.

On the way back home, stopping off at an all-night deli on First Avenue for a container of hot chocolate mixed with coffee and cream and lots of sugar, and a bag of potato chips, a five course junkie meal to carry me through the next day's run. In subzero icy wintertime, catching a jitney cab, gratis, whose jarvey was some pallid, gaunt, scurvy-faced young maniac who knew me as Robin's spurious pimp and that she'd be good for some head later on as payback. Before they were shut down, my first choice spot was right across from my Dantean digs on First Street, running over in my deshabîlle for a quick score and a container of Bustello at three, four, or five a.m.—just one of the boys in the neighborhood. This was my *tranche de vie*, Loesida, and there was no place I'd rather be. Crazy.

However, going out into the strange night world of the old city to cop during Matins and Lauds was always a tense endeavor fraught with peril, for one such lone gull is just the target which the stickup man has his radar attuned to. Chances are good that a kithless junkie moving furtively through the deserted shadows is either going to cop or returning from his score. Either way, moola or dope, the cocklight addict is ripe for the harvest. From sunset to dawn the streets become the patrimony of brigands and thugs, its very numen, moving like a mirage through the brume which lay across the ambit like a curse. Therefore, those dark hour runs, of necessity, subsume alertness and stealth irregardless of one's casual veneer. Otherwise the pigeon is just begging to be plucked. Despite my sometime nonchalant façade, for me, copping was always serious business demanding my unswerving, staid attention. Only once during my ten year run as a bum on the New York City streets did I fall quarry to the stickup man and that was a setup by my archfiend of a ex-flatmate Robin (rotten bitch) and a close call it was.

I loved to walk the city streets in the zodiacal light during the dewy dampness before daybreak, through the gossamery fog drip, the impression of a fresh oil painting, still wet, glistening, you can't help but touch it and a little sticks to your finger, rubs off on you. Everything is whist and perfect in its rendering. The still city; the not awake yet city. As I would range the downtown streets in the gauzy aurora of first light, I would glimpse not only the start of a new day but also the remnants of last night's folly. The signs in the street, the signs of our times were right there in my face to read, to interpret, the genesis of the city, the foibles of its inhabiters, that feeling of knowledge being akin to power.

Was I in my wanderings searching for the gospel, the truth, the meaning of life? I thought I'd found all that out long ago. Everything is bullshit. Example: Many bums are the by-product of substance abuse and the irony of it all is that the situation was created—the trap set—by the government itself, the power elite. Drug laws, similar in many respects to Prohibition whereby liquor was verboten so politicians could profit from supplying it, are part of America's economy, major industry involving millions of people and billions of dollars.

First, laws are established with stiff penalties against drugs. Then the government supplies the drugs and encourages addiction.

Next, police, FBI, ATF, DEA task forces are inflated to go out and catch those subaltern criminals. Then, prosecutors, courts, judges, lawyers, warders, counselors, doctors, with their contingent support systems of tailor-made buildings, offices, holding pens, special vehicles, all the customized equipment too extensive to detail, each comes into play. Then follows the prison system. Those multibillion dollar facilities alone employ a flabbergasting number of the civilian work force and offer Corrections Officers ridiculously high salaries and benefit packages to attract recruits into one of the worst possible jobs (COs have the highest alcoholism, divorce and suicide rate of all American professions)[1] costing the American taxpayer in excess of seventy billion dollars annually to operate nationwide. Finally there is the parole, probation and rehabilitation divisions and, as is most often the case, rehabilitation doesn't work and so it's back to square one for both addict and task force and repeat the cycle over and over. Most perpetrators realize all this and so it becomes a contest, a game between both sides of the law, a way of life for each.

The upper class does not want to stamp out crime because it doesn't affect them, it's good for business, keeps the economy rolling along, a platform for reelection. What's sad is this is old news. Things will never change as long as there's a class system with the upper class the fiduciary of American finance and jurisprudence. So, what to do? Be a bum. Go on relief. Our contemporary American culture is geared to this, breeds it, nurtures it, encourages it. It's so easy to live on the dole, so many handouts to be had. The price of conscience for a society that steadfastly refuses to acknowledge the consequence of their folly and the steadily rising number of homeless, like refuse. Refuse-strewn municipalities.

---

1 Ted Conover, *Newjack: Guarding Sing Sing*

What I found amongst the myriad and multitudinous refuse-strewn New York City host was a subculture within a subculture, an entire workforce comprised entirely of bums. Homeless professionals. Professional transients. Wave upon wave of bums working for a living yet residing either on the street or in flophouses, shelters and resident hotels. I was living in a shelter when a fellow resider quit the place because he couldn't find a suitable parking spot for his brand new car. I lived in a shelter where it was mandatory, a requisite to have a job and a bank account. Working and bumming on the street are much more common than one may think. In fact, many bums would be hard pressed to survive without some element of employment. Many homeless bums are those whose independence is often mistaken for laziness. People who are often willing to work but just not to be tied down.

There was a six-week period when I handed out menus for PG's deli on Forty-Fifth Street at Lexington Avenue, before I let my hair grow, dressed in my black-and-white waiter's attire and carrying a briefcase I passed for an office worker. For four or five hours a day, Monday through Friday, I trekked from Thirty-Fifth Street to Fifty-Fifth Street (a big spread for lunch delivery), up and down Lexington Avenue, Park Avenue, Madison Avenue, Fifth Avenue, Avenue of the Americas, Seventh Avenue, Broadway, and hit every single office in every single building, fifty-story skyscrapers nearly every one, buildings with tight security that prohibited soliciting—Colgate-Palmolive, Warner Brothers, RCA, Helmsley Building—sneaking up freight elevators, past lobbies where ID's were required, running down stairways, being chased by security who followed me via camera/radio relay; it was a game I was determined to win. Many of those skyscrapers have their own cafeterias but nothing attracts like the forbidden.

I beheld offices the likes of which I'd never imagined: sky-high outer walls of glass, elevators opening into reception lounges, shafts cut through ceilings with spiral stairways, atriums, offices decorated like Victorian mansions, English hunting lodges, Oriental temples, power chambers, pampered parlors, oil paintings, sculpture, meeting receptionists with personalities from twittering sweet sixteens to Katharine Gibbs herself. Always asking if I could leave a menu before I even produced one from my briefcase. I worked that job as much for the insight into the top New York office world as I did for my pay of a free lunch and six clams per hour. And the PG's staff cheered me on as the phones began ringing like never before. I was uncheery when that job ended, even though I came close to arrest a couple of times. Handing out menus in New York's top worldwide firms. What a laugh.

On the flip side of the coin, I had been offered a job of handing out flyers for a pizza shop on Thirty-Fourth Street at First Avenue nearby to a welfare office where I applied for restoration of the electric service in my First Street abode as I'd recently acquired a full-time guest (Robin). It was dead winter and I was flat broke, having gone to the welfare office smashed on D and found myself turned out on the spot. I stopped to beg a slice from a nearby pizza shop and the boss asked me to return in the morning to stand on the corner of the block in the hyperborean ether and hand out flyers to passersby who didn't want to be bothered. When I accepted the appointment (for the free lunch) and was thus sent forth into the arctic void with the handbills, I directly dropped them into a trash basket and walked home, telling Robin that the job didn't work out. Some jobs grab you and some don't.

Obtaining money while living as a bum is a nagging problem. While food and even shelter can be had for free, cigarettes, alcohol and drugs require a Bohemian charge account (cold cash). Panhandling is an occupation almost as bad as working, requiring one to stand in the same spot for untold hours, arm extended, asking for a handout. Even though it almost always yielded rewards, I hated panhandling and would go without funds endlessly before I would succumb to some subway conduit and ask working people for money. Embarrassing. Yet, I did it repeatedly out of necessity though it was always the last of the last resorts. I would rather work for a day than ding a stranger for a nickel. But, all too often, I would go to the employment agency, day after day, and not be given a ticket to work. One time as I stood in a subway station with my hand out, a pair of young bums approached the token booth to exchange their munificent cache of coinage for greenbacks and, noticing me (a less fortunate spanger), contributed their pennies to this insignificant person, a good three-pound bindle—a solid three banknotes' worth. Sharing the honey pot. Sometimes bums have the biggest hearts.

When I had my boom box I never minded playing along on my practice pad to music with a cup out for tips. Then I was doing something useful, something enjoyable, providing passersby with a return for their contributions. But the pigs would never leave me alone to pursue that harmless endeavor, feeling the need to push me around, to brandish their authority. Another ready-made hard money pursuit was the diving for coins in fountains or pools in front of many of the large skyscrapers or in parks or even churchyards—any place there was standing water people would toss tin rocks in and make a wish. But often those aquascapes were watched by security guards and all of the good ones were watched by bums. Yet I have recovered ten to thirty shekels in change at a clip from such lucrative sources that never seem to dry up, rolling up my pants' legs and going in barefoot like some renegade urban naiad. You just have to locate a few good pools and keep watch on them. They fill up fast.

With the exception of my callow days with crack, when I experimented with stickups, I never succumbed to out and out robbery. The temptation can be mighty strong, to grab the pelf from a cash register, especially if you're working at the concern. But I was never willing to risk going to jail, to be brought to book for my improprieties. Also, something held me back from stealing whatever I could get just because the opportunity presented itself. I had a temperate though pragmatic approach to thieving. For instance, even when I had a spot to snooze at (a resident hotel for example), I would regularly need items like bar soap and toilet tissue. Those staples I would filch from lavatories in restaurants or AA meetinghouses. But I only took one bar of soap or one roll of tissue at a time. I never gave in to the inclination to hoard supplies, to establish an inventory of pilfered items. I lived day to day. Even with foodstuffs, for instance: I would regularly rustle stalls at the Farmer's Market or a passing deli but I only took what would satisfy me for the present—I was hungry, so I ate. (Convenient, how easy it is to rationalize that taking food when one is hungry is remissible, while stealing cash is wrong.) Cigarettes—I would hunt for large butts in the gutters or rove the sidewalks looking for someone about to light up and rush them to ask, "Could you spare a cigarette?" Sometimes I'd do that for an hour, garnering enough smokes for the night. That was as far as I went with stockpiling goods to tie me over. Sometimes I'd take some food from the Catholic Worker and keep it in my room for a day or two: a peanut butter and jelly sandwich or a box of outdated cake that were often handed out when loads of day-old bakery goods were dropped off. Sometimes some fruit. I never had a refrigerator in my hotel room until the advent of the hamsters so my cooler was my room's windowsill during cold weather.

When I lived in a hotel or shelter or flophouse there was never enough room to store extra items like clothing that were not used on a regular basis. I developed a lifestyle, to which I adhere to date, whereby I don't accumulate things unless I have a daily use for them. People who harbor effects from childhood, magpie stuff they haven't looked through in thirty years, I don't live like that. Sentiment has only kicked me in the arse my whole life—my family, my friends, my bedmates, my jobs have all betrayed me and left me flat. Only my pets have remained true.

For those bums who decide to work at legitimate jobs (in places of business) for god's penny, there are certain occupations more appealing than others, such as running messages, factory work, unloading trucks and moving freight. But the most popular category of casual labor, for bums, by far is the fast food service. There are employment agencies that specialize in casual labor where, for a small fee, you can work for the day in a field of your choice and earn cash in your pocket per diem, at the close of the workday. ABC Employment Agency (downtown on Fulton Street) caters to plebian eateries such as delis, diners, coffee shops and similar fast-food concerns. And it was ABC I patronized for all my casual working needs. Working for the day through ABC was a great way to procure a free lunch as well as incidental money. And you could have any attitude you wanted as long as you performed because it was for the day only, who gave a damn? The only mandate was that you had to be fast. Sometimes a place would want you to stay on so you'd work a few days, a week, two weeks, as long as you could take it. You owed the agency a fee of five dollars per day or twenty dollars per week. The agency collection man came around to each worksite every Friday, there was no escape from paying.

For me, the ABC experience began slowly, early on in my food service career. I would go to the agency on my days off from my regular (career) job as a chef or food service manager just to earn the extra cash from a day's work, desirous of augmenting my income with a legitimate hustle. But the ABC fieldwork was drastically different from my normal duty in college, airport and office building cafeterias. Those (ABC) low-camp eateries are a world unto themselves. At times, when I was forced to take off from my career job for a two-week vacation, I would apply at the agency and work (a busman's holiday) for those weeks in coffee shops or delicatessens, learning the craft from a short-order standpoint in a profit and loss operation, as opposed to the subsidized accounts of the large food service companies that employed me. That was before I entered the fine restaurant and hotel divisions of the trade, only to wind up back in the coffee shops and delis at the close of my twenty-five year food service career.

It wasn't easy learning the skills peculiar to short-order work; those were not delineated in *The Professional Chef* nor taught at the Culinary Institute of America. As in a medieval kitchen, such trade lore was jealously guarded, much like an early Portuguese navigation chart might be concealed from prying eyes. And so by long, slow, painstaking perseverance did I glean the secrets of how to wrap a sandwich so that it wouldn't open accidentally; how to slice an egg salad sandwich so that it wouldn't squish out the sides (without double-wrapping it); how to wrap a hot sandwich in foil without moving the sandwich onto the wrapping paper; how to seal the top of an aluminum take-out tray in one smooth motion; how to ensure a lid is secure on a take-out soup or coffee container in one sure movement; how to pick up exactly one (or two) napkins at a time; how to fill a squeeze container with jelly or mustard; how to break the yolk of an egg without touching it; how to make a hard clump of lettuce lie flat for a sandwich; and a hundred other offbeat techniques all designed to save time. These, too, were the "tells" of how experienced a man was, as well as the speed and composure with which he performed under pressure. It took me many (frustrating) years to grasp it all. And many cuts and burns as well.

Most of my years working through ABC were as a counterman making sandwiches, although I also spent some years at the griddle which was not worth the dollar more per hour it paid. Six bucks an hour for the counter, seven chips for the same slot at the griddle (they don't pay bums a decent wage). Sandwich man required little more than speed. Coffee man demanded both speed and precision. Griddle man was a hectic spot, ending your day with cooking a couple of cases of bacon for the next morning, up to your eyeballs in grease. Packing for take-out could be feverish in a busy store with a dozen delivery boys worrying clamantly for their orders. I worked as a salad man at McAnn's Bar, 11 Stone Street for six months—that job was a piece of cake. Sandwich man at a hot steam table could be a messy slot, what with the hot fat on the joints. Working the griddle for lunch was much easier than breakfast. Lunch was hamburgers, grilled cheese, Reubens and omelets, tuna melts and maybe Monte Cristos. At breakfast your griddle was covered in fried eggs with the bacon causing the eggs to stick, poached eggs, omelets, pancakes, French toast. You needed a memory like a computer and nerves of steel, all the while with buns toasting in the salamander under the grill. Broiler or charcoal grill can be a very tough spot at lunch with steaks, burgers, liver and fish, it's blast furnace hot and easy to overcook. And the *prima facie* methodology peculiar to all those greasy spoons is "rough." I've been reprimanded by the boss in one establishment for sautéing the filling for a western omelet before adding it, and for grilling the tomato slices prior to placing them in a grilled cheese and tomato sandwich. You have to work like a schlock in a hash house or you don't fit in.

A head chef position in a coffee shop or in a deli with a hot steam table and cold salad bar requires real knowledge and expertise. You must be able to make many varieties of rice, pasta dishes, entrees, from meatballs to lasagna, from chicken croquettes to chicken pot pie. Quiche, spinach pie, potato pancakes, kasha varnishkas. Pie crust, pizza dough, and every kind of salad; chicken liver with schmaltz, and rice pudding. These are a few of the coffee shop menu items that you'd better be able to produce or get thrown out on your ear. You go into a place of business and the boss turns over $20,000 worth of inventory to you and a kitchen full of equipment and it's no joke. And you must have it all ready by eleven a.m., *ventre à terre*.[1] No wonder so many of those guys drink.

Where do bums learn to do all that stuff since few of them went to school? They learn in the field, by observation, by being a cook's helper, bosses teach them and, like myself, by watching their mother and reading. My first head chef job I inveigled my way into, and then withdrew twenty books from the library, a book on every aspect of cooking, and fudged my way through an entire summer as the head (bull) chef in a quality establishment. (My mom always told me, "You can learn how to do anything from reading a book.") That job cemented my confidence and gave me a solid CV on which to build. I learned because I had to learn. I also worked with chefs who were willing to teach me, beginning my career as a lowly minion in the food service industry. And I asked questions of professionals in the know: old time kitchen personnel, cooks, chefs, butchers, garde-mangers, bakers, patissiers, food service managers and directors. And I went to school. But, as in all professions, you need to have the right attitude which means a desire to learn. If you don't really want to do it, you'll never make it.

I've worked the chef billet in coffee shops on a few occasions, have even been asked to return and stay, but it was too much like working a real job. It was a real job. Insofar as you had to care, to pay attention fastidiously, conscientiously. Whereas with the line positions—counter or feeder or packer, even the griddle—all

---

1 At great speed

you had to do was be fast. The counter jobs were so easy, as far as the actual tasks you had to perform, that you could do them by rote. But with a chef function, with food boiling on the stove and roasting in the oven and frying in the pan you had to be continually on top of things, orchestrating a multicourse meal to come out on time and your mind could not be miles away. And it was as thankless a gig as a line position so who needed the added stress? I only accepted chef jobs when that was all the agency had to offer and I was hard up for the bread. My ego didn't require that arrogance anymore. Chefs in coffee shops may be top dogs but they're just as overworked and abused by the bosses as any other mutt in the place.

There was a job I once took from ABC as a delivery boy for a flower shop off Lexington Avenue at Grand Central Terminal. I thought, How hard could it be? Earning tips. Well, little did I guess—all of the deliveries were in vases filled with water (at eight pounds per gallon). The damn things weighed a ton. And I was such a naif, too green to think of dumping the water out. From office building to office building, changing the weekly floral display in the lobbies, not even seeing the client (forget about a tip), to restaurants where a stern-faced owner looked on critically (no tip), to a funeral home all the way in Chinatown (no egg roll), and to apartment house residences where I'd be required to leave the arrangement with the concierge in the foyer (no tip). That was one of the most depressing, discouraging jobs I ever took from ABC.

Another delivery job I once accepted was as a lunch delivery boy for Kosher Delight on Broadway at Thirty-Fourth Street. What a beat that turned out to be. First of all, one needed a twenty-dollar bank for a lunch delivery job, having to pay the house for the order before they would entrust it to you to deliver. (Who wanted to work if they had twenty bucks?) That place made the delivery boys wait at each feature station in the restaurant for each portion of the order, last to be served after the cash customers, waiting five to ten minutes at each post—you could waste thirty minutes putting your order together. Then they gave me a delivery all the way to First Street at Second Avenue—thirty-five blocks each way plus five long blocks crosstown—an unheard-of distance for delivery service. It took me a good forty-five minutes race walking to cover round-trip. But the climax of that debacle was that the cheapskate customer didn't even give me a plugged nickel tip. Kosher Delight was a place nobody at ABC ever wanted to work at, the agency could never supply enough delivery boys. Now I knew why. And Kosher Delight didn't even provide their delivery boys with a sandwich or drink. They were so stingy, they didn't even smile.

I've gone to work at places where I was fired for drinking a soda, kicked out for drinking a container of coffee, and terminated for drinking a bottle of beer. Most places will only allow you one beverage per day with your lunch and places that have a soda fountain won't allow employees to drink bottled beverages. Many places will not allow conversing amongst employees while on duty. I'm telling you, agency extras are treated like dirt, not even clean country dirt but oily, greasy, city grime. Some agency extras retaliate against ill treatment and abuse, making a bad situation worse for the rest of us.

I worked at an uptown catering house one time where the boss advanced us agency extras each five smackers from our (prognostic) pay so we could go across the street and buy our own lunch from a delicatessen. This from a purveyor who called the agency for a garde-manger. Most of the agency workforce didn't even know what that was nor could they pronounce it. So I arrive at the workplace and the boss inquires, can I make sliced melon and fruit trays. When I answer in the affirmative he asks to see a sample. So I whip one on him and he's satisfied. "Okay," he tells me, "Make up six of them." I no sooner begin to peel the melons than he sets me onto another task. I spent all day doing other chores the boss kept piling on and at five o'clock, after eight hours, I asked for my pay. The boss says, "What about the fruit trays?" I answered, "You should have thought about that while you were giving me other work to do." I told him, "I've had it with this place, I want my gelt." And I walked out with the green, the boss shaking his head in dismay.

On another occasion, after waiting most of the day at the agency and not receiving a ticket to work, the dispatcher announced a job as a lavatory attendant at a wedding reception that evening by an exclusive caterer (Adam Caterer) in Brighton Beach (a good hour train ride from the city). Being down-and-out broke, I accepted. The only requirement was white shirt and black slacks which I cobbled together from the clothing room at Saint Joseph House of the Catholic Worker.

Well, the proprietor of the concern, Adam himself, an eight-hundred-pound behemoth, as priggish and supercilious as he was gross, had me stationed outside of the men's room with instructions to only enter therein every fifteen minutes to check the toilet tissue and wipe down the sinks. No discourse with the clientele. Not that I could expect a dime from any of those snooty skinflints, the parking lot filled with Caddies, Lincolns and Lexuses. And not a bite to eat for the extras at Adam, not even a measly hors d'oeuvre from the passing trays or a soda. There was a begowned harp player at the main entrance, a harpsichord player in the bar along with six (6) three-hundred-pound ice sculptures, a dessert board of the Hawaiian islands complete with palm trees made out of chocolate, and live parrots and cockatoos in the ladies lounge. Yet only six lettuce leaves per hour for the agency extras. It's jobs like those that make crime look very attractive.

There was a six-month period when I hired on at Indiana Market & Catering on Second Avenue in my East Village alentours. A mandarin, top-drawer establishment in the locale, highly esteemed and in clover. They waged me well and I was able to produce much of the elegant, high-grade work in which I specialized: decorating whole poached salmon (twenty pounders), concocting gourmet soups like Petite Marmite and Stracciatella, making hot and cold hors d'oeuvres, crab cakes, artisan breads like fougasse, pâtés and tureens, and feature desserts like savarin and mint brownies. But I dropped a couple of bricks there, too. I worked legitimately (on the books) while I was signed up for welfare and, after tax season, my wages were discovered by the Fed and my welfare benefits were reduced until those extra earnings were repaid. And, I started to drink on the job, becoming more and more obvious until, lo and behold (surprise) they didn't need me anymore. Just went to show that I couldn't hold a straight job by fair means or foul, couldn't cope and was out in left field. And I could only work for cash (when I could work at all).

To emphasize the point of my being out to lunch, I had gone back to work (weekends) for a catering company of long acquaintance, Newman and Leventhal, the largest kosher caterer in New York City. I had begun working for that concern while still employed at "21"; everyone working for Mona (Leventhal) was moonlighting and one had to be employed by an A-1 firm in order to qualify—Mona employed only the best and paid well and in cash. But one could never turn her down if they were needed, you could never miss a scheduled slot. Mona's chefs worked on location at the city's most prestigious hotels (Plaza, Pierre, Waldorf-Astoria) whose ballrooms could accommodate parties of 1,000 guests, serving only the finest of everything. I started to drink at her jobs, missed once and that was it for me, I was history. And that work was a prime opportunity to showboat and learn and pick up top pay. Oh well, when you burn-out you burn everything—bridges, tunnels, ferries, the whole shooting match.

Other than my few coffee-man jobs for bagel shops, at which I excelled and harmonized with, I was hardly loved, often barely tolerated by many of my temporary employers in the delis and coffee shops at which I engaged as an extra. For one thing, my aversion to and distaste for that genus of the trade was hardly veiled and the only thing saving my place was performance. The bosses and owners, whether Korean, Greek, Indian or Jewish had no love or compassion for the bums they employed as extras from the agency, just as the agency had no concern for the suitability of the worker for the job; their sole interest was to fill positions as quickly as possible and to collect their fee. In many shops, if you stepped out of line just once—ignored a customer or gave too much product on an order (like too much butter on a roll or an extra slice of cheese or tomato on a sandwich)—you were out on your grass in a flash. Those places had no mercy. There was so much competition, so many prospective employees on line waiting for a job, that one slipup and you were history. Move too slow and you were replaced in ten minutes. You had to learn fast and stay fast (and accurate) or you had no job.

I've sometimes gone into work at those establishments stoned on scag and been nodding at the counter while making sandwiches, or pumping coffee in my sleep, the jefe watching me, waiting for just one flub. I've worked next to guys who wanted to punch my face in as soon as they had a break because I'd make them look bad or wouldn't suck up to them. I've worked with guys who'd wait for just the right moment to sabotage my work so as to make me look like a novice, to jam me up so they would look good by contrast. They spread lies and gossip, try to have me fired—petty kiddie-city bullshit is the norm in those cutthroat concerns; jealousy, envy, theft—it's horrid.

Approaching the curtain of my inhabiting New York City, I gravitated towards being a coffee man (feeder) in bagel shops, happily gave up the sandwich counter and the godforsaken griddle for my newfound mommy track. And, too, there were periods of sloth and indolence, of not working, not doing anything, times of deep disquietude and depression. Lost in a city that was a dynamo around me, a leaf being whirled in a dervish of aimless confusion and desire. Even with the necessities of shelter and food in hand, it seemed to always be a worrisome situation; someone (threatening) was going to come to the door, my welfare would be canceled, I'd wind up in the hospital. There was never a shortage of worry. Part of the doomsday mentality of the street.

Working the city's coffee shops and delis are an experience unique unto themselves, whose foreign owners face continual harassment from Consumer Affairs and other city agencies trying to close them down for absurd violations. For me, the practice of working as an extra for the day through ABC agency began in any number of the thousands of coffee shops in lower Manhattan's Financial District and Civic Center areas, busy places all. In those days (1970s) the businesses were owned mainly by Jews and Greeks, later (1980s) infiltrated by Koreans and India men, manpowered in back of the house inexorably by blacks and Hispanics, waitresses (almost) always Caucasian.

Even Eisenberg's Sandwich Shop (Fifth Avenue at Fourteenth Street), a quaint little relic sporting an aging mirrored backsplash and a narrow marble counter complete with old fashioned soda fountain, which touts Best Tuna Salad, is now owned by a Korean who, in carrying on the shop's hopeful Jewish tradition, tried to cheat me out of my full pay by asserting, "But you get tips!" to which I shot back, "What tips I get or don't get are none of your concern."

And it's not only the hospitality field whose ownership is changing nationality. Why is it that all the city's candy stores and news-stands, which used to be run by Jews, are now owned by India men, and the fruit and vegetable stalls, which were the domain of Italians, have now been taken over by Koreans? And nail salons are suddenly all Asian-run, while gas stations have been usurped by Hindus. Even taxi drivers used to be of European descent; now they're all Arabs.

Getting back to ABC. Whether I would be sent out as a counter (sandwich) man or griddle man or as a packer or coffee man—to reiterate, for emphasis—the main requisite common to all those positions was you had to be fast. All else was secondary to speed. And all the while the boss is watching you like a cat at a mouse hole: "Come on, Hurry up, Let's go." To the waitresses: "Pick up these orders, Let's go, Hurry up, Come on," a constant litany. And how I hated those places. I've hated most of my jobs (with the exception of "21"), a lifelong distaste for and discontentment with my profession, what began as an enchantment (in college) and devolved into a revulsion for the entire industry. Case in point, the coffee shops and delis: appalling working conditions, most of the establishments (behind the scene) were so dirty you would never want to eat anything in any of them. That food poisoning didn't affect everyone who ate there is miraculous. I exaggerate not. Rats, mice, flies, roaches and their excreta, fetid sewage in the basements, smoking foaming deep fryers never properly cleaned, filthy floors, walls and ceilings, contaminated work surfaces never sanitized, infectious sinks, dripping germ-accumulated grease everywhere, pots and pans inadequately washed, putrefied mops, filth encrusted toilets, a nightmare eatery.

In one place, the chief cook and bottle washer used to clean the toilets and mop the floor at day's end and empty the disgusting mop bucket into an equally disgusting sink in the basement. Next morning, after boiling the corned beef, brisket and pastrami, he would place the hot joints of meat in the same corrupt (mop) sink, forever unwashed, to cool. I had wanted to make myself a nice brisket sandwich but, after I saw that, I never ate anything in that place.

In another house, I opened a cabinet under the sandwich counter and a mouse looked up at me. I quickly closed the door and said to the boss, "There's a mouse in there," with which the boss walked over, opened the cabinet, reached in and slammed down his hand, Bang!, closed the cabinet door and walked away wiping his hand down the leg of his pants. I bent down, opened the door and peered inside the cabinet. There was the mouse, squashed flat, left presumably to grind up with the next day's meatloaf.

One store where I worked for awhile sold frozen yogurt (which I love). It so turned out they never emptied out the soft-serve machine (a daily requirement by law) in order to sanitize same. Day and night, week after week, fresh yogurt mix was added to the machine as needed without ever cleaning the equipment. When I commented on this oversight I was told that the machine didn't need cleaning as it stayed on (cold) continuously. "Don't worry about it," they said, "You don't know what you're talking about" (with a snort). Korean sanitation.

One shop which featured fresh squeezed juice never washed the juicer. Overnight, day after day, the carrot pulp was left molder-ing inside the juicer, scooped out only when the juice ceased to flow—built up, slimy and rotting and stinking. No wonder they didn't sell much. I love fresh carrot juice but I'd be damned if I'd even touch that juicer. That was the same place where, while I was working the breakfast counter, a customer asked me, "What kind of muffin is that?" pointing, so I held up said muffin to the boss and asked, "What kind of muffin is this?" and the boss answered, "It's a nice muffin, Give it to him." So I told the customer, "It's a nice muffin," and the customer said, "I'll take it." What a joke.

That same eating place used to keep their hamburgers in the freezer. Every morning the boss would remove more than enough hamburgers to cover the day's forecast of business and he'd spread the patties out singly on a table in the hot kitchen, open to the air and uncovered. The raw patties thawed quickly and were allowed to sit out all day in the blistering summer temperature, turning brown, flies and roaches crawling all over them. At day's end, the unsold hamburgers were returned to the freezer for the night, only to be removed again the next morning, often the same meat going back and forth day after day, putrid and slimy and reeking. Those burgers must have had all the texture of wet sawdust. They never sold well. Who would return for such a meal? Those ignorant Indic babus also kept the fifty-pound plastic bag of carrots out in the tropical kitchen where they began to sprout and rot in the bag. I would tear holes in the bag to allow some air to circulate therein, only to be admonished by the boss for mutilating the bag. When I tried to explain that the carrots should be kept cool so they wouldn't deteriorate he told me to mind my own business and to stay out front and not to worry about the kitchen. I would have liked to hang a sign in that place proclaiming, "Sanitation Is Our Middle Name." But what did I care? I only worked there part-time to earn enough scratch for my daily pint of aquavit, pack of fags and bag of weed.

I'd leave work each afternoon right after lunch was over and shoot over to Stuyvesant Polyclinic for my daily acupuncture treatment which was supposed to remedy my alcoholism. I'd leave the treatment room and hop right across Second Avenue for a quart of beer. So much for that cure. I only enrolled in the program in order to extend my welfare eligibility. I also signed up for psychoanalysis. What a sham that was. The psychiatrist kept wanting to hear about my dreams. He told me I was longing for my mother's affection. Well, I didn't need an MD to tell me that. What son doesn't long for his mother's affection? That charlatan kept me out of his group therapy until he thought I was ready. When finally he asked me to join the group, I asked him how many were currently enrolled. He told me two—four others had just dropped out. I told him, "Thanks, but no thanks." I could go to an AA meeting for that. A plastic shrink, the guy struck me as a gestaltist, as I have found most standardized programs conform to such an approach: Who can be bothered with individually tailored treatment? The head pill pusher there was always trying to put me on medication. He'd see me and say, "How ya doin'? You look depressed." So I'd rejoin vaguely, "Naw, I'm alright," and keep walking. I went to see their neurologist who prescribed Carbamazepine for my leg pains. I looked it up in the PDR and found it was given for seizures. That bottle of pills went right in the trash. The pain in my leg was diagnosed as sciatica. But do you think I could get a painkiller from those quacks? I'd have a better chance of being struck by lightning. An industry of worthless treatment offered to the "tired, poor, huddled masses yearning to breathe free"[1] who go right on suffering. Yet, of one thing you can be certain: the doctor's bill goes out.

The coffee shops and delis relied heavily on extras to staff many positions, especially in back of the house. Holes appeared in schedules constantly, employees taking off for heaven knew what reason: out sick, vacation, domestic trouble, days off, promotion, demotion, transfer, arrest, accidents, termination. Some positions were manned exclusively by extras. There were a few agencies who catered to the fast-food line and of them all ABC took the lion's share. And of all the extras supplied, ninety percent or better are bums. Bums of every stripe—family men, husbands and fathers, as well as transients, drunks and addicts. What gives so vast a spread the common moniker is attitude. Those men, most of them, are there to work for the day only. No company men at ABC. A few hope to fall into something steady but are just as ready to throw in the towel if the slightest thing goes wrong. Professionals all, you won't find any amateurs at ABC, though

---

1 Emma Lazarus, "The New Colossus"

the corpus of their knowledge is restricted to the fast-food field. Moreover, those are city pros, as unique to Manhattan as the vernacular they speak, a mandate nomenclature specially tailored to the trade in New York coffee shops and delis, as telling as a password and ritual as a secret handshake. All waitresses and cooks and line personnel must be versed in this lingo for it is often spoken exclusively.

A *combo* is ham and Swiss on rye bread; a *radio* is tuna salad on white bread; a *Mickey Mouse* is peanut butter and (grape) jelly on white bread; a *jack* (gac) is grilled American cheese on white bread; a *Jack Benny* is grilled American cheese with bacon (also called a *jack back*—gac bac); a *full house* is grilled American cheese with bacon and tomato; a *cowboy* is a western omelet; an *egg roll* is a hard-fried egg (broken yolk) on a kaiser roll; a *stack* is an order of pancakes (3), *short stack* (2); a *farmer boy* is a short stack with a fried egg on top, bacon and sausage; *Cajun skillet* is a mountain of corned beef hash and home fries, bacon and sausage with a fried egg on top and toast; a *BLT* is a bacon, lettuce and tomato on white toast with mayonnaise; a *number one club* is a triple decker BLT with sliced turkey breast; a *Reuben* is sliced hot corned beef, sauerkraut and Swiss cheese with Russian dressing on rye bread (buttered on the outside) and griddled (like a grilled cheese sandwich) until the cheese melts; a *Monte Cristo* (or *Croque Monsieur* or *French Dip*) is ham and Swiss cheese on white bread dipped in egg and milk (as for French toast) and griddled until the cheese melts; *down* means toast (if you say, down only, it means white toast); *whiskey* is rye bread; *mahogany* is whole wheat bread; a *British* is a toasted English muffin; *high and dry* means no butter or mayonnaise; a *slice* means slice of onion; *tommy* is sliced tomato; *grass* is lettuce; *LT* is lettuce and tomato; *AC* is American cheese; *marijuana* is fresh parsley (chopped or sprig); *schmear* is a light spread of cream cheese; *mazy* is mayonnaise; *bun* is a hamburger bun; *roll it* means the sandwich is on a kaiser roll; a *pair* means two of the same item. *For the money* means regulation in quantity the way an order would be filled for the full price as listed on the menu. This is opposed to specials, for instance, AC on a buttered roll at breakfast will be one slice of cheese on a lightly buttered roll for one dollar. At lunch the same item will be four slices of cheese on a moderately dressed roll with lettuce for three dollars and fifty cents. So, AC on a buttered roll for the money, when called at breakfast, tells the counter man how to build the sandwich. *Seaboard* or *airborne* (or *put legs on it*) means an item is for take-out and therefore wrapped accordingly. (Packers must know what accompaniments to include for each take-out order). *All the way* refers to breakfast platters which are to include home fried potatoes in addition to toast. Otherwise, a customer may only want a sandwich. *In the well* means well-done; *deep in the well* means very well-done (hamburger for example); *popcorn* means well-done also but is used at break-fast for eggs, say, scramble two popcorn. *Twenty-one, forty-two, sixty-three*, refers to egg/plate ratio, for instance, eggs over easy forty-two means four eggs over easy on two plates or two eggs over easy a pair. *Late flash* is an add-on after the order has been initially given; *express* means you need it instantly; *echo* is asking for the order to be repeated. *Ordering* means giving a new order; *pick up* means the order is being handed over to the waitress. An order may be called and then picked up ten minutes later. "86" means something has run out or for something to be thrown out (it has spoiled) or to cancel an item (a daily special) or to cancel an order. *Chopped liver* is an expletive used in a derisory manner to express irony or disdain such as, "What do you think this is? Chopped liver?!"

Thus a single announcement may be called:

"Ordering: combo takes AC on down LT takes mustard; Ordering: jack Swiss tommy on whiskey; Ordering: egg roll takes AC mazy;

Ordering: chicken salad mahogany down no grass; Late Flash: combo takes a slice; Ordering: hamburger in the well with French fries airborne; Ordering: full house takes ham with French fries airborne; Ordering: Reuben with French fries airborne, make it a pair. Pick up: cowboy all the way takes French fries; Pick up: radio whiskey down; Pick up: blue cheeseburger rare; Pick up: indi tuna platter mahogany down high and dry; Pick up: sesame bagel down cream cheese smoked salmon for the money takes a slice; Pick Up: Swiss cheese omelet roll it takes mazy no grass; Pick up: 86 the BLT make it a number one heavy mazy, pick up!"

ABC is the only casual labor agency I ever worked for. Open at five a.m., this is New York, and you had better be waiting on the sidewalk for the dispatcher to arrive if you want to be sure of getting out. A crowd of hungry smiling faces pushing their way forward all at once to be sure of being seen and remembered, "I was here first," the opening dispatcher, as anxious to get through his morning as those guys are to work, leads the way in, the throng "opening and closing around him after the manner of Moses with the Red Sea,"[1] his coffee and Danish on the way, the phones ringing even as the lights are turned on. With the exception of bimonthly days when welfare checks issue forth, the austere waiting room is packed to overflowing with better than sixty bums all hoping to be selected to work for the day. There are so many places to work—coffee shops, bagel shops, pizza parlors, delicatessens, diners, caterers, cafeterias, chain franchises, concessions, trattorias, bistros—one could work a career and hardly ever work the same store twice.

---

1 Elizabeth Eyre, *Death of a Duchess*

Despite the racket of the phones, the desks, friends of the dispatcher crowding around him rapping (the bums), there was a somnolence throughout the waiting room, the bums packed into their battered folding chairs and nodding even amongst the din that at any moment could be given over to an eruption, some altercation between two uptight bungholes. These could be serious as many of the guys carried knives, brass knucks or, like myself, a meat cleaver. And so would come into play the resident bouncer. Always big, simple and sadistic. And effective. Most of the guys had come to ABC to work though some came to cause trouble. The bouncer would put the offenders through the meat grinder right before your astonished eyes and then turn to the waiting room and ask, "Anybody else?"

I had a meat cleaver, a small mid-weight one that I carried around with me when I went out. In the cool weather I wore a nylon bomber jacket that had an inside slash pocket that was custom made for the cleaver. It rode balanced just right, was right there to be brought into action. One shot from that cleaver would split a collarbone or sever a shoulder or elbow cruelly, from its own weight and momentum. A brutal weapon. I was comfortable with it, it was part of me, made me feel secure. Much more effective than, say, a switchblade. But violence on the street is something one living on the street wants to avoid at all costs. Unless you're the type who revels in violence, that is, the stickup man who doesn't give a damn. Usually, no one wants a dead body on their hands so fleecing is achieved by guile, trickery and deception.

Towards the phase out of my years as a New York City bum, I worked almost exclusively as a coffee man in bagel shops—at Wall Street, Madison Square Garden and City Hall—never becoming deadass for the luxury of its simplicity and sensual appeal. I was so smooth and fast and efficient, I was begged to stay by the bosses one and all. I did stay, one place for over a year, and another for half that time. Me and my coffee urn. The aroma, the cleanliness, pumping coffee for New York's multitude. But you better be fast. One hundred containers per minute at breakfast.[1] One jaded New Yorker gave me the highest compliment by saying, "He makes a nice regular." Regular coffee. Only in New York. Barely medium amount of milk with no sugar. Put the milk in first so it mixes evenly. And clean your urn everyday including the glass registers and spigots.

A good coffee man (barista) should be able to make a perfect cappuccino. Hold the steam nozzle just below the surface of the ice-cold milk until a thick head of foam has developed, then submerge the nozzle deep to heat the bulk of the milk. Decant the espresso last. Skim milk will froth more readily than whole milk but I always used whole milk unless the customer specifically requested skim. I could always detect the recondite Prince Alberts when they ordered a campy iced decaf latte with skim milk. Latte and cappuccino are virtually the same item save that latte doesn't require the thick head of foam.

Early mornings, from where I'm working the counter at Croissant & Gourmet, I gaze upon the ladies of the night coming in for their breakfast, all smiles, straight from a good night's hustling, ordering quiche Lorraine, a chocolate brioche or almond croissant and a flavored coffee—the most expensive items; their money hard-won and freely spent on indulgences. Seldom seen luxuries for their set; everyday tidbits for their clientele. I observe such contrasts as I serve each class of patron, rarely partaking in such upper-crust delights myself anymore, having joined the deadbeat strata and lost my taste for such fancy fare in the

---

1 To move at that speed requires a good 48 pounds of pressure, or a full six-gallon urn, using a double-urn system.

process. Though I enjoy bearing witness as the whores pamper themselves with a slice of ambrosial pleasure—heaven knows, they deserve it.

There is much to be said for personalized service, a disproportionate overbalance of appreciation to be had from the slightest recognition, for the particular effort in remembering the name of someone's cat, or that this person doesn't like their tomato placed next to the cheese on their sandwich, or that one wants the tea bag on the side. Sometimes a customer will travel extra distance for just such personalized service, for having their order filled as soon as they are spotted in line, without having to repeat themselves day in and day out. And it is often such small singularities that can make or break the mood of a person's entire day. The unwrapping of one's sandwich at their desk and savoring the item exactly the way they like it, affirmation that at least one thing in their day will go right.

Too high a volume of business and too low a caliber of personnel frequently combine to yield a uniform non-personalized service for a customer at sea in an oceanic city that is indifferent to their individual quirks and whims. I had a favorite customer, a corpulent, middle-aged black woman of loyal acquaintance, who liked her breakfast roll toasted lightly yet evenly with a light, even spread of butter on each side—a simple order though one nonetheless that she found impossible to acquire, searching from deli to deli for an accommodating counter man until, one day, she spotted me (again) in a deli and exclaimed, "There you are!" And every morning thereafter, that lady would arrive with a big smile and, holding up her finger say, "I'll have mine."

Christmas season was payback time for a year's worth of remembering a customer's every idiosyncrasy and serving them fast and accurate. For if New Yorkers are arrogant and demanding they can, in equal measure, be generous. "We're from New York!" SMACK, as a twenty-dollar bill is slapped on the bar or counter as a tip.

Exemplified by gregarious New Yorker Jackie Gleason who, when he was broke one night, borrowed $1,000 from restaurateur Toots Shor and then turned around and gave $500 of it to the firm's maître d' as a tip. In the coffee shops and delis, those of us working out front would place an empty two-gallon glass jar on the countertop or on top of the cash register (throughout the month of December) for the customers to contribute—sometimes with a red ribbon tied around its mouth or a handwritten sign taped to the jar proclaiming TIPS. At slow times (in Bagel Maven) I would insert the long handle of the coffee urn brush into the jar and klang it back and forth as I rejoiced, "Merry Christmas!" while the cashiers and female packers peed in their pants laughing. It was nothing for us (6) each to pocket $50 daily from that jar in the week preceding Christmas (almost double our salary).

In reconnoitering all the different downtown locations I've worked over the years through ABC, it's amazing how complete an inventory I've racked up in such a concentrated area. And, in retrospect, the only thing I can say that all those eateries share is the pure unadulterated attribute of speed. I have traveled through (and lived in) every geographical area of our US of A and I can attest, first hand, that nowhere holds a candle to New York City for hustle.

inding out about soup kitchens took a lot of the stress out of living on the street. There were a good half dozen in the vicinity that I ran, the Lower East Side and environs—land of graffiti by Chico. The Church of the Nativity on Second Avenue at Second Street gave the most munificent spread every Saturday. Hundreds of ravenous bums would gather from all over the city for that eat, always including entire welfare families, queuing up an hour in advance. The large recreation room could accommodate near one hundred needy souls at a single sitting. There was meatloaf, mashed potatoes, winter squash, lima beans, corn, green salad, macaroni salad, Parker House rolls, sliced bread, margarine, salt, pepper, ketchup, coffee, tea, real milk, sugar, ice water, cake, apples, oranges, bananas, and it was all you can eat, unlimited seconds. People would take a whole meal with them when they left. There was enough food to feed an army. Servers pushing carts around the dining room replenishing your plate. Red and white checked tablecloths, napkins at each place.

During the week, there was Saint Joseph House on First Street and Mary House (for women) on Third Street, both of the Catholic Worker; Trinity Lutheran on Ninth Street; Diane's on Avenue C; Bowery Mission on the Bowery—all for soup lines. Holy Name Society on Bleeker Street at Third Avenue for showers. Most of those charities handed out secondhand clothes on select days of the week. Additionally, independent groups would frequently park a van on Houston Street at First Avenue or at Tompkins Square Park on Avenue B and hand out food: Indian food, natural vegetarian, outdated boxes of cake. Another reliable food source for a wholly first-rate bag lunch was a church on Seventeenth Street at Third Avenue, opposite Stuyvesant Square Park, a quiet, tree-shaded harborage which handed out bag lunches Monday through Friday to anyone who came to their door. Oft recurring were tuna fish sandwiches, a rare and costly treat from a charity handout, always included was a four-ounce can of apple juice, a packaged sweet and fresh fruit.

Besides the soup kitchens and charity handouts, there were a few other esculent expedients in the Lower East Side circumjacencies. The A & P Supermarket at Union Square boasted a steam table with a mélange of hot take-out selections from ragouts and macaroni and cheese to grilled chicken and barbequed ribs. At thirty minutes prior to closing time (around nine p.m.), all of the hot items were reduced to half price. At closing time, the same were thrown out. That was a cornucopia of affordable (or free) fresh, homemade meals. Another benevolent bonanza was a pizza shop on First Avenue near Eighth Street. At closing time (about ten p.m.) all of the day's cooked merchandise was donated to the Catholic Worker. If you were a bum in the neighborhood you could take your pick of pizza, calzone, Stromboli, whatever was on hand. Furthermore, there were pushcarts with griddled chicken pieces or lamb chunks (souvlaki) served on heros, located around hospitals and downtown business districts—those wagons served a lunch trade only and if you waited around until they were packing up, their leftover cooked fare was gratis for the bums. A morning trade pushcart, also around business areas (like City Hall) that served coffee, rolls, donuts and bagels would often give away unsold merchandise when they were shutting down (around 10 a.m.) and ready to be towed away. Often the same held true for hot dog wagons if you could catch one as they were hooking up (around dusk) to be pulled back to the garage. When you're a hungry bum on the prowl, you always have an eye peeled for handouts. Though, once you had a line on the soup kitchens you needn't go hungry. And (ultimately) I had the inside track to those charity kitchens as I became one of their cooks.

My gastronomic discursion began while I was a resider at Trinity Lutheran shelter on Sixth Street between Avenue B and Avenue C. By the time I was ready to move into a shelter I was at my wit's end, a defeatee of siege mentality. My humble self was a nervous wreck, having not been able to sleep securely for some months. I hated to do it but this mortal entity had to have rest. I had no misgivings about being a bum, if anything that stumbling block of not being able to rest hardened my resolve. Those were but early rumors of my new career, mocking me at that pivotal point, the terminal moraine of my previous life bemoaning the blurry romance and roseate memory of an obtuse, obdurate past against the dawning, daunting uncertainties of my present Homeric endeavor. Yet I would not second-guess myself, would not be swayed, my will was like steel, I just needed to get up my second wind, to step back and reevaluate my situation, revamp my strategy, and to carefully devise my extended, enduring campaign. I would abidingly mortify my reliance on the Establishment, sever all ties to my bygones and waver not in my fixity of purpose, my labor to be asunder, to disaffiliate from mainstream society. All in all, I figured I had better than a Chinaman's chance.

Alack, after much Socratic consideration and under the reign of prudence did I seek admission to a shelter, a judicious metathesis in my predicament, a timely *pis aller*. I went to Saint Patrick's Cathedral on Fifth Avenue, they conducted a philanthropic program, Our Neighbors. I had once been one of their volunteers—such was my advantage. They referred me to Trinity Lutheran (a non-partisan shelter in the *vieux jeu* area of Alphabet City), made the call and arranged an appointment. I went over to the Ninth Street at Avenue B (soup kitchen) location like a beggar or a holy man and was interviewed by one of the volunteer officers, Carmen. The whereabouts of the shelter proper would not be divulged until one was accepted for enrollment. I didn't know that neighborhood yet, Alphabet City, an old ghetto pungent with urban rot, where the topsoil of civilization is often a shallow veneer over the naked clay of a primal and savage reality, of crowded tenements, shabby taverns and seedy bordellos, run-down and abysmally strained, whose inhabitants all bore the stamp of poverty. An alien geography, Alphabet City is laced with menace, reminiscent of the area's drug wars of the mid-1980s, when shoot-outs in the middle of the streets were commonplace and the black market was flooded with heroin and cocaine like it was going out of style. A zone of mystery and privacy whose membership is grudging and conditional based upon privation, prejudice and praxis.

This was a corner of the East Village where, during the 1980s, one quarter of the buildings were abandoned by owners who stopped paying mortgages and taxes, a shaky period in New York real estate that left many buildings abandoned and open to squatters who took over those deserted tenements and fixed them up, which became the era of the East Village radicals.[1]

Alphabet City at the time of this story (1980s and 1990s) was the only area of my intelligence (which encompassed the entire southern portion of Manhattan from Central Park to the Battery) that actively recycled. There were bins and containers on every block for different types of refuse: glass, cans, plastic, paper, clothing. It seemed to me that it took the most fortuneless, flagitious community to take recycling seriously, to place a real value on consumer products and their impact on the environment. Exactly the opposite of what a middle class, moderately educated taxpayer in fact does in his land of plenty, the first one to criticize and ostracize the poor.

I told Carmen my sad story, my mien was good, I was mellifluous and urbane. I explained how I had gone down to the south dock offices of the steamship companies (Steamship Row) and tried to hire on as a chef for a cruise liner. One needed to have a union card (I had a card from a different local) in order to secure a position and one couldn't obtain a card unless they already had a job. Catch-22.

---

1 Peter DeJonge, *Buried on Avenue B*

It was conceivable that I could have imposed upon Mr. Jerry Burns (co-owner of "21"), to use his influence to secure the appointment I sought. But I wanted to reserve that boon for having my cookbook published, and was in no condition to entreat Mr. Burns at that time.

I thought a cruise-liner job would be a sure way to accrue a forced savings, as employees were paid at the conclusion of the cruise. Away from the ominous temptations of urban vice. I explained to Carmen that I was already working part-time as a waiter but was burning out fast. I laid it on a little, I needed this break. It seemed that Carmen was favorably impressed and he recommended me to Charlie, Trinity's director, and I was in. It was a relief to be in a secure environment, under the aegis of the shelter, in order to rest and sleep. But adjusting to the polity's regimen was irksome in the extreme.

It was high summer, deathly hot, and we weren't even allowed to buy our own fans to create a little breeze, a nocturnal palliation to allay our misery (too much electricity). The army-style cots had vinyl mattresses that were straight out of the Inquisition, upon which we lay bound at night as to the wheel, like Santa Caterina di Alessandria. It had to be over one hundred degrees in that crematoria during the hours of sleep. And the requirement of having to vacate the premises by eight o'clock in the morning and be locked in by nine in the evening was another bitter pill. And, always, Charlie watching over us like a mother hen. Discussions on how we were doing. When all I really wanted was a place to flop.

It was worthwhile, no doubt, the security, the warmth and bountitude. And we could lounge around the living room; but if I had known about flophouses at that time, the flop would have been my choice. Because I really wasn't interested in getting off the street. It was a forced move due to intolerable circumstances. Even at that critical stage in my stalwart hazard I had a presentiment that the street would prove to be my karma, my kismet, my key to kingdom come. But I still lacked practical hobo experience and needed to call forth opportunities and resources as they presented themselves, for I was ever cautious in the hellish depths of that snake pit of a city and would, with meet sapience, alter my course to the best of my advantage. Amen, we all there at Trinity made the best of it.

I finally sobered up after our potentate, Charlie, warned me about coming in so "effervescent." It just seemed like more of what I had given up in taking to the street to begin with. Following orders, living up to someone else's standards. I did give it the old college try, out of necessity. As the harsh seasons mounted—autumn, winter—I kept plugging away, from one crisis to the next. I broke my ankle, I lost my waiter job, and eventually moved into the Catholic Worker as part of my nisus to become situated in my own hearth again.

I was forced to go to work for the city as part of that era's work-for-welfare reform, a vain attempt by the city to prop up a vision of a fading industrial order. And that, coupled with shelter tenancy, inhibited any drinking or drugging. I knew I'd have to fly straight in order to succeed in saving enough mopus for a grubstake, to set myself up on my own again. By the time I landed back on my feet, with a top chef job in a swanky new restaurant on Park Avenue, I was right back where I started from when I'd dropped out from it all, and with an all too familiar *Anschauung*[1] to boot. I had rejoined Alcoholics Anonymous while at Trinity Lutheran to help me attain sobriety. Going to AA meetings and having a sponsor to pal around with seemed like just another step backward in the big picture. For what I really wanted all along was to be a successful bum, not another Mr. America. Well, I would get my wish but I'd have to work at it a little longer.

---

1 Attitude

Trinity Lutheran shelter inhabited a medieval citadel, the lower outer walls covered in graffiti (Jimmy loves Maryanne), built by the Tammany Society at the herald of the twentieth century to house orphan boys, coinciding with the seminal electrification of New York City. This fell in with a trend of the late nineteenth century of orphanages and other child-care institutions which in 1890 New York, the Children's Aid Society cared for 4,000 boys and girls.[1] No longer an orphanage, the shelter occupied the entire fourth (top) floor of that massive red brick edifice, yet with beds for only ten patrons—(there was room for thirty beds). Appointment for admission was by reference only. Of the ten available beds, never were more than six occupied at once. You had to be serious about getting off the street. You needed to have a job, part-time was okay. You had to open a bank account. Your progress was reviewed weekly by the live-in director, Charlie. A program of up to six months was offered. Complete self-sufficiency was the objective. This was truly the Rolls Royce of shelters.

The entire interior was simple but cavernous and spotlessly clean. Every room was cleaned daily by the residents. And all of the furniture was moved every Saturday for cleaning. The job assignments rotated weekly. There was a television with VCR, books, magazines, daily newspapers, lots of reading material. Everyone had his own bedside dresser. The bathroom contained a shower, two commodes and a large sink. The living room was friendly and inviting with its hardwood floor, carpets, couches, armchairs, tables and shaded lamps. The walls were generously apportioned with sizable windows, artifacts of a bygone era, through which we were wooed by foreign clamor from the residential street below, intruding from outside all through the night—shouts and screams, breaking glass, bludgeoning of ash cans and parked cars, gang

---

1 Kenneth L. Kusmer, *Down and Out, On the Road: The Homeless in American History*, statistic

challenges, inebrious brannigans—the poor adolescent minorities at their depraved leisure recreation, contributing their callow fervor to the summer heat wave and their sunless Erebus.

The hours we were allowed inside each day were limited. We had to be out of the building by eight a.m. six days a week and by nine a.m. on Saturday (owing to moving the furniture). No exceptions. I had broken my ankle and was in a leg cast, on crutches, but had to be out on time like everyone else; to spend my day drowsing in the public library on Fifth Avenue. There was no sleeping allowed in the library so I learned to sleep while assuming a reading posture. If you were caught sleeping you'd be ejected.

(Dealing with the disaffiliated guard): "Can't I just take a book before I go?"

"No book. You come back later. You sleep now, you out now…. You want me call the police?"

In the evening, at the shelter, the doors opened at four thirty p.m., not a minute sooner, rain, sleet or snow. Once inside, it was the chore of the last person in to go down and deadbolt the front door for the night. There was no smoking inside the residence. Smoking was allowed only in the hallway outside the main entry and that door closed at nine p.m. so you had to get in all your smoking by then. More than once I smoked two cigarettes simultaneously and was made sick from inhaling so much smoke so fast.

Trinity Lutheran was my first acquaintance with a shelter and thus I was unduly reserved. One fellow guest, Rob, left shortly after I enrolled, to join a detox. I was surprised at that as Rob seemed like a sober confederate. Another guest, Samba, whom I espied copping dope at Avenue B one morning, stank so bad that we petitioned Charlie to have him bathe. Samba kept such a low profile of dreamy mentation I wondered if he were autistic. Much later, I discovered Samba's reticence to be an act. Next was Thomas, who used to vanish under his bedcovers after lights-out and read (a bible?) for hours with a flashlight. One clean-cut guest, Aaron, brought in a video cassette, *Caligula,* which was fairly pornographic (this was done on Carmen's watch). Aaron was the first of our company to acquire his own apartment. He used to play basketball daily at Tompkins Square Park. When he moved out of Trinity, Aaron had a big row with Charlie who wouldn't allow him to store some of his possessions at the shelter. Another fellow resident, Bob, eventually became my (temporary) AA sponsor when I was coerced to adopt temperance. A consummate joker, Bob, he once placed in Trinity's refrigerator a brown paper lunch sack across whose exterior was the inscription "1,000 roaches." At his own expense (towards which I later contributed), Bob bought and installed on the bathroom sink a contraption which connected the separate hot and cold water spigots into a single faucet appurtenance.

Bob once invited me to breakfast at a West Village eatery where he worked as a waiter, cashier and all around major-domo. After serving me, Bob took cash from a pair of customers, the sole other patrons of the moment. He then shined to my table, the tumid swell, and pressed upon me the receipt which he had just collected. I couldn't believe my eyes. Was this guy serious? Bob would soon thereafter be terminated for stealing. Bob finally landed a superintendent post in a borough apartment building.

Charlie was forever looming around, keeping an eye on his charges, an ever-vigilant presence, conducting his interviews or gabbing on the telephone at his desk in the kitchen, which was a continual sphere of activity. And who could blame him? We weren't going to keep in line of our own volition. Charlie was of the persuasion that we needed structuring, without which we'd be hard pressed to function on our own once we left the imposed order of the shelter. "One day you'll thank me," Charlie would portend as he obliged us to douse our cigarettes at curfew. Good ole Charlie. How many people would devote themselves to the well-being of such wastrels as ourselves?

Charlie advocated cultural excursions to which I readily acceded and he also urged that we read *The New York Times* daily from front to back, which advice I never followed. Carmen, on the other hand, loaned me a couple of welcome books by James Baldwin which I devoured. I consider my time at Trinity Lutheran well spent as part and parcel of my total homeless experience. A couple of years after I moved from Trinity and had subsequently left the Catholic Worker as well, Samba and Thomas would both inveigle their way into Saint Joseph House for which they appeared extremely joyous. Praise be. A couple of professional bums upwardly mobile. It takes one to know one.

Lastly (the high point at Trinity) was the tucker. We had to wash our hands in the bathroom sink with hot water and soap before being allowed in the kitchen, a mandate inaugurated by Thomas. The self-serve provisions were unrestricted. Boxes upon boxes of assorted dry cereal, granola, scones and muffins, bread of every description, butter, cream cheese, crackers, peanut butter, jelly, honey. There were Stouffer's microwaveable entrees in the freezers (every choice they make), and other main dishes like pot pies, pizza, Indian cuisine. There were two each stand-up freezers and refrigerators packed with food. There were always fresh sliced cold cuts by the pound in separate plastic containers: turkey breast, boiled ham, bologna, salami, roast beef, liverwurst. All you can eat. And sliced cheeses: America, provolone, Swiss, Muenster. There was fresh fruit, always bananas. And there were cakes: Danish rings, coffee cakes. Everything in such abundance. Of the two refrigerators, one (off-limit) was a back-up stocked with gallons of milk, gallons of fruit juice. And a back-up freezer with fried chicken and pizza (popular items). There were napkins to be had and paper towels, unheard-of luxuries in a shelter. Trinity was truly a beautiful place. And Charlie, whose mission this was, though somewhat reserved, was thoroughly devoted. An earnest chap, long and wiry, lengthy flaxen-maned ringlets, firm but friendly in his humanistic fashion.

And there was Carmen (Elvis, so dubbed for his resemblance to and affinity for the king of rock), another of our night custodians. Carmen was more lenient than Charlie and thus was a favorite. Over time, Carmen learned of my culinary background and, as he also volunteered at Saint Joseph House of the Catholic Worker, he approached me about cooking a meal for them one evening. "Give them something different from their ordinary, humble fare." Saint Joe's cooked for close to one hundred guests and volunteers each day (which was sometimes a sore spot), in addition to the soup line. "We buy ground beef twice a week and quartered chickens twice a week," Carmen informed me. At Carmen's behest, I drew up a list of a dozen chicken dishes. We settled on Coq au Vin (chicken braised in red wine) with carrots, pearl onions and a sauce so glutinous and viscous it virtually enveloped the skinned pieces of chicken in a glistening viscid sheath. Carmen warned me about the wine, "We have recovering alcoholics," but I used it anyway.

Well, I was regaled with such praise for that one meal, I was offered and accepted the job of permanent Saturday evening chef, a big night at the Catholic Worker. It wasn't hard to please them, they were so desperate for good food. I made them blackened chicken, fried chicken, chicken chow mein and meatballs diable. Peking chicken, lemon chicken, chicken a la king and Cajun meatloaf. Chicken and dumplings, chicken cacciatore, chicken normande and Salisbury steak. Side accompaniments, salads, dressings, desserts. I made apple pie in a sheet pan, the top crust decorated with delicate floral designs out of pastry, shellacked with egg wash and rimed with sugar crystals. All made with ingredients from their own larder. Sometimes, when skinning the chicken pieces, I'd pan-fry the skins to a crisp then serve them, salted, as appetizers to be munched with crisp bread—a very popular item. Those meals earned me much encomium to which I acquiesced with equanimity.

It was good for me in a couple of ways. Mainly, it opened the door of the house to me. I became a sort of libertine in whose favor all rules were relaxed. I could come and go as I pleased, I was issued a key to the front door (a rare privilege), as well as the combination to the pantry padlock. I was petitioned to cook for certain affairs. My presence in any part of the house at any time became inconsequential. I was invisible, I was deferred to, I was consulted. Through my cooking, I proved a *success fou*. Thus, I blended in with the woodwork at Saint Joseph House of the Catholic Worker.

Naturally, Saint Joe's was affiliated with many like-minded organizations around the area, the East Village and Lower East Side. And through this network I extended myself, through what Our Lady might have intended to take place for us: an awakening, a provisioning, a quest. And though now I was helping the Catholic Worker, they would in turn help me as well. Before my allotted time was up at Trinity Lutheran I moved from there to Saint Joe's, a big step wherein I possessed a front door key (as did many of the house residents), I could come and go at will. What precipitated the necessity of this move was that I began working again for a caterer which required me to toil late into the night, preventing me from returning to Trinity by curfew. And so I made the move to Saint Joseph House of the Catholic Worker at 36 East First Street in the Naked City—my new home. A parting gift from Charlie was a serious supply of cleaning products that included scouring powder, bleach, scrubbie, Lysol and Playtex Living Gloves—"for the bathroom," prognosticated Charlie with fatherly prescience.

The director of Saint Joseph House was Bill, a frisky good natured slob, dedicated and (though resigned) fully dogged in his vocation. He welcomed me with open arms and that was that. I was in.

Bill was a character. Easy going and laid-back, his main concern was operating the soup kitchen and issuing the newspaper, *The Catholic Worker*, which were (largely) the main functions of the house. Bill's bedroom looked like a bomb had gone off in it, yet in the same breath, it was welcoming and cozy. Bill could make a great potato salad that was half boiled potatoes, half hard-boiled eggs, half Manzanilla olives and half mayonnaise. A memorable and funny (if disheveled) bloke. Carmen, by contrast, paid attention to details: sanitation, a new coffee maker, patched the fractured kitchen ceiling. Carmen would put lettuce on the daily take-out sandwiches for the soup line or, when it was his turn to go shopping, he'd buy Captain Crunch cereal or Cocoa Puffs instead of corn flakes. Both Bill and Carmen were warmhearted and generous. And devoted. Together they lent a complimentary irenic officiation to the helm of the house.

A couple of residents with whom I was to share the fifth floor dorm loft, who each had his own separate bedroom, were Smitty, an elderly black shelter veteran who had been installed by none other than Catholic Worker founder Dorothy Day herself, and who worked at Madonna Residence (a Brooklyn Catholic nursing home) as a chef (yet lived at Saint Joe's rent free). Smitty would, on occasion, drink (vodka) in his room of an evening and, not infrequently, indulge in some type of self-flagellation—I would hear him slapping himself like mad in the night. Weird.

And then there was Bishop, a spindly, emaciated coelacanth who was the sweetest soft-spoken Christian, a bona fide Catholic Worker, he was the officious house secretary with the most careful, exquisite calligraphy I have ever seen, the more remarkable for his poor eyesight. Bishop would lead evening vespers in the house dining room for those who cared to participate. Bishop rarely ate the house meals. He would shuffle along to Veselka coffee shop (an eight block trek) each morning and order pancakes (drenched with syrup) of which he'd manage a scant three or four swallows.

For dinner, Bishop would sit in Saint Joe's dining room with a container of Dannon fruit yogurt, a pint of chocolate milk, and a Baby Watson cheesecake, all of which he bought and paid for from his Social Security benefits and which he never managed to put more than a dent in. Everybody loved Bishop. And a few were wary of Smitty about whom Charlie often inquired, "How does Smitty rate his own bedroom and, moreover, exclusive rights to the fifth floor kitchen." But Smitty was somehow grandfathered in his status and thus enjoyed such privileged exclusivity. Or enterprise. Or hocus.

In acclimating to my eyrie up on the pullulating if spartan fifth floor, I was oddly upset by a peculiar and baffling mystery of blood splatters on the sheets of my wood-frame bed. I studied those incarnadine specks with Holmesian intensity and flipped. How could this possibly have happened? The splatters were not unlike the sprinkle of blood one might spray onto the ceiling or wall after pulling out from an intravenous shot. Who on earth could have done this on my bed sheets, having had to pull back the top blanket to do it and then replace and smooth out said blanket. So improbable and yet not impossible in that permissive, Borgian environment. Weirdoes abounding. As it turned out, the blood droplets were from bedbugs, by the score, painlessly drawing one's blood while they sleep, then scuttling back into the mattress roping. Leaving a speckled trail of blood and the victim's legs peppered with tiny red welts that would itch for days. Just something to get used to living as a bum.

Another sore spot up on the fifth floor was the bathroom. With up to a dozen bums using the facilities, without continual wiping down, the scabrous soap scum and rank toilet spatters were often out of hand. Yet most repellent were the two guests who used bedside urinals, one who emptied that repulsive container into the fifth floor kitchen sink, the other who dumped his foul detritus into the bathroom sink. I would lean over to brush my teeth and be assailed with such a vile, feculent odor as to make me wretch. I complained to Carmen about this abhorrent practice yet, despite the culprits' vow to modify their invidious deportment, nothing ever seemed to change.

On the lavatory's brighter side however, I would often gaze out the fifth floor bathroom window into the city's caliginous gloaming of full night, the art deco skyline: the Chrysler skyscraper in all its floodlit, spiky glassy armor—medieval, mysterious, majestic; the Empire State skyscraper in its bold holiday color filters—red for Valentine's Day; green for Saint Paddy's; red, white and blue for July Fourth; orange for Halloween; red, white and green for Xmas. Classics of New York City's grandeur. The metropolis' unique proclamation of the Empire State's eminence. Things would get better for me, or things would get worse, it didn't matter for I was content, at one with the prana, the grass roots of the city.

Saint Joseph House of the Catholic Worker was hardly a cloistered residence, nothing like the strict, highly supervised, fail-safe environment at Trinity Lutheran from whence I'd come. For one thing (in addition to its function as a shelter), Saint Joe's was a soup kitchen and as such had a daily traffic of hundreds of calcified homeless psychopaths moving through there *ad nauseum.* Additionally, there were a dozen Catholic Worker volunteers living there, plus a half dozen superannuated fossils, antiquated pet relics who had been allowed to petrify within its unassuming rooms and around whom that ideationally inviolable asylum operated and was probably built. As well as extending a helping hand to those whom the street had done for, threw upon Christ's threshold, beached and helpless—another dozen full-time guests that included psychotics, sociopaths, alcoholics and drug addicts of the first water.

Some of the derelicts required only short-term crisis intervention, until they enrolled in either detox, rehab, Bellevue, public assistance or, like myself, saved enough income for a private residence.

And there was Tommy, the long-term, po-faced resident Caliban, a hopeless alcoholic who began drinking at seven o'clock every morning and was falling down drunk by the afternoon, claiming to suffer from recurrent seizures as a smoke screen for his often bruised and swollen face. Tommy would, at some point, conspire with Brad (another resident alcoholic snitch) to have me ejected from Saint Joe's. There was Preston, a geriatric scarecrow and dour sourpuss who carried around his own salt and pepper shakers in his shirt pocket and kept complaining, in his querulous cackle, that the house residents should be served (their meals) first. Mr. Wong, a skeletal Chinese Methuselah with his corrugated and camphored hide, who could be cantankerous and who I never heard speak a word of English. Amiable Alex, a plump, jovial old soul who, like Preston and Mr. Wong, lay low all day down in their murid repository, obscure in the crepehanging desuetude and dust of a damp subcellar, gazing out the grimy windows like submerged Captain Nemo caricatures, conning a museful Nautilus—trance-like in deep privacy, capsized in time. And there was Whiskers, a hyper, bellicose old curmudgeon with a long white beard who, despite his contentious disposition, was always willing to work like a horse and of whom everyone was fond. Those were a few of the more senior guests extant (well into the Medicare years) whose permanence in the house was legendary and who all had their own income (SSI) and yet received free room and board from the sympathetic largess of the Catholic Worker.

Continuing with the occupation of the house: the newspaper—*The Catholic Worker*—was mailed out from Saint Joe's (so there was the newspaper staff), as well as mass celebrated, parties held, clothing distributed, laundry washed, showers allowed, loitering permitted, constant scullery bustle, US Mail call, pill call, telephone calls—it was a bedlam of activity and confusion. None of the five floors were immune to the direptions of second-story thieves and cat burglars. I've woken up in the middle of the night to catch some afflicted wight insinuating his hand into my suitcase. I've had a fellow guest comment on the contents of my secured locker. A volunteer in the bed next to mine had his Walkman radio stolen, cash money disappeared regularly, and I've caught scurrilous dope addicts wandering around restricted areas (the women's floor) unchaperoned, more than once. All in all, an indomitable house, well spavined and typical of the general shelter environment as a whole. Yet it was better than the street by a long shot and much better than drop-in centers where security and supervision are nonexistent.

Drop -in centers are merely a last ditch refuge from the elements. Resembling nothing more than a meager waiting room, drop-in centers offer none of the amenities of a proper shelter such as beds, blankets, tables, cooking facilities, often without windows, sometimes lacking even toilets. My sole experience at a drop-in center on Twenty-Eighth Street near Lexington Avenue supplied nothing more than rows of long wooden benches packed with predominantly black vagrants, many of whom were women with small children. As I awaited my screening at the admitting desk, threat to turn out my pockets, I observed a swarthy malefactor firing up a crack pipe as bold and brazen as you please right in the middle of the ruck. A woman sitting near the rogue, looking terrified with her clutch of wee bairns, was ineffectually attempting to distance herself from the scene by scrunching against her neighbor on the bench and focusing on her fidgeting offspring. Farther back, in the funeral shadows of a rear corner, occulted by some standing bucks, was the unmistakable piston-like motion of a kneeling woman's head as she performed her duty for, no doubt, payment in crack. The place was packed like a sardine can, the persistent babel of voices and clamor of hotching youngsters, the threatening presence of the bucks in that dim, smoky atmosphere impressed me with pandemonium. Already I had ascertained some case-hardened hoodlums leering with their canine grimaces, sizing me up as I abided my vetting. There was no space to sit down, the benches already crammed, standing room only. I thought, this place is a panic waiting to happen and thus I retreated to the familiar quagmire of the street with its prowling bushrangers, the oppugnant hinterland of the dark city.

Some few churches open their doors to the homeless after vespers as a drop-in center, allowing the bums to doss down on the floor in the narthex, but I never patronized any of those flops though I've seen them firsthand. Also, a couple of first-rate full-course dinner charity kitchens (both at which I've eaten) I believe allow homeless to kip for the night: The Coffee Cup on Lexington Avenue in the mid-Twenties and Saint Vincent de Paul on West Twenty-Third Street. Drop-in centers (and shelters for that matter) were never my cup of tea.

Saint Joe's was at least locked at night and it was warm and dry. And the laissez-faire, non-polemic atmosphere was more congenial and relaxed than the Gestapo-type control of some residences where Big Brother always has his nose up your arse. I really liked Saint Joe's, as did all of its long-term guests. This was largely a reflection of the casual yet compassionate approach by prefect Bill, Carmen, Irish Roger, Martin, Sioban and Annie (to name a few volunteers). None of us desired close custody at the cost of freedom. We looked after ourselves and each other and accepted life as it was. Nobody wanted to live in a prison.

What the soup kitchens with which I'm familiar share in common with each other are, firstly, an appearance that is in harmony with their clientele. Antediluvian buildings that had once been East Side tenements for the blue-collar immigrants of the nineteenth and early twentieth centuries have had little, if anything, done to them by way of remodeling, short of expanding the kitchen or removing a wall to enlarge a dining room. Flooring, wall coverings, windows and stairs are much as they were when the buildings were erected, save a more worn and weathered condition. The reason for such a negligent approach, other than penury, is to conform with the living standards of the homeless who are their patrons. To make the bums feel at ease, as it was so tactfully explained to me once. However, this blanket explanation connotes a slight understatement.

At Saint Joseph House of the Catholic Worker, much of the kitchen equipment looked as though it had been through the American Civil War. Dented, pitted and blackened aluminum pots, rusted iron skillets and roasting pans, cooking utensils that seemed better suited to a prairie kitchen, which may have been their heritage. Cracked, mismatched ceramic plates and bent, tarnished cutlery. With the commercial twelve-burner sauce top, double oven, patched and blackened cast iron range a relic from a bygone era with more character and reliability than ten modern stoves. I loved that old stove, which had a temperament all its own and upon which I created many a loving meal. The spice cabinet looked as though a hand grenade had gone off in it and if one dug through could uncover some unusual or exotic treasures like star anise, fenugreek, coriander, allspice, marjoram, savory, celery seed and mace.

All of the Catholic Worker volunteers had to make soup for the soup line and their learning endeavors could have some interesting results, not least of which was pottage carbonara (burnt soup). And despite fastidious cleaning and two four-pawed mousers the house, like so many New York City buildings, was plagued by mice and roaches, another amenity to make the bums feel at ease. The dining room/kitchen area had worn and cracked linoleum flooring, water-damaged walls and ceilings, dilapidated refrigerators and coffee urn, and scarred and gouged wooden tables. Yet it was cozy, comfortable and lived-in, Saint Joe's, no doubt, home sweet home to a passel of homeless, both affluent (volunteers) and fulsome (guests), bums all of variegated stripe. Organization and sanitation was not going to make the house more attractive nor more efficient. That would be merely an affected stagy façade, a veneer of someone else's idea of ritual Christian standards or values which, conversely, would alienate the contingent clientele for whom the shelter functioned. Long live Saint Joseph House of the Catholic Worker in all its archaic splendor.

Saint Joe's location in the East Village, district of many of the area's soup kitchens, developed around the vicinity's first breadline where Fleischman's Model Viennese Bakery on Broadway and East Tenth Street handed out leftover bread to hungry tramps, right next to Grace Church.[1]

Next in common to each soup kitchen is the bill of fare: soup—or mulligan stew might be a more appropriate term. Made from some type of dry legume—split green pea, white navy bean, black-eyed pea, lentil, pinto bean, black bean—with beef or chicken soup base (bought in bulk) added to the water and plenty of chopped vegetables, courtesy of charity donations which assorted collection volunteers pick up (unsalable fresh produce from various distribution markets) weekly by the truckload. This includes almost every vegetable imaginable; you name it, it all goes in the soup. But, never garlic for no matter how desiccated and old, garlic is too valuable to give away. Leftovers from dinner like macaroni or rice might go into the soup (depending on the cook), and Siobhan used to buy chicken with her own money and contribute it to the pot when it was her turn to make soup, while Annie always added a pound of margarine to each twenty gallon pot to eliminate gaseous side effects.

---

1 Christopher Winn, *I Never Knew That About New York*, statistic

Collateral to the soup are: plenty of stale bread of infinite variety, similarly collected by charity volunteers and dropped off daily by the carload. Tea bought in bulk and boiled up (never steeped) daily; sugar; salt; reconstituted powdered skim milk; margarine served by the kilo; and hot sauce by the gallon, brewed up weekly at each individual house, made from city gin, vinegar, ground cayenne pepper and paprika. Some houses made a limited number of bologna (or other inexpensive processed lunchmeat) sandwiches each day to be handed out in bag lunches for those who didn't care to come in and sit down, as well as dispensing soup in take-out coffee containers. Saint Joe's made sixteen bag lunches per day. When questioned as to the seemingly arbitrary number of sandwiches, Brian replied, "That's how many slices come in a (one-pound) package." Soup is served in thirty-two ounce aluminum or stainless steel bowls, plastic mugs for tea, assorted mismatched flatware. Eighty to one hundred gallons of soup is made each day at each house—(That's from three to four hundred servings.) Lines of bums stretch around the block undiminished for three hours, eleven a.m. to two p.m., Monday through Friday. Come in, sit down, be served, eat, be gone. Monitors watch the toilets to discourage shooting up and crack smoking. Lines are patrolled to stop cutting in. Dining rooms are supervised and still fights break out regularly. A disaffected if not volatile atmosphere.

At Saint Joe's the dining room accommodated only about sixty persons at one sitting, thus a line was formed outside and an orderly entrance effected whereby a door guard regulated the admissible number. In the bitterest weather, a good hour on line was not unusual, stomping their chilblain tortured feet and slapping their equally sore ungloved hands,[1] a dumb procession of the uncouth poor and needy, those whom the street had claimed

---

1 Theodore Dreiser, *Sister Carrie*, paraphrase

and now owned. The median age of those soup line patrons I estimate to be twenty-five (male and single); although there were a fair share of eld, as well as mothers with youngsters, the street does not abet longevity. Some curious statistics concerning homeless women are as follows: "In 1987, females made up twenty percent of the homeless population; in 1993, forty-three percent; in 1996, thirty-two percent; and between 1982 and 1992 the number of homeless families in New York City increased five hundred percent."[1]

The assignments that the volunteers would perform each day rotated, such as shopping, making soup, dispensing medication, running inter-house errands, washing laundry, and being "on the house" which meant "in charge of the main floor" which involved answering the front door, answering the phone, giving permission to use the lavatories, permission to loiter in the dining room, permission to make another pot of coffee and so forth. Mattie (personality forthcoming) would never miss an opportunity to (he believed) ingratiate himself with a volunteer (especially a female) by remonstrating another guest loudly for the benefit of all and sundry: "You have to respect the person that's on the house!" as if to remind us all that he (Mattie) was ever cognizant of that maxim and, good little majorette that he was, could be relied upon to inform others of such. I would become embarrassed for Mattie at those times I'd witness this transparent ruse to bolster his insecure acceptance at Saint Joe's. While Mattie would stand his ground with his bulldog face, challenging anyone to contradict him, and the volunteer in charge would let out a long sigh at this one more absurdity with which they had to deal, the infantile behavior of their Romper Room clientele.

---

1 Kenneth L. Kusmer, *Down and Out, On the Road: The Homeless in American History*

Weekday mornings were a busy time at Saint Joe's, the kitchen crowded with galley lackeys, making the soup for the soup line, making sandwiches for take-out, assorted stewarding such as receiving and sorting donated merchandise and storing it downstairs in the pantry and walk-in cooler by way of a bucket brigade arrangement, taking inventory, determining the lunch menu for the house residents, answering and interviewing callers at the front door which opened to every Lazarus in the neighborhood, fielding phone calls, dispensing medication, pot washing and cleaning up, setting up for the soup line, and dealing with any number of emergencies which would invariably crop up. Therefore, the kitchen area was a hectic work site leaving no room for intermittent guests ambling in for a casual English breakfast. Thus, a Continental breakfast was offered from a self-serve table set up in the dining room consisting of assorted dry cereals, peanut butter and jelly, cakes as were on hand, bread and toast, margarine, reconstituted powdered skim milk, canned evaporated milk, fresh fruit, sugar and brewed coffee. On Sundays, a bacon and egg brunch was prepared, often with eggs cooked to order, occasionally expanded to included hollandaise sauce (Latin Roger) or bread pudding (myself) or oatmeal (Siobhan) or beignets (Annie) or pancakes (Carmen). The first time I was asked to cook Sunday brunch, when I was a newcomer at Saint Joe's, I scrambled all fifteen dozen eggs (one half case) at once, thinking that everyone came down at the same ding-dong time as at other meals, not knowing that on Sundays the house members dribble in at their leisure. When Bill came down and saw what I'd done he gently put me wise. I felt so bad despite Bill's consolation. At least I hadn't burned the bacon, a recurrent bungle at the green hands of many house (would-be) cooks.

Lunch for the house residents reflected what had been donated, often including cooked dishes from restaurants or hotels (leftovers from parties) which could be quite elaborate. Otherwise, whatever could be slapped together, reflecting what foodstuffs as were on hand, and the ingenuity of the cook; sometimes leftovers from last night's dinner, sometimes a rice or pasta ragout with beans and vegetables which were usually very tasty (depending on the cook), and always the day's soup which, if nothing else, was substantial. Dinner, as lunch, was prepared by staff members on a rotating basis. The chicken and ground beef nights (two each) were invariably good, twice a week were vegetarian dinners prepared (at Saint Joe's) by Mary House staff and were frequently disasters unless cooked by Kassie. Friday night was fried rice (both vegetarian and pork), charitably donated by a Asiatic-owned Chinese-style restaurant near New York University at Washington Square. I sometimes marveled at the systematic generosity of a business which would donate freshly prepared (delicious) food for one hundred people and always hand it over with a smile. And there was (24/7) always peanut butter and jelly (by the number ten can). All in all, a reliably gratifying feed of which I, ever and anon, considered myself fortunate to be allowed to participate in.

Not infrequently, during the late night hours of communal fraternizing downstairs in the kitchen/dining area at Saint Joe's, as we middle-aged resident bums and privileged local familiars (like Big John and Mattie) sat around enjoying a reprieve from our afternoon boredom, smoking cigarettes, drinking coffee, watching television and shooting the breeze, someone would spring for a dozen eggs (purchased from the corner bodega) and we'd all scoff a midnight snack of fried eggs and toast and coffee. Tommy (after polishing off twelve quarts of beer) usually paid for the coffee, Whiskers bought the eggs, and I invariably got roped into the short-order job, while Brad remained bromide, and Big John faked chest pains, dropping his Di Nobili guinea stinker and grabbing a chair for support, as Mattie looked on in compliant conviviality. We would never be allowed to pull off something like that at Trinity Lutheran or Bowery Mission or any other shelter of my intelligence. It's not just nostalgia that makes the old regime at Saint Joe's the best.

As for the acknowledged administrative director for both Saint Joseph and Mary Houses, there was Frank, the distinguished, white haired, live-in (Mary House) CEO and chief honcho of the NYC Catholic Worker organization, as saintly a personage as I have ever met, whose persistent idiosyncrasy which comes to mind was in telling everyone to cut costs. The resident Catholic Worker volunteers each received a five dollar stipend per week for personal necessities. Frank made the post office run each day for the houses and managed to keep the charity fund in the black. Everyone loved Frank, the Catholic Worker's very own confessor and spiritual confidant.

There was some sibling rivalry between Mary House and Saint Joseph House of the Catholic Worker; mostly a condescending, holier-than-thou prospect on the part of Mary House even though they relied on Saint Joe's to cook their evening dinner. Saint Joe's, in Mary House's estimation, was the pits, the bottom of the rebarbative barrel, reflecting the clientele they served. Whereas Saint Joe's was on the front line dispensing and ministering full-bore the *de riguer* ethos of the Catholic Worker while Mary House luxuriated in playing house for a select sorority of country-club bums amongst whom, outwardly, many seemed kind and jocose, though inwardly bore a decidedly devious cruelty, as how they seemed to waltz around with their noses in the air. This superior attitude was illustrated by an incident during a Christmas celebration which took place at Saint Joseph House at which I was in attendance.

It was an occasion of gift giving, festivity and refection during which time a representative contingent from Mary House came calling. With much pomp and ceremony, Mary House feted Saint Joseph House with their gift in honor of Christ's birth: a used toilet seat, splattered and soiled, not even cleaned. Ha ha, big joke to show Saint Joe's just what we think of you. I was floored at the base, vulgar reproach which that gang of whited sepulchers had the audacity to presume. I felt like spitting in their falsehearted simon-pure faces. Meanwhile, I've witnessed a couple of senior Mary House volunteers (I'm married to Jesus) drinking beer out of cans while sitting on a Third Street tenement stoop, cementing their special (secret) comfortable relationship while impersonating a couple of Mrs. Grundys. Boston marriage in the cloisters?

In living at and cooking for the Catholic Worker, my life continued to improve. I began collecting welfare, working weekends, saving my income, staying sober. I attended mass regularly at the nearby Church of the Nativity (Second Avenue at Second Street) where I met Julie who was involved in every function and ministry on offer. She persuaded me to sing in the choir every Sunday, I recited biblical lections on the altar during mass, I was invited to participate in Julie's singles' ministry for which I prepared food. I was asked to be the leading man to Julie's leading lady in the upcoming Christmas pageant, and was invited to Julie's (home) Christmas party. Julie and me were spending more and more time together. Out to dinner. Gift giving. Phone calls.

Who can say what incidental notion catches a girl's eye and causes her to take a shine to a fellow, it's one of the mysteries of love that make the world go round. Though, after her Sunday puppy love crush, I purposely drew attention to myself by surprising Julie's ministry, to which she'd invited me, with handmade canapés. After that, things progressed steadily, especially with an unexpected Christmas gift for this vibrant jewel.

Julie had confided to me her distress over the demise of her much favored aloe vera plant, one of the high points in her cozy one and a half room crib. Having been invited to Julie's upcoming

Christmas party, I scoured the plant district on Sixth Avenue until I located a suitable (and affordable) aloe vera plant which I purchased and wrapped and presented to my earthangel on Christmas Eve. Upon accepting the evident plant (though covered with wrapping paper) Julie dutifully (and unenthusiastically) thanked me with the remark, "I know what it is." I'm certain she expected it to be a poinsettia (how drab) which were in abundance everywhere one looked, particularly in church where we were nightly rehearsing for the upcoming show. Upon my arrival at Julie's home for her holiday soiree, I was rewarded with a serious show of ardor that made the earth move. With the aloe plant prominently displayed on top of her refrigerator, Julie couldn't express her gratitude sufficiently. Our relationship soared.

So everything was hunky-dory until Julie learned I was homeless and had a past. Up until then, she had seen me for what I was, my actions, my personality, my vibes, my image. And she had liked what she saw. I think I should have been given the benefit of the doubt and not only judged by my immediate presence, behavior and character, but admired for my courage, ambition and fortitude in overcoming such a formidable obstacle, hurdle in my life, my circumstances, rather than rejected for not, perhaps, having a sterling track record, an unblemished background that would have made me less than the seasoned trooper that in fact I was. And for not meeting the à la mode standards of the ton, if such were conceivable in the punk, biker and New Wave East Village. A hypocritical judgment call, I feel, since Julie had a tarnished past herself, having been married and the hallowed sacrament annulled, so that Julie was not the unsullied maiden that she purported herself to be, playing at being the vestal virgin. She was just doing the best she could for the moment, starting over, taking it from this day forward, the same as myself yet, somehow, thinking she was better than I, holier-than-thou, her crap didn't stink. I've no time for playing those kinds of make-believe games as if we were all fresh faced kids with no mistakes behind us. And after we'd shared so much for three or four months, Julie didn't even have the civility to face me. A real cupboard lover.

I recall the night it all happened, when Latin Roger (a Catholic Worker volunteer and ex-paramour of Julie's) decided to jam me up once and for all. We were having lasagna dinner at Saint Joe's, me and Roger sitting next to one another at a table, when I was summoned to the telephone (a call from Julie). Upon returning to my seat, Roger inquired, "So how's Julie?" to which I replied, "Okay, I guess," not letting on that the call was from his lost love. But, of course, who else would have phoned me? I tried to steer the table conversation in another direction, discoursing on different styles of lasagna (Roger was an accomplished cook), all the while noting the smirk on Roger's face. He was no doubt planning, then and there, to put the kibosh on my success with Julie (on whom Roger still had a major crush) because it was the day after next that I discovered I no longer had any audience with Julie, Roger having spun his damnifying parable *à outrance*.

I had carved Julie a butternut squash vase with three owl faces in relief around the outside, having gone to the New York Public Library on Fifth Avenue to research owls in their picture collection, selecting an owl face to copy (owls being a fancy of Julie's), and filled the hollowed-out vase with hand carved flowers out of carrots and scallions, and was to present this exquisite labor of love to Julie at the coffee and cake reception after mass on the approaching Sunday. I had the surprise gift stashed in one of the cafeteria refrigerators in the basement of the church where we would all gather after mass.

Well, Julie didn't even want to look at me or speak to me and when I pressed the handcrafted arrangement upon her, she stared in shocked surprise and then turned away, not wanting anything to do anymore with me or my fairing. Bupkes. That Julie turned down such a personalized, lovingly executed handcraft, something which obviously took a great deal of work and time (and talent) to accomplish, really hit me hard. What a mug I am for any sweet chuck who's nice to me. And all the while, I'm not good enough no matter what I do, the fact of homelessness eclipsing all other acts of reformation and related agencies. What a waste. Lost to a past that no present or future will ever rectify.

I remember a conversation I once had with an employer at a coffee shop whence I was relating how difficult it was to meet a nice girl. And he advised me to go to church. Now, I don't know if he was suggesting that I pray for a miracle or if my attendance might reform me or that church was where a meeting with a nice girl might occur. I admit that I did meet Julie in church and that I considered her to be a nice girl although, after all was said and done, I didn't get anywhere with her. Advice is a fugitive thing, simple to give and iffy to follow.

For the most part, the girls I ran with on the street (both real and imitation) I considered to be very nice (and nasty) although I don't think the average person you'd ask would agree. Certainly Julie wasn't a hooker or a junkie but, in the end, she turned out to be, simply, another pious fraud. Just about everyone has the capacity to be two-faced. Perhaps others perceive me as being duplicitous. Maybe I'm in denial and deceive myself, believing I'm honest. I think now that it's not so important whether one's background is good, bad or indifferent as long as the chemistry is right and the sparks fly.

Holidays were always a big deal at the Catholic Worker with much anticipation, fuss and effusion. Christmas, which was ever accompanied by gift giving, was an especial favorite. Even myself and Mattie (personality forthcoming) received Christmas gifts from Saint Joseph House, along with all the other resident and transient guests (scarf, hat and gloves). At Thanksgiving, every bum on the soup line received a minipack of cigarettes. Every popular holiday—New Year's Day, Valentine's Day, Martin Luther King Junior Day, Easter, Memorial Day, Fourth of July, Labor Day, Saint Patrick's Day, Halloween—were all cause for maffick jubilation involving elaborate meals and, sometimes, outdoor barbeques. And there were other special events too, like birthday parties and weddings. I have attended three weddings at the Catholic Worker where volunteer couples have tied the knot after a year or so of working together at Saint Joe's. Any excuse for a lavish feast and hoopla to break up the frenetic monotony of daily life in service.

And all the regular star cooks would vie for the opportunity to chip in and ham it up, myself included, along with Smitty, Kerry, Kassie, Latin Roger, each aiming to outdo the other and always a feast fit for a king (or queen). Smitty always cooked Thanksgiving dinner, my favorite meal at Saint Joe's, he could make stuffing and giblet gravy the absolute best. Too, holidays were occasions for special desserts and baked goods as well, eliciting rare expenditures from the usually frugal house budget. For the daily staff and resident guests, meal service was for around seventy-five people, consisting of Mary House as well as Saint Joseph House, whose finances came solely from contributions. So we all especially enjoyed and appreciated those beggar's banquets, always a high point in our mean and marginal lives.

My weekly duty as Saturday night chef at Saint Joseph House was an all-around good thing, as well as a reaffirmation and measure of my worth, merit and ability, plus a boost to my ego which, often, was a little deflated in my homeless days of bumming around the streets of the unremitting city. It meant more to me than almost anything I did all week during those times of travail and solicitude. And it was an impalpable blow to me when, after years of unflagging service, I was suddenly forbidden to cook there anymore, no reason given, not even anyone willing to face me and tell me. My slot was just one day filled by someone else who informed me, when I showed up to cook, that they had been told by the staff to take over.

It was the new regime. After Bill and Carmen had left, a new breed of pharisean volunteers took over (this was during my second stay at Saint Joe's). That was when I was ejected from Saint Joe's on an arctic day in January, to wander the streets again, homeless, by the new self-styled satrap in charge (Joe), a COO (chief operating officer) manqué, who told me I had been snitched out by fellow fifth column guests for drinking (beer) while living there (what else is new). And I had asked Joe, what about those self-same lickspittle rats who drank daily and were allowed to remain at the house, and he told me, "This is about you, not them." And so I wound up that night...

Roweling around in the deep, starless, silent snow, there is nowhere to rest. I enter the emergency room at Beth Israel hospital and am ejected for loitering. I eye a mammoth refuse container parked curbside, beside the ER entrance, about eight feet in height, and climb atop it for safety. I lie down on a spread of cardboard, an innocuous, immanent part of the trash, refusing to acknowledge my slothful indolence, my stupidity for allowing myself to fall victim to such miserable circumstances. I only know that I must get through this one frigid night in the ultima Thule of my crusade and resolve to renounce my indifference, to never again be caught out so naked and vulnerable in the insuperable harshness of Old Man Winter on the complacent, unforgiving streets of a cruel implacable city. And thus I pass the hours of darkness, arising brittle and prickling with numbness from exposure, frost rimed and dehydrated, a human ice cube. That's the kind of vicar Joe was.

But I suspect a more devious intrigue was afoot. There was another player in this framework, in the subtext of Sabra, an associate volunteer at Saint Joe's whose role, like Joe's, was to assist in the ministry which was the devoir of the Catholic Worker. As it so happened, Joe and Sabra were soon to be engaged and summarily wed (gratis the Catholic Worker) and, until my expulsion, by Joe, from Saint Joseph House, Sabra had been sympathetic to my plight and my efforts, as well as being a felicitator of my cooking and supporter in my ancillary persuals (such as medical treatment). And thus did Sabra regard me in a worthy light as though I were some strange young Heathcliff by whose very need she might realize her calling.

Poor Joe. He was ceaselessly vying for Sabra's attention, I couldn't help but notice his coxcombry and pedestrian antics to win her admiration. And it came as no surprise that Joe conveniently removed what he jealously perceived as a contestant for Sabra's affection. A regular Rasputin, Joe.

I've encountered, all too often, young philanthropic volunteers, like Joe, who assume as evinced by one's homelessness or alcoholism that they're stupid rather than troubled or simply rebellious or even withdrawn. It always seems to be the nescient ones who think that way.

After Bill abdicated his authority, Carmen took over as steward of Saint Joseph House, but Carmen was on frequent hiatus at home during which opportunities Joe took on the role of parvenu and made great strides in cleaning house, exercising his newfound plenary power, irregardless of its mere provisory status. For instance, Joe and Sabra painted Saint Joe's dining room and kitchen walls (for which Joe was unduly proud) in a "tasteful" color-coordinated scheme. Subsequently, I fell under Joe's hatchet as part of his bang-up clean sweep campaign. For I religiously failed to kowtow to Joe since my life as a bum was not relegated to paying homage or playing games. I had one face only on the street, which I trust I maintain to this day. Like it or lump it.

A final reflection on just what a duplicitous ingrate Joe was. The wedding of Joe and Sabra was attended by not only the thirty or so extended Catholic Worker staff and doubly as many of their friends, but the forty resident guests at both Catholic Worker houses, plus a half dozen elderly welfare pensioners from Brooklyn who ate dinner nightly at Saint Joseph House, who were referred to, with some derisive sympathy, as the deli crowd. During the reception feast in the auditorium of Mary House, at which the guests were scattered in enclaves amongst multiple round (rented) tables, Joe, as the triumphant groom, made his postprandial way around the assembly (the toplofty benedict) bestowing his regards and respects amongst the attendees, and as he dutifully hovered over the table at which I was seated, Joe turned to observe the neighboring table at which the Brooklyn pensioners were gathered and, addressing our table with a conspiratorial smirk, slurred, "The deli crowd," in a tone dripping with contempt and disdain. I almost choked. Those people were Joe's guests at his very wedding which was a donation from the beneficent Catholic Worker. How could Joe be so insensate, unvirtuous and cheap to those of his constituency and on his wedding day. Joe's greatest failing, his feet of clay, was in not appreciating the tempo of the (Saint Joseph) house, its people and its calling. It appeared to me as if Joe would whitewash Saint Joe's into a clone of Mary House, creating a kind of private club, and in so doing completely efface the *raison d'etre* of that noble house, making a sham of the Catholic Worker and its mission. A man who had his own ideas, Joe would bull ahead and, like Robert Moses, woe be to any who stood in his path.

But there were equally iniquitous volunteers at Saint Joes, same as everywhere I guess, there's just no getting away from the B side of even the most earnest seeming people. Here's another example. A very popular couple of volunteers at Saint Joes were getting married, Annie and Don. The entire wedding reception was being donated to the couple "on the house" from the Catholic Worker. Lasagna for over one hundred guests was being made by Kerry (a professional pastry chef) who donated her time and labor. Music on the piano was being played by Barbara (one of my criminous girlfriends) who bestowed her talent ex gratia. And Annie asked me, with measured pudicity, if I would make some edible decorations for the head table, which I consented to do, contributing my time and expertise in the spirit of the occasion.

I made for the newlyweds' table the following exquisite centerpieces. I bought, with my own money, a three quart clay flowerpot in the shape of a bowl. This I covered in pastry, which I made and rolled out, and then applied an upper and lower pastry border of vines and leaves and a central floral motif from pieces of pastry I cut out of a rolled sheet, then egg washed the entire vessel, and baked it in the oven so that the finished product was of a japanned pastry bowl decorated with flora. Into this bowl I piled a bouquet of fried potato roses made out of thin slices of raw potato, folded together in petalled layers to make individual posies, which I then toothpicked together and deep fried so that the result was a rose made out of potato chips and, after removing the toothpicks (the starch in the potatoes held the petals together once cooked) I piled around a dozen of the crisp roses into the pastry bowl. That was one display.

For the second piece I produced one of my gourd vases from butternut squash, carving into the khaki-colored rind a bright orange relief of three Chinese characters signifying health, happiness and longevity, edged top and bottom with the Greek border for eternal life. This urn I hollowed out and filled with a bouquet of radish chrysanthemums and scallion paintbrushes, each which I carved and placed on the tip of skewers which I ran through green scallion leaves. These I arranged in the carved squash vase, adding some additional scallion leaves (dipped in hot water to render them pliable) with a coiled spiral of thin copper wire run through them to create some curly loop-the-loop leaves into the nosegay. All the squash and radishes and scallions and wire and skewers (as well as sculpting tallow) I bought and paid for myself.

For the third piece I carved, out of butternut squash, two sparrows in flight (wings separate and toothpicked on) the bright orange flesh facing outward, which I attached onto alligator clips so as to be able to clip them onto the tallow-coated tree branches, facing each other, beak to beak, like two lovebirds kissing in a tree. I couldn't find a suitable branch, trees being almost nonexistent on or around Second Avenue—virtually no verdant vault in that vicinity. And so I asked Annie for ten dollars that I could buy from Petland a plastic faux branch (sold for bird cages and fish tanks). I was running out of time, it being only another couple of hours until the reception and I couldn't find a blowdown or afford an artificial branch. The birds were already carved, the wax to laminate the branch already tempered. I'd like to interject that those centerpieces were worth at least one hundred dollars apiece at a top hotel. In response to my request, Annie told me (in high dudgeon), "I'm not going to give you any money. You're an alcoholic and a drug addict and you'd only spend any money for alcohol or dope." I couldn't believe my ears. That blasphemous cheapskate who was getting a few thousand dollar wedding for free wouldn't spring for a measly ten bucks. I had already spent a good five clams of my own bread on food cost and was doing this specialty work for free, and Annie had the nerve to condescend to me like that. Unbelievable. Well, I hit Carmen up and he gave me the cake. Boy, I'll never put myself out again for ingrates like them. A couple of bums masquerading as missionaries. Sanctimonious ringers.

PS: My centerpieces were the talk of the reception; no one had ever seen anything like them. Naturally.

PPS: To be fair though, it was Annie and Don who once loaned me a sawbuck (out of the house fund) to redeem my hamsters from mass genocide, a crisis which I will later relate.

An afterword on one member of the deli crowd—Evelyn, the most considerate, sweetest, placid soul; chubby, well-scrubbed and proper, with whom I always conversed each evening at dinner, confided to me one time at Saint Joe's as she set the tables in the dining area: "You know, David, there's these black kids at the projects where I live who are giving me a hard time and I'm afraid to say anything to them." I absorbed this intelligence sagely then, later, approached my fire-eating friend Gene, who was a neighborhood regular at Saint Joe's dinner. I explained how poor Evelyn (whom we all loved) was being victimized by a crew of young punks from Brooklyn. "We should go over there, Gene, and straighten those jaspers out," I advised. Gene nodded his head gravely.

Gene was a large badass of some repute on the street, a seeming benign soul, always with a paperback (Robert Ludlum) whom one wouldn't want to be on the wrong side of. We also recruited Gene's sidekick, Jonathan, another seeming good-natured worthy of the gutter who could turn psycho in a heartbeat if provoked. Between myself with my cleaver and those two seasoned streetfighters we were a formidable crew. All this gangland strategizing taking place in the soteriological precincts of Saint Joseph House of the Catholic Worker while a couple of whores seated closeby strained to eavesdrop.

Our rencontre with a pair of the ne'er-do-wells in Prospect Park proved anticlimactic whence they prudently backed down, claiming ignorance of the charges levied against them. "We've got her back," warned Gene (speaking of Evelyn) as we cut the no-goodniks slack, turning and walking away first to grant them the appearance of face. We never heard any more complaints from Evelyn.

At first, living at Saint Joe's was an opportunity to revitalize some of my old talents and skills. My big moment each week was my Saturday night cooking for the house. All of the motion, the dynamics came back to me with delicious delectation, the genesis of creation, the palette of aromas, the melody, the orchestration (of gastronomy) were all mine to relish and command once more. This was more than just contributing to the organization which was assisting me in my endeavor to become self-sufficient. It was a honing and polishing of techniques which I'd need to be razor sharp in my upcoming reentry into my profession at the top level. Also, it was a long neglected inflation to my ego which was instrumental in developing the appropriate attitude of someone stepping into a position of authority and leadership. Yet, above all, it was a welcome sense of satisfaction in doing something at which I was accomplished and for which I held deep affection. And, thusly, my cooking at Saint Joe's served me in multiple ways to which I looked forward each week and when it was revoked, years later, for drinking, it was a kick in the arse by a faction that I'd served loyally, if not intrepidly, through thick and thin for years. Nonetheless, my early months at Saint Joe's were filled with hope and achievement.

I began carving my gourd vases (reliefs carved onto hollowed out butternut squash) up in my attic room during the evenings and keeping them wrapped in plastic film and refrigerated so that by the weekend I had four or five such, of divergent design, to bring to the Union Square farmer's market to peddle—Manhattan's largest farmer's market, the Green Market. I'd wheel the shelter's grocery wagon up to Fourteenth Street, complete with a large piece of cardboard to use as a tabletop on the wagon, and would drape a white bedsheet over it like a tablecloth: my little stand. Then I'd display my vases and carve flowers out of

251

radishes and carrots and scallions in front of the customers and make bouquets right before their very eyes. But it was dead winter and my wet hands were numb from the cold and, although I always had a crowd, I sold only a couple of vases, less than half my stock. Very discouraging. Nobody wanted to come across with a piddly twenty bucks though the vases were worth five times that much.

A major hindrance to my squash vase enterprise was that the city's farmers markets (at that time) did not allow crafts to be sold. All of the items peddled had to have been grown or produced locally. So where did that leave me? Besides costermongers, there were wine merchants, jelly hawkers, chevre dealers complete with live goats, breads and pastries—aren't all those crafts? After all, I was using Long Island grown squash, scallions and radishes. But I was forced to set up on the periphery of the marketplace, off the radar of the patrolling market officials. And yet, guitar players and small ensembles were tolerated. Bums never get an even break.

I settled into the most laid-back routine at Saint Joe's but, in reality, I was biding my time to get back to the street or, at least, to discover a way to beat the system. That achievement I ultimately succeeded in when me and Robin entangled our lives together and turned my First Street apartment into a crack house (description to follow).

All through my shelter life, even though I was making concessions, my spirits were high. I was still sidestepping the Establishment, maintaining my objective, my walk in life, as a professional bum. This was just another rung on the ladder, a necessary step in the total experience of street life. I would not be beaten. I used every facet of my new occupation as a brick in my fortress of resistance against a system, a society that had let me down or, however, in which I could find no contentment. I would make my solitary way and prevail in spite of all the obstacles set against me. A warrior, an explorer, a hierophant. I always divined being a seer, a paladin for the underdog, yet to gain the necessary experience to qualify as a street savant was a long and arduous track, requiring a great deal of bad living, of durance vile to accrue the necessary wisdom of which I would not trade in order to shield myself from experiencing those harsh lessons that street life deals so incessantly, especially in the bowels of the city.

My assets were formidable. I was determined to win. I would prove to myself and the world that one man alone could triumph over insurmountable odds and prosper. My emotions, so finely tuned, although agonizing, were my greatest quality—a barometer, a gauge, a water pool in which to scry. My attraction to things sinister and taboo, which had led me to the street to begin with, had an open road of opportunity as a bum, I felt, at least for one as adroit as I. I had reached a stage in my life whereby I could gain access, like Mercury, to the seedy and dismal levels that pass for life in this city and flourish there, not only an observer but as a participant, and to endure to cartograph a map, a route through the hair-raising chicanes of paradise—the sewers and blind alleys of America's greatest city.

After around six months of living at Saint Joe's I had saved enough money for an apartment. Following much hunting around, I moved into a studio directly across from the soup kitchen on First Street, which allowed me a gradual acclimation towards complete independence. And I landed a prestigious job as head chef in one of the tony new high-end restaurants on Park Avenue, which was molded in the olde Front Porch flavor; back on top as I was when I last left the profession at the Ritz Carlton and "21." Earning big money and an egregious vanity to match.

I began drinking almost immediately. All my enablers in place once more. I began smoking crack. With my newly enjoyed wealth, I began to realize a lifelong ambition, pipe dream really, of having my entire body tattooed. Over the next year I would spend well over ten thousand dollars on tattoos, attaining half body coverage. Complete chest and back pieces to start. I began shooting coke, drinking more and more. After one year, my work began to suffer. I was coming in late, falling asleep on the job, making inexcusable mistakes. That continued for another year until the owner had his fill of me and my act and put the skids under my industry, giving me the gate at last.

On unemployment—land of enchantment—I was free to run to my heart's content, purged of the pervasive helotry of civilization. I had no use for the straight life any longer. It took me a good couple of years but I would be back on the street once more. Along with flophouse bouts at the Samovar, the Sunshine, and the White House, as well as a second extended stay at Saint Joseph House, I was still winging it on the street for some six months before I moved, as a bum, into the Kenmore Hotel on East Twenty-Third Street between Second and Lexington Avnues, a run-down welfare hotel, the Hotel from Hell.

During my post years as a guest of the Catholic Worker, I would often roll into Saint Joe's after a two or three day coke run, so obviously wiped out and wasted, scoffing anything in sight, having fasted for the previous few days, and I'd get these pitying looks from the house staff as if in remonstration while I'd think, "Hey, I'm not here to live up to your expectations." Very few of the volunteers had the heart and soul for a vocation in charity ministry. Most of them were merely side tripping, doing their bit for the Junior League, serving their temporary stint to both salve their conscience and see how the other half lives while arbitrarily passing judgment. The true dedicated standard-bearers like Irish Roger, Charlie and Carmen are a breed apart, with hearts of gold and saintly souls. And they have my undying gratitude. Nonetheless, this is not to disavow the well meaning efforts and compassion of many of the prevailing Catholic Worker volunteers, some of whom have been friends indeed when I lacked such. Nor to refute the helpfulness of all such houses of succor, without which many homeless bums might very well perish.

Life on the street demonstrates how solitary people without families create their own network of friends and support systems for, despite their shortcomings, such people intuitively gravitate towards each other and devise the faux families that they need. Inventing for themselves the institution that is the very cornerstone of America. And for many whom houses like the Catholic Worker are paramount.

It was somewhere around that time, newly unemployed, that I determined to seek work as a barman. There were ample bars and clubs around Alphabet City and the East Village that I felt confident of success. From one watering hole to the next I beat a path, only to discover that it was the age of the barmaid; no place wanted a male bartender. Even a transvestite club had real girls behind the bar—a GLBTQ scandal. All the way to the tourist traps around McDougal Street and Waverly Place in the gay West Village I found only busty female barkeeps. Surely that was sexual discrimination. And the end of my dreams of free drinks and lusty lushes to procure.

First Street, between First and Second Avenues, is where I lived for about four years and it is typical of the East Village neighborhoods which it exemplifies. A relatively quiet street for all the wailing sirens on Houston Street, one block over, where ambulances and fire trucks are routed, and with the crowds of homeless swarming the sidewalks daily for Saint Joe's soup line. A mingling of declining tenements and commercial trade and traffic far removed from the surrounding skyscrapers of the metropolis; a ghettoized throwback whose like pockets dot Manhattan Island, where the rank-and-file order of New Yorkers dwell in the manner of persistent memories that keep intruding on modern times. The block was made up mainly of red brick and brownstone, five-story walk-up railroad flats, each with a high stoop of sandstone steps reaching the first floor, a perron, beneath which was a sub-basement whose entryway was a few steps down below the sidewalk level with doors and windows facing a dugout under the first floor soffit. Those buildings were both historic and dilapidated, infested with roaches, mice and bedbugs, were considerably overpriced and yet had waiting lists for occupancy.

My building was owned by two NYC policemen who resided on Long Island and I ultimately vacated the premises in arrears of my entire second year's rent which was seven hundred extortionate dollars per month. My studio apartment was on the second floor at the front of the building, facing First Street and the Catholic Worker where I'd lived for almost a year before securing (this) my own domicile.

A twenty-unit brownstone structure with conventional twentieth century size windows, not the oversize windows so common one hundred years ago in brownstones all over the city, especially uptown. Such were the few modern touches to my apartment house—new sash windows, self-closing glass front doors, an intercom system. But there all progressive pretense ceased. The interior hallway and stairway floors were of a worn stained linoleum, the sagging staircase a creaking wobbling relic whose wide turned balustrade of dark mahogany still evoked an inherent dignity and class far removed from modern dwelling embellishments, narrow unilluminated hallways, peeling plaster walls and ceilings in the public areas, with dark scarred solid wooden doors to each apartment (another throwback to a bygone era). And it smelled old and uncleaned; nothing you could put your finger on, short of cat smell—no urine or onions or cabbage—just a worn mildewy neglected aroma, stale and stagnant and dead.

At the closest (north) corner to my residence, First Street and Second Avenue, was a gas station (one of the few on Manhattan Island) and a deli (south corner) owned by Arabs, above which was an eight-story apartment house. There was a trendy bistro next to the corner deli (on First Street), Orpheo's[1], which specialized in cuisine cooked exclusively with steam (only in the Village). Next to my building, beneath the neighboring tenement, was a Latin social club (you had to speak Spanish to be admitted). Next to the gas station on Second Avenue was a dime spot that sold little else (other than coke), with a notice on their plate glass window stating, NO LUCY. Saint Joe's soup line (opposite my tenement) stretched to Second Avenue and the gas station. On the adjoining side of Saint Joe's (towards First Avenue) was a cardboard manufacturing factory with a loading dock fronting First Street. Next to the factory was a 24/7 bodega selling twenty-dollar grams of coke and fresh brewed Bustello coffee.

One day, the *New York Post* ran a story of a neighborhood grocery store whose personnel (three of them) had been slain; speculation being they had all been shotgun blasted in the face, so absolute was the bloody ruin, only to be determined later that the damage had been caused by bludgeoning with baseball bats—a barbaric yet effectual warning conveyed to the trade that commerce at that particular spot was thereafter banished. And, lo and behold, the address was on First Street. We all ran out to look and, sure enough, the coke spot was closed down. Never reopened, unlike many spots that get popped and are back in business the next day. Scuttlebutt had it that it was the police themselves, the elite, who had attacked the spot, a story which had some validity in the area. Those executions happen not infrequently when, for some reason, the law determines that someone has to pay for something that wouldn't ordinarily be prosecuted through

---

1 Now changed to "Prunes"

normal legal channels. The elite bust dope dealers and then sell the dope themselves. They recover stolen merchandise and keep it for themselves. They shakedown businesses and rationalize it as they are the ones who have to always deal in the ca-ca. They never consider getting a little more education and then changing professions. Why should they? They reap million-dollar returns from their dirty business; the biggest case ever during my own (1980s) street years, the much publicized Michael Dowd and the Seven-Five police scam—just another drop in the NYPD pork barrel.

Now, that coke spot wasn't forcing anyone to use their product. They weren't giving it away to school children. They were providing a public service for adults who chose to indulge in that commodity. They were business people, fair, honest and discreet. And for the tec op's to go in there and murder those merchants because it was determined that they deserved to die for offending the sensibilities of morons with a little power who can't even think for themselves without a rulebook is wrong, unconstitutional and plain evil.

The elite are a self-styled justice system operating above the law. They alone decide if an alleged perpetrator is too dangerous to entrust to the courts. They are highly evolved vigilantes, modern hypocritical moralists who are judge, jury and executioner all rolled into one final arbiter. Archaic American justice is alive and well in the twenty-first century. Every working taxpayer contributes towards his salary and may have a false sense of security in knowing that he's out there but beware that average taxpayer or their farrow doesn't step out of line and become themself a target.

Power and control are the name of the game and fear is the engine by which those ends are achieved—the old Black Hand axiom to demonstrate what can and will happen if you don't toe the line. With so much scientific gadgetry and weaponry at their disposal, not only the elite but the de facto government are always looking for new targets on whom to bestow their maleficence, be they foreign agents or their own homegrown constituency.

The prophecies of *1984* and *Brave New World* are within the lives of Americans today, having been subliminally incorporated by a paranoid oligarchy that has stolen the Constitutional rights from every American taxpayer. Big Brother is already in every American's living room, monitoring you, compiling data. Phone calls are scanned,[1] plastic purchases documented, bank accounts catalogued, library withdrawals surveyed; media manipulated. The Orwellian nightmare is already manifest within our borders. Land of the free has become a misnomer. Terrorism is America's latest buzzword, the galvanizing rallying battlecry. But if America were not the domineering bully boys of the world there would be no threat of terrorists. The American government has created a problem which threatens their own countrymen so as to guarantee their homeland supported dominance and control. They are so slick, and the mass populace so gullible, that the Fed can orchestrate a fiasco like 9/11 and get away with it. Heaven help us for we are in the grip of the most heinous devil: our own misguided culture's power elite, the superclass which has been obtruded upon by shadowbosses—government employee unions.

All this theoretical philosophizing and doomsday prophesy from a lowly bum. Why should I care? I care because it's my world, my planet, my creatures that are being victimized. The birds, the fishes, the forests are being sacrificed for the reckless, selfish greed of mankind. I am sick and helpless over this sad state of affairs and much of that helpless frustration has encouraged me to drop out, to become a bum to begin with, for I cannot move the mountain of insane kleptocracy and have, in a sense, become insane myself, another victim of our great American culture. So pour another round gang and fill the pipe, and let's have a toast

---

1 Using clandestine data collected from concealed sensors in mobile phones of over three million drivers, Zendrive reports motorists spend 7% of their driving time on their cell phones.

to a better life at our own expense. Let the chips fall where they may for I've got mine. This is our modern American mantra.

Across the street from that now historic coke spot on First Street was another bodega, Jose's, which extended credit to locals, and sold lucys (loosies—loose cigarettes), and also fenced small stolen goods (and always had a half dozen goons on duty loitering around the store—the San Juan syndicate). Both bodegas carried a full line of groceries. Between my tenement building and Jose's was Fun City tattoo studio where I received most of my tattoo work.

Tattooing is part of the street principally because it was (at the time of this telling) still illegal in New York City; that it carries the mystique of something taboo, a mysterious blend of Oriental and Occidental ritual and secret rites, the swashbuckling romance of privateers and true corsairs, not to mention its indelibility, stiff price and piercing pain. Tattooing in New York City is still situated largely in the Lower East Side and downtown areas from whence it evolved one hundred fifty years ago and has developed from the seedy, cigarette butt littered, unsanitary stalls of yore into a high tech, hospital clean environment operated by self-popularized artists whose rates reach a ceiling of $150 per hour. From the exclusive, appointment only, custom-work specialists to the mundane, walk-in, stencil jockeys whose walls are covered in standardized flash, tattooing remains an underground venue which still carries the stigma of the occult, the sinister, the rebel.

Having been outlawed in New York City in 1961 after an alleged outbreak of hepatitis at Coney Island in the late 1950s, tattooing has ben relegated to the back room parlors of secret locations, only to have made a recent resurgence of blatant storefront ateliers (one such workshop right on Second Avenue in the East Village, whose proprietress opined, "Nobody seems to care. A fifty-dollar fine and we're back in business.") and commercial entrepreneurs who advertise in popular trade magazines like *Tattoo, Outlaw Biker Tattoo, International Tattoo* and other high gloss pulp rags.

Additionally, periodic tattoo conventions, held around the country, are an occasional opportunity to obtain quality work in areas that have no reputable shops, or to patronize artists from out of town whose work one admires. Tattoo conventions are a unique experience with all the excitement and carnival atmosphere of a circus where tattoo enthusiasts can indulge in all the hoopla and visual addiction that this cult's advocacy has to offer. Live bands, booths buzzing with tattoo guns, shirtless people milling around wearing only their tattoos, competitions for cash prizes, refreshments and souvenirs all contribute towards a memorable experience. And it's worth mentioning, for those contemplating their first tattoo, a oft-reflected sentiment, to buy a big one as initiates frequently wish their tattoo were larger after the fact. Convention schedules are publicized in tattoo magazines.

Everybody should have at least one tattoo, deems Jonathan Shaw of Fun City Tattoo in NYC's East Village, whose studio bears the legend: "Good tattooing is not cheap, Cheap tattooing is not good." There's nothing like a fresh tattoo for exciting erotic hype. Flash your trash! And, oh yes, they do hurt—the entire tattoo bleeds.

Attached to Fun City studio was an occult boutique, the Crypt, that sold witchy, devilish talismans (rings, scarabs and aigrettes), whose keeper was a tattooed sorceress with whom I never had any dealings (she had a dog). In the middle of the block was a faddy haunt/whiskey bar, an *estaminet* that held an open house amateur night where anyone could stand in front of a mini theater and perform—sing, dance, recite poetry. I had taken up there one night and sang one of my songs, "Pea Soup," which received honest applause. At the First Avenue end of First Street (south side) was a kiddie park, fronted by a small cooperative garden. On the opposite (north) corner was a Caribbean restaurant, next to a juice bar, next to a small café that served a very good cheesecake (but not as creamy as mine). And interspersed along the block were residential tenements, a wholesale meat butcher, an overgrown vacant lot—house sparrow sanctuary, and a commercial gambling equipment supply that manufactured roulette wheels, felt-topped card tables and related gear.

Such was my block and it was ideally located at the edge of the heart of all the action that circumscribed the area known as the East Village, on the periphery of the nexus, a quiet residential street between two avenues and parallel to the main thorough-fare of Houston Street. During the summer months, First Street hosts two block parties, complete with live bands, stands selling homemade foods and moonshine, card games and dancing in the street. A pleasingly arrant milieu in which to dwell.

Those East Village tenements, for all their yearlong staid and stodgy gravity, would come out of the closet at Christmastime and transform themselves into a gala Mardi Gras glitz with straggly strings of multicolored electric lights hung (almost) straight down from every floor's random windows, giving the effect of an exploding Roman Candle. Those lengths of (Japa-nese) holiday lights were handed out free of charge to neighbor-hood residents every December, by a local charity group, with the condition that the lights be haphazardly thrown out of the windows on the street side to hang straight down ("The way we do it"). Surprisingly, everyone complied and the effect, other than the unique, generic design, was of a unity or solidarity that I found acutely emotive. The whole area, by that one gesture, became "ours."

The superintendent of my apartment house, Mattie, and his uxorial, common-law (junkie) wife, Marion, were right out of *Avenue D Comix* or *Bizarre Life* magazine. If you were to look up "dysfunctional couple" in the encyclopedia, they'd have Mattie and Marion's picture. They lived on the third floor of our tenement and you could hear their ruction and screeching throughout the building (Mary and Vinnie in *Last Exit to Brooklyn*). Marion had AIDS (very advanced), weighed about seventy-five pounds, used to be a hooker, an ex-taxicab driver, was on a Methadone program, made average crack addicts look like teetotalers, a sly flimflam artist, and she couldn't even boil water, clean or wash laundry. Mattie worked nights as a porter in a skyscraper in midtown (in Marion's parlance, Mattie worked in a "Building"), union job, made good money (but was always borrowing from the local loan shark), was illiterate, an ex-gang member, and hired prostitutes regularly for philandering (they all came over to service Mattie and make their quick Jackson). Mattie and Marion were completely codependent. When Marion died of pneumonia (from AIDS), Mattie intentionally contracted AIDS and wouldn't take AZT and died within a few years.

Mattie would yell and scream and holler and bang things and throw stuff and punch Marion—she'd often have a black eye and puffed lip. She'd rob him while he slept and spend his money on drugs. Mattie would trash and wreck their apartment systematically, lock Marion out and abuse her relentlessly. But he'd give Marion most of his pay for coke while she collected SSI as well.

Mattie would snap at Marion for the least thing. For example, Marion would ask me to, "Hand me some of that roast beef in the refrigerator," (sliced barbeque roast beef that Mattie had bought for her the night before). So I'd open the fridge, remove the take-out tray of meat and pass it over and Marion would say, "Not all that, I only want one piece." So I'd say, "Well, take what you want," and Mattie would suddenly shriek, "Marion, why don't you stop bothering people. You don't know what you want, so just shut up!" And Marion would lose interest in food altogether while Mattie fumed around the kitchen as I stood there, the straight man, marveling that those two existed in such perpetual turmoil and friction.

It seemed that as Mattie's rage brewed within him he was cruel to Marion (whom he needed), as she quivered in apprehension, and finally he would lash out at her in a fury (which she may or may not have precipitated). Then Mattie would brood, feeling badly and sorry for reviling Marion, yet he was awkward and unable to show his love or repentance (for by humiliating Marion, Mattie humiliated himself). At that point, Mattie was ripe for Marion to play him for a twenty so she could go out and cop a gram of coke. This was a recurrent cycle which those damaged people seemed to thrive on. Half the time, Mattie despised Marion (for her weakness at being an addict) yet it was transference, a displaced self-reproach for his being deficient in the qualities he coveted in his surrounding paragons; a *mal à propos* defeasance or dissatisfaction insofar as Mattie had much to be grateful for. Perhaps Mattie had a genuine chemical imbalance or some genetic lesion in his makeup which caused his fits of manic depression and bouts of violent psychosis. At any rate, Mattie was good for me as both a lenient building superintendent and as a friend who was a full-blooded product of the street.

Mattie's rent was free for his super pay. He would routinely give me a double sawbuck to swamp our building's hallways (a twenty-minute job) with a mop so foul and decrepit it seemed counterproductive. Between visits to Mattie and Marion, me and Robin, and Karen downstairs, there were always up to a half dozen whores in the building at any given time. Mattie dined at the Catholic Worker while Marion had Meals on Wheels delivery, though Mattie would also buy Marion prepared food from neighborhood eateries. She rarely ate though, all the food piled up and spoiling in their refrigerator. Marion was a very sick girl. Always had pneumonia, always in the hospital.

The best meal I ever witnessed Marion enjoy was she sitting on a brownstone stoop on First Avenue near First Street, attired like the atrophic house bum that she was in a wraparound shift, during early morning rush hour of demolition derby traffic and surly sidewalk marathoners, next to a busy delicatessen, plopped smack dab in the middle of it all, having her breakfast of buttered bagel and container of coffee, tearing bite-size pieces off the crisp-shelled bagel with her fingers and softening them up in her mouth with the coffee, munching with her toothless gums—that being the most I ever saw her eat in one sitting in eight years, imbued with her element (the bustling East Village), as evocative a bare bones illustration of the Lower East Side as is effable.

Me and Marion accompanied Mattie one day to his job site to scare up his wages (in secret hopes of benefitting from Mattie being flush). As we passed a midtown tobacconist, Marion asked me, "Do they have loosies?" Which cracked us both up as such a snobby, world-class proprietor would be scandalized at our slummy suggestion; loose cigarettes being strictly a ghetto commodity. After Mattie had collected his remuneration, and we were retracing our steps home, we heard, loudly, over the bustling din of traffic, "Hey, yo!" And Mattie responded, "Fuck you 'yo,' I got the pay." For that was the one time per week that Mattie was truly in demand—his wife, the loanshark, the whores all gravitated to Mattie for a portion of his hard-earned bread. Even I was inquiring if Mattie wanted our tenement swamped.

Mattie and Marion had five cats (four tabbies and a Siamese tom), two finches and a gerbil. Mattie was cold sober, didn't smoke or drink, but he enabled his wife and the neighborhood hookers with dope as a form of displaced directorship. Mattie and Marion were so bizarre they were funny. May they rest in peace.

I never seen a deuce of stupider people. Yet, for all their verjuice and doltish antics, Mattie and Marion were content together. Even idiots, it seemed, could find someone in life. What the hell was wrong with me? I would look at those two condescendingly and sneer, "What jerks. Pathetic." But Mattie and Marion, in their ignorant misery, were happy. It was I who was pathetic; though I would, with perseverance (and luck), make my grim reality work.

Marion was queen of the gaff artists, a natural born yegg, always chousing somebody, especially her old man Mattie. She was forever filching the cash he gave her to pay the phone bill, the electric bill. Mattie couldn't read (or write) so Marion always got over on him until the electricity or the phone service were disconnected. Marion would borrow money from Jose's bodega and tell Mattie she had charged food, running that scam into the ground until scotched. She'd euchre a neighborhood wench and the fuzz would come to Mattie's door looking for Marion and Mattie would have to make good on the snaffle. One had to be virtually Argus-eyed around Marion. If you were getting high with Marion you'd better not take your eyes off your gear or it would vanish like magic. She used to enter my apartment while I was out (something I cheesed pronto) and steal cashmere sweaters of mine and sell them at a secondhand shop. She'd also search around and set my alarm clock so it would ring unexpectedly and flip me out. She began to swipe my unemployment checks from my mailbox until I put the brakes on that dipsy-doodle mighty quick. That's just the typical personality, the character of all the street hustlers, the shifty dopers who learn to nobble anyone, any-where, anytime; it's just their felonius nature, Intro to Survival at the school of hard knocks. And naturally they don't trust anyone since trust is a foreign concept to them. There is no such thing as trust, it's a synonym for gull. I had a special tool (miniature melon carving gouge) which I used for scraping down the inside of my crack stem. Somewhere along the line I couldn't find it anymore. Months later, I spotted the tool in Marion's crib. "Oh, that's yours? I don't know where it came from." And yet, Marion and Mattie were my friends. I liked them both. They were real.

Neither Marion or Mattie had any teeth, though both were only in their late twenties; Mattie wearing a perpetual scowl, while Marion affected a suffering, martyred countenance. Two worn-out casualties of the street, still standing after most of their compatriots were already in Abraham's bosom. How fleet and efficacious does the street deal with its fodder. Where making it into one's thirties is regarded as a good run.

Mattie's home life was a disaster. His junkie wife lent a dissolute quality to their entire domestic endeavor. Thus, the only structure in Mattie's life came from his job, over which he had no control—he was merely a porter whose sole function was to move freight and remove trash. Therefore, at his leisure, off the job, Mattie found organization and community at Saint Joseph House of the Catholic Worker, across the street from his private hellhole, where he was welcome and respected. There, one could often find Mattie staging around in his gray job uniform, always keen to exhibit that he belonged to the Establishment, unaware in his self-estimation of how nuts-and-bolts of the city machinery he truly was. And in return for such open door neighborliness as extended by Saint Joseph House, Mattie was ever ready to repair a broken toilet or replace a faulty door hinge as the resident volunteers were more of a spiritual and less of a mechanical nature. And thus was Mattie allowed to take his meals regularly with the (Saint Joe's) house staff and residents, which is where I first met Mattie, who was instrumental in helping me secure my apartment in his building when the time came for me to develop that area of my life. As an aside, Marion was likewise welcome at Saint Joe's as Mattie's terminally ill wife, though she rarely put in an appearance there save when searching for Mattie. On her good days, Marion was still an attractive fox, a congenital rakehell and New Age bawd. The first time I clapped eyes on Marion and Mattie

267

together I was stunned that caveman Mattie could attract such a sexy wench. I was such a yardbird then and hadn't yet gotten to know either of them who, it turned out, were fortunate to have found each other. They were both good kids at heart, just twisted around by poverty and ignorance and dope and the slums—the perverted street which would claim them both in the end, those whom it had spawned.

Mattie and Marion's two-and-a-half room apartment contained a walk-in closet in the living room, in which Mattie had a little writing table of the like which might be found in a small child's room. One day, while in their abode, I happened into that closet and espied on top of the miniature desk some writing paper upon which were carefully written out some hieratic signatures of Mattie's full name, over and over. A penmanship exercise obviously exacted with great care and persistence. A valiant effort at learning to write his own name. Mattie I doubt knew the alphabet but had mastered his own signature, undoubtedly under Marion's patient tutelage. A touching example of Mattie's striving for literacy, which brought me back to elementary school and my own efforts with my Palmer Method workbook, under the strict supervision of Sister Mary Edwardine, and my struggles with the alphabet, the difference between "p" and "q," and the same sound for "c," "k" and "q," and the lilting jingle of singing my ABCs to memory. Long lost remembrances of diagramming sentences and long division and multiplication upon the (real) blackboard, of confusing rules, like "i" before "e" except after "c," but for weird, their, reign, feign, vein, heir, heiress, forfeit, seize, being, either, height, leisure, heifer, codeine, foreign, deity, weight, zeitgeist... of a child at sea in a grown-up world.

Occasionally Mattie would phone Marion in the middle of the night from work and have her pick up a sandwich or platter for his dinner from the Greek diner on Second Avenue and Fifth Street—meatloaf or roast beef. This order Marion would have to deliver by taxicab to Mattie's job in midtown, her reward usually being a Jackson so she could go cop afterward. They spent money like water. After a generous tip to the cabdriver, Marion would hobble all the way to Avenue D for her score because a girlfriend had come by and told her, "That spot on Avenue D that got popped day before yesterday is open again and their shit is kickin'."

Sometimes, if a coke spot changed location, say, as a result of too much heat, a counter clerk from the spot would traverse the neighborhood sidewalks for days on end, handing out business cards to local dopers with the spot's new location printed on it. One would present the card to the server when patronizing the new spot for the first time, as a kind of ID, so that they would serve you. If a runner knew you well, he might give you a few cards to pass on to your friends. That was one way of a new spot to establish a clientele in addition to the verbal junkie grapevine as alluded to (Avenue D) above.

In the outdoor macadam-topped plot contiguous to ours and the neighboring tenement on First Street, Mattie would sometimes compose planned or impulsive displays of his fancy. One such annual theme was his Halloween exposition. A sitting room tableau consisting of an area rug, loveseat, wingback easy chair, coffee table, and a honest to goodness gallows. Scarecrow mannequins were arranged dressed in both antiquated and modern attire complete with wigs and macabre masks featuring bloody lacerations, cracked skull, rotted teeth, hairy boil, and mutilated eye; one corpse hung from the gibbet; a full skeleton, severed head with gore and bloody hatchet, tombstone, a moth-eaten stuffed mongoose and cobra in mock battle royal; candles in candelabra... the gruesome works. The extensive assortment of scenery was impressive. The period vesture wondrous strange. The number and quality of hideous masks incredible. Such detailed devotion to nightmarish death; an obsessive predisposition imprinted by street life. O' Mattie, tortured soul, the shadowing pall that tracks us all.

Of another occasion, Mattie carted around fifty wheelbarrows of topsoil, removed from the backside of our apartment house (bordering Houston Street), around the block and into the fenced-in lot next to our building, creating a twenty by twenty foot corner "garden," about two inches deep, edged with gray two-by-fours, that was too shallow to grow anything, but gave the illusion of greater depth. Mattie the farmer. Sweet and sad in his heroic tragedy.

A sorry incident occurred early on in my First Street flat when, after Marion and her nominal sister Arleen had dropped around, I couldn't find my rent check that I'd hidden before they arrived. I was convinced that they'd filched it. I put a stop on the check at the bank and borrowed money from my job to cover a new check. Ever after, when I saw either of those two trimmers (who were often together), I seethed over having had my hospitality violated and been played for a sucker. Around two or three months later, I found the check in my kitchen where I had hidden it so deep that I'd accused two innocent victims of larceny, branding them with my imagination. Proof that I had (at least on occasion) lost my mind.

One day a conspiracy of our crowd were hanging out in Mattie and Marion's living room, sitting around on the floor (because there weren't enough chairs); Karen (character to come) was in attendance as well as a couple of local whores (to Mattie's delight), and in blows Robin (my future houseguest), the only one of us who was flying high, and she's brought a huge bag of corn chips. Everyone perks up as the chips are passed around and, as suddenly as she appeared, Robin is out the door, only to turn and reenter the room to (with some demurity) collect her chips. It was an instance in which those chips represented all the food any one of us might see for the whole day.

Some very special evenings I'd share with Marion. I'd creep up to her crib in the dead of night, scratch scratch on her door, she'd silently open up after spying me through the peephole, finger to her lips while pointing at Mattie asleep on his suspended bunk, constructed during one of his architectural joyances. I'd slip in and Marion would motion to the kitchen where I'd tiptoe like a feline shadow, to take my place at her kitchen table—my privileged space for our ebon flight. While Marion resettled herself in her corner of the living room, if settled could be used to convey the wired fidgeting that was her wont; in sight of one another through the opening over the breakfast nook, encompassed by a shemozzle of cats; each with our own supply of the magic white powder—two naughty children at midnight in Hannibal, Missouri. An intimate scene as we each joined and shared our private dope world, crack life, whisked from the seedy squalor of our poor surroundings to the Midas ecstasy of paradise, Nirvana, with the swiftness of an inhalation, of a shot, bang!, an injection of euphoria, soaring with the speed of light through space, floating, as quiet as mice (a misterm since mice can be some of the noisiest buggers). We'd better be quiet and not wake Mattie (the sleeping giant), trying not to laugh as we flaunted every law of Gott, clay and reason; rash in our cabalistic madness, as close as twins in the womb, our symbiotic, spiritual soul mating. Aye, those'd be rare and special shared times of virtue and sin under the blessed palladium of Quan Yin.

As tiny and overpriced as it was, my First Street two-and-a-half room apartment was a snug, sweet little chimney corner, essenced with a wayworn geniality despite its up-to-date conventions. There was a brand new ceiling fan in the living room and wall-to-wall carpeting. The kitchen had a vogue black and white checkerboard tiled floor and featured custom kitchen cabinets, spanking new. There was a small hall closet and the bathroom fixtures all appeared to be new. The airtight sash windows were all like new and the front door boasted a Fitchet lock. The steam radiator, though barely adequate in polar wintertime, was amply buttressed by the kitchen stove's oven (gas supplied courtesy of the landlord) which provided thermal climate control at the turn of a dial.

Although I never intended it, I systematically destroyed that household which, unfortunately, became just an innocent bystander that fell wounded, a victim besieged by the violent consequences of crack. At first, I started to decorate, going out of bounds, Andy Warhol's east side factory. A midnight ceiling in the living room. One wall was papered in a decoupage of newspaper pages hodgepodged in an abstract collage of doomsday headlines, all with an overcoat of orange shellac. Two walls were scrumbled in an undercoat of brick red with an overcoat of flat antique ivory, which I gouged away in swirls using the comb edge of a mason's trowel. I went on a scavenger hunt for furniture and picked up a flower print Castro sofa bed; a four-drawer chiffonier that I painted pink; an aged wooden desk with three drawers, above which I hung a large salvaged four-pane window frame, flush against the kitchen wall, a glossy erotic detective magazine behind one of the panes; a couple of sturdy wooden chairs (one in need of a replacement seat); an octagonal presswood end table with a cabinet underneath that I painted purple. I picked up black venetian blinds for one window and bamboo roll ups for another. The place looked pretty groovy, my heretical hideaway, and then went into decline as garbage and trash began to pile up when I started to drink and drug myself back into the Stone Age.

The accumulation of garbage grew rapidly, which included food wrappers and cartons from take-out meals, coffee containers, beer cans and bottles (some containing urine), glassine bags from cocaine and heroin by the hundred, used syringes and their packaging, candle nubs, paper bags, pizza boxes, cigarette packages, match-book covers, spent disposable lighters, candy wrappers, potato chip bags, soda cans, empty gin and *Cisco* bottles, baking soda boxes, plastic shopping bags, dirty clothes, empty crack vials, plastic juice containers, cigarette butts, uneaten food remnants, broken glass (from crack stems and shaker bottles), and mojo gear of every description including high heels, nylon stockings and underwear, skirts and dresses, gloves, wigs, makeup, costume jewelry, masks and shower caps, clothesline and plastic wire. There were pillows, sheets and blankets, including a king-size knitted afghan in a riot of bright colors, and huge piles of used clothing collected from all over the neighborhood. Empty wooden farm crates such as from vegetables that were used as tables, a couple of ironing boards (used as tables)... The deeper and more foliated the mess grew, the more fun it was to go rummaging through while tweaking on a big blast of crack or a bionic shot. Grubby company never felt ill at ease in that place, the OD Lounge as one of my houseguests (Robin) dubbed it.

One day, a neighborhood drag-in-the-mud dropped by and (amidst her obsessive persiflage) asked could she park a large plastic garbage bag there, filled with clothes, until she found a new crash pad. I assented. A week later, I noticed a foul smell coming from the bag. Upon inspection I discovered a melted, moldering, rotted half gallon of vanilla ice cream that was swarming with roaches. Well, the entire apartment was infested with mice and roaches. During crack runs, I'd sit at my desk on my seat-less chair frame, naked, and allow the roaches to crawl all over me and bite me (strange stimulation) until I had my fill, then I'd catch and eat them and spray myself all over with Raid, my crack cologne.

There was so much junk, clothes and garbage strewn about the floor that the mice could move about as through labyrinthine tunnels. One night as I sat at my desk with my crack, I noticed a mouse sitting up looking at me no more than a couple of feet away. Thinking, in my narcosis, that I could communicate with that tiny creature, I began to speak to the mouse in a soft squeaky onomatopoeia while augmenting my articulation with concentrated, canalized eye contact. I made peculiar friends as a bum.

My IV usage (shooting) really began in earnest in that First Street apartment. It started as an erotic clou and quickly took hold. It didn't take long before the needle eclipsed even crack or whiskey as my quack remedy of choice. Everything about it appealed to me: the needle itself (a contender for a hot crack pipe), the blood, the tracks... And it was faster and less trouble to prepare than cooking up crack. Not that crack or whiskey had lost their appeal—never—but shooting-up, by far, took over as the main seducement for me. I quickly became a degenerate junkie. And was always OD'ing as I kept increasing the potency of my shots. By the time Robin moved in and christened my cave the OD Lounge, I preferred shooting above all else. When Robin would come home with a gram of C and cut out a shot for each of us, I would watch in dismay as she cooked the remainder, wanting (if the choice were mine) to shoot the entire bag. And that addiction to shooting kept me hooked for a good five years, a period of time during which it's a miracle I didn't kill myself.

After a year of living in that grungy condition, and to appease my new housemate, I cleaned up the mess with the help of Mattie who dragged out about a half dozen ash cans of trash. We rolled up the broadloom, swept, mopped and scoured—a complete redd out—and my new roommate, Robin, was in the pink when she saw the place. "You cleaned up!" That's when we colluded and went into business, opening the place up as a crack house.

But in the early months, while I was alone in the haunt, I used to throw my cigarette butts on the kitchen floor, from the open bed, through the living room doorway, too lazy (or drunk) to get up to use an ashtray. The smoldering butts left a galaxy of burn marks on the white floor tiles that invariably had to be replaced when I vacated the premises. I also spray painted the kitchen cabinets with graffiti which, surprisingly, Mattie was able to scrub off; one of the lines I sprayed on the cabinet doors read, "Easy Does It," a mocking affront to the AA motto.

But perhaps my most noteworthy disaster was the fire. By the time that debacle occurred, my electricity (that is to say my incandescence) had been long disconnected and I was using candle power at night, my eldritch radiance. Usually, only one or two candles were alight at a time—a twinkle in an island universe of blackness—as the cost of even the cheap tallow dips could add up, especially (unemployed) when every cent went for drugs. At night, with the windows blacked out (to prevent spying eyes from looking in), it was as "dark as the devil's basement"[1] and, illuminated by only a single swimming chatoyance, a glimmering gleed, to say it was eerie is to put it mildly; it was downright uncanny.

Witchy, dreamlike and hypnotic was the candle-glow—shimmering nimbuses and lambent aureoles and waving shadows ever so compelling, evanescent and dazzling. It was often difficult to see well enough by the diaphanous argence of only one dip to hit a vein for a shot, especially when my vision was bleary to begin with and I was shaking to boot. Sometimes, I was forced to abandon my cave's caliginous umbra and go out into the actinic albedo of the hallway to shoot up. But occasionally, like when I'd first receive my bimonthly unemployment checks, I'd stock up

---

1 R. Garcia y Robertson, *Werewolves of Luna* /(Isaac Asimov, *Moons*)

on candles, buying longer, more costly tapers, spreading them throughout the flat, disposed like sorcerous lusters tipped with dancing jinni, creating a phenomenon that was nothing short of magical. The desk, alight with coruscating bougie, became a field of fluttery penumbrae moving in an endless whispering masque. Those were my favorite nights, forted up safe and sound in my spectral setting, solus with my coke, copybook and pen (I kept a crack journal), in the somber hush of the darksome night, the witching hour, with no one to bug me, spellbound. Those were the best of times.

On one noteworthy occasion, no doubt after a long hard coke run or perhaps after shooting a couple bags of D or maybe swilling a pint of gin, I passed out with a desk full of candles alight. When I awoke, it was into the thick, raven obfuscation and bickering fulguration of the desk and the abutting kitchen wall in flaming conflagration, smoke billowing and prowling everywhere, the desk had a hole burnt through its top and the kitchen wall was burned to its armature. Providentially, there was no smoke alarm, otherwise the entire building would have been alerted. I scrambled around in the smutching sloe dousing and smothering the flames, opening windows, and going downstairs to the front entrance of the building and chocking open the doors to outside, allowing a draft to draw through my apartment doorway and open windows. What a mess. It took hours to air the place out and it was the dead of winter. I remember being bundled up in my greatcoat, covered with blankets, freezing in the Stygian gloom of my lair, hoping the landlord wouldn't find out. Mattie came by the next day and observed the damage and merely shook his head, no doubt having seen worse accidents in his calamitous life, on his daily journey through the charnel house of his world, his despair, the ossuary of his faith, a small fire being par for the course in the infernal regions through which we all moved.

Another passing episode of note happened one night while Mattie was at work and Marion somehow jammed the lock on her apartment door and was beside herself with worry over what Mattie would do to her for breaking the lock. This, it so happened, occurred during a period when me and Marion were palsy-walsy for the nonce and so I volunteered to switch doorknobs, mine for hers, how hard could it be? I unscrewed her doorknob and removed it and likewise with mine and, shit, the blasted things fell apart like Chinese puzzles. I never could have imagined such a mess of little pieces, like the scattered works of a clock. High-tech Fitchet locks. There was no way I could reassemble those damn things. Mattie came home and went ballistic, an avalanche of fury. Marion suddenly puts all the blame on me (Pearl Harbor), she tells Mattie I did this for no reason. What a disaster. We had to wait until the weekend when the landlord came out to fix the door lock. It took him a good hour of fiddling with Mattie's doorknob to reassemble it. I didn't want the owner near my apartment (which was a wreck) so I never let on that anything was amiss. Forever after, I needed a screwdriver and pliers to open and close my door.

One time, I OD'd on a shot of coke and tried to get out of my fortress but I couldn't open the door using the pliers (I was vibrating so badly) and wound up in convulsions on the floor of my living room. The heavily tattooed domina in the apartment across the hall heard me frantically rattling the doorknob and sent her boyfriend out on the fire escape to peek in my window and I could hear him out there saying, "O my God," as he observed a vision of hair-raising jim jams whence I lapsed into a syncopal swoon.

As the success of our crack house flourished, there seemed to be an inverse relationship between the degree of activity in our humble household and the attitude of my neighbor's dog towards me. The more night traffic we attracted, the more ferocious the attacks by the dog which, lucklessly, reflected the bad vibes and animosity from that across-the-hall witchwife and her medicine man. She and her toy poodle, whom I had once been on happy terms with, had become a maggot in my brain.

Around that solitary winter period with the coke and the candles in my First Street abode, officially unemployed and delving deep into my addiction, my eyebrows began to fall out. I recall sitting at my kitchen desk in the candleglow, sweating profusely from the monster blasts of crack, and wiping the running beads of perspiration from my eyes and brow, noticing my eyebrows coming out in alarming clumps with every swipe of my hand. I say alarming for the simple fact that despite my rabid headlong plunge into the hellish depths of degeneracy, there still remained a significant remnant of the original old me, ever observant of the shock value my escapades elicited, evincing delight therefrom. I was amazed at how readily those tough old hairs surrendered their hold and just wiped away, my hemorrhaging perspiration acting like a depilatory. The few stubborn survivors were easily yanked out with some fastidious obsession. Afterwards, friends commented, "You shaved your eyebrows!" I wondered at the time if those brows would ever grow back, as my curiosity led me to the far side of strangeness.

I would become so numbed from smoking a lot of crack, its effect on the nervous tissue was such, so as to induce a kind of neuropathy, that it took something equivalent to an electric shock to affect a fried crack fiend like myself. Thus, the self-inflicted first and second-degree burns, then my custom, were necessary irritants to provide stimulation, incessantly of an erotic property. The tip of the glass crack pipe (just a tubular glass stem) was a neat fat little O which, when firecracker hot, lent itself to peculiar sexualized applications. One not uncommon brand, which brazen addicts would proudly or shyly wear, was the seared circular marking on the back of a left hand, between thumb and forefinger, a temporary stylized proclamation of one's irrepressible bent and dedication to crack sex. I've frequently noticed this mark on wayward birds about town and found it very arousing. Also, I've been caught out at work (at the Ritz) wearing such a distinct ID and was hard pressed to offer an explanation. Another prevalent area for this bizarre annular branding is on the upper thigh, oftentimes in a linear file of three succeeding circles—I've seen a few photos in assorted magazines displaying this singular manifestation: Hot, hot, hot! One step removed from some of those more routine practices of mine (including the singing of erogenous zones) was the occasional stubbing out, upon my bare stomach, of lit cigarettes (700°F at the core). I was the human ashtray, or subhuman as the case might warrant. How much more evidence does one require to qualify as clinically insane? My life space was a funny place full of weirdness and perversions. A real sicko. What irked me was being surrounded by crack fiends who kept their (displaced) sexual aggressions buried, refused to face the facts, and carried on in extreme frustration and denial. "I ain't no pervert!" as they jabbed the needle into their ravaged arm and lusted in secret and masturbated behind closed doors. What a waste.

Later on, when I expanded my cocaine addiction to include intravenous injections, I was able to broaden my masochistic pleasures through the employment of the syringe's needle whose naked steel was edged with razor sharp slicing blades, along either side of the sticker, by which I enjoyed ceaseless, lovely, inventive play. One recurrent amusement which I utilized with this cutting toy was, upon pulling out from a shot (overcome with the rush) and delusional in my hellish glory, I would indulge in scarification upon, but not restricted to, my arms by tracing the mirage of patterns projected there (as though with a planchette) slicing away until the rush subsided, leaving a trail of blood lines, sometimes of a design or, more frequently, an aimless vanity of chaos. I just loved being a dingbat, a practice I found safest to enjoy in private, always needful to be on the defensive when engaged in blood sport in mixed or strange company for fear of being victimized and assaulted. This is why those with whom I could share such teratoid proclivities did I truly cherish and love. Like Wanda, my Isis, my deified vamp.

Yet, to be honest, to complete the picture, for all Wanda's tolerance of my peculiarities, never once did I witness, either in fact or any evidence of, Wanda engaging in self-debasement or self-mutilation. Wanda was an inveterate whore, yes, but her profession was a means of supporting her drug dependency and of appeasing her somewhat ginchy nature. For despite being "like Vesuvius on the verge of eruption with a libido of igneous magma,"[1] Wanda had the heart of an angel. Her aspiration, if there were an overlaying or underlying goal for which she strove, was (I believe) to be the perfect courtesan or concubine. In these, our different ambitions, did we sometimes clash yet, for all that, did we neither demean or vilipend ourselves, nor did we indulge in any humors black. I always enjoyed a most kindred spirit in Wanda. Though "it was madness to allow our secret love to kindle within me, which could only lead into miry wilds whence there is no extrication."[2] Still, I wanted to jump the broom with Wanda at one point but I feel I proved too unstable and flighty. Not a very credent character reference for the sacrament of matrimony. Just another pipe dream to add to the vapors of the street.

———————————

1 Carlos Ruiz Zafron, *The Shadow of the* Wind
2 Charlotte Brontë, *Jane Eyre*

I had a couple of vintage, knee-length dresses, short sleeve, print, collared affairs, consisting of a one-piece corsage and skirt, V-necked with little circular glass buttons down the front to the waist, faded hues in brown and in grey, patterned and silky smooth of a worn combed cotton, very slinky for all their once proper guise. Either of those articles were my favorite apparel for evening wear when home alone in my OD lounge, seated at my kitchen desk, Beelzebub on his throne, engrossed with my coke and related agencies, the garments made all the more enticing by their repeated saturation with urine, upon whose crumpled heap I would contribute regularly, until they acquired all the rank odor of a subway platform piss corner. Warm silky aroma, extremely arousing to my atrocious, licentious turpitude.

I once was able to share this perverse fetish with a lovely damsel in distress on a fortuitous occasion as follows. I had picked up one wasted and forlorn young addict on the block, Michelle, upon whom the street and drugs and her godforsaken profession had taken an early toll and, together with a goodly supply of coke, I easily coaxed her home with me. I perceived at once that Michelle was pleased with the condition of my shambles which was a "very sink of filthy debauchery"[1] and, thus, I suggested, would she care to try on one these nice dresses?, which I proffered. Smiling coyly, she forthwith donned the raiment (which stank to high heaven) and genially acquiesced to the seat at my battered desk which I graciously inclined. Next, I offered her a shot of C, which I generously piled upon the cluttered desk and of which she demurely fixed up and, by my oath, which she made a brutal mess of, exquisitely missing (and abscessing) in her valorous attempts until the blood was streaming down her arm in ramate rills of erotic testament that, as she stood, all apologetic innocence, and offered up to me her ravaged arm to lick, by this truth we were

---

1 Fyodor Dostoyevsky, *The Brothers Karamazov*

both slaves to the game, "like chained maledictions."[1] My girl! And although I was convinced that succubus carried AIDS, I did what I must for I was vivified.

I needn't detail our ensuing bliss, with all that our bodies and needles and hot crack pipes could conjure, but that I think of that poysnous bosom snake to this day, and that she jilted me for a fifty-dollar bill which she managed to hornswoggle with deft celerity while my back was turned. I confronted that mazed minx on the street some days later, though I couldn't bring myself to commit battery upon her, even after she had confided to me that she secretly desired to be marmelized. I ran into Michelle a year hence, in Chinatown, a restored and rejuvenated magdalen, whence she informed me that she was enrolled on a Methadone program. I wish her luck. She was pure, right down to her natural blondie (which we shaved).

I experienced plenty of paranoia in that First Street apartment. The cop/landlord had an undercover agent stationed in the empty first floor studio, opposite Karen's, below me. We all knew this, we'd see him watching through his cracked-open doorway or peeping past his drawn window shades, but we'd carry on as blatant as you please in spite of it all. Once, I conspicuously left some empty crack vials in the hallway for the hawkshaw to find. When me and Mattie cleaned out my nest, I twigged the narco rummaging through the filled ash cans at curbside, in front of the building, lifting out spent disposable lighters and looking up at my crib.

I was always convinced there were spooks looking through my windows from the building across the street, from the rooftops, with their spyglasses and cameras. Sadistic Mattie loved to feed into this obsession by telling me, "The landlord is planning to bust you. They'll be stationed in the empty apartment down the hallway on a Friday night and at midnight they'll rush your spot."

---

1 Carlos Ruiz Zafron, *The Shadow of the* Wind

So I'd go through a period of hiding my works and stash under the stove or hanging out the bathroom window from beneath the embrasure but it was hopeless. We were always using in that place so there was always dope and paraphernalia lying about. It's amazing that we were never popped since the whole community knew that both me and Karen downstairs were operating crack houses. Like the three wise monkeys, the citizens of East First Street neither saw nor heard nor spoke. I loved that neighborhood.

In between extended runs of illicit drug usage (when I was socked in broke), my time was spent reading. The public library became my escape from reality, the egg in my beer—a phrase my mom used on us kids when we would complain, since we had everything. "What do you want, egg in your beer?" And when all else failed, I would read my dictionary (my *vade mecum*). "Our dreams are real / Our lives are bitter lies."[1]

There were a number of exquisite patisseries and candy shops on lower First Avenue, of which I would occasionally patronize, splurging when I was flush, for some scrumptious delicacy. On one such occurrence I purchased, from the Black Hound, a gorgeous miniature confection of frangipane and chocolate, planning to crown my day's end with its enjoyment. My only problem was in preserving that lovely morsel until late in the evening, safe from the depredations of the legions of marauding roaches that swarmed over every square inch of my humble redoubt. My solution was in hanging the wrapped tidbit from the ceiling fan cord where, dangling in mid-air, it would take the roaches some hours to devise the route to that delectable gem, by which time I would have dispensed with it myself. I knew that fumigation of my funk hole was way overdue.

By the time I got around to fogging that apartment, the roach infestation was lawless. I set off ten roach bombs throughout

---

1 Warren Carrier

the premises, being chided by the clerk who sold them to me for my substandard housekeeping (this from a shiny wog with putrid smile who looked and smelled as though he never bathed). The cloud of noxious mist throughout the flat was so deadly that I was forced to camp out in the hallway for the night, setting up a bivouac on the floor outside my apartment door (whose perimeter I sealed with duct tape), much to the amusement (and relief) of my neighbors. The morning after the holocaust, the litter of dead bodies throughout my abode would have rivaled the sands of Iwo Jima, a hellish side effect of paganish urban dwelling.

When I first moved into Trinity Lutheran shelter, and was working my lunch job as a waiter, I bought my first boom box, for which I was reprimanded by our liege Charlie for squandering my money. I was earning more tips than I declared (to Charlie) and would buy pot each day at the Queensbridge projects. I had a safe deposit box at a major bank right across from Naturally Tasty on Fifth Avenue where I'd make my concatenated deposits of my tips. I was making good money for only a few hours work—thirty to forty dollars daily, fifty on a good day. I was able to secure the bank box without having an account at the branch. The custodian in charge of the safe deposit boxes was an agreeable old soul who rented boxes to a host of limousine drivers (all Arabs) who declined to offer ID. But I'd hold back fifteen possibles a day for my pocket to spend on boo, ciggies and gin. Yet sometimes I'd keep all my tips, there seemed to be more than enough lolly coming in. For some reason, I wanted to be able to lay my hands on my brass whenever I wanted it—weekends, late night—plus, I never liked the idea of proper banks with capitalistic autocrats in control of my wherewithal, reporting my fiduciary to the Fed and so on. Thusly, I would walk across the Fifty-Ninth Street Bridge (en route to my pot score) carrying more dinero than I wanted to have on my person. So I made a cash stash on the Queens side of the bridge under the southern ramp coming down from the overlay, next to the massive stone colonnades around which grew a thick coppice of prolific vegetation in which I knew, without doubt, took place every kind of illicit activity, from sex to dope, by every scoundrel the vicinity had to hand. That was a spot that would be searched and searched again by maniacs who had nothing better to do. Yet secret my boodle there I did, digging down, burying and camouflaging over, where my nest egg grew and grew into a tidy sum.

One sunny day, as I reached the Queens side of the bridge, near the Queensbridge projects, still wearing my black pants and white shirt of my job uniform, I decided to change into something more comfortable that I carried with me, some neutral-tone stretch lace pants and an open back vest. I went into one of the vicinity's plenteous factories' rear loading dock bays and undressed, my carpetbag and boom box up on the dock and, as I stood there in my underpants and socks, a local two-legged mongrel approached from the street and I called out, "Whatta you want!" and he replied, still approaching, "You got a cigarette, man?" and I answered sternly, "No man, sorry," by which time he was abreast of me and he reached out, grabbed the boom box, turned and bolted. I was hot on his tail, we were running like banshees but the monkey was faster than me, boom box and all, and suddenly my ankle twisted coming down on a curb and it must have been fractured, I was stopped dead in my tracks. Whereupon the bloody eggplant had the gall to turn around and flash me a toothy smile. At that point, I realized that my clothes with all my money were back at the dock and so I gave up on the boom box and returned to retrieve my remaining property. I was so despondent over the loss of the boom box, complete with the "OJ's Greatest Hits" tape, that I limped to my bank beneath the bridge, harvested all of my savings (around one hundred fifty dollars) and went and spent it all on crack. During the ensuing crack run my ankle became numbed and I walked on it back across the bridge, all the way downtown to the shelter and, by the next morning, the ankle was swollen to twice its normal size, whenas having it X-rayed it was fractured. Put into a cast I was down for the rest of the summer, jobless and all. (A hindsight comment from the peanut gallery: that $150 would have easily bought a new boom box, tape and all.)

The inhabitants of the shelters in which I was a resident were comprised mainly of two groups. There were the officials of the organization, of which there was sometimes a hierarchy, consisting of a managing director with a compliment of multifarious subordinates and, then, there were the guests, the patrons for whom the house of goodwill functioned. Amongst the guests were, as a rule, the dregs of the street, the mentally imbalanced, handicapped, malnourished, schizophrenic, manic-depressive, alcoholic, drug addicts, AIDS and hepatitis victims, feeble and disabled, fugitives, sociopaths of every description. Desperate characters all. Often, the yeoman's service was to have the guests bathe, wear clean clothes, practice basic hygiene, as well as assisting with dispensing medication, cleaning up after the incontinent, providing basic rapport and counsel by which to learn about, reassure and assist guests in attaining reasonable objectives like, say, staying sober, seeking medical treatment, becoming employable. An admirable, necessary, usually thankless service that too often is only a recess, a pit stop for the guests as many are hopeless cases, lifetime victims of the street. Sometimes there were long-term guests among the resident patrons and, often, shelters would provide food, clothing and showers at specific times for the general homeless population.

When, my playing Cassandra's advocate, postulating the frequent futility of such charity work with Bill of Saint Joseph House, at the (first) time of my moving on from there, he reminded me that, "We succeeded in helping you," and I was admonished at my censure. That I wound up on the street again two years later has nothing to do with the fact that I would have never been able to land a top job in my profession, secure a costly Greenwich Village apartment, develop my physical and mental posture, and accrue all the necessary adjuncts that reentering society requires, without the protracted support and assistance freely given me by Charlie and Carmen at Trinity Lutheran and Bill and the dedicated staff at the Catholic Worker. And of those homeless victims less fortunate than myself who reap only a temporary furlough from the terrors of the street during their transient residence at the shelter, it is always a crucial respite that provides them with faith, hope and charity, so important, in however small doses, which bolsters their courage if not their overall well-being. And thus, the shelter system becomes an integral, inseparable component in the very stuff of the homeless and their exegesis.

To be just, Alcoholics Anonymous is as much a part of my story as is using drugs and alcohol. It is something that was always there, like the employment agency for a day's work when I needed cash. Likewise, the twelve-step meeting rooms were always there to welcome me when I needed to sober up. Going to AA is something that, usually, seemed to coincide with living in a shelter and was an anchor for my faith, like a place of worship. Many advancements in my life were a by-product of AA involvement, although I am not an advocate of AA, nor do I twelfth-step people. But during my years as a bum on the Lower East Side of New York City, I made the Fourteenth Street meeting rooms (at

Second Avenue) my home group and found friends there, as well as a girlfriend (the thirteenth step), something I'd always sought through the fellowship and was jealous of (in others) and it finally happened to me. Her name was Cathy and, ultimately, I was bad for her as I picked up again and tempted her to do the same (she refused) although Cathy was a (classic) compulsive personality looking for an enabler, a job I didn't want. I just wanted a party companion, though we did share copious fun and some sensuous moments. And the Fourteenth Street meeting rooms were always conveniently located as a lavatory stop and rest stop, to sit down and get warm or dry with a cup of coffee. And they have continuous meetings, so expedient for imperative moral and spiritual elevation.

One of the first noticeable side effects of sobriety was not being broke all the time, the ability to hang onto and accumulate money. During one such period of wondrous accretion, I purchased a pair of secondhand cowboy boots. I was so pleased with that new acquisition until, alas, one of my pet hamsters made a nest in one of the boots, chewing the padded lining to smithereens. He nested in that boot forever after. A worthwhile end use for extraneous clutter.

Unlike many of the downtrodden who mainly have an abject, downcast gaze, I ordinarily looked at the tops of buildings, at their trimming and embellishments, details that seem divorced from the contemporary architect's ken. Not that I dismiss the drama and majesty of simplicity like, say, the aluminum-encased Citicorp skyscraper, with its monolithic solar panels, the New York by Gehry skyscraper with its rippling waves of stainless steel, the marble-sided United Nations building with New York's earliest glass curtain wall, and Freedom Tower (World Trade Center)—New York's tallest skyscraper; or with eastern influence like, say, Frank Lloyd Wright's Guggenheim Museum, or the New Wave Juilliard School at Lincoln Center. But I redound with reverential passion by dint of the archaic pride and glory within the master craftsman's art in gargoyle and statuary, fretwork, tracery, fresco, cornice, frieze, architrave, bas-relief, arabesque, corbel and finial from Gothic to Art Deco. And usually the outer ornamentation is only the facing on the structure.

Having more skyscrapers than any other city on earth, New York is home to many exquisite jewels. From the top of the Woolworth skyscraper to the Little Singer Building, the New York World skyscraper, the Metropolitan Life Insurance skyscraper, the interior of the Cunard skyscraper, the mezzanine of the RCA skyscraper, the Potter skyscraper, the Lyceum Theater, the New York Public Library on Fifth Avenue, the Met, the Plaza Hotel, the Dorilton, the Dakota, and St. Nicholas Russian Orthodox Cathedral. The corridors, lobbies and elevators of the Chrysler skyscraper, the General Electric skyscraper, the Empire State skyscraper. The daring fashion of the Flatiron. The art deco Century Apartments. The Babylonian Jefferson Market Courthouse. The façade of Loew's Canal Street Theater. Along with quirky New York landmarks such as Village Cigars (store) where Christopher Street slashes Seventh Avenue—the *sine qua non* of the West Village. And "Subway Map Floating on a NY Sidewalk" in SoHo. Or the largest mural in the world in the American Express Tower. Plus the Empire Diner in Chelsea (renamed the Highliner), a giant step back in time.

Continuing with Manhattan architecture, building detail like the Chanin tower fresco, the old Grand Central Terminal façade, the vanishing tessellated mosaic work of the subways, including the secret cathedral of the subway (the now closed City Hall IRT station), pentimentos of a bygone era. Those were sources of endless hours of pleasure, right under the noses of every New Yorker, many too busy to notice all the incunabula that make

New York great. I've spent hours studying and contemplating the woodwork in the Church of the Transfiguration on East Twenty-Ninth Street; the interior of Saint Patrick's Cathedral on Fifth Avenue. And the Cathedral Church of Saint John the Divine on Amsterdam Avenue (the largest cathedral in the world).

I took day-trips into Brooklyn, walking the Brooklyn Bridge, touring the Transit Museum. And Manhattan's cultural exhibits: Black Heritage Museum, Museum of the American Indian, Chelsea Market and Gallery Center, the burgeoning Bowery, SoHo art galleries along Greene Street, random wandering, not knowing one gallery from the next, potluck—nothing I ever tried to acquire any connoisseurship in—pearls before swine. But one needn't be a chef to appreciate a good bowl of soup. Isn't that the beauty of art? The ability to touch an archetypal chord, to cross every boundary—the sound of music, the look of love. The entire city was one huge art gallery and I, the Norman Rockwell "critic," gazing up at my own reflection, holding a dripping ice cream cone behind my back. Skyscraper Museum, Tenement Museum, Jewish Museum, Fire (Department) Museum, New York Historical Society (museum), Museum of the American Gangster, Madame Tussaud's wax works, Museum of the City of New York, even a New York City Police Museum (be they ever so humble). Plus, downtown's ethnic and maverick neighborhoods (surrounding Greenwich Village and environs)—an archipelago of cantons, insular little irredentas of persistence that help signify our great city: Hudson Square, West SoHo, NoHo, South Village (no such thing), Nolita (north of Little Italy). Days spent in Central Park, the branch libraries, JP Morgan library, Nassau Street, the waterfront and South Street's Pier 17, the Farmer's Markets, three or four hours browsing *Balducci's* on Sixth Avenue was nothing, especially when the old man was still alive. Even trade shows at the New York Coliseum (at Columbus Circle): this took some ingenuity—either steal in or connive someone to bring me in on their pass. And the Museum of Natural History where I knew how to sneak in, having worked there in the cafeteria during the Pompeii exhibit.

Many of my cultural forays were made in sobriety as I bounced in and out of AA, through the revolving door as they say in the meeting rooms. But until Woolly and the hamsters, and Polly, sobriety was an iffy thing. For me sobriety usually coincided with residency in a shelter since few shelters will tolerate active addicts.

There was a time during my second stay at Saint Joseph House when I would have to deposit, with the house, a major portion of my welfare allotment each month (as a savings) from which I would periodically embezzle a sizable chunk and disappear from the shelter for a night (no one ever noticed as I was closeted up on the fifth floor) and rent a room at the Saint Mark's Hotel on East Eighth Street and hole up (with my doppelganger) smoking crack, shooting C and drinking gin until dawn. Then I'd crawl back to Saint Joe's like a thief in the night, up to my fifth floor hoosegow unnoticed, to sleep all day. If questioned, I told the truth. They'd heard it all already anyway so better I stayed out if I had to use.

In the earliest days of my peccant relapse into the dome world, while I was still residing at Saint Joe's, near the conclusion of my first installment living there and just prior to my moving out on my own, I went to cop a Grant's worth of crack near the south end of Avenue D (of all places), dressed like a yuppie in my six hundred dollar (gift) modish leather jacket. The grubby, loitering youth whom I approached had me wait while he ran to re-up. Like a lamb awaiting slaughter, I stood conspicuously on the sidewalk until, ten minutes later, I was surrounded by a gang of ten straightly hoodlums who instructed me to lie down on the ground. I complied. This was an electric moment when anything could happen; the gang, though predisposed to robbery, were ready and capable of rendering me anywhere from unconscious to graveyard dead. And, knowing this, my focus was on survival.

I was quickly searched and relieved of my script and, as quickly, the gang dispersed, leaving me lying, broke, on the ground. The jokers were bigger dopes than I. They earned five beans apiece and could have been injured (remember Bernard Goetz). Mainly, they were dumb enough to overlook the expensive leather jacket. I was lucky not to have been stabbed. Just another random lesson of the street where life is cheap and any ill-gotten gain or thrill is worth the effort or risk.

I had been living at Saint Joseph House on First Street for some six months, working for welfare in the mailroom at City Hall and moonlighting for a catering company on weekends, banking every cent, preparing for my reemergence into mainstream society. I had, by then, been homeless for around fourteen months. Having landed a head chef position for a posh new restaurant nearing completion on Park Avenue and having saved enough change to afford an apartment, in sobriety while religiously attending Alcoholic Anonymous daily, I took the plunge. Booze at first, then crack, and finally intravenous coke and dope. The free-fall from grace was dizzyingly rapid. How I managed to acquire a costly apartment in the East Village, start the new job and hold it for two years is a miracle. Within months my rent was in arrears, my thousand dollar a week salary didn't cover my drug usage, I was always borrowing from the waiters, had overdue tabs at the neighborhood bar and bodega, was constantly late for work, was falling asleep at work, getting into street fights, coming to work bruised and broken. That was the beginning of the end of my being employable and sociable, traits I carry still to this day. It seemed I was just waiting for a place (the shelter and privacy of my own rooms) and the means (a steady income) to jump right back in the beanbag.

One episode of note from that period, when I picked up,[1] soon after the commencement of my new job, culminated in my breaking the middle knuckle of my right hand; a major embarrassment as it necessitated four weeks of convalescence when the restaurant was just getting off the ground. A neighborhood strumpet, Pepsi, had robbed a half dozen kitchen timers from a Bowery restaurant supply, of which I purchased one for work; hence she cajoled her way into my flat whereupon I left her there to shower while I dashed across Second Avenue for a few drinks at the Mars Bar. Upon returning home, I found Pepsi asleep on my couch whence I proceeded to awaken her in a most sensual manner. The shrew came awake as nasty as you please and, resisting my advances, informed me that she was going to shower. I told her to, "Get the hell out," but she flew into the bathroom and locked the door. I was three sheets to the wind and fuming as I pounded on the bathroom door, which remained locked while Pepsi cursed me from within. At this juncture, the bathroom door was kicked in, I grabbed Pepsi by the hair and yanked her out while punching her in the head, dragging her, screaming, to the apartment door, where I threw her out into the hallway, stark naked, flinging her *choses personal* after her as she scrambled, wailing, down the stairs. My right fist's middle knuckle was broken which I did not discern until the following morning.

Pepsi later sought retaliation by enlisting the sympathy of a local Sicilian palooka, Big John, who approached me after the fact, inquiring if I knew one Pepsi. Of that hussy I denied any intelligence, to which Big John quipped, "She says she knows you," at which I scoffed, "She's got me mixed up with somebody else." And that was the end of the matter. Me and Big John were acquainted through Saint Joe's and I doubt if Big John wanted to muddy those waters by mashing me. Not to mention that

---

1 started drinking

nobody can take the word of a whore. During my ensuing recuperation, I made redress by attending AA meetings where I poured my heart out over the (I didn't mean it) domestic assault my latest transgression had led me into. Like a broken record, the same old sob story, save only the details and date on the calendar ever change.

What I sought on the street, as a bum, was freedom. Freedom from all the expectancy and laws and customs of civilization. As a shelter resident, at the end of my first year and a quarter homeless, I was in a position to not only reenter but to flourish in society again. I had every chance, the golden opportunity to regain my status as an independent scion of my profession's *corps d'elite*. And yet I found that, once more, it was not what I wanted. I did try. I gave it my best shot. But ultimately I had to face facts. I disprized modern Americanism. Society was no longer my cup of tea. I was antisocial. Everything was bullshit. Although I realized that, on the street, I had to make concessions daily—to forage, to obtain medical treatment, shelter, and so forth—I did not have to join the ranks of the working class, pledging allegiance, paying taxes, measuring up, fitting in, concerned with appearances. I did what I had to do when I needed to, the bare minimum, and that was it. All the trappings of society to which I'd been fettered—the nicely furnished apartment, air conditioning, a muscle car, club membership, quality apparel, entertainment and color TV—I now eschewed, were no longer wanted in my life. Many of those things would one day again be important but, for now, they were ligatures that restrained me, reminding me that my life was a sham and I wanted shut of them.

What did I care for money, for luxuries once I had what I needed to live. As Confucius say: "What the superior man seeks is in himself; What the mean man seeks is in others." For what did I seek? Would I mold myself after those whom I despised? "A man does what he has to. And sometimes, you just have to give up some dreams. As you get older you find out most of your dreams don't really come true anyway. They keep you going, but they don't often turn out. Still, without them a man never would amount to much."[1] How many people, I asked myself, ever get to do something like this—to just close up shop and blow off all past relationships and routines and start all over again. I was now sharing in the primordial sense of exploration, some atavistic adventure renewed with every step, this synthetic chemical metropolis of desire—my provenient destiny—a New York City bum.

There was a wonderful feeling in being a doper and a bum; of passing by, for instance, a heavily patrolled housing community and apprehending the vast gulf that separates you from them, and luxuriating in that expansive freedom, the freshening sense, first hand, of how distant you are from that nailed-down life-style of morality and approbation that must, ever vigilant, be defended tooth and nail against the likes of you—from which you ran for your life. Of which you chose to be an archenemy. Whose reproachful, challenging eyes pursue you as a reminder. And speed your glad flight.

It's funny because we all pay for the things we want. I remember one time, my girlfriend Wanda telling me as we walked down the sidewalks of Alphabet City and passed some gentrified buildings where yuppies now resided, speaking of the inhabitants and the high rents they paid, "You know," lectured Wanda, "those people will eat three string beans for dinner just so they can live there." Meaning that their rent cost left no money for food. And I wanted to remind Wanda, "You live in a cardboard box just so you can have all the coke and dope you consume each day." But, of course,

---

1 Elmer Kelton, *Pecos Crossing*

I didn't say that. I'd never want to hurt Wanda's feelings. And so, as for myself, I spent much time going cold and hungry just so I didn't have to work. Everything has its price. The trick is to find the right balance where you're satisfied. And I was resolute, determined to find satisfaction, contentment as a bum.

One of the tantalizing things about crack in the 1980s was its newness, both in originality, as well as being a schism in the drug scene, for all its other-worldliness. And thus a special feeling in belonging to such an exclusive group, being so set apart in society, like another culture or race, segregated, ostracized minorities, or worse, subversives, GLBTQ troopers, *enfants terribles*.

And, so, to be such a dissenter amidst the mobbed congestion of the city was to feel esoteric, singled out, and hunted all at once. Such was my stamp, my ilk, and I totally loved it. I was a new breed of dissident all rolled into one: most hunted sniper, a real-life war game, the underground railroad, spy versus spy, the war on terrorism, the war on drugs, secret meetings, safe houses, jacklighting, smuggling, midnight runs, shaking a tail. Rama of the Jungle, Captain Black, Lorne Campbell, Guy Fawkes, Charles Manson, Frank Zappa, Jim Jones, *Zap Comix*, crashing through my brain, slipping through a fifth-floor window in the velvet pitch. These were the switchbacks of crack, up-down, round and round as I head-spin, looking in a mirror, the magic eye sees all, making a run, a strike, divvying up, vanishing. With crack I ran and ran, flirting with opportunities, sudden death, coming and going, always on the move ... the city was my arena, all night long, daytime interludes, and night again, nonstop action, that special scene, the new hot crack scene. Hey!

Preparing for my interview as a top chef at a new exclusive restaurant on Park Avenue at Thirty-Fourth Street took a serious, concerted effort on my behalf by the officers at Saint Joseph House, especially Carmen, plus my new AA sponsor, and a sustained regime on my own part to focus my mind and energy in order to develop and project the moderate disposition of a sane and normal member of society, accomplished professional and enthusiastic director and leader *au fait*; to convince my prospective employer to invest the future success of his enterprise into my guidance and keep. And to pay me one thousand dollars per week in salary. Those were my motives for inducing my lapse into convention and morality once more, abandoning what had taken all my nerve and so long to appease—my heart and soul—being abandoned by my inculcated mind, all for the woeful lure of deep pockets, or the mean green.

In the mid 1980s, one thousand dollars per week for a chef was good money in a profession notorious for low pay. Especially when contrasted with a coffee shop or deli that offered little better than two hundred dollars per week for a counter man. Of course, the technical requirements between the two disparate positions were more than slightly unlike. Be that as it may, all this from a bum, an outcast and dropout from society, living on the street, addicted to drugs and alcohol and suffering from psychosis and paranoia and depression, invariably looking and acting the part. There was much work to be done, great distance to cover, to recover, not only to condition myself mentally and physically, but also to accumulate all the necessary appointments in order to create a veneer of respectability and the acumen to carry it off. This was a mega goal, to reinstate myself at the top of my profession, and I was resolved to succeed.

I attended AA meetings daily, faithfully. Took a fade and a do (haircut and style). Bought a Timex watch and wallet, tie tack and college ring (second hand), wool suit (brother-in-law). New shirt and silk tie from Saint Joe's clothing room. London Fog trench coat from Holy Name Society. Florsheim kicks from a secondhand shop. I had business cards printed, *très chic*. Adolfo cologne. To affect such *soigné* habiliment, such preciosity was as natural to me as is water to a fish. This was the apparel with which I had been raised, my natural element, my everyday attire for many years in my managerial profession. I was never more at ease than when accoutered in formal wear, putting on the dog, unlike some poor uncurried schlemiel who is uncomfortable when spruced up in a monkey suit, having to observe ritual politesse and decorum. Thus, the donning of such splendid raiment only endowed me with a confidence which subsidized and enhanced my cavalier image. I subscribed to a telephone answering service and recorded a singing message in Italian. I phoned the chef emeritus from "21" and prevailed upon him to speak with the new restaurant's owner on my behalf. I read cookbooks and menus and refreshed my memory as best I could. I centered myself and I prayed. I was ready.

I made the appointment for my interview. I arrived early, freshly showered, shaved and caparisoned. I was nervous in the extreme. I tried to be eloquent but my anxiety was evident. Yet I landed the berth. And the emolument. I was more discomposed afterward for feeling giddy. I was flush with optimism and great expectations that this job was the ticket to prosperousness and triumph. All that was required was that I deliver what I knew how to do best. A cinch.

I set about refurbishing all my tools. Repainted my toolbox. Scoured, shined and oiled all my apparatus. I would be making all the desserts; all salad dressings. I'd be making all the hot sauces, and every known hot soup, plus cold soups. For the daily lunch display, I'd make pâtés and terrines, as well as decorating whole poached salmon. I had to perform garde-manger alternately with sauté position at lunch. Plus I had to cook for the staff daily. And occasional parties.

I worked twelve to fifteen hours a day, six days a week. I had one excellent man whom I relied on heavily, Frankie, who knew the entire kitchen and was fast. A couple of my chefs were slackers as the following account illustrates.

It was Mother's Day, a Sunday, my scheduled day to open the restaurant and cook brunch, working the range unassisted— omelettes, eggs, French toast, quiche, my own bread and butter pudding. I had made a dinner reservation for that evening at LOLA to commemorate that special May day with my AA girlfriend Cathy and was anticipating the shift change at three p.m. when my relief, Carrol, would arrive to take over the kitchen for the dinner trade. Three o'clock rolls around and, as yet, no Carrol. By and by the office phone rings and it's Mrs. Carrol calling to inform that her husband is ailing and won't be able to report for duty. When I ask to speak to him, wifey informs me that Carrol is too sick to come to the phone. I'm fit to be tied, hung up yet again by that lazy, good-for-nothing blackamoor, causing me to not only work a double shift to cover for his worthless black derriere but, also, to cancel my dinner reservation and stand up my date into the bargain. So I tell wife to inform Carrol that I expect him to present himself at the restaurant forthwith, the alternative being that he can remain at home forever. Needless to say that I worked through the night, having to cover the grueling positions of both sauté and grillardin single-handed, my malingering, tit-ular sous-chef (Pepe) being on retreat in Puerto Rico with some psychosomatic malady, seeking a respite, I expect, from a barrio witch doctor named Ron Bacardi. Happy Mother's Day.

Monday morning and I'm back on the job as the sparrows are singing, plodding through another day of responsibility as I rack my brain over finding a replacement for my Abbevillian swing chef. The restaurant owner offers no assistance as the kitchen is my plenipotent domain. At two p.m. a waiter comes to inform me that Carrol is downstairs changing into his whites. I seize this opportunity, this *casus belli*, to vindicate myself and encounter Carrol in the crowded locker room where I apprise him of the actuality that he is no longer employed by this establishment, on which note that 800-pound decerebrated gorilla hauls off and punches me in the face, battering me back out the door into the hallway, succeeding in fracturing my jaw.

I'm next off to the hospital for X-rays, a process entailing around four hours and am fortunate enough that my jaw does not require wiring. Back to the restaurant, my face swollen and already turning a rainbow of colors, to be admonished by the owner for having offered myself up to that koolokamba like a sacrificial lamb. Moreover, I was expected to perform in Carrol's stead for the remainder of the evening shift, irregardless that I looked (and felt) like I'd just been hit by a city omnibus. By then, two double shifts in a row and having been passed through the meat grinder for good measure, I was fuming to put it mildly.

The following days found me moiling overtime as well, down in the courthouses at City Hall to obtain a restraining order, thence to the appropriate (police) precinct house to enlist a patrolman to accompany me to Carrol's second job to serve the papers, filing a claim in criminal court for battery, all the while holding my own at the restaurant as my face took on the hue of a pending thunderstorm. I had counseled with the restaurant owner seeking legal representation in my suit against Carrol, only to be browbeaten once more over inviting disaster by confronting the rabid simian unabetted. He (the owner) refused to incur a $150 per hour expenditure to defend his chef who had been assaulted on his own premises by one of his own employees. Finally, a month later, on the morning of my scheduled court appearance with Carrol, I received a phone call at home from the restaurant owner, inquiring if I planned to show up at work. I reminded him that this was my date to appear in court and how I'd arranged with the sous-chef, Pepe, to cover for me. Owner tells me that Pepe is bellyaching about being overworked and that I'd best abandon the court action and focus on my bricks and clicks. Thus did I forfeit my retaliation against Carrol and persevere on the job, continuing to perform Olympian feats of production and culinary gymnastics simply for, in the end, what amounted to be my considerable salary. Money, money, money, and it was all spent on alcohol and drugs, so miserable was my life, and my work efforts no more appreciated than as if I were a well-oiled high tech machine. This is what I'd worked so hard and so long for, getting off the street, attaining sobriety, rehabilitation, repatriating back into the body politic, only to wind up right back where I started from when I'd thrown in the towel four years earlier and retired from my lifework and society, thereby sundering myself from every opportunity which with result in the formation of all the rapprochement as are the warp and woof of our culture; an outcast from life's velvet. How many trials and errors does it take before the penny drops and comprehension sinks in and I break the mold of conditioning, sever the Gordian knot, and forge my own apostatized pathway, however hermetic or peripatetic. For two years did I endure that vainglorious torment and eventually was terminated. The restaurant closed its doors one year after I left. That was the grand finale, the encore of my professional career which, at last, I saw for the velleity that it was. My devolution with feeding the rich in quality establishments. Finis.

My Dad was always self-employed, disseminating the credo that he could never work for another man. I, on the other hand, had always liked the security of knowing that if I did my job, a weekly paycheck would be waiting for me. Even though I always harbored an aversion to authority, I spent half my adult life working jobs that grated against my bias. Until I found crack. For, if nothing else, crack enabled me to turn my back on a career which did not quite suffice—that, for all my entrenchment and its vocational appeal, was bad for my health. Hence my years searching on the street, homeless and adrift, until I too (like my pater) wouldst never again do another man's bidding.

Once I'd started on that (new) job and moved into my First Street apartment, I bought my second boom box. In unpacking the sound system in the outlet on Fourteenth Street, I was so rattlebrained, I discarded the detachable electric cord, thereby rendering the unit useless without eight D size batteries. I would sometimes bring the boom box over to the Mars Bar where I'd play along with my drumsticks on the wooden bar rail to prearranged tapes. At other times, I'd blast the music in my apartment while beating along on a hunk of metal, well likkered up, an intrusive serenade for my poor inoffensive neighbors. Eventually, as I became more addicted to crack (and more broke), I sold the boom box to the owner of the corner grocery store, as oily a mullah as ever oozed through the cracks of immigration, who tried to wheedle me down from my rock bottom price of twenty beau dollars (the cost of a gram of C), complaining that the batteries needed replacing. When I went to fetch the Saracen bossman of that Arab trading post at his dwelling place on the ground floor of my tenement, where the entire deli staff (and then some) lived, their door opened upon a scene straight out of the Old Testament. Assailed by a sonorous skirl of zither, tabla and recorder, there whirled in a dervish of choreo-drama one of the young Sufi tribesmen clad only in a pair of briefs and covered in a glistening sheen of perspiration like some revenant marabout, surrounded by a squatting clan of his trance-like Bedouin brethren. All male. Far out.

During my first year with the new chef job, in my new First Street flat, before I started shooting coke regularly, I would consume a gram of crack and a pint of gin on work nights. Those forays took on some bizarre twists as one memorable evening comes to mind.

I had been painting my new digs in a kaleidoscope of colors and had around a half gallon of green paint left. In my pioneering the outer limits that night, I painted myself green, head to foot, hair, face, hands, legs, arms, the works. Then, while the paint was still wet, I decided to go out and buy more crack. Into the hyperborean hale of winter's tooth, wrapped in my full-length Soviet peacoat (still naked and all green), I went around the corner to the crack dealer (an out-there cat named Twiggy), where the vapid, frost-fettered crowd exclaimed, "It's the green man!" and from that night onward I was known to them as the green man. Just another crazy New Yorker.

The refurbishment of my crib came about during America's gunboat diplomacy termed Desert Storm, where this country's brainwashed perdus were scrabbling to go abroad to kill some commies and wogs. On one of my living room walls, which I covered in newsprint front pages, were headlines that coincided with my own personal battlefield: JUST DO IT; BOMBS AWAY; TAKE THAT. The good old Fourth Estate doing its part to drum up patriotic home front fervor. There's no right or wrong. Only winners and losers. "From sea to shining sea."[1]

After I became an IV junkie, I would sometimes carry premixed shots around with me. One evening, I went to pick up my mistress Wanda at her tabernacle in the kraal on Allen Street, carrying a shot of C all set to go, priorly drawn into my syringe and zippered into my bomber jacket sleeve's pen pocket, the protruding plunger held in place with masking tape, my ever ready rider. The stroll was crowded with baddies, each one hard done by and war-like and, once inside Wanda's hut, a privileged guest, seated on her

---

1 "America the Beautiful"

doss, I was dead game of what must clearly have been a delusion, imagining that I was in control of a situation, an environment that was pure phantasmagoria. Therewith I unlaxed my wary vigil.

I had just done my shot and was weaving to and fro when I spied the enemy through the veil of the cuddy, walking back and forth fast, slithering black wraiths gliding like ghostly afterimages, casting their furtive glances past the fly into Wanda's sanctified chapel, clocking us, eyes glued to me because they knew they were eyeing a pigeon and were getting ready to pounce, while I registered all this yet was powerless to do anything to stop it, swooning and helpless as I was with the shot still coming on and real fear takes hold just before I'm hit and taken out... ah-ling-da-sa-wa-see-ee-ee-nee-yee-ah-wah-na-sa-boing-oing-nee-dee-see-na-ya-ya-la-de-da-ha-ya-ya-ying-yang-chang-sooki-ooki-you-ah-pa-kah-ha-ha-ing-sang-tong-soonki-inka-chaka... and Wanda cometh to the rescue! *Mighty Mouse*, my shero, chasing off those pesky old rapscallions in all her terrible fury. Saved.

For all my years on the street and in getting high, Wanda was my favorite companion by far, the one I truly loved. Pretty as a picture, the only chuck I ever really laughed with. A femme fatale. Tiny and pert like a sparrow, though for all her petiteness Wanda was a brick house, supple and firm and curvaceous. Strong. Always clean and neat. Designed and sewed her own clothes from trash remnants. Kept the nicest cardboard cote, all fixed up and cozy inside. Always wore high heels and a skirt. Made more money on the Allen Street stroll than anyone. My best (social) times ever as a bum getting high were with Wanda. I've never met anyone looking so good, like Wanda, so consistently living on the street. I've accompanied Wanda on many twists and turns into secret flash houses where I could not have passed save in her company. And I always felt distinguished in her presence. Wanda cultivated few, if any, close friends and I like to consider myself her chosen soul mate.

Wanda, besides being a holy terror, was fearless. I've witnessed her standing up to guys twice her size (she was little) on numerous occasions. It was a rare scalawag indeed who would challenge Wanda. Wanda was my maiden liaison on the Allen Street stroll whence I first went there, unknown, amongst the consolidated coke spots, to cop on my own. I had picked Wanda out from the stooging horde, an iris amidst a bog, and approached her with my query: could she go into a spot and score a couple of grams of C for me? For which I'd reward her with ten dollars. Upon giving me the once-over with her eyeballs, Wanda held out her hand for the green with which to cop. In and out of the spot in a flash, I then followed Wanda into the corner deli. When I asked for the drugs, Wanda required that I pay her first. And thus did Wanda honestly exchange forty dollars worth of coke for a measly ten dollar bill. That was the beginning of a long, loving, tumultuous relationship I will forever cherish; and may her spirit and soul rest in peace when she crosses over.

Wanda would get some strange ideas, natural for her but foreign to me. We'd be in my hotel room with enough coke and dope to choke a horse. She'd want to put crack into plastic drinking straw segments of around one inch and sealed at the ends by a flame—(homemade vials). She thought we could sell them and make a profit. Me, I just supplied over two hundred mint leaves worth of drugs, and even after the last nickel has been spent I won't give a crap about jack. But with Wanda, like most of the street's vulpine vamps, it was inbred, a matter of survival to turn whatever was at hand into cash; anything, as long as it was illegal, deceitful or underhanded.

Wanda would accuse me of things. I was once housing a local hooker from the stroll who used to be a barmaid at the Mars Bar. Wanda, scowling like an angry sibyl, would charge, "You picked Robin instead of me. It's because she's white and I'm Spanish, right?" I didn't pick anybody. Robin moved in with me all on her own, showed up one day with a pocket full of coke. Besides, Wanda had never intimated that she desired to be my housemate. Or, Wanda would come over, well supplied with dope, coke, take-out food, Little Debbie cakes, all kinds of provender. She'd arrange my living room into two distinct halves and say, "Okay, this half is yours and this half is mine," and I'd bite back, "This whole dump is mine and you can get lost." But I always felt like a heel after I stood up to Wanda.

There was a vacant lot opposite the stroll on the west side of Allen Street, near Rivington Street, whose chain-link frontage was accessible only to those, like Wanda, who were privy to its mystery. Hemmed in on either side by neighboring buildings, the lot was a full block deep, reaching through in the rear to the backyards on Eldridge Street. I accompanied Wanda into this cul de sac one day to shoot up, where we were completely visible from the front of the plot, through the fence from the sidewalk on Allen Street. It was a trap, with no escape route if we were spotted, the only egress being through the front whence we'd come into the lot. I observed as much to Wanda who blew me off with, "Don't worry, I come here all the time." In we stole, to the far reaches of the empty field where, in a dim corner overhung by a boscage of leafy boughs from some backyard shade trees, there was a small table of sorts, a wooden plank set upon a couple of rusted oil drums, at which me and Wanda stood. We each fixed up our shots, myself cold shaking a healthy dose of C in my shaker bottle, using some of Wanda's portable water supply, and Wanda choosing a bag of D, stirring up the smack in her trusty soupspoon, an old-fashioned four dram, oval, silver piece of cutlery whose handle had been neatly severed at just the precise length so that the top edge of the concave bowl remained level when resting on a flat surface. It was a unique, customized item and a treasured part of Wanda's dope kit. We each squeezed off, Wanda hitting only half the bag of D at first, leaving the remainder dissolved in her spoon, myself banging home my customary blockbuster of a shot, zonk, reeling with the surge, and as I gazed in the direction of the front of our lot, Mayday! Here comes bloody Kojak straight out of a junkie's nightmare, striding determinedly towards us, me and Wanda with the smoking guns in our hands and I'm like, "O shit!" I fling my works into the grass and knock Wanda's spoon behind the table while I alert Wanda of the encroaching danger as I begin wobbling in the direction of the approaching gumshoe who's asking us something in Chinese and I mumble that we were just leaving and, somehow, I'm past the dick and out on the sidewalk, moving away, fast, and here comes Wanda from behind, livid, wanting to know why I ditched her spoon and didn't I know there was still a shot left in there, and I'm like, "Baby, we were as good as busted," but Wanda's in a twist and, to complicate matters, the whole slither of protohuman saurians leeching round the stroll are observing the fracas (and I'm holding, still soaring in the stratosphere) so, leaving Wanda fulminating in the dust, I skedaddled out of there hell-bent for leather. I don't think Wanda ever forgave me for losing her beloved spoon. I feel really bad about that too.

Percy was a young black cat who had a second floor apartment right on Allen Street, near Stanton Street, of which the neighborhood whores made ready use. There were private bedrooms and the housekeeping was tubbed and tidy and Percy charged as much as the traffic would bear (not much). Percy's was primarily a hot pillow joint for the simple reason that he was renowned for squeezing crack addicts remorselessly for his own gulosity. One time, together with Wanda on the stroll, after we had just copped, too lazy to walk the two blocks to my own coop on First Street, we decided to duck into Percy's for a quick get-high. Thus we advanced, myself posing as a john whom Wanda had just hooked. We took a room for a Lincoln and were about to cook up the coke when I discovered that we had no baking soda. This required asking Percy for some of that product, which was a tip-off to what our business really was. Wanda was fuming at this oversight (my fault, of course) but she managed to connive the bicarb from Percy. Upon exiting the room, there's Percy, wroth sentinel at the door, holding a bayonet and demanding a sop for duping his lobotomized noodle. What a jerk. Like I was supposed to worry that clown was going to stab me after dealing me a flat rate? Hobson's choice.

I started renting out my First Street apartment by the half hour as a crack house. The OD lounge. Scary place where for five dollars (per thirty minutes) you could do whatever you wanted. The joint became crowded, six dopers at any one time smoking crack, cooking crack, shooting up. There were certain rules. No cruising; no styling; no squeezing the customers; if you dropped something, it was lost; bend down to pick it up and it cost you five dollars—"Hey, what are you doing? You can't do that, I'm gonna have to charge you for that."

I'd also let out the whole apartment to select slags to service their johns. This meant considerable cake but I'd have to vacate the premises (into the bathroom). More than a couple of times me and Robin pulled the husband comes home trick (Murphy scam). I'd be outside and Robin would come in with the mark. She had to have his money in five minutes because that's when I'd be coming through the door. "What the hell's going on?!" (to Robin) "You pulling this shit again?" (to the mac) "You, out!" Never failed. Well, Robin would pick the right marks. There was also one guy who made bogus Polaroid camera boxes with no camera inside. He'd make up the decoys in my living room and pay rent for the privacy and convenience. I even had transients crashing, to kip down on the floor, and paying; everyone always paid.

We made out pretty good there with our chicanery for almost two years. Free food from the soup kitchen across the street. Coke spots three to a block. And Houston Street with its taxi hub and ancillary stroll, entertainment dives, bodegas, crack houses and shooting galleries. There was a funk and spicy atmosphere around those stomping grounds—Houston Street and First and Second Avenues with their brio and hustle really was like a dream at the time. And, a singularity worthy of notice are the many (80) lampposts in that vicinity (Mosaic Trail) whose plinths have been plastered over by local artisan Jim Power in a charm-bound harlequin of shells, beads and bits of glass—a kaleidoscope mosaic circa flower power vogue—ideogrammic cairns of runic East Village characterization.

"The East Village is mystic; it is wild. An escapist's Utopia, it is what you will. And it withstands all interpretations."[1] Strategically situated near some of the most colorful landscape on Manhattan Island, from the East River's Alphabet City to all the ethnic projects and tenements down around Knickerbocker Village—Chinatown's eastern frontier, from the Lower East Side due west to encompass localized clannish and lineal (hereditary) slices of spice, the very extremes of the city, all profligate in their piece of mud, the very pulse, the heartbeat, the lifeblood of the street—this was the raging main through which I ploughed.

The manner of living over round the Allen Street stroll was very minute by minute, without any planning or foresight at all, with an overall air of *dolce far niente* (carefree idleness). One's entire waking existence, which was often incessant for days at a time, was directed towards getting high. Get the money, cop, get off. That was the closest one came to a schedule or routine. A corky lifestyle of sudden explosions and recoils, a quintessential happy-go-mania for the rapparee. Were I to have wistfully designed the ideal utopia in which to embark at that episodic era of my life, I could not have done a better job.

We thrived on the adrenalin rush of danger, fear and madness. But we didn't always see it, recognize it as such. It was more like

---

1 Julian Smith, *Crossing the Heart of Africa*, some words and phrases

an amusement park funhouse—close call scary, sneaky Pete tricksy, hurdling hazards, pulling a fast one—all designed to thrill but not harm. And that was the rub, the denial, the illusion. For this was serious, deadly business, one in which the odds were stacked against us and one in which, in the end, the house (the street) was always the winner. But who cared? We were players in the game; every trip to score was another narrow escape, every IV shot a risk of an OD, every kiss a new disease. This is what made our spirits soar, our enlivening exhilaration, our life of herald or peril. Cheap thrills, the easy way, fly now pay later.

All during my post First Street years, even after my installment at the Kenmore Hotel on East Twenty-Third Street, my roving of the polymorphous city intensified even if its focus became more narrow and concentrated. From Houston Street to Canal Street and from West Broadway to Essex Street and East Broadway, this geography included the fringes of Tribeca and the West Village, SoHo, NoHo, Little Italy, and much of Chinatown, plus the remnants of Polish, German, Irish and Jewish enclaves and a more recent hiving of Hispanicism; altogether lending that entire region a patina of surrealism for all its interfacial ethnocentrism. And containing myriad specialty food shops, the finest authentic ethnic foods from every corner of the globe. For, "New Yorkers think of their communities as if they were miniature countries with their own histories, rules, customs and identities."[1] A wonderful, stimulating, gustable sphere containing not only the haymarket hum of Orchard Street, Delancey Street, West Broadway, Broadway, Canal Street, Hester and Mott Streets, Essex Street and East Broadway, but also the slums of each ward, the Bowery's skid row,

---

1 William B. Helmreich, *The New York Nobody Knows*

the Village's tin pan alley, Alphabet City's urban tobacco road and the reduced sector from Essex Street to the FDR Drive. This was the world in which I was lost and found, a xenophile at one with his element.

There were a few bootleggers whom I patronized in Alphabet City, not moonshiners but retailers of popular brand liquors sold at slightly inflated prices by the pint and half-pint. Those distributors (blind tigers) operated at all times when ordinary liquor stores were closed, such as all through the night and early mornings and on Sundays. My most frequented bootlegger was a large, late night Latin grocery store at the corner of Second Street and Avenue B (a notorious dope and needle corner) which had an after-hours service window expressly for the hooch trade. My usual Sunday morning bootlegger, patronized before the Second Street bodega was open for business, was deep in a vacant lot on Sixth Street between Avenues C and D, not even visible from the street for the thicket of overgrown shrubbery, trees and fencing. There, in a small weathered wooden shed, surrounded by the Hispanic mafia, business was conducted as from a package store. An alternative recourse for strong waters was an apartment in a tenement on Avenue C between Sixth and Seventh Streets, whose proprietress (an ebony hag) I suspect was not alone in her crib. All three of those concerns stocked Gordon's Gin in factory-sealed bottles. Vice around-the-clock in my East Village vicinage.

First Avenue south of Houston Street becomes Allen Street and runs down to Chinatown. But unlike northbound First Avenue, Allen Street runs both north and south, four lanes in each direction, with a wide concrete median lined with towering maple trees. Within this island, this esplanade, is an unblessed cardboard settlement, lined by rows of park benches and an enclosing balustrade of ornamental iron work. And this section of Allen Street, this dystopian upas, stretching the couple of blocks between Stanton Street and Rivington Street is the stroll.

The Allen Street stroll, whose contumacious inhabitants would go about the cyclical chaos of their byzantine existence craven, dejected and sullen; clustered tares like vermin on the murk and ferment efflux of their lives. Or fresh recruits, the intermittent precocious young ingénue or budding epicene rarity, fresh to the life, just starting on coke, who are all smiles—impulsive and generous and fatuous—not yet jaded and made bilious by the paradisial world which has ensnared them in its tender trap. Every one of them isolable because of their inanition; aimless and forlorn and not knowing how to love. All the sentiments of compassion, of benevolence, of pity, all twisted or buried; unmannered, rough, intractable, as well as ignorant, thinking sex is love and then wondering why it isn't all that it's cracked up to be. Confounded by their yearning hearts which can find no outlet, no peace. Frustration building into an uncontrollable, destructive force, wondering how it was that they had become what they were, barely human anymore. Tragic lives punishing themselves for being the wretched wrecks that they are. These are the aggregate lost souls of the homeless, the hustlers, the addicts, spiraling down the Ruritanian back alleys of the city, the cold and empty boudoirs of the street, epitomized in the Hades of the Allen Street stroll whose Lethean waters are their only respite, and for whom death is a companionable kind of suckle.

Accompanied by Mattie one time on the stroll where he stopped at a cardboard hutch to speak with some acquaintances, he observed to me with ill-concealed disgust, "These people all used to have apartments." And I wondered, at the time, at Mattie's concern over the fate of those hapless forsaken. Perhaps it was that Mattie tried so hard, was so diligent in his efforts at being accepted, coupled with his lack of confidence for being illiterate, that he felt an empathic disappointment over someone who had shent that which they had finally achieved; the same upon which Mattie placed such high regard. And yet, for all his transparent sensitivity, Mattie was a deeply troubled individual, splenetic, truculent, erratic and dangerous.

The corner of Allen and Houston Streets was a taxi hub for refueling at the nearby gas stations on Houston Street between Bowery and Lafayette, where autos could receive a Whale of a Wash, and for parking and loitering, where cab drivers became prime customers for the stroll's trepanned trollops, the mewling, homegrown dope addicts whose endemic faces change every three months like the seasons, to be replaced by fresher, younger faces, gamines who just disappear into the bowels of the city: murdered, suicide, OD's, kidnapping, jail, nervous breakdowns, many become lesbians, some get beat up so bad that they can't work anymore and enroll on SSDI and a Methadone program, some fall victim to the final KO from AIDS. The Allen Street stroll is where all my girlfriends worked: Wanda, Barbara, and Robin—hoydens, harridans, harlequins all.

An oddity I'll observe here is how, at any given time, day or night, there could be either a flood of whores mobbed round the stroll, or nary a one for hours and hours. Why, one would think, did this occur? What was the reason for this baffling continuum, where (according to Mattie) when one had monkey grease, there were no tricks, and when one was skint, the block was thronged with strumpets for sale. I think it came down to the whores being lousy or flat-ass. When they had the wherewithal for dope, they were hole up getting high, until such time as it became necessary for them to go back to work when they would reappear, like a recurring golden dream.

Although the whores of the Allen Street stroll were the dregs of the gutter, when they dressed up, many of them were knockouts. For many of those girls were naturally pretty prior to burnout and, given a hot set of rags, some decent kicks and a coif, they could hook any cat who wasn't careful. Those chicks knew all the tricks, as the seasoned veterans often assisted the novices. There was enough business for everyone. After all, the seasonal turnover always left ample room in the ranks. And thus, the selection of whores at any given time was often a varied as well as contradictory mix, evincing the entire spectrum from fresh to ripe to rotten. A sampler to fit every mood and pocketbook. Although my steady girlfriends were top of the line, I too enjoyed the scuzziest of skanks, depending on my current level of degeneracy. From five star to closed by order of the Board of Health.

The buck niggers had their own camp. A strip of once pristine sward along the north side of Houston Street at First Avenue, now defiled and trampled into a multifarious regolith of broken glass, cigarette butts, spent disposable lighters, discarded hypodermic syringes, empty crack vials, and glassine dope bags. The once quaint, wooden, benches that lined the promenade have been broken up and burnt in open, rusted, hundred gallon drums billowing noxious plumes of acrid smoke in a vortex of ritual around which the resident contingent latrate and quit themselves like ululating goblins in the night, or dance like maddened imps, snorting their dope, smoking crack and drinking cheap wine. That once lovely, peaceful oasis has been destroyed, turned into a dump by the grotty black hoodlums who have commandeered its sanctuary. My apartment building super, Mattie, makes friends with them by bringing them things to burn—chests of drawers, wooden chairs, tables—whatever he can scrounge or steal from evicted tenants. "I'm a Black Panther!" Mattie shouts to the street, though he's a white Irishman (ignorant of the provenance of the militant black organization), saying anything he thinks will earn him acceptance.

The fierce black street arabs tolerate his presence because he's bringing them fuel for their bonfires. I once braved the roistering gaggle and tried to buy dope from one of the curs who just smiled at me as he snorted a bag right in my face (dropping the empty bag which spun like a samara as it fell) then turned back to their obstreperous shivaree. You could hear them howling, bickering and braying a block away. Always loud, niggers, it's part of their identity.

Although homelessness affected all age and racial groups to some extent, the new homeless of the post 1975 period tended to be much younger than their skid row predecessors, and they were far more likely to be black (43 percent) or Hispanic (12 percent). Such overrepresentation by minorities can be attributed to demographics such as economics as affected by the recession of the early 1980s, along with racial discrimination, as well as massive urban renewal projects which left poor minorities with no alternative infrastructure. And the imbruement of crack. However you slice it though, it was a foreign country out there on the street, particularly for a li'l ol' white boy of the Third Estate.[1]

In my purlieu of the East Village, Second Avenue is a sidewalk bazaar at twilight—an irrepressible spring, a sultry summer's eve, a susurrant autumn, a dissolute winter dusk—mortal souls strolling at leisure experience the Village; want to buy, to purchase something, a memento, to add to, to signify, to memorialize their endeavor, their plight. Anything will do. And thus the street beggars ply their trade, spreading out their blankets on the sidewalk, or no

---

1 Kenneth L. Kusmer, *Down and Out, On the Road: The Homeless in American History*, paraphrase and statistics

blanket at all, bums doing business with little more than rubbish, with no more merchandise than dreams.

A girl and a boy, together, yearn to make real their hopes and dreams, the moment, boundless, in a photograph, a snapshot of happiness, proof of a good time immortalized. And so the bums prowl the shoal with Polaroid cameras, "You look so happy, Only five dollah your pitcher." Whores read your aura for three dollars and do a good job of it for they are all clairvoyant, having the third eye trained and practiced at reading the *mise-en-scene*, a prerequisite of their stock-in-trade.

Second Avenue, traveling north from Houston Street: At First Street, the soup kitchen of the Catholic Worker; Second Street, a clubhouse for Hare Krishnas; Third Street, clubhouse for Hell's Angels; Fourth Street, a motorcycle museum; Fifth Street, a square gay bar; Sixth Street, a stroll with signs posted;

Seventh Street, a Korean deli that stocks one hundred different brands of beer; Eighth Street, Saint Mark's Place with its name-sake ancient stone chapel fronted by a quaint little green where buskers doodle and croon and Mary Jane and Coca-Cola are sold to cold-coppers; Ninth Street, Dr. Sally Haddock's Saint Mark's Veterinary Hospital (tweet tweet). And all along the avenue's community length, between its primary streets, stand the shops by which Second Avenue notoriously attracts both tourists and locals alike: Restaurants, some of them surprisingly inexpensive and cozy—Mexican, Thai, Indian, Italian, Latin, Greek, Ukrainian, Caribbean, German, Chinese, Polish, Kosher, Southern, Vegetarian (pareve); and Korean delis with their smorgasbord and attached florist; coffee shops; Indiana Market and Catering; spice shop; coffee importer; Indian grocery; Gem Spa for every magazine on earth, complete with soda fountain featuring egg creams; liquor stores; Cuban sandwiches; cuchifritos; pizza; gyro; taquería; cigar and candy stores; saloons; check cash; chain supermarket; meat butcher; Teutonic bakery; thrift shop; juice bar; health foods-cum-holistic center; bodegas selling lucys and coke; antique theatrical accouterments; Olga modiste; botanica specializing in the occult; tattoo parlor; leather shop; fabric shop; hardware store; laundromat; locksmith; pharmacy; barber shop; shoe repair; public (branch) library; Stuyvesant Polyclinic; Ronnie Wood's (Rolling Stones) art gallery; Woody's (Rolling Stones) nightclub; and rising above those commercial enterprises loom soiled and hoary brownstone and red brick tenements, studios and lofts accessible by narrow interior stairways up from the sidewalk. A drop in the East Village bucket, so much color, life, eclectic, eccentric, esoteric, vibrant, salt of the city, heart of the city, nerve of the city, real true everyday life of the city. A round-the-clock urban bazaar. My front yard.

Additionally, there are so many bars and clubs in the precincts of the East Village—First Avenue and Avenues A and B, along every primary street from Houston to practically Fourteenth Street. Each and every night trap unique and eccentric because they're East Village—featuring punk rock bands, female rock bands, transvestite clubs, biker dives, avant-garde cabarets, heavy metal—live bands in every hole in the wall; for "it's in holes like this that the real stuff is being born."[1] On weekends, the Village streets shimmer with the tremolo of the corners, like a poltergeist fog enveloping the neighborhood with a spell of mischief. I never patronized any of them (short of the Mars Bar) to drop my bread on such frivolity. I was already living what many of those (tourist) patrons were looking for: Dancin' with Mr. D.

---

1 Lou Reed, from *Transformer: The Complete Lou Reed Story* by Victor Bokris

My most frequently patronized restaurant during my life as a bum on the Lower East Side was Princess' Southern Touch on First Street at First Avenue. Firstly and secondly because it was dirt cheap, and thirdly because it was so convenient to my First Street flop—at the end of the block and across First Avenue. My introduction to Princess' Southern Touch was through a girlfriend (whore) who coaxed me there with the prognostication that I could eat a full dinner for under five dollars. Princess offered three choices: fried chicken, fried fish or pork chops. All were accompanied by cornbread, collard greens, pureed sweet potatoes and maybe another vegetable. The entrees and accompaniments never varied and all the vegetables were sweet sweet with added sugar. No beverages were served (BYOBeverage)—although on one occasion when I brought Cathy there and asked for coffee, Princess said, "I'll make you coffee" which turned out to be instant with powdered coffee lightener. Princess weighed around 500 pounds, was the color of ebony and sang gospel after everyone was served and eating. When I continued to talk with my date during Princess's performance, she stopped singing to scold me for being rude—upon which I paid my check and left (dragging my date after me). It was a small (20 seat) operation, always packed by locals because it was so cheap and good home cooked eatin'. And since Princess worked the dining room (taking and serving orders) in addition to cooking—an honest to goodness one-person operation—no tipping was required.

Other fair-weather bazaars to browse in the neighborhood that were always gratifying for idle wanderings of a few hours are: Orchard Street, between Houston and Delancey Streets, a pedestrian mart of shops and stalls with merchandise literally hanging out of windows and from fire escapes and awnings, tables and shelves of clothing, shoes, notions and tchotchkes blocking the sidewalks, encroaching into the middle of the street; a glut of objects, a riot of goods, a wild mosaic of color, activity and katzenjammer of sound; the Jewish stallholders hawking their wares where money talks and nobody walks.

Alternately, there's Eighth Street/Saint Mark's Place, between Second and Third Avenues, a hodgepodge of shops and sidewalk hucksters catering to the esoteric, the whimsical, the eccentric: costume jewelry and bibelots, tattoo stall, tobacconist-cum-head-shop, offbeat bookstore, flash clothing and *dernier cri*, too-too shoe stores, new take boutiques, leather, the occult, religious sex shop, novelty shoe repair, confetti-colored tables of used paper-backs and bondage magazines, "a Chinese luck shop where you could buy tables of numbers, systems for various games, jade charms, money-drawing oil or ancient coins that concentrated the good fortune of many centuries, as well as aphrodisiacs such as powdered rhinoceros horn and ginseng root compounds;"[1] a blazonry of counterculture merchandise and pedestrian activity, the peddler's blandishments gyrating through the jumbled crush of patrons, and the mazy Saint Mark's Hotel—a webwork tangle of rooms for all pocketbooks. Plus, Saint Mark's Hair Creations, three floors of far-out hairdos. And, for those tiring of the life, the sprawling Living Now meeting rooms of Alcoholics Anonymous, perched atop most apt courthouse-like steps. This geographic location was close by to where Stuyvesant Street cuts diagonally from Ninth Street at Third Avenue to Tenth Street at Second Avenue—the only true East-West compass plot on Manhattan island.

Next to Living Now, up an additional flight of stairs, was an office of some allied alky referral which found temporary housing for those attempting to achieve sobriety or related victims, or at least that is what I assumed, maybe it was a satellite of Alanon, I had never been in there before. But on a subzero winter night when I was strung out, broke and gelid with nowhere to go, I went up there and lamented that I wanted to sober up, could they

---

1 Stephen D. Becker, *The Chinese Bandit*

let me stay? There was one stern faced bloke at a desk and one frightened-looking woman with a toddler in the waiting room. The clerk looked me over (an open book) and said, "There's a place in the Bronx by Yankee Stadium, Take the Ⓐ train there," (the Ⓐ train doesn't go to the Bronx), and he wouldn't let me stay but kept on about the Ⓐ train and the Bronx and he kept asking me if I had the directions right and I could see that the bugger was just yanking my chain, getting rid of me, playing me for a chump, so I had no recourse but to back out into the hyperborean wasteland of the city to beat the street, a walking icicle.

Additional curious excursions, a fifteen minute walk from the East Village pale, will take one into the exotic realms of Chinatown, Little Italy and the West Village, telluric journeys to alien planets, each unique neighborhood an outlandish bazaar in its own right.

Catty-corner to my First Street apartment (at Second Avenue) was the Mars Bar, where I would often hang out drinking Singapore Slings, playing Sade and ZZ Top on the jukebox, joined through alcohol in silent or conversant coalition with the ranks of neighborhood barflies. During my first year of installment at my First Street bedsit, as a high-end piece of chef, dressed in my worsted slacks, cashmere sweater and leather jacket, I cut the rakish figure of a roué. By my second year (approaching unemployment) I resembled one of the area's blowsy bohemian artists. Jaunting on the funicular social ladder: bum going up, yuppie coming down.

Some of the regular crowd at the Mars Bar (all lushes) included a married couple, he a landscape architect, and she a computer programmer; a limousine driver who brought in his dog, a wirehaired terrier that drank milk out of a glass at the bar; a bald British real estate agent; a young transvestite guitar player (I could go on tour); a groovy guitarist (scag head) who had a solo act in a club at Houston and Lafayette Streets and was Mars' barmaid Robin's one time beau who would always greet me with a hug; a French sculptor whose girlfriend was another of the Mars' barmaids; assorted wigged-out painters; assorted punks complete with piercings, spiked Day-Glo hair and tattoos; a schoolteacher (I want a few intelligent friends); a long-haired, dark shades biker who rode a Harley Electra Glide festooned with a confounding surplus of chrome, mirrors and folderol; a couple of Chinese gangster hit men; Fifi (personality forthcoming); a couple more female impersonators (both of whom I dated), the one (transexual) introduction made through (Dateline) a dating service, which passed her off with the curious notation, "No charge for this introduction" (ho ho); a couple of real girls with whom I had worked at Indiana Market & Catering, one who had a pet parakeet; and the long gray-haired Cuban Mars Bar manager, Jay (I like everything, if I'm in the mood). An eclectic if not cosmopolitan group containing a fair proportion of eggheads as well as dilettantes. The place became crowded of an evening. Pan-East Village personified. On busy nights at the Mars Bar, when the electricity and fervor of the crowd combined with the earthy artistic ambiance of the resort's Zeitgeist, it took on all the unrestrained passion of those tie-dyed enclaves of ferly which give New York City its depth, its pulse, its very *éclat*.

At the Mars Bar one could view the latest neighborhood artistry (including the punk barmaids). The paintings of those uncelebrated local artists were, for me, pure and vital expressions of the city's New Age art world in Greenwich Village, long famous as a mecca of turgid sensuality and cutting edge innovation. The displays, hung on every square inch of wall space at the Mars, would change monthly, often a few of the same artists repeatedly represented, and were largely lurid in their permutations. One such artist, whose acrylic paintings appeared regularly at the Mars, a favored talent of mine, used his name as an integral part (often the focus) of his subject. This maven, Bob, printed his name in glaring stylized characters reminiscent of the lettering on Bambu rolling paper packages, and his rathe themes put me in mind of a cross between Andy Warhol's tomato soup cans and Bob Indiana's cardinal numbers. The first study I ever remember noticing was nothing more than a colorful canvas boldly proclaiming: It's Bob. The following canvas I recall showed two yellow smiley faces (ideograms), the topmost face (in usual smiley fashion) with the caption: Before Bob. Below was an identical face save the mouth turned downward in a frown and the normal button eyes were X's, conveying a blotto visage with the caption: After Bob. Later on, there appeared a canvas depicting a collage of haphazard domestic and garmenture images, deviantly bursting with the unclean tinctures of corporeity, which could have reflected a mad dreamscape, perhaps the artist's real or imagine habitat, nonetheless psychologically revealing, in which was prominently flaunted, Bob, in a bewitchingly tantalizing and suggestive manner. The subsequent paintings progressed in this vein, growing gradually more intricate and Freudian until, over a year gone by, there appeared a scene of a girl (?) in a one-piece swimsuit and bathing cap, sitting on a Turkish towel (leaning slightly back on one arm with one leg contracted and bent at the knee) on a cement terrace beside a small, blue, sunken swimming pool with a blasé *Beaver Cleaver*[1] family in the background (kids with beach ball, Mom couchant on a cheap *Woolworth's* chaise lounge, Pop in boxer swim trunks complete with thick glasses and briar), enclosed by a chain-link fence adjoining a cheesy motel (Bates Motel?), with the caption: "Real life with Bob," which (following the sequential themes over the preceding months) suggested, to me, gender reassignment surgery (or facial surgery and breast implants) by none other than Bob him/herself. May the force be with Bob, whose twisted work invoked certain of my tortured, erotic sympathies.

Moving along at the Mars Bar, one showing by a talented painter of the gritty, renegade Ashcan school (who I believe moved on to

---

1 TV sitcom, *Leave It to Beaver*

notoriety) was a series (in oils) of urban street scenes in which a number of studies actually employed garbage cans as their focus. Washed-out backgrounds of ghetto storefronts, save that the old-fashioned covered garbage cans were painted bright green so as to jump out at the viewer. In other works, paper money was the focus, involving street action such as a bright green banknote being slapped from one black pimp's hand to another's as in the manner of a give-me-a-five handshake; another study showed a gigolo lighting a cigarette with a flaming bright green banknote in the face of an astonished lady passerby. I was intrigued by those genuine renditions of city street scenes.

Often, neighborhood painters and sculptors would bring their latest creations into the Mars and set them on the bar or a table, sometimes passing them around from hand to hand. I once bought, for twenty dollars (a steal), a scrapbook of India ink drawings by a bellwether and obviously disturbed artist whom I'd gotten to know at the Mars—those drawings were the stuff of shpilkes and shirty nightmares. Such vaward of the art world would never make it to the pantheon of galleries in Chelsea or SoHo, yet, for me, they were the genuine article of modern urban America; starving beatniks literally living for their art and displaying it in seedy hovels, selling it for a meal.

And I, in my itinerant street life was living it, an undiscovered rogue work of art, some imaginary New Wave artisan with a mad desire to capture the authentic spirit of life; adding my life essence, my genius, my *élan vital* to the licentious flame of our current urban times. For aren't all of our culture's outcast behaviors but manifestations of displaced sexual aggressions? Bank robbers, cat burglars, smugglers, confidence men, gamblers, counterfeiters, hackers, grand auto thieves, gigolos, courtesans, they all document the pages of psychology texts and contribute grist to the hypotheses of those experts who would invent work—a profession—for themselves. And yet, in the same breath, society accepts the day

trader, athlete, jet pilot, astronomer, clergy, rocket scientist, surveillance detective, fashion designer, hairdresser, plastic surgeon,
astronaut, submariner. Those are celebrated professions though no
less displaced in their dichotomy than their ostracized counterparts.
And can I, in all my ostracized, dichotomous artifice transpose
my experience into a testament, a fusion of poetic and noetic
prose, a virulent prescient ennui that might endure on a shelf in
a hovel in Greenwich Village, a permutation or merely a signpost
of our times.

One barmaid in particular at the Mars Bar, Gina, an exotic so
perfect one might think she was synthetic, always had the place
packed when she worked. I'd sell her cartons of Marlboros (for
twenty smackers, plucked from the register) procured on credit
from the Muslim Shiites across Second Avenue on nights when
I was strung out broke, then copping four caps of rock on the
corner before crossing back to my crib. "Cigarette man!" the fox
would cry as soon as she saw me walk through the door. That
scam lasted until the Bedouin bossman cut me off, knowing that
I smoked Camels and smelling "something rotten in the state of
Denmark"[1] with my charging ten packs of Marlboros every night.
Those snide bandogs would pad my bill every week anyhow, the
usury levied for running an account there.

Some nights at the Mars Bar, after the joint had (officially)
closed for business (4 a.m.) and shut the door, when the last of the
vulgar masses had dispatched last call and gone home (and when
Jay wasn't there), around six of us hard-core regulars would remain
and the dive would turn into a shebeen. Those were roistering
times reminiscent (I imagine) of the wild west when bottles of
liquor would be placed on the bar and we one-toke-over-the-line
alcoholics could help ourselves, when bawdy cracks and prattle
were blatantly hurled at the barmaid turned B-girl while she raked

---

1 Shakespeare, *Hamlet*

in enormous tips, lusty mercenary that she was, having shed her T-shirt and working in bra or topless. Those were sublime occasions (for those of us who could remember them).

One afternoon at the Mars Bar, I was conversing at the bar with a fellow regular, a schoolteacher, when he learned that former Mars barmaid, Robin, was my houseguest. "She's selling her body!" the educator exclaimed, as if such were a close-lipped scandal of which I should be made aware. When I remarked that Robin could do whatever she pleased, the nerd proclaimed, "You're her pimp!" And I just took one last look at that jerk and turned away. There's always some doggy with their nose up someone else's arse. That guy was probably Robin's first customer.

On the street it always winds up shit with those worthless hophead chicks, it's just a matter of when. You can't trust a junkie or a whore and Robin was both. So I can't blame her for running her subliminal game on me; I left myself wide open for her treachery. I wasn't firm enough with Robin, not ruthless enough, not sadistic enough to keep her in line. I didn't have the right stuff of a true pimp, I was too kindhearted or just plain lazy. Robin had me pinned for the soft touch that I was and she kept pushing till I snapped. We had such a smooth operation going there for awhile and then, somehow reflexively, we became like a uroborous (the self-devouring snake), recreating the cycle of our lives—of the street.

On the day Robin showed up at my First Street apartment and offered to move in, I was just leaving for detox, as I was strung out broke, with no prospects of income for a week until my unemployment checks arrived. And Robin offered to keep me high in exchange for shelter for herself. It was winter and life on the street, homeless, during winter can be mighty tough.

Of course I agreed, I was only going to detox out of desperation, not for any desire to be sober. And Robin was a Grade A barn burner, not long on the street and just starting to shoot so she still had her youthful bloom, a freshness which could be preserved indefinitely with proper enabling. A foursquare pixie, Robin was a practical investment.

The Catholic Worker was directly across the street from my abode for free food, clothes and sundries as I still had a front door key from when I had lived and cooked there. Robin was streetwise and with her sultry looks and ambition she could pull in a bundle every day. And that was how it started. With me, she was sequacious and unctuous, endeavoring in her feeble tendencies to be convivial. She would come back to the apartment every hour or two, a returning tide after the ebb, and we'd both get high, then she'd go out again, make a quick twenty, forty, fifty bucks, cop, return to gas up, out again. I'd have food ready and waiting, fresh clothes, toilet articles laid out. This would go on nonstop for days on end until we both passed out for a day or so, then the pattern would start over again. It was perfect for both of us. Robin also kept me in cigarettes and cheap wine when I could inveigle it out of her. I had keys made for her to the building and the apartment. I would cajole toiletries from the Catholic Worker, as well as bedsheets and towels. I kept the flat clean, it had been trashed when Robin moved in, although it retained the tag OD lounge. And every two weeks I would receive five hundred heavenly blessings from unemployment at which time Robin would refrain from working for as long as that ooftish lasted (two days).

Robin's act for her work was predominantly fellatio. Performed in hot pillow cribs or in taxis remotely parked (the drivers knew where). The stroll on Allen Street (the whores' business promenade), one block south and east of my apartment building, was a conflux of taxi routes, the cabdrivers invariably Hindu or Sikh, whom all the erring sisters liked to service because they would climax right away. A chick like Robin (or Wanda or Barbara) who were clean and pretty would earn twenty bucks a pop easily. As their looks, appearance and overall style deteriorate, as they will from hard living, fear and drug abuse, they are reduced, in decrements, to trey bag hookers.

During one evening's festivities at the OD lounge, as I passed through the kitchen en route to the head, I spotted this cat Ronnie, who occasioned the premises, a friend (and customer) of Robin's, as he crouched against a wall in the gloom like some grotesque caryatid, wild-eyed and frantic, gamely attempting to inject himself with a syringe whose needle was bent at a right angle to the barrel. I was momentarily struck dumb by this grim feat of desperation, made the more inconsonant for Ronnie's usual blithe and swaggering manner. He was a pensioning dope fiend whom Robin would hook regularly as he made his recurrent foray from his uptown men's resident hotel down to Chinatown where he received his daily Methadone ration. He would occasionally stop in our crack house and feign ingratiation while he boasted of his past heroics—"I'm a second story man," Yada, yada—posturing around while he appraised our humble cottage industry with a discerning eye. Once in a month of Sundays Ronnie would bring over some junk he scavenged from the street—old clothes, a battered lamp (we had no electricity)—as though such largess would excuse him from squaring the five blunt cover charge for customers because he was only paying a social call. Just another dead rat that I allowed the cat to drag in. To be fair though, Ronnie did once contribute ten dollars on a frigid arctic morning when me and Robin were strung out broke. And, another time, he gave me a shot of C when I barged in on the two (Robin and Ronnie) having a jittery bender in the jakes downstairs at Karen's. I suspect that was the shot whereby I contracted hepatitis, only a guess but sometimes you intuitively know things, like when a woman apprehends the moment of conception. My baby.

327

Ours was less a proper crack house—meaning we didn't sell crack, one had to supply their own drugs—but more a crack usage spot or flash house and shooting gallery. Addicts always needed a safe haven in which to employ their dope, especially in cold and inclement weather. There were always goings-on at our walkup, the door and intercom buzzing constantly, feet tramping on the stairs, a dead giveaway to the neighbors; day and night some of the seediest chancers, hoods and two-timers on the block; all one needed was the five beano cover charge and our door opened. Many of our clientele were steady customers and some were wayfarers just stopping in to scope the place out. Every last one a hardened career doper, every one desperate and dangerous. The atmosphere was rarely cheery, rather the climate was edgy, what with everyone clocking each other, keeping track of the dwindling drug supply and concentrating on how to transfer some of yours to theirs, myself and Robin key players in our own scam.

Mattie was a frequent visitor, vicariously enjoying the show of pathetic addicts revealing the worthlessness of their escapades— perhaps such a display allowed Mattie to feel superior in the shadow of his own impotence, feeding off of the weakness of others, as well as relentlessly shopping for new whores to dominate (Mattie being the only one permitted such blatant conduct in our humble harborage—gratification for granting us the liberty to operate thus). Such was our home life lookout.

There were the occasional repulsive patrons who visited our enterprise, such as one scuzzball Robin brought home a couple of times—only that he paid us each a shot of C did he make it through the door. Surly, high-handed and offensive, he stared with crazed gray eyes, his skin a pallid, ghostly white, maculate with blackheads peppering and flanking his nose; rotten teeth, barfy halitosis, with weather-wasted shoes and smelly. He wore a shabby black trench coat in the blistering summer, for what purpose I never ascertained since he shot only into his right hand (between thumb and forefinger), the most repulsive vision of self-mutilation

I had yet to witness with the needle. He would brag about his wife and daughter (heaven help them), his job (?), his limpid boasts a transparent echo of my own corrosive loneliness of which I was in fierce denial—part and parcel of the pathology of an addict. For such was my intense loathing of this creature that I may have envisioned myself in that likeness—straight out of the sewer. And he was fastidious with a pledget of toilet paper to sop up the blood as he jabbed into his suppurating ulcer, dab dab, such a gentleman. Yet the polish on this gem was when he'd finally spout out, "Daddy got a hit!"

Another guest of note was Baby, an acquaintance of Robin's who was cuddly and cute, a fresh-faced fruitcake for all his unhallowed experience. I invited myself into the bathroom after they'd (Robin and Baby) been in there an hour, Baby with a gun sticking into the back of his hand, both of them yukking it up, writing a play (to which I was welcomed to contribute). It struck me, watching them so gaily immersed in such a flakey occupation, that I was jealous of the airy-fairy caprice of the two, overcompensating for my resentment by criticizing them in my mind, then stewing at my own pettiness. It marked a point in time of unsettled malaise for which I had no solution.

And there was Heavy, a huge, obese black crack addict, who came by nightly like clockwork, one of our regulars. He worked by day moving furniture for a streetside antique lot at Houston and Lafayette, hefting dining tables, credenzas, hutch cabinets and highboys like they were nothing, and keeping watch over the merchandise spread out on the sidewalk along Houston Street. Like many addicts, he was withdrawn though considerate and respectful. Unlike some hopheads with roving eyes and high anxiety that kept the entire room on pins and needles.

Yet my favorite customers by far were the whores (providing they weren't too slick), many of whom were friends who, for the most part, were genuinely thankful for the safety and respite from the threats and dangers of the street; who could relax in confident security and just be themselves and, sometimes, even sleep (if it was down time).

Purling from the rubric of the OD lounge, Wanda arrived one evening when we were doing a brisk business, the place was crowded with paying clients. In pushes Wanda, immediately making a pest of herself in her irascible, fractious *modus vivendi*. Me, Robin and smarmy Ronnie (who was visiting) attempted, hopelessly, to placate Wanda who persisted in being pugnacious and contrary, as was her custom. After ten minutes of this outmatched sparring and upon Wanda's refusal to vacate the premises, Ronnie grabbed Wanda in an armlock from behind, at which moment I joined in the fray to assist and together me and Ronnie dragged Wanda, screaming and kicking, out into the hallway, down the two flights of stairs and out the front door where we deposited her informally on the sidewalk. "I'll call the cops, I'll call the cops," wailed Wanda, to which I threw back, "You can call the Pope for all I care." Out she went. Obstinate to the last. Upon reentering our party pad, I discovered Wanda's handbag, which I forthwith threw out of the second story window (for show) to the sidewalk below where it flew open, scattering the contents willy-nilly in an unholy mess, for which I incurred my first pangs of remorse for defiling Wanda's personal property.

By the Eos of first light, Robin established that Wanda had bilked her for her new (used) shoes. Egged on by Ronnie, to replevy the pirated property, I tracked Wanda through the dawn's nebular mist to the stroll, asking the whores lined up there for the morning trade, "Where's Wanda? She stole Robin's shoes," to which I was apprised, "If Wanda's got them shoes on thay'll be wore out by now." I spotted Wanda across Allen Street and, upon my approach, she bolted and raced down the block, with the callets yelling in chorus, "Go Wanda, go!" Later that day, some junkie, Dennis, who had been downstairs in Karen's crack house at the time of the prior evening's fracas, asked me, "How many flights of stairs did you throw Wanda down last night?" Much later, after our reconciliation, Wanda observed to me, "You wouldn't have kicked me out if it wasn't for Ronnie." (Which was true).

Robin, before becoming a hooker, was a punk barmaid at the Mars Bar, bald-headed, sporting an atomic symbol tattoo on the side of her skull ⚛, plus a silent defalcating partner in the firm and, prior to boosting the till, had been a member of a modern dance troupe. A smooth charmer, Robin could also be risible. She had a chawbacon one time who inquired, "You don't shoot dope, do you?" Robin foreswears, so the john demands, "Let me see your arms." Robin rolls up her sleeve and there's dried blood in rivulets sheathing her forearm (she had forgotten about) and the mug cried, "Look! See, see!" and Robin knee-jerked, "Fuck off, you faggot." I could just see her, hands on hips, leaning slightly back, looking down on her mack with derision even, somehow, if the berk was taller than she.

And we both cracked up when, one day, Robin found one of my old shopping lists in the flat from before she moved in, when I would write down all the supplies required for my long-awaited run, when my unemployment checks arrived, so I wouldn't forget anything in my excitement, as my bimonthly hopes ran ahead of me.

15 coke	300.00
5 dope	50.00
3 syringes	5.00
1 stem	3.00
1 bk. soda	.50
5 lighters	5.00
5 Camels	20.00
3 *Cisco*	7.50
1 pantyhose	2.50
5 Good News	2.50
4 juice	8.00
6 candles	3.00

331

Robin also composed some good songs. Late one night, Robin got us going beating on the living room floor with drumsticks, completely spaced out, boomba boomba, ("And the queen spun her flax/While the bees made their wax"), unknowingly bugging out Karen below us who, the next day, complained to Mattie. What a creepy fink. She should have banged on the ceiling or the risers for us to shut up. Instead, she notified administration while she was running a crack house downstairs. A real two-faced doody hole.

I knew from day one, Robin didn't hide her feelings, that there would probably never be any bodily love between us as Robin got her fill of naughty bits on the job and what she cherished most in our living arrangement was relief from that demand, to be able to relax in safety, to have her solitude respected, and liberty to get high without worry or expectations to be met or roles to play. And in that understanding and acceptance was left room for mutual affection and exploration in a strife-free atmosphere of platonic regard. We grew close very fast, probably too close, too fast. And then we each somehow felt betrayed, aspersed, and blamed each other when in fact we both were guilty of shortchanging one another— *folie à deux*—forsooth none of that was necessary save the insidiousness, the internecine certitude of the disease with which we were both afflicted. And finally, acrimony led to turmoil.

I'm not sure in what order, but these things happened. I wasn't paying the rent; we were already without electric, burning candles all night. I could have evaded eviction, the landlord was lenient. Robin offered to keep working if I used my unemployment money to pay the bills but I let it go too far. Then I was going to bank my future cash at another Catholic Worker (Mary) House, the one for women, a few blocks away, but they wouldn't allow me, told me to go to Saint Joe's, but I knew that place as too wild and that my cash wouldn't be safe there. So money to move to a different location was never saved and Robin was hurt by this, I could see that plainly.

Enter Karen. The raving lunatic who lived in the apartment below mine, Karen, was operating a crack house also. Squat and toad-like with a broad, dished face, fulvous hair exsiccated to brittle straw, piggy-eyed, thin-lipped, and a nose not quite falcate, Karen was the essential true-to-type mug shot. Cold as charity and gloomful. She was always yowling, hurling invectives at her two sons (ages 14 and 15), who were learning the drug scene from a pro (mom). Karen had received forty grand ($40,000) reparation from welfare and blew it in a few months. She didn't even pay any rent. She became a dope addict (again). She would rail at her kids, sending them out to strip cars and rob grocery stores to augment their income. Karen couldn't talk without screaming. She was a cross-grained madwoman though a conversant Job's comforter.

Karen was insane. Her studio apartment had two Hollywood beds that were the only furniture in the entire abode. Guests disported themselves on the floor, cooking and smoking crack. Karen cracked the whip over a black druggy, Freedom, who worked for her selling dime caps of crack on First Street, outside our tenement. A household of crack fiends ruled by a psychotic Ma Barker. Karen bought herself and her sons each a cheap attaché case and equipped the cases with a Pandora's box of crack gear: mirror, shaker bottle, stem, screens, lighter, baking soda, water bottle, chopstick, razor blade, scraper, and insisted that her non-age maintain their own autonomy as far as crack cooking and smoking went. As Karen swirled a rock in her shaker bottle she would wrawl at everyone watching her, spraying anyone near with saliva—a spitting cobra—"Don't *anybody* even *think* of asking me for a hit." She had drabs from the stroll crashing at her pad (for a small fee). It was a simulation redolent of what me and Robin were doing upstairs.

Karen would rant and rave about her hobo days, as a dope addict, living in a cardboard box in a kampong at City Hall Park: "I had a refrigerator (aluminum bread box) and I kept a package of chicken in there and even though the chicken was rotten I could show my friends and say, see, I've got chicken in my refrigerator." Vauntful in her pathetic pride over her pitiful circumstances. As Karen boasted of such puerile bygone exploits, replete with hyperbole, the day was rapidly approaching whence she'd be back on the street (and on the block), strung out broke, shivering dope sick in a frosted cardboard igloo in Sarah D. Roosevelt Park, another city desperado. A born, perpetual, masochistic victim. Living the dream, as would we all; one, at least, to be redeemed to tell the tale, many others to perish, culled and threshed by the supreme, unconquerable street, the omnipotent city. How many countless souls and dreams does it own?

One night, flying on crack, Karen and I went out for Chinese food (Karen still flush with the green), swashing around affably, having a potty good time. We traveled by taxi to an Imperial restaurant in Chinatown with a great bronze moon-gate flanked by obsidian-like dragons, where Karen ordered almost everything on the menu—shopping bags full of food—hundreds of dollars worth of lobster, shrimp, the most expensive dishes (I requested scallion fried rice). While the Chinks were preparing our order, we went across the street to a huge souvenir shop where Karen bought clothes for her kids: jeans, sweatshirts, tee shirts, windbreakers, jackets, she kept piling the goods on the counter.

Karen insisted on rigging me out as well. At first, Karen suggested a wristwatch. "What?!" was my shocked veto. Then she offered, "How about a nice wallet?" Are you joking me? I was confounded by such asinine proposals, the last two things in the world I wouldn't be caught dead with. Was this chick for real? At least a necktie (comparably objectionable) could have been used to tie-off for a shot. Nevertheless, Karen allowed me to select my own choices.

I donned a skintight black disco-satin tee shirt by *Chanel* (outrageously overpriced), a pair of tight white jeans with a narrow yellow and black imitation snakeskin belt, a pair of shiny black leather pointy-toe Cuban-heel shit kickers ($240), a pair of long dangling hammered brass multi-feathered girandoles (which I brutally jabbed through the long-closed piercings in my earlobes), capped off with a floppy, feathered, lavender felt hat with a wide brim that I pinned up on one side with an ornate silvery brooch and creased the crown like a fedora. I looked for all the world like a pimp which, in effect, I was—armed and dangerous. As Karen gazed at me in approving adoration I was suddenly lionized. Super-Fly. *Sacre bleu!*

My name for the night was Slavery and I was going to bang Karen as a reward for being so nice and splurging on everyone. On the way back home, we stopped off at a bodega at Ridge and Rivington Streets for a deuce of eight balls, as seedy and desperate a locale as was Avenue D to our own heath where, as Karen began flashing the green, a crew of rancid greasers started surrounding us, closing in to rip us off, a rabid situation fast like sin acquiring an aura of menace, and myself armed with no more than my trusty meat cleaver against a half dozen or more slobbering gangsters. This called for some pawky thinking (and acting) *tout de suite*, especially burdened as me and Karen were with six stuffed shopping bags. Warily edging out of the coke spot, feeling the cynosure and tensity of all eyes upon us, I stopped dead in the middle of Ridge Street, putting my shopping bags down on the blacktop and turned to face my pursuers, reaching into the inner depths of my bomber jacket to grasp the cleaver's handle, intending the bluff to appear as though I were heeled with a piece in a shoulder rig. We were between Stanton and Houston Streets, the tableau frozen as the bête noires halted in their offensive, not desirous of being ventilated, my stance and aura and very glamour daring any of them to try it, showdown at the OK Corral when, lo and behold, here comes a taxi, cruising through that remote region at such a forlorn and darkling hour. Our deliverance. As me and Karen jumped into the magic pumpkin our mirth was unrefined, having four-flushed the would-be mother jumpers, their disappointment and our relief fading into the evanescence of the Magian night. As we rode home, Karen kept addressing me as "Slavery," which pleased me no end. Karen must have dropped two large on that single outing.

Karen discovered, upon unpacking at home, that the sleazy mama-san had swindled her for a couple of sweatshirts that she had paid for, deriding her as a "slant-eyed yellow hide." And we all ate for the first time in two or three days and Karen made the boys each take showers before anybody could smoke. And Robin pointed out that Karen's two studs were white Slavery and black Freedom. And Karen wouldn't let me do her in front of her kids so I had to drag her upstairs where she punked out.

The younger of Karen's two boys had a stammer and was always being picked on and blamed for everything by Karen and elder brother. One time, Karen suspected five hundred dollies stolen and of course they blamed hopeful son. Like, where and when was the poor pup supposed to spend it, they were always together. Although, youngster did swipe fifty berries out of Mama's box while she was passed out, afraid she would spend their last drop of moola on dope. When Karen found the needful missing, right out of her private parts, she went nuclear. Another time, Karen suspected that her Methadone had been watered down and, while Mom and older brother accused junior of taking the Meth, they both watched, like hawks, for him to go into a nod, which never came to pass so it appeared like just another of Karen's scams to juke money from Mattie, the compassionate sap, so she could buy a bag of dope. Once, Karen corralled me going into a coke spot and asked me for a C-note, offering, "I'll pay you back triple." I told her, "Sorry, I don't have it," (I did) and she feigned mock indignation, bemoaning, "I just thought I'd give you a chance to make some money."

One evening down at Karen's, she had a full house of guests, everyone flush with drugs and green, the dope flowed freely while runners ran in and out bringing snacks, paper towels, drinks, a regular party. Not content to play hostess, Karen announced that she was going to make tomato sauce and spaghetti. (That would have truly been "speak spaghet" had it ever come off.) Mustering her two boys, plus Freedom, Dennis, me, Robin, and who all else, we were sent hither to purchase olive oil, tomato paste, garlic, oregano, parsley, pasta, salt and pepper, and probably disposable plates and forks and a pot since Karen never cooked. The last I remember is everyone moving through the kitchen to the living room, back and forth, glancing less and less at all the ingredients piled on the counter while Karen descended into one of her waxy bipolar tirades.

I never cared much for Karen, she was a catty, hard-hearted junkyard dog, devious, manipulating—an innate control freak. Perhaps merely a scared little girl beneath it all, though such are many of society's most heinous butchers—that's no excuse to feel for them. Whereas, on the other hand, Robin and most of the tarts of my circle were rollicking, good-natured party people trying to do the best they could with what they had, burdened by neither acrimony or animosity towards anyone. That is, until the street and their profession and their addictions masticate, digest and void them as something undistinguishable and unredeemable and, alas, unemotionally forgotten.

One night, Karen was having a party and begged mine and Robin's attendance and so gave Robin a money shot for not going out to work that night; accordingly, Karen would supply the drugs at the party, so Robin and I attended. Since me and Robin weren't sharing any venery and Karen commenced in giving me the eye, I made the moves on Karen, in front of Robin, and Robin was cut by this so she left the party and went upstairs, keeping the hundred bucks, and downstairs we could hear the furniture being moved above us. (Like, did I owe some loyalty to Robin who worked as a trull?) So I went upstairs to find that Robin had rearranged the furniture (sofa bed, chiffonier, tables, chairs, vegetable crates, stacks of clothes) in the living room, where we mainly lived, to create a separate space for herself, leaving only the lonely couch in my portion of the room. She made herself a cozy bed from crates and piles of clothes, the chest of drawers somehow became a wall, in fact, Robin's new little creation was the most inviting area in the whole apartment. She explained (somewhat eristically) that she didn't feel good, was why she left Karen's, to which I sized up, "And moving the furniture made you feel better?" Well, what the hey. It was either let her have her own little corner or throw her the hell out and Robin was my steady drug supply, so now Robin had her own room. And the beginning of an ever-widening rift between us.

After that, Robin started to bring guys home and they'd go into the can and get high for hours. I was getting mighty tired of her colubrine act. Then she lost her keys. Like, how the hell could she lose her keys? I went from hiding grams of coke in Robin's things for her to find, to ripping her off while she was asleep. She said she'd go along with some role-playing for which she knew I held an affinity, but then she'd be churlish and indifferent, like she couldn't make that one small effort, a pro who does that crap for a living.

My biggest pet peeve with Robin was that I had to crack her back ten times a day until I wanted to crack her in the mouth. This involved us standing back to back; she'd hook her arms under my arm pits and lace her fingers against the back of my neck. Then I'd bend forward at the waist and she'd be lifted off the ground, her back arched backward against my forward leaning back. When she was six inches off the floor I'd bend my knees a few inches (a sissy squat) then straighten my legs up fast, still bent forward at the waist, and she'd fly upward, bent backward, holding on laced through my arms, and fall back down onto my arched back with an audible crack.

Alas, Robin was always OD'ing when squeezing C. Sometimes I thought she was just doing it for attention. Like once when I was trying to sluice a visiting young chuck in my living room and Robin suddenly summoned me to the bathroom where she was leaned over the sink in only bra and panties, sweating profusely, head hanging down, holding the needle, blood running down her arm, and she asked me to open the window, she couldn't breathe, and I'm like, damn, Robin wants me to swyve her now just when I was moving on the hot one in the living room. When it rains it pours. But, often as not, I'd have to watch over Robin after a shot and talk to her, opening a window, until her heart rate settled down and she could breathe normally. Nobody likes to babysit an OD.

All the little things I used to do for Robin I now felt I had to do, like I was her valet, and I was weary of it. She became a slob and I was always picking up after her. She would throw food (such as donuts) around the clean living room which, in turn, attracted the roaches which had been localized in the kitchen. I would fume over this practice. By that point, Robin's welcome in the flat was wearing right thin. She never made the slightest redress or propitiation for her misdeeds. I couldn't find my comb one day and Robin said she took it and lost it. Then I couldn't find any works, when we had about a dozen sets the day before. Later on, while Robin was out, I found about twenty combs and twenty sets of works, each in separate kitchen drawers. What the...? That was the telling writing on the wall. Robin had been conspiring with a girlfriend, out of earshot (very suspicious), not an hour before and I became convinced Robin wanted to kill me.

It was night. I dressed for the road, fixed my apartment door-knob so it couldn't be opened, told Karen downstairs what was up and she gave me fifty clams and I split. Word goes out that

Robin's trying to put a hit on me. Karen downstairs won't let Robin back into the building, "How could you be such an ungrateful bitch!" Robin is out on the street again, homeless, all her tackle locked in my apartment and I'm on the run for my life, paranoid into the twilight zone, imagining tracking devices secreted in my clothing, my shoes. I start to undress and throw away my clothes, undoubting they have homing signals in them. Every cab driver is working for Robin, radioing in my location as they spot me. I'm running downtown, crouching behind parked cars with each approaching headlight, coronas of radiance popping like flashbulbs, dodging through rubbernecking crowds in Little Italy, Chinatown, so they can't get a clear shot at me. I'm the running man and time is running out. Tick, tick, tick. I've got delirium tremens from crack and I got it bad. I go to Mary House of the Catholic Worker, it's past midnight, I pound on the door, clearly deranged, "Please, I need a change of clothes." "What are you crazy? Go to Saint Joe's." "I can't go there, the place is watched." "Get out of here, I'll call the police!" I know those dirty rat bastards are in on the scam. I'm convinced that Karen's ex-old man, Blackie (who gave me a chapeau to wear as part of my disguise—a trick!) is helping Robin, looking to kill me for her.

All through the Cimmerian darkness and into the wolf's tail of false dawn I am chased by the ghouls of my fears. I hie to Avenue B and cop fifty shekels worth of coke and return to the source of my cruciation to face my destiny. I ask Karen, who a few hours ago gave me half a hundo to help me escape, if her dissociated husband is trying to kill me. With some acerbity she says, "Why don't you go ask him, He's up on the roof." Climbing the stairs is the longest walk of my life, crestfallen, treading the corridor of death, with all the premonitory foreboding of my own execution dragging at my heels, flooding my mind, from whose destiny I could no more turn away than to still my hammering heart. I find Blackie on the fifth floor landing, morose in his marital proscription, and ask his face, "Do you want to kill me?" And he replies, "No, man, Hey, What's the matter? No, I don't wanna kill you." And I sink to the floor with relief, seeing it all now, how the paranoia was all me, Robin was just messing with my head and I've probably set guys looking for her, how all this psychotomimetic waggery is clearly insane so I may as well shoot up all this coke I just copped, not even thinking of giving it to Karen who paid for it, and I'm sitting up there, back against the wall, cooking crack and up comes Mattie, Mr. Super, who looks down at me and says, "Come on, You can't stay up here, Come downstairs." Karen was caterwauling that I ripped her for fifty bucks. And so me and Mattie finally get the door to my apartment open and it's the most desolate place, I don't even want to go in there and I see now just how wacko crazy I am and I'm sick and despondent.

What followed was (Robin remained history) the landlord had Mattie put me out so Mattie took me into his apartment to live with him and terminally insane Marion, and then Mattie wanted me to be his girlfriend and I flipped out because I thought Mattie was my pal and I told him, "I can't go for that." Happens all the time, some guy sees me in a dress and high heels and thinks I'm gay—ticks me off. This was a reflection of Mattie's outlook, whereby if one became dependent on him, then that one need be submissive to his personal (sexual) demands. Instance: There was a glabrous old sundowner, Sal, a regular patron at Saint Joe's, who was tolerated as a habitual loafer, whom Mattie once allowed to camp out in the fenced-in vacant lot adjoining our tenement, to whose gate Mattie retained a key. Sal made much ado over his good fortune in acquiring such a secure nesting site at which I catechized Sal's mode of recompense for his squatter's rights (knowing that he performed unnatural acts for Mattie), to which Sal readily admitted, "Sometimes you gotta do things." I recall once when Mattie gave a local quean a Jackson, gratis, with the prognostication, "Next time you know what you gotta do." Thus my new status as Mattie's lodger reclassified me as his catamite, to which I said, "No way, Ray!" Hence, Mattie pillaged everything in my crib and sold it and he wouldn't let me back in the building. So now I was back on the street, homeless, with not even a pot to piss in or a window to throw it out of. That's how fast one's fortune can change living as a bum (especially when one is unwilling to do things).

Well, I sobered up quick, had to snap out of my rut as soon as it turned frigid that hard winter's night. I cobbled up some wampum somewhere because I moved into the Samovar, a flophouse on Fourteenth Street near Second Avenue, as decrepit and loopy a place as I ever flopped in. It was freezing cold out and I became deathly sick with pneumonia. There was no heat to speak of at the Samovar with hyperborean drafts blowing through the window frames of my spartan room and the place was filled with low-life crack fiends making such a racket at night, tearing the place apart, it was bedlam. I just wanted a safe warm room where I could relax, get high and dress up. Not a chance of any of that at the Samovar.

There was a four-inch space between the top of my room door and the lintel above it and the incumbent, unhinged maniacs were peering through into my room; I'd hear them out there and open the door and some creepy goon would fall off a chair propped against my door and he'd laugh, "Hur hur, You got a cigarette, man?" The lunatic across the hall was tearing his doorframe apart when someone came by and banged on my door, "Did you see Crocodile?" I was so sick that I could barely stand up, couldn't stay in that insane asylum, that pandemonium. I had paid for a week but I wandered the streets on my third night in the freezing rain (overwhelmed with my pneumonic disorder, chills, bronchial wheezing, migrane), spending the wee hours at the counter of Veselka coffee shop (Second Avenue at Saint

Mark's) over a cup of coffee until the Catholic Worker opened in the morning. They had no vacancy at Saint Joe's but, for pity's sake, let me sleep on one of the kitchen tables after they were through chopping vegetables for tomorrow's soup, which went on until ten or eleven at night. I was a mess at that time because I was so sick.

I eventually made the rounds of, and crashed at a few of the fleabag flophouses on the Bowery—the old six-foot square cubicles in skid row hotels, aka cage hotels circa post 1945 era. The Palace, the Sunshine, the White House, places whose condition and accommodations were the inverse of their names. Those were five by seven foot cubicles, about one hundred cages per floor, a bed and a two-foot strip of aisle per box made by partitions, with a wire screen covered top. Ventilation from windows at one end of the hall; one toilet for every thirty to forty occupants; bedbugs and lice.

The term skid row originated in antebellum logging camps such as Seattle and Bangor, where seasonal (hobo) workers camped along roads where logs were skidded. However, the nascent emergence of skid rows in American cities didn't take hold until the latter part of the nineteenth century, abetted by police forces intent on localizing such riffraff. Up until that period, the homeless were spread out in neighborhoods known for their poverty and vice activities, frequently passing the night in cheap lodging houses or police station-houses. By the 1890s, New York's Bowery eclipsed the skid rows of Chicago, Philadelphia, Detroit, Omaha, Minneapolis and San Francisco.[1]

The Palace Hotel on the Bowery at Second Street was a dross flop and crack house most arrant. Completely overrun by black crack dealers, one had to shoulder one's way through the swarm

---

1 Kenneth L. Kusmer, *Down and Out, On the Road: The Homeless in American History*, paraphrase & statistics

of scurrilous workers crowding the interior stairs to reach the hovel's second floor quarters proper. I'd never beheld such blatant criminality in a place of business, and I'd seen some (though I had yet to experience the cat's meow of them all in my upcoming installation at the Kenmore Hotel). My intention at the Palace Hotel had been to acquire a bed for the night but I was forestalled by the action taking place in the stairwell, never even reaching the front desk at the head of the dope-defiled stairs behind whose bulletproof Plexiglas I could discern a cowering dharmic gook. I tramped the streets of the Lower East Side on that occasion, the soughing night breeze cold and sibilant, opting for discomfort over certain assailment. Thus I consider that episode as an experience at the Palace Hotel.

The Sunshine Hotel on the Bowery near Delancey Street, a dirty scab of a place, had no vacancy, not even a bed in their large open dormitory room with dozens of cots lined up like an army barracks. I used the bathroom where the toilets were similarly collocated, featuring no partitions, to discourage shooting up (and other nasty business), and as I was ensconced on the throne I addressed the passing rabble who came to get a glim at me, "I been holding this crap for two days," at which they smiled knowingly. Back at the desk I was persistent so the clerk came up with four walls that had no lock on the door and no light, a tiny closet of a room, completely barren save for a rachitic iron cot, sans pillow or linen. I took it. Ten dollars (which undoubtedly went into the crook's pocket). The janitor rigged an extension cord with the only light bulb found in the entire dwelling, a 125 watt lamp, blindingly bright, that I threw a shirt over which caught fire.

I was in my room preparing a shot when I heard a crowd, must have been a dozen deranged coons, climbing the outer walls of my pale to look in over the top (the pasteboard walls stopped two feet short of the ceiling). I was the only white-bread in the entire hotel except for the desk crook and janitor. And I heard the nosey jigaboos conversing as they watched me from over the top of my enclosure, "O man, Look at dat. Imagine livin' like dat." And I yelled back as I plunged the needle into my arm, "Get lost you fuckin' creeps!" I didn't sleep at all in that place; left early the next morning, girt for travel, out into the subzero elements, duffel over my shoulder, lugging a steamer trunk. Up the Bowery, dogged in my exhaustion, buffeted by the commiserating wind, cold as a welldigger's arse. I walked to Saint Joe's where I dropped off the trunk. Then I hopped on the Ⓐ train to Twenty-Third Street, to the Kenmore Hotel, where I checked into a room for thirty dollars. It was a Friday and the maids wouldn't be back until Monday so I had the whole weekend for the inflated price of a one-night stay.

I slept for two days straight, rising every few hours to go down to a deli for a buttered kaiser roll and coffee, then back up to bed. The accommodations did much to propitiate my harried circumstances. The room was airy, eleven by seven feet, with a large window facing Twenty-Third Street, on the fifteenth floor. I had a view of all southern Manhattan and the room was toasty warm, the bed linens fresh with a batik sateen coverlet. There was a sink, a closet, a sizable three-drawer lowboy with a large vanity mirror on top. Plus a small table and chair. To me, it was like the bridal suite at the Pierre (the most expensive hotel room in Manhattan). And it was quiet. I arrived that Friday with two twenties (2 grams) of C and a pint of gin. After a nice hot shower with soap provided by the hotel, a complete body shave and dried off with fluffy Turkish towels, also complimentary, I was so rejuvenated that I remained exhilarated all afternoon even after perfunctory assuagement. Sitting at my little table in skintight mojo gear, gazing out my window at the bleak winter cityscape, a panoptic vista, cooking and smoking crack, nibbling a buttered kaiser roll, sipping coffee and gin with nobody around to bug me, I was in seventh heaven. My cozy bed beckoning with promises of sweet dreams, a complete about-face from the previous twelve hours. What a merry-go-round. Months later, I would move into that curate's egg of a hotel full-time for five years, my last residence in New York City from which I was thankful and lucky to escape.

The White House on the Bowery, between Houston and Prince Streets, the cream of the flophouses, allowed guests to lodge for only one day less per month than the number of days in that month. For instance, September has thirty days, therefore one was only allowed twenty-nine consecutive days habitation for that month. Something to do with their license. Though many lodgers did leave their property in their rooms without moving it out, they had to sleep elsewhere for that one night. The price was six dollars per night. The rooms, though private, were poky, seven feet by four feet, bedighting a flimsy bed (with bedbugs), Mickey-Mouse nightstand, and weeny closet—the aspect akin to being entombed in a coffin. The walls were so thin (Masonite) that you could hear your neighbor breathing. If you listened closely, you could follow his every movement precisely. I had a little radio that I kept on constantly to mask my illicit activity, predictably, smoking and shooting coke. You could hear every click of the lighter, so I kept a candle burning thus having only to depress the lighter's thumb lever and hold the escaping butane to the candle flame for my incendiary device. The rooming house was pretty well emptied out daily by eight o'clock a.m. as almost all the residents worked, a not insignificant portion of the city's vast homeless workforce. A White House clerk would traverse the hallways of each of the three floors every morning calling out, "Five o'clock wake up!" And the day's bustle would begin. Loud bustle as many of the residents chinwagged freely with one another, having lived there for years. The cycle was repeated each evening around five p.m., even more robust, as the men returned home.

The main floor was given over largely to a community room containing long wooden tables with benches where the men would eat their brought-in meals, the walls lined with well-worn easy chairs, small wooden end tables with soft-lighted lamps for reading, the main desk a lookout post, and a large lavatory. Showers were in the basement. I lived at the White House happily for my first month during which time I clocked the patterns and movements of the place pretty well.

One garrulous old-timer and permanent fixture at the White House was Wally, whose second floor room abutted that floor's lavatory—a busy confluence of comings and goings. Either seated on his bed or leaning in his doorway, Wally would gab and gossip with all passersby; his room's door perpetually open to display his walls covered in glossy color photos cut from nudie magazines, of women in various extremes of undress and suggestive poses. Like a huckster peddling smut, Wally would point out one or another snapshot while looking at you, "You like her? Or maybe you like this one?" To which I would reply, "I like them all." And everyone gathered around would guffaw. I tried to avoid that head and used the one down on the main floor.

All of the flophouses on the Bowery were exclusively for men. If there were similar dwellings for women I have yet to see them (save Mary House), though I believe they do exist somewhere south of Delancey Street, less visible and profuse than those for the men. At that point in time, Karen had also been evicted from the First Street tenement and was living in a cardboard box in Sarah D. Roosevelt Park and hooking on the street, randomly protected by her now roving sons. As I entered into my second month at the White House, I bumped into that thrice condemned daughter of Belial on the Bowery one day and told her of the groovy digs I had and would she care to join me there for a little party. I described how the stairs were immediately to the left of the entrance (I lived on the second floor) and she should follow close behind me, head lowered, as we quick and deliberately passed throught the tiny window of observation by the front desk directly opposite the entrance. In, up, and to my room we went, safe inside, door locked, radio on, side by side on the bed. "How do you like it?" "Hey, this is great." Out comes the coke, shaker bottle, syringes. Knock, knock on the door. "Shhh!" Pounding now, "Come on, open up." Karen is in the closet. I open the door. "Yes?" "Where is she!" "Who?" "The girl!" Two men from the front desk, one pushes in, squeezing past me, going directly for the closet, the only place to hide, opens the closet door—Karen gives her winningest smile. That was it. I was barred from the White House for a year, never went back. At least I was given a refund and permitted to check my possessions there for a few days. I think those clerks really got a kick out of the entire vignette but were powerless to look the other way. I mean, when we reached the main floor there was a small crowd gathered, observing us intently. Me and Karen wound up getting high at her new home turf, a vast necropolis of the once alacritous and swift, crowding the park like some invasive bracken, refugees reduced now to existing in a cardboard huddle amongst the bundu—a woesome and dreary place to be—where at night the wind comes moaning across the lorne expanse specifically to haunt the sorry lot encamped there; a cipher of the life, of the *annus mirabillis*, the empirical dream.

Ah, the trials and tribulations of being a bum. That many of those incidents even occur often stems from the bum's prevalent attitude of not caring, which either put him where he is in the first place or at least helps keep him there. A great obstacle to overcome if and when he finally decides to reenter society, which would be from necessity and not desire. For me, the necessity was being a bundle of shattered nerves, paranoia, fatigue. Without considerable help, it's frequently impossible to get oneself together enough to quit the street, especially as you wish you could somehow continue as is, and not really, truly, suddenly start caring about conforming, responsibility, and so forth. It always seemed a catch-22 situation. You must be crazy to be on the street to begin with, then, you can't become responsible because you're crazy.

Blanket pro-bum programs do little good because often they're staffed by administrators and counselors who care less than the bums; the programs are exploited by directors who inflate their fees to insurance payers while collecting graft. I have witnessed such malversation. Then, the bums see no advantage than to extend their existing benefits. For instance, one must be enrolled in a rehabilitation program to qualify for substance abuse bonuses. Another catch-22 pretzel program that is all smoke and mirrors. Why do rehabilitation programs fail to achieve lasting results in their alumni, rather than so many repeaters, failures and dropouts? And welfare doesn't seem to catch on to this endless cycle. Or, more likely, welfare is part of the scam, not desirous of rehabilitating anyone because poor, ignorant addicts are the easiest to control, as well as being grist for the entire jurisprudence system—a major cornerstone of our economy.

What works is truly caring individuals like Charlie and Carmen at Trinity Lutheran, who carry on their own mission and provide adjuvant assistance personally to sincere bums in need. Those types of helper are too few and far between, too rare, to make a noticeable dent in the homeless epidemic and yet I see little else that is truly viable, save Catholic Worker ministers like Bill and Irish Roger, et al., who are effective in the catholicity of their approach.

Meanwhile, cash contributions from would-be well-meaning donors, funds that go into large charity organizations, are invariably lost in the shuffle, often winding up in pork barrel slush funds or the pockets of the depressed country's junta, serving mainly to salve the consciences of the concerned grantors. The only sure way to win the game is to not get on the dime (become a bum) to begin with, or to qualify for SSI, or perhaps commit self-murder. Because what I have seen confirms that once a full-blown bum,

always a bum. There is never truly a pure reentering into society.
At best might be complete self-sufficiency like the many steadily
employed bums which make up so large a work force in the city.
But the seamless blending into society is forever severed once the
plunge has been taken. It is an attitude, a frame of mind that
belongs to the bum, which, once assimilated, is indelibly impressed
upon his character. It can be likened to one who has served hard
time, a telling; for the bum there is that which lies just beneath
the surface, a manner that will not be defined yet is nonetheless
ever-present. And it is that manner which forever separates the
bum from society, cannot be papered over or erased, will not go
away. I have it, and I see it in my brethren.

I observe people today with homes, jobs, spouses, children,
and can usually tell if they've ever been a street person, a bum.
They can be so fragile as to be only a slip or an eviction notice
away from that place they hope never to return to. Like the
sober alcoholic who is merely a drink away from the detox ward,
the bum is always a sidestep away from being homeless, living in
society under disguise, lost in the dark, hostile, often unfamiliar
landscape of civilization.

And I remain on the street as the months, the years roll by;
Where my motley life bursts into bloom.

Sitting in my room at the Kenmore Hotel (a resident now), bordering the palmy Baruch College (CUNY) campus and Gramercy
Park locale, mid-afternoon on a dank drizzle October Saturday, I
became negligent at the end of a two-day run, still pretty flush
with green, I decided to go down to my old (Loesida) neighborhood

for one final score before crashing. I chose to take a bus down Second Avenue to Houston Street in the adumbrating clabber of a buttermilk sky—my favorite type of weather.

I went to cop at a twenty spot on Ludlow Street, four bags, and who do I bump into coming out of the bodega but Robin. She looked beat and haggard, really a sorry sight, a chanteuse who had lost her glitter and (so quickly) turned into a trey bag hooker. She just didn't have it in her to look out for herself like, say, Wanda or Barbara who were both impervious to anything the street could throw at them. Me and Robin were both surprised and stammered, "Hey!" "Wow!" "What's happenin'?" Robin had just seen me come out of the cop spot and I saw her standing in the gutter so, just for old time's sake, I sez, "How about a shot? Is ther someplace we can go?" She motions to a tenement across the street and sez t'me, "I don't have any works," so I sez, "You can use mine," then she sez (pointing), "Up on the roof but what about water?" So I sez, "We'll take some from a puddle" (it was raining), and she sez, "Whaat?!" And I sez, "We'll boil it," so she consents. As we approach the building, Robin sez t'me, "I know these two guys" (a couple of skeevy black hoods leaning against the building like bedraggled crows). "Let me try and get some works," which she does, and we climb the stairs (the street door was open) to the roof where we found an *Evian* bottle of water (popular spot). As I'm mixing up the shots, here come up the stairs the two corvine goons from the street. Uh-oh. In order for them to get up close to us, the weasely one says to Robin, as they top the landing, "He wants his works back," and I shoot a glance at Robin who gives me a quickening look of incredulity and surprise—like all whores, Robin was a self-styled thespian, well-versed in the art of histrionics. I would have been surprised if she hadn't launched into such a pat performance. Next thing I knew, there was an iron tube—zip gun—pressed against my temple (the weasel needed both hands for this), and he snarls at me with some asperity, "Don't move or I'll blow your fuckin' brains out. Gimme all the coke." And I, very slowly, reach into my pants pocket and hand over the C to his partner, Jumbo. Then weasel says, "Now money," and again, I slowly reach into my other pants pocket but, before I can comply, that emotionally unstable Child of Ham girns, "Hurry up!" and I rap back, "It's comin'," and I hand over my cash. He snaps, "Is that all?" (sixty dollars), and I nod, and weasel turns to Jumbo behind him and asks, "You good?" and Jumbo growls, "I got mines," and, with that, they both turned and raced down the stairs. I was shaking like a leaf and sweat was running down my face like raindrops and as Robin squeezed past me for the stairs, feigning crocodile tears, she said, "I'm sorry, David."

What a filthy slut. Did she think those slimy maggots were going to give her a cut? She wouldn't even get the shot I had offered. It was just for old time's sake. I had to stand there leaning against the banister for a good five minutes before I could even move.

I've never beheld a more dirty, death-dealing, homemade shooter than what that gunsel was pressing against my head. And he was dying to drop me with it. I could actually feel the venom emanating from him, a lifetime of hatred about to be unleashed. What made him hold back, I'll never know. I remember the thought flashing through my head, "So this is how it ends. What a damn shame."

I never saw Robin again after that, she vanished into the void. But weasel I did cross paths with one last time and it wasn't pretty. I doubt the bastard will ever raise his left arm again. Maybe now he can qualify for disability.

I walked from Ludlow Street, still trembling, a few blocks over across Houston Street to a candy store on First Avenue where I had a cash stash. It's where I bought my cigarettes, stems, screens, shaker bottles, and lighters throughout the week and, each time my unemployment checks came, I'd pay my tab and usually leave a twenty or forty dollar reserve, like a retainer, with the Indian bossman for safekeeping. Just a little bank in the neighborhood where I ran. So I went straight there and withdrew my double sawbuck balance, copped a gram of C across the avenue and walked the one block to Saint Joe's where I sat in the dining room for the half hour or so it took me to calm down. What a close shave. And fortunate I had a bag of C to take home along with my life.

When I would receive my bimonthly unemployment checks, I would often seek companionship for my first run. A chick as crazy as myself who was always happy and eager to join in the spree as long as the dope flowed. And of the flood of sex slaves in the local harem from which to choose, my all-time favorite, by far, was Wanda, bound as we were by amative friendship and dangers shared. On one memorable evening, I went to find Wanda at her cardboard bothy amidst the picayune misery of the Allen Street stroll, midway between Houston and Delancey Streets. With the owl's light just turning tenebrous, my quarry was home and, as usual, looking as fetching as though she'd just stepped out of a beauty salon, fawn hair brushed and shining, smoldering amber cat eyes deliquescent in the half-light, decadent in all her callipygous and sonsy rondure. As we saw each other and I inquired, "Is Wanda home?" my Venus pouted, "O Hip City, I'm depressed!" to which did I retort, "Well, Get undepressed, I came to take you out." At which my leman rejoined with the assent, "O Hip City, You make me feel brand new!" And we hugged.

I could see Wanda was doing her best to shake off sleepiness, having no doubt been up for a couple of days. She asked, "Can we stop for some food?" and I said, "Anything you want." First item to go was a shrimp vindaloo from some Indian bistro on Stanton Street where Wanda timidly informed me, "It's twelve dollars." Next was a toasted cinnamon bagel with cream cheese and a container of coffee from a bagel joint on Houston Street. It seemed Wanda was well known at both stops as she harried her dismayed servers on, "Come on, I want more shrimp than that for twelve dollars," and "Put more cream cheese, more, more!

We were cavorting around by taxi, into the heart of the deepening night, stopping for coke (ten grams) and dope for Wanda (five dimes), whereupon the pusher remarked at our approach (seeing Wanda), "Here comes the troublemaker." Though, nary the gravest of Wanda's acrimonious failings cast the least blemish upon her sweeping merit in my estimation. Wanda spilling coffee as she bent to rescue bags of coke and flying Hamiltons and Jacksons I was letting slip in back of the cab (the jehu wise to our act), scolding me, "Hip City, you're dropping everything, Look, What would you do without me, Here, Try some of this," shoving the shrimp at me, then, "Here, Have some bagel." Then, "Do you like this top? I made it myself." A hot, provocative, peekaboo pullover made from a lawny rice sack laced with tiny colored glass beads (recovered rejects from jewelry shops around Canal Street) and ruched with passementerie, looking like the latest bon ton from some chichi East Side boutique. In response to her query I answered, "I like," while sampling the merchandise. Wanda is truly amazing. I love everything about her.

When we arrived at my room in the Kenmore Hotel, Wanda scrutinizing every night prowler we passed in the hotel lobby ("That girl is following me, do you see her?"), the first thing my sybarite demands is, "Before we do anything I want some sex." And she is up against the wall, skirt up, panties down, arms around her back, hands promulgating herself, and she's turning her head saying, "Come on, you're not gonna deny me."

My hotel room was pretty well trashed, partially from neglect but largely an intentional creation to suit my usual overall mood: Pigs in shit. Wanda could conform to almost anything, but I think she thought she was doing me a kindness as she decided to clean

354

up. She's clearing the floor in a plethora of verve, pushing the layer of trash into a corner, slopping water onto the floor from the sink, then she's on her hands and knees scrubbing with wads of crumpled newspaper, saying over her shoulder, "See, I know how to clean," and I yap, "Forget that crap, C'mere, Wanda."

I've pulled two chairs up to a three-drawer chest onto whose top I'm laying the table. Ten grams of girl, five bags of boy, a small mirror, business card, cooker, baking soda, shaker bottle, glass stems, screens, scraper, lighters, chopsticks, razor blades, packs of new syringes, absorbent cotton balls, toilet paper, narrow maniples of hemmed silk sash, looped and knotted at one end, water bottle, ice, cigarettes, ashtray. We'd stopped in the bodega downstairs and bought ice, juice, beer and soda, all of which are in the sink chilling out, the inverse of us; the purple evening oozing through our open window, the ambient street sounds and sidewalk traffic comforting portamenti of the city, like the dreamy chuckle of a burbling brook.

"Wanda, c'mon, leave that."

Wanda will do the cooking, she's a five-star chef, there's nobody better. I'm already fixing a shot of C for myself, my favorite choice, and Wanda will start with a shot of D, which seems to affect her like a shot of speed and acid, I've never seen anything like it. She's transformed into a holy terror, a magical specter, enameled in a sorcerous glamour, eyes swirling, whirlpools of molten lava, beautiful, dangerous, compelling. Bang! I blast my shot. Wanda turns to regard me, a delectable morsel, needle waving like a wand, she wants to see what I fear, there is nothing, I belong to her, I am her toy, her factotum, her cat's-paw. I want to be taken, to be used for her pleasure, to soothe and accompany and assist her; to join and share in the immensity of this woman, the street, the city and the night. She is a harpy, salacious, yet cannot face me down, sees me willing, waiting for the needle to jab, not certain if she's satisfied. The needle is flying about my face like a mosquito, aims at my eye and I involuntarily twitch. "Aahh," purrs Wanda. She has found my fear. I am helpless, holding her gaze, pleading. She relents, knows she owns me. Our opening shots have been played. The party has begun. Ah, Wanda, my high fidelity, my houri, my inamorata.

The mechanics of getting high (or more appropriately, getting stoned) are fairly complicated. You need works—disposable hypodermic syringes (disposable after you can't sharpen them anymore), each sealed in its own little plastic package. You need a shaker bottle—a fireproof glass bottle the size of a twelve-gauge shotgun shell. You need fresh baking soda. Very cold water. A glass stem—a five-inch long fireproof glass tube whose circumference is the equal of a common lead pencil. Smoker's pipe screens. A pencil or chopstick to fold and compress the screens and to push them back and forth. Disposable high flame lighters. A metal bristle from a street sweeper vehicle brush to scrape down the sides of your stem. Absorbent cotton to protect your point. A two-foot length of material to use as a tourniquet to prevent your vein from moving. This was quite a kit to carry around. And points always had to be sharpened—pull the needle between two pennies (usually warped and verdigrised) to remove the large burrs, then sharpen the tip on a new matchbook striker.

In the early days, when crack first became popular, the clear plastic vials (bottles/capsules), which were about 3/4 of an inch in height and about the diameter of common lead pencil, were the only packaging in use. There was nothing deceptive about those containers and, packed with three or four chunks (rocks) of crack, the price was $10. Those vials had tightly fitting colored stoppers, like a cork, made of slightly softer plastic than the hard plastic vial itself. The color of the cap became a signature or trademark of the product—red top, blue top, green top. And, the variety of colors which the stoppers came in expanded to include every shade of the rainbow. As the years rolled by, slowly but surely, there came onto the market a frightful array of optical illusions and bogus bottles, all designed to trick the customer into buying a pig in a poke. First there appeared a somewhat shorter bottle, slightly more narrow than its predecessor, which sold for five dollars. This was a sensible modification as crack addicts were often hard-pressed to cobble together ten greenbacks at a time. Soon, there started to appear significant variations in the standard five and ten dollar size bottles. The height and diameter of the vials began to vary, the thickness of the clear plastic container increased, false bottoms became common whereby the bottom of the vial gradually climbed to the middle of the bottle. Jumbo vials appeared—one third to one half taller than regulation yet contrived to contain less product. As time pressed inexorably onward, one didn't know what they were buying until the material was finally dumped out of the capsule. Three dollar (trey) bottles came onto the market to corral the desperate dire crack junkie trade. The outer circumference of the standard crack vials were octagonal. In the pioneer days of the crack trade, the counts were always healthy. As the thickness of the plastic bottles increased, the octagonal shape served to better obscure the material contained therein. It became practically impossible to determine how much product was actually in a given bottle, especially in the dimly lit, hurriedly transacted deals of the street. Hence, the beat artist came into his heyday. By the time this evolution was transpiring, I had given up crack for awhile in my early homeless days on the street. There was a candy store on Houston Street, near First Avenue, that was a wholesaler of those little plastic crack vials. I was astounded at the selection of deceptive bottles available, all of which the crooked dealers made ready use. A tromp l'oeil effect. Some head shops retail crack vials by the gross. As an aside, small glassine envelopes, of the type used for heroin and cocaine, are available at the Thirty-Fourth Street *Woolworth's*, in the basement, where they are sold in a full line of sizes for stamp collectors, precious gem merchants and dope dealers. By the time I secured my First Street apartment in the East Village, I had graduated to buying cocaine in powder form and cooking (freebasing) my own crack, as was the common practice amongst my new circle of friends in that glut of a drug market, the Lower East Side. Buying crack in caps has devolved into a certain swindle, thus the crack smoker of today is advised to cook their own.

The cooking (catalyzing the powdered cocaine hydrochloride with an alkaloid—freebasing): For each amount by volume of powdered cocaine going into the regulation shaker bottle or 1½ ounce test tube (no more than half a teaspoon/a gram/a twenty dollar 1990 NYC bag) add one third (⅓) part of baking soda (sodium bicarbonate). The ratio is three parts coke to one healthy part soda, yielding four parts mixed powder. Then add enough water to make little more than a paste, drops only are needed, just enough water to liquefy the batch: wet your finger and run it against the lip of the bottle into the opening or slowly squirt drops of water into the bottle from your syringe. The volume of solution will be slight. Then boil the batch, uncovered, by holding a high strong flame (lighter) beneath (or over a gas stove burner), while swirling the bottle. All the while, holding the shaker bottle in one hand and the lighter in the other.

Once the batch boils, swirl it around a few times, boil it violently for twenty seconds so there's no doubt that it's cooked, always swirling, and then kill the fire and fill the bottle up immediately with ice cold water while you swirl it around. And, abracadabra, there will be your rock, bright white, hard as nails, the size of a sugar snap pea. Sometimes, if you don't boil it enough, or if there's too much water in the batch, it will colligate dark and gooey and stick to the sides of the bottle like molasses. That's all right. Just let it dry and it's as good as any. I actually prefer the gooey style, it used to hit me like a kick from a mule, often to the dismay of my cohorts. They all liked that nice white look. The perfect cookie. You can always recook an inferior yield. Add a few drops of water and an additional quarter (¼) teaspoon of baking soda and repeat the process. It is always expedient to add extra rather than too little baking soda. An alternative method of freebasing, which requires no cooking, is to add ammonia to the batch in lieu of water (omit the baking soda), enough ammonia so as to be able to swirl the batch easily. Your rock will appear in three swirls. Rinse with cold water.

It may be of interest to mention that the catalyzing of coca has been going on since time immemorial. Aboriginal tribes the world over whose culture revolves around the cultivation and chewing of coca, have discovered long ago the advantage of mixing an alkaloid substance with the coca dip to enhance its effect. Such is coca aidful that it remains a (flavoring) ingredient of Coca-Cola (which began as a patent medicine) to this day, save the intoxicant has been removed by the USFDA, much like decaffeinating coffee. Today one may enjoy the payoff from cocaine in any priest hole.

To increase the height of the flame on many disposable lighters, remove the C-shaped metallic housing from around the gas nozzle, beneath which is the plastic flame adjustment lever. With the protective housing removed, you can push the plastic lever upward with your thumb, which should increase the amount of butane released significantly. Or at least that was the case before anti-crack technology came along. If you are unable to locate a lighter whose flame can be raised through such tampering, you may have to resort to purchasing a butane torch which are not as handy as lighters but which work like a champ. Those devices connect directly to a canister of butane, which are sold to refill butane lighters. Once lit, the flame can be adjusted manually and will burn continuously until closed off. Crack cooking and smoking requires a high constant flame.

Shaker bottles and stems and screens are available at most tobacconists and candy stores in Greenwich Village or depressed areas (ghettos). You have to ask for them (discretely) at the counter. Don't present yourself looking like a cop. For hypodermic syringes (and coke or dope spots), enlist the aid of a prostitute—don't neglect to tip her for her assistance. Hookers are good compradores for any illicit business. Don't fall for the line, "Give me the money, They won't serve you." It's the hooker's job to vouch for you—that's why you're paying her. Have them introduce you to the source and make your own deal. Don't pay the slag until after the transaction.

There is a phenomenon, when shooting coke, known as hearing the bells. This is an intensifying of aural sensation, often manifesting itself as an outright audial hallucination of the most convincing (though not quite seraphic) order. I've frequently heard bells clanging and reverberating inside my skull after a kick-ass shot, bong bong, the hunchback of Notre Dame quaking with orgasmic repercussion. One recurrent empirical contingency of my overwhelming nocturnal shots was the distortion and magnification of the staccato concussion of vehicular traffic speeding over a large steel plate covering an excavation in the roadway, outside my apartment house's window, on Second Avenue. I was convinced that this echoic booming thunder was the sound of heavy cargo being off-loaded from tramp freighters docked at Canal Street (some few miles distant). Iregardless that I knew there to be no docks or waterway (or ships) at Canal Street, the visualization of Chinese stevedores manhandling huge containers on the age-old wooden slips was too delicious an impression to be obtruded by logic or reason. Crash, boom, the resounding steel plate were the derricks dropping their massive loads amidst a flurry of coolies wielding their long iron boat hooks as they swarmed the (projected) docks in the darkle of the mystical night. ("Ah so, ah so, you chickie Chinee?")

When shooting up, you had only a split second to pull the needle out of your arm otherwise, often, you wouldn't be able to extract it (being too stoned) and you'd mutilate your vein. I used to tie off, wrapping a nylon stocking or length of silk around my bicep, and make such convoluted knots that I couldn't undo them after I'd shot and would strangle myself in the arm. Psycho-junkie bondage.

Booting is the partial squeezing off of a shot, allowing the needle to remain in your vein with a portion of the shot still in the barrel, sometimes taking up to five minutes to inject (the shot). In the old days, before disposable syringes became readily available (and affordable), homemade works consisted of a glass eyedropper (barrel) with a steel needle pushed onto the narrow end with the aid of a torn corner from a dollar bill for a collar or gasket and a latex baby pacifier for a bulb, rubber banded over the large opening as a pneumatic plunger. The softer the pacifier the better. (They don't manufacture them properly anymore—another anti-junkie strategy.) Booting with a set of those homemade works encouraged blood to enter the glass dropper as pressure on the pacifier was relaxed, allowing the level of fluid in the barrel to remain fixed as the subsistent shot mixed with blood until one sent it home. The purpose of booting is to prolong the rush as the shot is introduced by increments. However, this is playing with fire as one can lose the dose surviving in the barrel if the blood begins to clot before you are through playing around with it. I've booted in the old days, shooting speed, using homemade works but I always preferred to have the shot in my bloodstream as quick as possible and not make a game of it. I've seen junkies reel around with two and three hypos hanging from their arms and hand. That was never my scene.

The advantage of using cotton in drawing up a shot is that it protects the point of the needle. Also, the cotton absorbs and holds the fluid in a localized area while acting as a filter as well. And the tiniest pieces are used, one quarter the size of a bulb on the head of a *Q-tip*. Or the same quantity of a soft, new cigarette filter. Drop the cotton into the dissolved solution of your shot and press the point of your needle into (or onto) the cotton as you draw the fluid into the syringe. It's not necessary to heat a shot's batch to any extent since anything that doesn't instantly dissolve with a cold shake isn't coke or dope. Use the thumb end of your syringe's plunger to stir and break up any lumps. Some people, including Wanda, liked the old fashioned tablespoon (the original cooker when dope was boiled before drawing up) which protects your point without cotton, being able to lay the needle on its side as you draw (although Wanda always used a cotton). I always liked using a shaker bottle for dissolving a shot. It was securely contained yet transparent, it stood upright and handled comfortably, and it was one instead of two things to carry around. But it did horrible brutality to your point without a cotton (my style), and subsequently to your arm and vein. I almost never sharpened my needles. My beautiful veins were soon degenerated to collapsed wraiths that defied injection. I would swing my arm around like a windmill, forcing the blood to the lower arm, then tie off quickly. Or, for a leg shot, jump up and down or run in place before tying off. Sounds like a lot of trouble? All these little inconveniences were merely drops in the bucket of getting high; each drop a welcome extension of the habit. Well, I wore my affliction like a coat, a badge, a flag to wave. But I never succumbed to that savaging, self-hatred of gouging my veins repeatedly in a scourge, a bane that produced those hard raised tracks, like faux bodybuilder veins, along the inside forearms. When you see that, you know you're looking down. Yet there is one step lower, always one step lower, and that is the ineffable, incontinent, continued shooting into a single location, like in the pilca between thumb and forefinger or somewhere on the back of the forearm, excavating to a deep venous mother lode. Those pyemia-producing areas became suppurating, purulent cesspools the size of a dime, ulcerated, septic and stinking, and could cause me to be nauseous. Sickness upon sickness.

When injecting a shot, it is necessary to know if you've hit a vein. Such is effected by drawing back on the syringe's plunger to see if blood enters the barrel. This is known as a register. If you haven't entered directly into a vein, then the plunger will suck back, as if from a vacuum. It often takes multiple tries before you succeed in getting a proper hit. This is due to dull points, collapsed veins, dim lighting, moving veins, dehydration, scarred and callous skin, shaking hands, stuck plunger, blurred vision, clogged needle, or all of the above. A little *Vaseline* on the rubber plunger gasket helps it slide, and sharpening the point also helps, but nothing beats a new set of works. Also, it's not unusual for blood to enter the barrel and then for you to slip out of the vein for some godforsaken reason and then, while you attempt another register, the blood in the barrel begins to clot, and to dry in the needle, thereby hindering and sometimes blowing your whole shot. Then you're tapping the barrel with your fingertips trying to move the blood clots to the back of the syringe, pressing the plunger to dislodge the clogged needle, running water over the needle—a nightmare. A sharp needle, a good eye and a steady hand are key to a successful shot—none of which most junkies ever have. That's why most IV addicts' arms look like a lawnmower ran over them.

To demonstrate how impulsive overbold actions can lead to disaster, I once moved to relieve Robin of a shot she was losing as blood commenced to clot and clog her gun while she deteriorated in her efforts to make a hit. I impute that blint meritorious credit for having the acumen to exclaim to me, "No! Different blood types." Whence Robin's observation was the last of my considerations, having already disregarded AIDS, STD, or other blood-born pestilence in my blind junkie single-mindedness. That is, the desperation for a shot overrides all else.

It's a serious situation when a shot is in jeopardy due to clogged works, as I once recall hearing the unmistakable tap tap tapping of a fingernail against a plastic syringe barrel coming from a toilet stall in a welfare office men's room, accentuated by a black buck swearing. I removed myself from that vicinity whip and spur. As in fast.

Shooting up is messy business. Anyone who has undergone phlebotomy can appreciate how a direct puncture to a vein can cause a bleeder. The junkie does not rely on a handy supply of pledgets or *Band-Aids* to staunch the flow of blood. Blood runs freely down one's arm, dripping all over the floor, while they reel around, too smashed to give a damn. I have shot up in public lavatories that I used regularly, one even in a clerical (priest's) office, and had to crawl around in horror (beadle knocking on the door) wiping up the venous blood that looked as though someone had been shot. Thus, it was not uncommon for one to walk around with blood smeared and streaked down their arms, as appearance was the last thing addicts were concerned with. And abused points of entry often turned black and purple and yellow so that a junkie's arms often looked like the ravaged war zone that, in fact, they were. A dead giveaway.

Once I titrated, adjusted the shot (the coke being the reagent), which took a few trials, I could judge how concentrated a solution would deliver me just to the brink of expiration. Of course, IV drug abuse is an OD trip, the very playbook of death, always pushing the limits, taking just a little more, never satisfied until you are over the edge. Thus, many addicts are always OD'ing. I would black out, periodically, from overdoses—it was the nature of the addiction. Subconsciously aiming to scare myself. And succeeding.

Junkies are always shooting up, it's minimally a six times per day activity, which involves getting the dope, preparation, doing the deed, and the aftermath. There is no such thing as a quick shot. When someone goes into the bathroom for a shot, it's forty-five minutes to an hour before they come out again. (And public lavatories contribute an unsanitary element to an already dirty business.) At best, the junkie exists in a state of continual euphoria, injecting a shot, riding the high, another shot, another high, and so forth until the dope runs out. Then the pendulum swings back to getting more money, more dope, until one is riding the high once more. It's a full-time occupation. And it is an obsession. Being a junkie means addiction and addiction is a jealous, dominant spouse. Addiction isn't a sometime thing, it is the lodestone, the cornerstone, the controlling focus of one's life. Nothing takes precedence over one's addiction, as the junkie quickly learns. Adios!

A junkie's world is never safe. The junkie is ever on the lookout for the police, the narco, the confidential informant, as well as his own confederates, the legerdemain, the jack-roller; whether ambulating home from a score, or merely carrying a set of works; the sound of feet on the stairs, the sudden knock at the door. An extrasensory perception is the junkie's constant companion, a radarscope, a high frequency direction finder; forever wary, for he is the hunted, and the hunter is out there, ever dogging his trail.

Alas, it is not uncommon, after you've already drawn your shot into the syringe and are ready to shoot, that you drop your gun onto the floor of the insalubrious public lavatory in which you've barricaded yourself. Now it's lying there amidst the remnants of all the loathsome filth which has never been effectively mopped up: urine, vomit, feces, blood, pus, phlegm, mucus, staphylococcus, shigella and other contagious pathogenic bacteria tracked in from the street, all sorts of nasty stuff. Your hands are shaking, it might be your last shot, or your first after a long forbearance, you're already tied off, hyperventilating, heart palpitating wildly. So you pick up the set and wipe the needle between your lips to clean it, and shoot it. You don't have to share works to share disease.

When I first began shooting, I was fastidious about sterilizing and sanitizing my works. Boiling water, isopropyl alcohol, bleach. Even storage was sanitary. It didn't take long, however, to abandon all pretence and succumb to careless indifference regarding sanitation of my appurtenances, even hygiene of my person. As I descended into the wicked helix of cocaine abuse in its most devastating forms, cleanliness became the last thing on my mind, save its use as an axiom against which to measure the depth of my perverse fetish for smut.

I would squirt from my syringe just enough water into a batch (a shot) to make it injectable. The more water used, the longer it took to shoot, the greater the chance of not extracting the needle from my arm. I made a concentrated shot, in and out fast, hoping my heart would take it. When shooting heroin, an intramuscular shot was permissible. To wit, if you're in poor light and can't see well enough to hit a vein, or if your veins are just plumb collapsed. But with cocaine (or speed) you had to mainline directly or you'd abscess. Sometimes, you could go right through a vein and out the other side and so abscess as well. After a day of shooting coke, you're usually so dehydrated and shaking so badly as you attempt a hit that it takes ten to twenty tries before you make the shot. Blood running down your arm, clotting up in your needle, a mess. Thus is IV cocaine abuse a scourge.

Often, when I would receive my unemployment checks and cash them, my hands would start to shake uncontrollably while still in the check cash, before I could even pocket the moola. As soon as the oof was in my fist, I'd start shaking. This was the apperception of what I was about to do, where that tootie would take me, and I was fearing with foreboding.

Sometimes, you could score a supply of coke that took more water to dissolve than normal. It would gel up with the usual amount of liquid and leave your arms so numb that, after a day of using that product, you'd have to switch to another spot to cop. They would cut the material with cheap intolerable substance that was okay for cooking, but not for shooting. It was not that rare for a clerk in a spot to inquire, "You shoot?" when they were dealing toxin to their clientele. But those discomforts are out of league with the bone crusher. With the bone crusher, you always go to the hospital and sometimes die. The bone crusher crushes not only your bones but your muscle, your water, your consciousness, your very pith, spirit and soul are snuffed out, you are left pyretic with fever, sweating, shaking, labored breathing, blurry vision, dizzy... This is the bone crusher, the hot shot. If you survive it. I had it twice. When a dastardly chick asked me if I ever had a bone crusher, I didn't know what she was talking about. Rotten bitch decided to hook me up. Another trial by fire.

What precipitated this backstabbing was as follows. I had collected Kathy, a foxy Latin Loesida strumpet and prestidigitator of long acquaintance, for an evening's companionable amenity. We had entered my tenement, having just copped a large score of C and D and, before ascending the stairs to my crib, I checked my hallway mailbox. Therein was a junk mail catalogue, addressed to me, offering all sorts of nonsensical notions: a contraption for nasal hair removal, whiskey-flavored toothpaste, aerosol pet repellent, horoscope guide, pack-at-a-time cigarette dispenser (holds one carton), weight loss kit, hair restorer, nine inch × one inch cylindrical vibrator (batteries not included), hooded rain poncho (folds to the size of a purse compact), nostalgic lamp globes with the legend BAR, marked poker deck, glitter nail polish, and so on. I remembered as a kid looking through those catalogues with my sisters, as though reading a *MAD* magazine, laughing and saying, "Do people really buy this stuff?" No doubt my name evolved onto their mailing list either from that earlier period c/o my parents, or myself falling into a high tax bracket, or as a registered voter, or a union member, even though I was currently collecting unemployment benefits, I was at the ceiling of entitlement. (How else are those mailing lists formulated?) All my adolescent friends' families received those same types of mail order catalogues, everyone the same socioeconomic background (white middle class)—thus my hypothesis on mailing lists. Kathy, on the other hand, had never seen such a catalogue, having been raised in poverty, her refugee parents probably never having voted, nor had a union book, nor paid any income tax, hence on no mailing lists for trifling articles of whimsy, and the poor ruca was enthralled by such sundry offerings and couldn't stop leafing through the tawdry pages, like a bobby soxer ogling a pop magazine. I noticed all this at a glance and, later on, up in my crypt (I wanted to hook up with that vulpine trull), I observed to Kathy how we were different (albeit completive), like a chiaroscuro, alluding (in macaronic argot) to our disparate socioeconomic genealogy, a grave error on my part as she promptly took offense, castigating me, "You shouldn't have said that," suddenly giving me a raptor-like gaze, then asking me, "Ever had a bone crusher?" She probably thought I was laughing at her, which I never did. I admired those chits for doing their best with what they had, felt a ruth for their suffering. "But unimpressionable natures are not so soon softened, nor are natural antipathies so readily eradicated."[1] Besides, you can't convince them, they all have a persecution complex and no self-respect. And some pros carry Drano or chloral (Mickey Finn)[2] for just such occasions. Luckily, I was cagey enough to recognize the subliminal irony of her inquiry because, quicker than a thimblerigger, she set up my shot with a bone crusher,[3] which I prudently set aside and ignored. Funny how only blacks can call each other nigger.

My first and worst experience with a bad IV shot, the accursed bone crusher, came about one Sunday morning when I was in my First Street apartment. I had awoken in my bombed-out disaster of a living room, which was littered with layers of trash and garbage and onerously infested and, there, sticking up from that blanket of foul detritus and effluvium was a syringe, point down in the graveolent rug, barrel filled with a kick-ass shot of C. In my haste, during my run of the night before, when the needle clogged on that shot, I discarded the whole gun and mixed up a fresh hit with a new set of works, leaving that bottlenecked dose in the barrel, thrown aside and forgotten. Until now. I sat there and eyed that gun knowing it to be a potent shot just waiting to be redeemed. Irregardless that there was coagulated blood in there, harmful bacteria and evil galore, with the point stuck into the most gruesome, grotesque, germ-ridden medium—all that became secondary to rescuing the shot. However I did resist for awhile and hopped across Second Avenue to Saint Joe's for brunch (a mere shuffling of the deck). Upon returning home and seeing the syringe once more, it became irresistible and I picked the forbidden fruit, transferred the dose into a working set of gimmicks, tied off and shot it. Well, I think I barely pulled the needle out of my arm before I was on my knees, sweating, bent

---

1 Charlotte Brontë, *Jane Eyre*
2 Name of bartender who popularized usage of chloral hydrate
3 Almost any evil impurity (i.e., toxic bacteria) can effectuate such a reaction when injected intravenously.

over with cramps, blurry vision, disoriented, ataxis, gasping for breath, Lord knows what all I shot but it had me on the ropes. I managed to wamble across the street to the Catholic Worker where they called an ambulance and I was brought to Beth Israel Hospital where I was admitted with a fever of 104° F (which they couldn't explain), maybe I had contracted Ebola. But it took some days for me to recover. I stayed in their detox ward for a week, living it up with room service, breakfast in bed, medication to relieve my anxiety and to help me sleep. I was lucky to have survived. That is the insanity that goes along with the life of a junkie. Reckless, careless, thoughtless behavior. No wonder AIDS is so rife. Hepatitis. VD. Not to mention malnutrition and psychosis. Many prostitutes can't wait to contract AIDS so they can receive SSDI.

I recall a comely young doxy of my acquaintance, Lee-Anne, who once told me, up in my East Village laboratory whence I'd gotten her smashed on alcohol and crack, how delighted she was that she'd finally been diagnosed with AIDS so that now she'd be eligible for lifetime maintenance from public assistance, meaning that her rent would be paid, meals provided, automatic Methadone program, medical treatment, and anything else she needed to live comfortably. This was a popular sentiment amongst many of the incumbent whores of the stroll who were sick of the wretchedness of their iniquitous profession and the unendurable living conditions of the street and were desperate for a means of relinquishing the daily struggle to maintain their drug habits and all the required supplementary upkeep necessary to enable them to attract customers for whom they must perform the most repulsive acts.

I was put in mind of a group of young female freedom fighters (unwilling to work at gainful employment) in a prior circle of hippies, with whom I'd lived years past who, upon many of the local male drug dealers being arrested and the girls' future in the commune thus threatened, were trying (and succeeding) to become pregnant as a means of qualifying for welfare whereby, as single mothers, they would be provided with an apartment, free food, health care, the works. Willing, one and all, to sacrifice their future for nothing more than a free ride.

This is not such an incomprehensible outlook as it may appear on the surface. When wallowing in the deep waters of the street and laboring about the dark wings of the night, faced with the multi-headed hydra of drug addiction, desperation, psychosis, and monsters who are your clientele, contracting AIDS seems like a prophecy fulfilled and one can finally lay down the flag and take off the coat and resign oneself to eating humble pie on the dole, and romanticize and lament all the high jinks and picayune concerns of a life which no longer affects them, however cancerous and graven on the memory.

Even I have fallen prey to the allure of a lifetime meal ticket when, at a low bottom, I sought to intentionally contract AIDS. It was a spontaneous, forlorn move in a wild befuddled moment of despair over the bleak prospects of my future as a hopeless drug addict. I had taken in a houseguest, Arleen, for a few days, a good acquaintance of mine and close friend of Marion's, who had worked the stroll in her heyday (though currently under 25 years of age), and was fairly wasted from AIDS (yet still bewitchingly attractive). In fact, Arleen would, like Marion, later die of AIDS. This was a girl who, when we first met, shunned my advances by admitting that she carried AIDS. Much later, after surmounting her resistance, as I defiled her in my lust, I spoke aloud (to our mutual astonishment), "Give me your AIDS." A futile, suicidal gambit. As it so turned out, I resisted the deadly virus. A stroke of fortune (or a miracle) which I can only ascribe to my well-knit immune system, then still intact, that may be attributed to my fresh juice regime to which I always religiously adhered. Silly moves, often fatal, the offhand decisions, those slight impulsive mistakes that could swell and become one's fate, all the reckless random behaviors of the street.

371

Before she crossed over into what I hope is a more peaceful plane, Arleen became pregnant. Tormented by her wretched circumstances which included homelessness, prostitution, advanced AIDS, heroin addiction and crack addiction, Arleen procured her Aceldama from a band of Asian predators who offered her a warm residence and some spending cash and all the crack she could consume in exchange for her baby when it was delivered. To this Faustian offer Arleen readily acquiesced. Arleen's best friend, Marion, upon telling her old man Mattie this news, sent him into a self-righteous uproar. I was indifferent. I knew the baby wasn't mine as I had never climaxed during my relations with Arleen. Those baby merchants are prodigious in the city stews, where a white baby will fetch a cool ten grand on the spot, no questions asked. Where they wind up in some Third World enslavement seems no worse than a fate of feticide or a life such as that led by Arleen herself or other comparable bar sinisters who can't even take care of themselves, let alone a baby. Wouldn't sterilization be a better answer to such a dismal dilemma for poverty stricken, diseased addicts whelping babies all over the tenement squalor and back alleys of the ghettos? Most of those parturient mothers aren't fortunate enough to find a baby broker to relieve them of their unwanted burden which, if the infelicitous infants survive, face a life of living hell. Whether sold at birth or abandoned to the streets to confront the untented ramparts of social class—the shibboleths of our prejudiced American culture—those offspring of depraved parentage face a life of miserable samsara that is as inescapable as the grave. Such is the underside of the classic American dream, a term which has become an anachronism. Land of the free? Home of the brave? Land of opportunity if you're born to it. Our disadvantaged populace tragically resemble our consumer products: disposable—use once and throw away. "Ah, but ain't that America."[1]

---

1 John Cougar Mellencamp, "Pink Houses" (recording)

I knew I was playing with fire but the drug, the addiction makes one not care. All that matters is getting more drugs. So many homeless live that way because it's impossible to change, to get out. I know so many addicts, they tell me they want to stop smoking crack or shooting coke, if only they had some dope. See the insanity of it all? Because crack makes you crazy. And shooting coke is the worst—expressway to doom. Yet, you can live a long life and die of old age on dope. (A sophistic oxymoron? Some dope to help make me normal and stop being so crazy.)

I was, for the most part, very fortunate in all my years on the street; plain lucky if not miraculously blessed. Be it the power of the mind or faith in Our Lady that kept me from that final tumble. I visited almost every Christian church in the lower city. From Saint Patrick's Cathedral on Fifth Avenue to Saint Patrick's Old Cathedral on Mulberry Street, from Saint Stanislaus in Alphabet City to Immaculate Conception Church on East Fourteenth Street, from Our Lady of Sorrows on Pitt Street to Saint Mary's on Grand Street to Church of the Transfiguration on East Twenty-Ninth Street (in whose Elysian fields are buried many of my little pets).

As I gaze up into the clerestory, bathed in the diffuse jewels of light bleeding through the stained glass windows, a multicolored magic carpet upon which to wing my reverie, listening to the celestial resonance of the pipe organ, I can almost smell the frankincense and hear the brass chain clink against its censer as I flashback to my boyhood, the cathedral-like atmosphere of Saint Ignatius Loyola and its hallowed wonder, a child immersed in the posy security and pious mystery of high mass—*Ad Deum qui lœtificat juventutem meam* (To God who giveth joy to my youth)—and marvel that for all my heretical complexion and humor, I still ween and trow to the old faith, a bit of revisionary obliquity in my rebel constitution.

373

I would visit those houses of worship just to gaze in wonder, to be awed or inspired in the presence of so much beauty. And always, "it evoked some longing in me, though I did not know for what, or whether it was more than merely a feeling of loneliness."[1] I would sleep in the pews, give thanks and ask for guidance, copy fresco designs for use in carving my gourd vases. During Christmas season, attending (for three nights running) fifty-voice *a cappella* choir concerts sung in Latin at Church of the Epiphany on East Twenty-First Street, the last evening accompanied by a thirty-member orchestra. A truly moving experience. It was the big Saint Pat's which, when I needed it, gave me the necessary referral to Trinity Lutheran Shelter. It never hurts to align with the divine.

During my ten-year career as a New York City bum, I took advantage of numerous city amenities which appealed to both my sensitivities as well as my purse. For almost a year (two semesters) I practiced with a bow and arrow as a member of the archery team at Baruch College on East Twenty-Third Street. I had been looking out the window from my room on the fourteenth floor of the Kenmore Hotel, directly into the huge windows of the college's gymnasium early one evening and saw a line of students shooting bows and arrows. I had always wanted to learn archery. So I ran across the street, weaseled my way into the building, found the gym, and approached the instructor. A young Korean sir, very well affected and accommodating. Sure I could join in, no fee, no student status, just show up. Twice a week for three hours per session (an arduous spell), one weeknight and on Saturday. The instructor had an ID made for me, allowing me unrestricted access to the building. I was issued my own bow, a thirty-pounder to begin with. What a blast. I learned to shoot.

---

1 Barry Unsworth, *The Ruby in Her Navel*

For the first day, I bopped over to a used clothing annex at a church and purchased a fresh shirt and slacks. My teammates (all students) were warm and congenial. The instructor took great pains for individual attention. (This was a competitive collegiate team.) He had a camcorder to make videos of us so we could observe ourselves shooting and critique our form. He would splurge for take-out lunch to be brought in on weekends. He put up novelty targets for a fun shoot as a diversion from the rigors of our instruction and training. All this generosity available to me, a bum, in the community spirit.

On a few occasions, during water outages at the Kenmore, I took luxurious showers in the college's men's locker room. At the end of the term I carved the instructor one of my gourd vases out of a butternut squash, Korean characters in relief around the outside, edged in the eternal life border. I went to the flower district on Sixth Avenue and scrounged a lovely bouquet from discarded remnants, arranging them in the hollowed-out squash and presented this to the master as a token of my appreciation for letting me join the team. This was a touching ceremony for which the instructor seemed genuinely moved. Those unique hand-carved vases were my big attempt at enterprise, yet they never caught on where I tried to peddle them. I was out of my element with that quality of craft in the plebian quarter of the metropolis and in trying to market them myself, sans agent. Just another starving artist.

There was Asser Levy Community Recreation Center at the east end of Twenty-Third Street that was very affordable—twenty dollars for a six-month membership. They had a complete gym with free weights and cables and an outdoor swimming pool. I joined up there for a couple of years while living at the Kenmore Hotel. I was able to work out all winter and swim all summer. Like all gyms, it was crowded (especially at that price) but there were down times, like early morning, when it wasn't too packed, you could do your circuit, your sets without waiting in line for a bench. The pool was always crowded, but at least it was wet on a sweltering day. There was also another gym I patronized fairly often in my early years over in Alphabet City, Gladiator's Gymnasium. It was largely a Hispanic crowd (their champion was Puerto Rican), and the place was small, but it was inexpensive and had a full line of free weights, cables, and machines, with lots of home-made equipment that was dynamite. Plus, there was an outdoor backyard for pumping iron alfresco. Very cool. A real homeboy place. That was one of my all-time favorite gyms, surpassed only by Better Bodies in Chelsea.

Another good time to be had, when I had the palm oil, was to spend a day at the Public Bath on Tenth Street in Alphabet City (the only public bath in Manhattan I ever heard of that wasn't gay). It was a mature Russian/Ukrainian crowd, and even coed on weekends. It was affordable and well worth it. They had six various temperature pools, from scalding hot to frigid cold. Whirl-pool. Sauna. High and low temperature steam rooms. Assorted massages, including Swedish and flagellation with birch branches. There was a health restaurant with a charcoal grill and rustic varnished wooden tables and booths and a television, the walls decorated with memorabilia (John Belushi was here), and smoking was permitted. There was a quiet dim room with bunks where one could take a nap. You were issued a bathrobe, flip-flops, towels and a locker (valuables were deposited in the front vault). Nudity in the pool area was the norm. Even the showers were out in the open. The place was ancient, completely tiled (Soviet style), subterranean and out of sight. I'd buy a copy of *Vermont Life* magazine and bring a bag lunch and spend the day for ten dollars. It was like going to a hotel in the Catskills for the ethnic lower class. A great way to spend a rainy or winter day.

The New York free public (branch) libraries were the most fre-quented amenity that I made use of during my ten-year stint as a bum on the streets of New York City. The branch at the west end of Twenty-Third Street specialized in westerns, and the branch on Twenty-Third Street between First and Second Avenues was only a block away from the Kenmore Hotel and they had a large selection of paperbacks. For research and cookbooks I used the Fifth Avenue lending library at Forty-First Street. The branch on Lexington Avenue at Forty-Fifth Street was almost entirely paperbacks. The Second Avenue branch in the East Village, next to Stuyvesant Polyclinic, was my regular standby, and I also patronized the First Avenue branch around Sixth Street, and a branch on Tenth Street between Avenues A and B, across from Tompkins Square Park. Those were all my stomping grounds. I almost always withdrew paperbacks, when reading novels, so easy to carry around and read single-handed, squashed on the subway or standing on a soup line or forlorn in some waiting room.

During the years of my extended association with Saint Joseph House of the Catholic Worker (beacon in the lightlessness), through the thick and thin of my often volatile circumstances, I developed an affinity with one of the resident volunteers, Siobhan who, for me, fit the classic image of My Wild Irish Rose. Petite and pert, with burnished red hair, Siobhan enjoyed much success from a ubiquitous wriggle of earnest admirers, all of whom she seemed to casually brush off. Nonetheless, with some bold daring, I approached Siobhan with the overture of our engaging in a dinner date together, anent which she assumed to be favorably disposed. Encouraged by the possibility of success, I scoured the vicinity within comfortable walking distance for appropriate restaurants. The selection was extensive. I didn't seek anyplace exclusive, Siobhan was an unpretentious lass. She did not deign to skirts or au courant froufrou, though Siobhan wouldn't be caught dead wearing sneakers. I scouted out five eateries from which my acushla could choose, collecting a menu from each, an opening ploy which pleased my prospective date. To my delighted surprise, Siobhan picked Pete's Tavern at Irving Place in the Gramercy Park vicinage, an establishment which boasts being the oldest tavern in New York City—doubtful (as might claim Fraunces Tavern on Pearl Street or the Ear Inn on Spring Street), though with all the ambience and charm to support its claim. Beyond the tavern room was as snug and warm a dining room as I could have hoped for, a puncheon grotto with worn wooden quasi-banquettes and a wall of large mullioned windows.

Prior to our rendezvous, I canvassed Sixth Avenue's flower district, collecting discarded fresh rose petals, which I scattered on the seats and table of our reserved booth. I had already reconnoitered the route along which I would escort my lassie, up Second Avenue over to Irving Place, inspecting each crosstown byway through or around Stuyvesant Square Park, selecting the most peaceful side street from the lot (East 19th Street—"Block Beautiful"). Confident of a most atmospheric course, I embarked to join our engagement. I was not disappointed. Clad in a plaid madras blouse, blue jeans and her signature black boots, Siobhan looked ravishing. Our stroll along my preordained path was delightful and I was pleased as punch at Siobhan's efforts at being congenial. The encounter proceeded in this vein, with Siobhan being receptive to my every gesture.

Throughout our thoroughly enjoyable meal, my colleen treated me to an intimate insight of her family's vocation in service by way of the Catholic Worker. Siobhan's father, Irish Roger, pro forma of Saint Joe's, while a youthful volunteer at that ministry, had met Siobhan's mother, also a volunteer there, and they were summarily wed. Devoting their lives to that benevolent philanthropy and within its framework, did Mr. and Mrs. Roger raise their family and, thus, was my duck's heritage. A noble tale. I was reverentially affected. And honored by Siobhan's disclosure. At a later point in time, while discoursing with Irish Roger, when I remarked on how he'd given his life to altruism, he corrected me with the distinction that he'd given two lifetimes. And I was humbled in the face of sainthood.

Wanda is the only girl from during that epoch who enjoyed my cross-dressing. She's one of only a few who were able to see (and appreciate) the whole me in all my myriad parts. Me and Wanda would be getting high atop a multistoried car park when she'd pull makeup from her purse and fard up my face with lewd and lurid war paint (while disclosing a latent lesbian fantasy). She's the only one of that period that I ever went to visit dressed to the nines. Wanda once gave me a small gift and it was wrapped in a two-foot square of white lace. I used that swatch of lace, that lagniappe, as a mask and would often be seen on the streets at night wearing it as a talisman, like Prince in *Purple Rain* or the Lone Ranger (whose mask was a torn piece of his murdered brother's shirt): I will avenge her to the ends of hell and back! (Who was that masked man?)

One night I went out to cop dressed up in a long sleeved ivory linen shirtwaist with a tight Chinese collar and the whole back panel ripped out, exposing my full back-piece tattoo. I had on a tight black miniskirt and my favorite red spaghetti-strap spike heels, corseted by a wide red patent-leather belt cinched tight around my waist, and my long hair was flying wild, with my face banded by the white lace mask. I got stopped twice going downtown by guys who wanted to pick me up. "I like what you like." One even gave me a cap.

The biggest coke spot right on the stroll, and I arrived at the island between north and southbound lanes on Allen Street and was headed to the spot when I saw Barbara over there in the middle of the median and she was bending forward, squinting at me, as she warily approached and was softly cooing, "David?" Seemed she had just shot a half gram of C and was seeing my lace-wrapped face as though in bandages and thought I was just coming from the hospital having had my face bashed in (Ha ha), so violent was the world through which we moved. On the way back home, I walked past the windows of an all-night diner on First Avenue (the Cosmos) whose clientele included cadets and rookies from the nearby police academy. As I flitted past a packed booth, I heard (right through the glass window), "Hey, look at that!" And the bozos all turned and gaped.

Barbara was another *fille de joie* who frequented both Saint Joe's soup kitchen and the Allen Street stroll, a true doyenne of over ten years on the block and a favorite of mine; she was a rarity for her longevity and, moreover, in that she was highly talented (concert pianist) and intelligent (MIT graduate). An overall alluring, lascivious wench, stoic and phlegmatic with the composure of a Grecian sphinx. We shared a chemistry that allowed us companionable ease together as well as a similar extent of craziness. When Barbara would come over for an evening and would say, "Let's do a shot first," I knew she was my kind of gal.

I had made a date with Barbara for one particular day that I expected my unemployment checks to arrive and, while I knew she waited for me at Saint Joe's (no doubt buried in a Stephen King novel), I went and got myself arrested for jumping the subway. As the clock ticked away towards five-thirty p.m. (when the check cash places all closed), I was being arraigned downtown, next to a macadam-topped playground (Columbus Park—Chinatown's only park) where elderly Chinese men, lined up like an aerobics class, performed their morning Tai Chi exercises; the same playground where adolescent Chinese gangsters rumbled by night; the juxtaposition of the arraignment bench,[1] and the cosmic Chinese Absolute,[2] and hatchet-wielding tongs,[3] a durable New Age riddle for the Muses.

It was already past five o'clock when I was released and I ambulated allegro all the back ways to our rendezvous where I made the check cash by the skin of my teeth (much to my and Barbara's mutual relief) and we were off to the races. Room 1407 at the Kenmore Hotel, whose walls tell their story on these very pages. There was never any eros when me and Barbara had an assignation, that was never our intention. Neither of us engaged in meaningful passion ordinarily and so, unhampered, we would carry on together like old shipmates. Me and Barbara were like bread and butter.

Barbara stationed herself, back to my room's door, close to the floor, sitting on an overturned box, her right hand in my closet next to her, searching, then in my toolbox, in which were knives for every occasion. Every knife a professional chef might conceivably need, whose function however mundane or remote, was in there. When Barbara grabbed a knife, I knew just what she was holding because I knew that knife intimately and, when she moved on to the next knife and the next, I knew each subsequent knife, its nature and spirit. For those knives had each in turn been extensions of my hand, the means of my livelihood, the tools of my art, my craft. I had purchased, lovingly, each knife that Barbara now so haphazardly rifled in her curiosity. I let her satisfy her casual interest. She was not unlike a kid with her hand in the toy chest.

One night, Barbara went to some john's pad for a trick and the berk started pinching her paps, hard; whence she resisted,

---

1 American jurisprudence
2 Tai Chi Chuan
3 Chinese-teen vice-racket brawls

the fish said, "Come on, you know you like it," and he kept it up, and when he finally paid Barbara she noted where he took his do-re-mi from. Later, Barbara and her boyfriend went back to the mark's flat with a gat and robbed him of all his whip-out and the sap was sobbing it was his rent money and while the posslq held the heater to lover-boy's head Barbara told him, "Act like a gentleman next time."

At one point, Barbara managed to enroll on SSI, enter into a Methadone program, and secure a (state-provided) furnished flat in Brooklyn, no doubt all part and parcel of the same package. I accompanied Barbara home afterward for a visit to check out her new digs, getting roped into making her a cake as it turned out to be her birthday. After sharing some birthday crack together, Barbara explained how she planned to cart her brand new uphol-stered living room set (loveseat and two overstuffed club chairs) into Manhattan to sell on the Bowery. I just absorbed this news as typical junkie behavior. Barbara then offered me her bottle of Methadone, as she preferred to keep doing dope instead. The Brooklyn apartment was merely a hideout, a bolt-hole; Barbara continued to spend most of her time on the street and working the stroll. Just a matter of taking all she could get, I guess. Why not?

Barbara had, by then, been arrested some eighty times for pros-titution, vagrancy for the purposes of, and possession. When she told me I was aghast. Eighty? Eighty! Most of the girls on the stroll couldn't even count that high. She related one instance that stood out from all the others. Barbara had just copped five bags of dope and ten bags of coke. The dope was inside her cigarette pack, behind the cigarettes, and the coke was in the cellophane wrapping of the pack. Enter New York's finest (the worst). They had staked out the coke spot and were doing a sweep of all the customers upon exiting. They thought they were onto a dope (heroin) spot. So they grabbed Barbara and, upon searching her and finding the cigarette pack, exclaimed, "Here it is, we found the dope!" whereby they confiscated the coke, thinking it was dope, and gave the cigarettes back to Barbara. As soon as Barbara was in lock-up she snorted all five bags of dope at once. And was said to have been mumbling in her cataleptic stupor, "Stupid pigs."

It's really funny how that bust happened, the rozzers not even knowing that dope is never sold from a store. Dope is always sold on the street where it, like a three-card monte game, can be folded up in a snap, scrambled into a snafu, nixed in a New York minute, and the dope dealing vanished before your very eyes. On the other hand, coke is always sold from a bodega where servers couldn't escape. I often wondered why. Cocaine falls into the amphetamine category of drugs, which is a misdemeanor, a venial offense. Heroin is in the opiate category and so is an automatic felony, a mortal contravention. Coke spots get popped in the afternoon and are back in business three hours later. Get busted selling dope and you're looking at serious time.

Arguably, heroin is controlled by Afro-Americans; according to a 1965 Time-Life report, more than half of the heroin produced in the world goes directly into Harlem; whereas the cocaine distribution in NYC is dominated by Latinos in such alsatias as Washington Heights, Hell's Kitchen and Alphabet City. From those primary wellsprings (*entrepôts*) does the contraband trickle down into multicultural components. Similarly, all the heroin and cocaine that enters the city is the same respective product, as per the current governing cartel. It only begins to differ as individual suppliers extend and adulterate the merchandise with their unique and varied additives—lactose, procaine, quinine—which give a (often nugatory) signature to their own material. It can be likened to a tanker of gasoline selling lots to *Mobil, Shell, Getty*, who each add either a blue tint or a pink tint or a detergent and then market their blend as superior. As we used to say on the street regarding competitive product, "There's five cents worth of difference between them."

Most of the coke spots were Hispanic grocery stores (bodegas[1]) although there were also (in Alphabet City, all Latino owned and operated) a bookstore, record shop, fried chicken shop, gas station, botanica, a vesperal parked van and, rarely, an empty storefront selling nothing else but coke. But the common bodega was the norm and, as in all of those spots, no querent palavering was required. Just step up to the counter (often enclosed by bulletproof Plexiglas) and pass your cash over. They knew what you wanted, why you were there. The amount of mopus passed told how much you were ordering. If it was a dime spot, denominations of ten. A gram spot, denominations of twenty. Few places sold eight balls (⅛ of an ounce, or 3½ grams) because they knew you'd buy the product singly anyway and they weren't, after all, discount houses (the price was low enough as it was). When you exited the spot you were encouraged to walk out with a cheap mundane product (gratis) like a container of coffee or small bag of chips or a small container of bug juice which was kept stocked for just such purposes (all under fifty cents). If you made a substantial buy, you could take a can of soda. You weren't expected to walk out onto the street empty handed. Sometimes, if there were legitimate customers at the counter when you arrived, you were to browse the store until you alone could approach the cashier. The law occasionally invaded those places but, because of the tight security, the product was easily disposed of and rarely did an arrest take place. The coke is what kept those places solvent. Free enterprise serving the public. Isn't that what America is all about?

I couldn't handle dope (heroin). It was a nonesuch which with I could not cope, something foreign to my nature. It made me sick, I'd vomit, then thirsty, drink water, vomit again. Constipated, couldn't urinate. It's overwhelming, soporific, demolishing

---

1 There are over 25,000 bodegas in NYC, Bodega Association of the United States

clout held no real attraction for me. And that is why I never developed a scag habit. (A chippie maybe, but not a jones.) Who wanted to be knocked out? Nodding? Sick? Though I used dope periodically to mitigate the shaky, snapping crash of a hard coke or crack run, dope was never my drug of choice. I was a speed freak from the word go, never happier than when I was jittering around in a flurry of ebullience. I didn't want to be mellow, or to chill out; nor to touch base or be on the same page, never to be user-friendly, or online, or to give anyone a head's up, nor to wake up and smell the coffee, or push the envelope—it isn't what it is. And I never, in a million years, plan on going forward. My trip was hopped-up, my act racy, risqué. Hype and crazy was the way to go for me—freaky, freaky, freaky. I mean, there was plenty of time to lighten up, to be cool, to chill out when I was six feet under. Get heavy. Walk on the wild side. Let it all hang out, was my motto. For my purposes, crack was the ideal drug. Having tried practically every get-high, I found nothing equal to crack for warping one's disposition, for inducing physio/psycho-trauma or transmogrification. People who try to act normal after a blast of crack make me laugh. Go with the flow, baby. Ah, the burning, undying energy of youth. Sayonara.

I was frequently surprised to discern that acquaintances who knew me thought I was a dope (heroin) addict. This is because most of them were dope addicts themselves and, I guess, it was natural for them to assume the same of their confederates. I often thought it was wishful thinking, like, psychological projection—misery loves company. Even Wanda, my loyal Egeria, routinely suggested my fixing a speedball when we were shooting up together. "Here, put some dope in there," coaxed Wanda as I fixed my C and Wanda fixed her D. "You trying to get me hooked, Wanda?" as if my drug habit wasn't bad enough already. Marion was also convinced I had a dope habit. She'd often ask me, "Are you straight?" meaning was I dope sick or had I fixed. Thank heaven for small favors. I could never see the sense of a speedball. You either did one or the other, first the C and then the D. Mixing them up seemed counterproductive, like a funicular, antipodes cancelling each other out. Similarly, I couldn't see chasing the dragon (smoking heroin). Like snorting coke—why play around with your drugs? Once you start shooting, it's the only way to fly.

I recall once speaking for the first time with some slag when she asked me, "Do you do coke?" and I answered, "I shoot coke," at which she seemed embarrassed as she mammered, "Well, Yeah, ah, I mean, if you're going to do it..." I always marveled at how those young chits affected such a bluff and tough manner, which only served to make them more transpicuous. Just part of the survival instinct of the street, I guess. Which brings to mind another piece of physical graffiti who once boasted to me, in her stroppy self-hatred, that she charges fifty dollars for fellatio. Haughty and challenging as if such a disclosure would elevate her in my estimation, would earn my admiration for her worthless, shit-hole of an existence. So many of them out there—on their knees.

Another acquaintance of mine, Sharon, whom I had just treated to a monster shot of C in my then current hellhole, shared her innermost desire with me (honesty in payment for the shot) by admitting that she secretly wished to die. She expressed it as "We all want to die" referring collectively to girls like herself—street whores, dope addicts, AIDS victims, etc. And in return (after my own shot) I admitted that I secretly desired to get my ass kicked—like I had it coming for being the shithead that I was by living as I did. This was, for real, the sad honest truth at last, the tragic fear and horror harbored by all the sick, hopeless street people who all wind up dead (at an unnaturally early age) just as they expect. I'm not sure about Sharon but she became very sick from AIDS soon afterward and went on a Methadone program, hopefully to save herself. But others, like Tina, who expected death daily and finally embraced it as she wound up dismembered under the Williamsburg Bridge; and Barbara, of the rare *jeunesse dorée* that fixed her last shot to the stars on the street she so loved. And as for myself, I escaped the beating as I escaped from the street, but I am a rarity, an exception to the norm. The point here is that the life of the street leads to an early grave and it comes often as a relief. And thus is the street tragic, the final price for a (seeming) carefree life of drugs, sex and violence. Yet the real sadness is that, for many, "the life" is the only choice they ever have. And it is that reality for which I blame America—the waste of its populace like the waste of all its natural resources and, as exemplified by the amount of garbage this country produces, a mirror of our society's attitude, our arrogance: America's population equals five percent of the world's total peoplement while, at the same time, we produce twenty-five percent of the world's garbage, of which twenty-five percent is food—that's no less than twenty-eight billion pounds of food annually—thrown away.[1] "One nation, under God, indivisible..."[2] or, "Sha la la la la la live for today..."[3] Reduced to a cliché.

But back to the police, who are unbelievably naive. I've gone into a coke spot to score and there was a cop in mufti at the counter trying to buy. I get the eye from the server, so I go browse amongst the aisles. After the narc leaves (being unsuccessful) I score and exit onto the sidewalk where the plainclothes accosts me and says, "He wouldn't sell to ya, huh?" I glance at him like he's got ten heads and continue walking, but the young cop is persistent. He walks along beside me, rapping, trying to bring up the subject of coke. I think he's going to grab me and I'm holding, so I jump into the busy street in front of a taxi and,

---

1 Edward Humes, *Garbology*
2 Pledge of Allegiance
3 Grass Roots, "Live for Today" (recording)

when the cab stops, I hop in, leaving the pig more frustrated than ever.

Another time I had just copped a dime of coke, my last tenner in the whole world. It was dusk and as I exit the spot and start across the street, I see movement out of the corner of my eye and there's two uniformed Dogberries emerging from concealment and crossing the street to intercept me. I take the glassine envelope out of my shirt pocket and pop it in my mouth. Upon seeing this, the fuzz rush me, I'm slammed against the wall of a tenement, arm twisted behind my back and one cop is clawing at my mouth trying to pry it open. I have the bag of coke between my gum and cheek so I could talk, open my trap and all. I'm frisked withal they find my stem, which had a whole cap only tapped into it and whose entire length was opaque, thickly coated with milky residue. There was more than ten smackers worth of crack in that stem alone. The stupid flatfoot is banging me against the wall in his frustration, scratching my lips bloody. I don't want to swallow the bag of coke, I have got no more cowrie, but I can feel the glassine paper bag dissolving with my saliva, there's nothing I can do to prevent it. The pigs see it's a no-win situation and so let me go, seemingly forgetting about the stem they have of mine which contained as much contraband as was then dissolved in my stomach. That incident later worked to my advantage when, one night, out to cold-cop some dope on Clinton Street, the roving dealer recognized me and commented, "I remember you, standing up to those cops when they were shaking you down over on Second Street," and I was surprised that not only had that episode been witnessed, but that I had been tagged and recalled as a local hophead who would face down the fuzz when under pressure. Not so much honor among thieves as that I would rather any consequence before I'd help the pigs.

On a late night deserted subway platform, wanting to beam up, I wandered into a train tunnel a good thirty yards on the catwalk whence I stopped to fire up. As I was toking and rushing with the blast, here comes a train, its headlight bearing down on me and, as I'm caught in the glare, I press back against the tunnel wall while the motorman speeds past, close enough to put his arm out of his window and touch me. I'm certain that he must have radioed in this aberration lurking in the tunnel since that is what those transit workers and their private police force do. Hence I make haste along the catwalk back towards the station platform and when I arrive into the glaring florescent light there is a transit cop coming towards me. And, I'm still clutching the crack pipe in one hand and the lighter in the other hand as I cup the contraband in my grip and turn my hands backward, doing my best to conceal this fell evidence in the face of the nosy bizzy who is inquiring as to my doings in the tunnel. I explain how I needed to take a leak and merely intended to duck decently out of sight. The patrolman lectures me that I only needed to request the key for the platform toilet facility from the token booth clerk—Yeah, right. I'd have a better chance of being struck by lightning before a token booth clerk would open up a toilet for some stranger, let alone the fact that those subway toilets are the most foul, reeking, disease-ridden cesspits imaginable (the stench permeating through the steel door). Now the bobby is reciting statistics on death and maiming in the subway tunnels as though such trope would impress me. Finally, I have no ID to produce, which the gendarme requires in order to issue me a summons and, Christ, I'm still clutching the crack pipe and lighter through all this, trying to play the straight man in this obvious gag. Is this cop serious? I'm at last able to verify my immanence by way of a phone call, and receive my summons, accepting the citation with my lighter-encumbered hand, the flatfoot having tagged me and done his pettifogging duty, and I'm released into the ominous night, ticket in shredded pieces on the ground, as I hurry to find a cowling blind in which to urgently beam up another blast.

Another time, I had just copped ten caps of crack (a C-note's worth) and ducked into the entrance of the Orpheum Theater to take a quick hit. My head is back, the stem to my lips, lighter flaming above, and suddenly there is a shield in my face and a dick holding it and he's saying, "Don't move, let's see some ID," and I blurt aloud, "O shit!" and bolt as if the hounds of hell were after me. I always carried my drugs in a pocket containing nothing else, to allow for easy access in just such a crisis as this. As soon as I turn the first corner, all the caps are in my fist and I'm looking for a place to throw them where they'll be retrievable. I spot a stack of empty boxes piled on the sidewalk and expertly fling the caps into an empty box as I fly by at fifteen miles per hour. I looked behind me and never caught a glimpse of the heat. After circling the block for thirty minutes, I recovered all the caps but one and was on my merry way. Still, your tax dollars at work. What's the big deal when one of us little fishes is scooped up? To keep the courts and jails running. A Sisyphean labor at best, serving only to provide an impression, a domino that the NYPD are hard at it to keep our streets clean, thereby helping to justify huge payroll expenditures and employment for so many inept bluecoats (tools), a smoke screen for law and order. We're all glad it's so easy and predictable. In a foreign country, it could be your life. Just to get high, to try and find a little relief for a few minutes from the overbearing and depressing miseries of living. With everyday impetus and values of hustlers and their clientele so opposite—strange bedfellows coming together for a trick. A putative conflation that surely shouldn't be illegal.

Coke spots were (are) a dime a dozen. It often seemed as though every other bodega or candy store in the ghetto sold grams of coke for twenty dollars. But dope (heroin) was harder to locate, not because there was less of it but mainly because the dealers moved around, on foot, on bicycle, roving from street to street, from block to block, sometimes in a vehicle. Dope spots that were stationary were rare and very popular. One such location was on Second Street between Avenues A and B. Dealing only after dark, until three a.m., they set up at the end of a hallway in a tenement, at the foot of a stairway. There were minimally eight workers in the team, possibly more. All Hispanic. There were at least four bruisers stationed on the sidewalk outside the building a couple of doors in each direction on both sides of the street. The door to the spot was manned (outside) and there was another monitor (indoors) keeping the line straight and against the wall. "Have your money ready, Have your money ready," a broken record, "Up against the wall, Against the wall; OK next, Go, Go!" The pusher (at hall's end) was flanked by a bodyguard like a Rottweiler. The pusher sized you up, "How many?" (Dimes only, only dimes in Loesida—price-fixing by the Dope Trust). He took your cash and carefully counted it, placing the bills around a thick roll he kept at hand. Then counting out the glassine envelopes of dope, cautiously bending each bag back and forth to insure single servings. His stash was in individual bundles of ten glassine envelopes (bags) per, each glassine bag *Scotch* taped closed and each bundle bound with a rubber band. Those bags had no markings, unlike the bags on the street, which were stamped with brand names and emblems, an inscription sometimes with an impresa, a logo: Polo, Acme, Hennesy, C-Town, Forsyth, Lifetime, Red Bag, Cash & Tango, Libra, DOA. This spot I'm referring to here did a whopping business, serving over five hundred customers nightly, usually fifty people loitering the sidewalk waiting for them to arrive and open, then all the dope addicts swarming the spot like a file of the afflicted descending on Lourdes, a bizarre processional of the damned, a cortege of zombies. And every Tom, Dick and Harry set up shop in tenement doorways up and down the block to take advantage of the traffic for the stand-pat spot. But often those transient black grifters would sell you dummies so it was always prudent to buy from the established business. And there was invariably a temerarious bad'un close by to every dope spot who was selling hypodermic syringes. "Works, Works, Two for five, Two for five," their litany. I always managed to inveigle three sets for five clams. Those entrepreneurs (crooks) would buy the syringes for ten cents apiece and sell them for two-fifty hard cash. It was not uncommon to see anabolic hunks who looked like cops buying needles from those sidewalk vendors. They were weight lifters buying works to inject steroids and would resell the hypos at the gym for five or ten dollars per set. When I was bodybuilding, long before I became a junkie, I used to pay such inflated prices. I've paid thirty-five dollars for a shot of steroid that should have cost five dollars. Capitalism in action on the black market.

Often, (like crack dealers) the needle pushers would have their stash in a crumpled paper bag, tossed on the sidewalk against the wall of a building nearby, so as not to be holding the evidence. When someone approached them for a buy, they'd look around and, determining that the coast was clear, go over and bend down and extract your purchase from the apparent garbage on the sidewalk. This always amazed me because it was such a transparent ruse. It would be so easy to collar those guys in any number of ways. Once, I scored (pot) from a crew in Washington Square Park where one cat picked up your dropped cash while another tossed your purchase onto the ground for you to bend over and collect while their friends all kept watch. Yet, that act too was obvious if observed from afar. As if the narcs would honor some ethical regulation according to Hoyle. But such is the capacity for self-delusion. Occasionally you'd come across some slick beat artist trying to sell used works that were resealed in the package. You had to look carefully to make certain that the plastic barrel of the set was shiny on the outside with no streak of *Vaseline* inside from lubricating the plunger. A neat trick in the shaky, hurried umbra of full night.

It was not unusual, when standing in line to buy coke or dope, to observe someone making a purchase with a crumbled wad of greenbacks that were covered with blood. The thing most notable about such a scary giveaway was that the dealers didn't bat an eye, they just straightened out the bills and accepted them as if this were normal—which (in that violent drug world) it was. There were so many desperados on the streets who thought nothing of killing you for your swag. Welcome to New York.

There was a pet peeve I had about dawdling when out copping. For me, copping was the all-important activity, the means by which to attain the moment of fruition, to be at the apex of my aspiration. There was such a priority, a premium on achieving that ultimate goal, the very act of using the drug, getting high, that absolutely nothing should take precedence, should stand in the way, until you're securely back in your hidey-hole doing the trick.

I've been with blockheads who want to stop for coffee on the way to score, window shop, talk to friends, cogitate over trifles, until I'm literally dragging them away from the diversion. And then, on the way back, while holding, an instant bust if you're stopped, these congenital imbeciles want to stall for an argument, yell and holler, litter, shoplift, jaywalk, anything to call attention to us. There are so many things that can go wrong on a drug run. How many times I've heard tell of the guy carrying an ounce of dope, ten thousand dollars, a gun, and he gets busted for jumping the subway. I mean there's dumb and there's asking for it. When you're out to cop, that's all you should be doing.

Another peculiarity I had was a unique way of folding my money, carrying it, and palming it over, developed expressly for copping. I continue to shake my head in dismay when I see some poor jerk on the street, in the park, the projects, in full view of the surrounding, gossiping populace while they count out the transaction cash, hand to hand, conspicuous greenbacks flapping in the breeze and, finally, crumpled into a wrinkled ball and shoved helter-skelter into a pocket. I am appalled at such slapdash carelessness, such blatant advertising of their hustle.

I folded my bills (with the dark side showing) in half, then in half again, to only one quarter of the bills' original size. No wrinkles or folded corners, the final fold left the denomination showing.

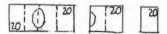

These compactly folded units were then arranged in a pack with the largest denomination on the bottom and smallest denomination on top, like a hand of cards, the denomination showing on the bills in the same ordered sequence.

This allowed me to count out the money single-handed inside my pocket, to hold the money and pass it, always palmed, never showing outside the boundaries of my hand. It allowed the recipient to see at a single glance, a quick flash, exactly how much there was being transacted and to accept the green as invisibly as it was handed over. So neat, fast, efficient. So cool. I've had more than one dealer remark on and adapt this method. And I always carried my cash in a pocket with nothing else so that the neatly arranged bills were readily accessible, unimpeded. My pants' front pockets were designated cash in the right and dope in the left. Both methods proved invaluable on more than a couple of occasions. And I never used one-dollar bills. Dealers don't like them, too bulky, too time-consuming, too amateur.

A run for me, and what might be considered usual or regular in the drug scene, is from two to three days in duration. That is the time one can be expected to stay up (awake) and continue imbibing drugs before exhaustion and sleep overtake you. It's not so uncommon to do a four-day run. But to stay awake and using for five consecutive days is rare. By the time you reach that point you are blacking out and nodding, often in the most unlikely positions, being kept from toppling over by junkie inertia. I may even have done a few five-day runs myself, it's hard to recall because one's brain is seriously snapping at that point. But when I hear someone bragging of having been up for seven days I know they're full of crap because nobody can stay awake that long. It's just impossible.

Everyone's body has its own capacity, its finite limit. When it comes to endurance, drugs can enable one's body to exceed its own limits. Yet even one's outer limits have their eventual boundaries. I have more than once imbibed a good quarter (¼) teaspoon of good speed (crystal Methedrine) at the limit of my endurance and immediately fallen asleep—a quantity of crank that would have kept a sober person speeding for two days. I have personally, and witnessed others, fallen asleep after a monster blast of crack when I had reached the limits of my reserves to remain conscious. So don't ever believe that you can rely on a drug to enable you to exceed your mortal limits, though you can have fun trying.

I recall falling asleep while speaking to an employee at my last career job; jerking awake while in the process of addressing him, with the wise cat facing me deadpan. Probably couldn't wait to gossip to his cohorts that the chef nodded out in the middle of a sentence. Embarrassing.

One of the certainties of remaining awake for days without sleep is the psychosis that results from the absence of rapid eye movement (REM), which occurs during dream time and slow-wave sleep, which is so necessary for the maintenance of sanity. Thus it is the lack of proper sleep, as much as anything else, that contributes to the derangement and insanity of so many street people and it is that factor alone, or lack thereof, that caused me to abandon the street for a shelter the first time and to finally settle into a resident hotel for the latter duration of my vagabond life as a New York City bum.

I will always laud the nutritional and rejuvenating attributes of fresh-squeezed carrot and orange juice for the drug addict in that one's body is run down repeatedly to so damaging an extent that massive doses of this juice taken during the time of or immediately following acute bouts of chronic abuse will ward off exhaustion and give one an edge over co-conspirators. I have regularly drunk, after a hard two-day run, a pint each of fresh squeezed carrot and orange juice and without so much as a short nap was able to go on boosting for another day as if I were starting fresh. I am convinced that this therapy has kept up my very vitality and health and immune system in the face of such corrupt lifestyle. Available at all Korean delis.

I had heard somewhere (through the junkie grapevine) on the street that people could sell their exanimate corpse in advance (while still alive) for $100 cash to a hospital, to be used as a scientific research cadaver after death. It was known as the body donor program and participants were supposedly tattooed on the bottom of their feet with some sort of identification so that, when they expired, the body would wind up at the institute to which they'd sold out. This is the sort of fantasy that circulates amongst street desperados. It was the latest get cash quick scheme for bums, much more lucrative than selling a pint of blood. Well, I gobbled up the gossip; I mean, I really put my hopes up and proceeded to truck from hospital to hospital (Beth Israel, Bellevue, Saint Luke's), following directions through labyrinthine corridors deep into the bowels of each hospital, to the offices of the body donor programs, only to find, time after time, that there was no cash payment for donated cadavers. One could donate their posthumous body if they so desired, but no one was paying for it. Well, that was a big letdown, only to be expected I suppose. Life is truly cheap in the cities and there just isn't the demand for fresh cadavers anymore, not enough that someplace is willing to pay for one. Unlike the 1800s when there was a brisk business in supplying corpses for medical study. I surely wore myself out trudging around on those expeditions, chasing a jack-o-lantern.

It seemed to me that I was always more fatigued and exhausted than should have been normal; even when I wasn't worn out from a drug run I seemed to always be bushed. So I started going for blood tests at clinics and hospitals asking them to check for any disease whose symptoms included lethargy and lassitude, such as diabetes. Time after time the results came back negative, nothing wrong, nothing abnormal. I was stumped. Until finally one doctor ordered a test for hepatitis and I scored positive for hepatitis B and C, and anemia. So then I knew why I felt tapped out. The life catching up *pede claudo*.

Back to street rumors: There was one prevalent canard afloat about that time (1990), especially amongst Spanish-speaking clans, of the Chupa Cabra (goat sucker) that slinked around the city at night killing its victims by inserting a long thin member and exsiccating the life blood or fluids from its host (like a spider). This story seemed to gain popularity as elderly West Indians and Hispanics elaborated scary tales with which to frighten their grandchildren. The myth originated, purportedly, when a dead goat was discovered on some tropical island, with no apparent cause of expiration. "Don't close your eyes or the Chupa Cabra will come and suck you dry in your sleep."

Getting arrested is always the ultimate bummer and Manhattan's detention center, the Tombs (a mock Gothic necrolith), connected to the criminal courthouse by the Bridge of Sighs on Center Street in New York City, is truly the pits. The initial holding tank, a temporary calaboose designed to jail fifty prisoners is always packed with two hundred of the city's hard cases, gangsters, jaspers, waddies, shtarkers, psychos, and jack-rollers, as well as jellyfish who are gobbled up almost as fast as they come in. Noisy, dirty, oppressive, standing room only, and the toilets haven't ever been cleaned since everyone makes a flying crap anyway. And you can be thankful, dear reader, that you need only imagine the odoriferous stench and its causative agents. Three meals a day: fried egg on white bread with a container of regular coffee; yellow American cheese (one slice) on white bread with bug juice; bologna (one slice—non-halal) on white bread with bug juice. Detainees should be put through arraignment in less than a day since the gears grind twenty-four/seven, this is New York.

Of those holding cells which "belonged to no one and everyone, a place through which all passed and no one stayed,"[1] and of

---

1 Nelson Algren, *The Man with the Golden Arm*

detainees as "people who had never picked up any sort of craft; it was not so much a lack of aptitude as, simply, feeling that no work had any point to it. They lived in prison much as they had lived out of it; not hoping or despairing, not worried about the future, or regretting the past, nor feeling any concern for the present. They had never learned to want. Secretly afraid of being alive and the less they desired the closer they came to death. They gave nothing because nothing had been given to them."[1]

This is the blanket outlook, the secret psychology of the hustlers, the whores, the aimless, ignorant homeless who infest the cracks and crevices of the mean streets and their shadow world, all those systematic rejects whose bids in the quod are frequently a relief from the nagging requirements of living. Society is the poorer (and not just in lucre) for those miserable defects of humanity, a sorry by-product of our great American culture.

I often marvel at the blathering stupidity of untold street people from the ghettos, the slums, as well as from privilege and prestige. It doesn't seem possible, yet there it is looking you in the face, that so many imbeciles are born, bred and reach adulthood with no more maturity than frustrated children—spiteful, jealous, malicious children with no skills, no heart, no understanding of anything. Pathetic in their infantile convictions and distorted superstitions, full of animosity and a feeling that society owes them something. An insult to and a drain on working taxpayers. They crowd the streets and they crowd the prisons; they are the aimless drug addicts, the petty criminals, masochistic prostitutes, dysfunctional perverts; a tidal wave of human garbage produced, not overseas like our consumer products but, with Made in America stamped all over them. As technology advances, America's populace keeps apace in direct contraposition to progress, such as, people can't add without a calculator, they don't read books

---

1 Nelson Algren, *The Man with the Golden Arm*

but rely on television for information. Americans can't think for themselves anymore—media-manipulated, misguided souls who (like the homeless and illegal immigrants) help to define our great nation.

All of my arrests during my NYC bum years (save one for fighting) were for jumping the subway turnstiles. And my sentences were always community service. One time, on my way to the Catholic Worker for dinner, I found a discarded full-length mirror that had only a slight crack in it, thus I took it with me to tape up at Saint Joe's. It was raining cats and dogs so I jumped the ⑥ train (from Twenty-Third Street to Bleeker). A plainclothes transit policeman approached me on the platform and asked for identification, a request that I ignored. But he was obdurate so I asked to see his badge, which he showed (could have been had from any joke shop on Forty-Second Street), thus I asked to see his gun, he refused, I turned away, he grabbed me, and I smashed the mirror to smithereens over his head, cutting his bloody cheek. In half a minute I was surrounded by three more plainclothes TP (doing a sweep of that station). By the time they bundled me into the waiting Black Maria, I was strangling on the bear-trap-tight manacles, my captors had made sure that my head hit every step going up the subway stairway and bounced off every surface along the way. I felt and looked like I'd been run over by a bus.

But, always, the likely and condign amercement—community service—was the easiest part of the whole program. Working in the city's parks: cut grass with a motorized lawnmower; pick up litter with a bimmy stick; sweep sidewalks; rake between shrubbery; paint anything paintable. Once, I disappeared for a couple of hours to smoke pot and drink gin, came back and everything was cool. The Latino supervisor was the most laid-back guy, afraid to tell anybody to do anything. I felt sorry for him so I always made a conscientious effort. I mean, you could go as slow as you wanted anyway. One time I cut almost all of Madison Square Park's grass in one day, the reeve was so thankful he was practically sputtering.

There was a girl named Fifi who frequented the Mars Bar, across the avenue from my First Street apartment. I had made her acquaintance some years earlier when I first moved into the neighborhood and began patronizing the Mars. Exhibits erotica—paintings by disturbed and gifted artists—and foxy barmaids were the dive's saving grace. Fifi was petite, lithe and very attractive. An exotic Oreo. Always in a dress and heels. I never in a million years would have guessed she was a guy. My Chilean friend Ernesto was good at spotting drag queens a mile away, but I went so far as to pick Fifi up still thinking she was a real girl. What a witchy surprise when we fell into her bed. And Robin was living with me at the time so I was given the knowing stare when I came home. Seemed Robin knew all about Fifi's scene, Robin having tended bar at the Mars.

At Fifi's pad on Carmine Street in the quiddative West Village, we passed by her ground-floor residing flat (complete with walled-in backyard parterre) and ascended the building's staircase to her second-floor party flat. Fifi held forth how she never entertained guests in her domicile proper; that the upstairs *pied-à-terre* was her sporting den—what kind of bucks did this trick have? Those West Village apartments didn't come cheap. Fifi explained that she was an amanuensis to a dame magazine editor (evidently wise to Fifi's transexuality). That Fifi never allowed smoking or drinking in her sporting lair. That she used rubbers. (How many rules were there?) The place was clean and tastefully furnished. Fifi then proceeded to show me some "before" photos of herself as a high school all-American, a good-looking kid. She only cruised East Village bars to pick up guys... I appreciated the case history, but, I mean, "Let's go, honey."

It was so pleasurable, I remember, a relief to be with some-one like Fifi. Gentle, loving, caring, clean and cuddling. Eager to please. I can't help myself from doing whatever I can for them. More of a girl than the majority of butch dykes on the stroll. The most touching moment of the whole affaire was when, in the morning, Fifi gave me cab fare home. It reminded me of when I used to do the same for dates leaving my Asto-ria flat the morning after. Naturally, I walked home and kept the cab fare.

We are relentless, we are remorseless. There is no stopping us. We are hellcats. Spawn of the street with no future and no past.... Out on the street, on the corner, making our score, making the scene, getting the skinny, pulling a caper, ripping a john. We've got it all, youth, freedom, savage fury. Some of Chico's renowned epitaphial spray paint graffiti eulogize on the tenement walls of Loesida: In memory of Sunny, Rolo, Kiki, RIP. In memory of Flash, Mickey, Speedy. A final placa or cenotaph for all the departed cholas and cholos: Con Safos. So many of my own crowd gone west even as I chronicle this memoir, outworn before they're thirty: Marion, Mattie, Tina, Arleen, beautiful Barbara, Tony the Artist (who drew the portrait of me in the back of this book). I used to bring Marion bags of coke to the hospital during her final throes of pneumonia from AIDS, cooking crack in the bathroom, couldn't eat but still smoking. Shooting dope to the end. The hard, fast, wild life of the street. Never backing down, game to the end. We are slum life, slum vitality, slum venery. We are style. Refractories. Recalcitrants. Recidivists. As I squeeze out the final draft of this manuscript from a jail cell. Eat my dust coppers, you can all smell my grass. Rebels even to the grave. We are a product of the class system, proof of all that's wrong with apartheid, blood, sweat and tears as sport for the affluent, cracks in the mirror of America.

When I used to accompany Mattie to visit Marion ("She got the ammonia again.") at Cabrini Hospital in her final days, a drained, sepulchral skeleton lying in her deathbed with the waxen *memento mori* of enervated hopelessness, she would rally upon seeing us, ever ready for one last get-high. Propping herself up in a half-hearted effort of vitality, Marion would feign interest in her untouched meal tray by picking up her fork and then, unconsciously, putting the handle into her rictus of a mouth as though toking on a crack pipe stem. Conditioning doth prove.

En route to Cabrini (a public assistance hospice), Mattie would dispatch me into a coke spot, having given me twenty lovely dollars with which to cop. Oddly, for all his enabling of dope addicts, Mattie was ever cold sober and would never venture into a spot himself to cop for his wife. Flush with the score, in the hospital room, me and Marion would slip into her private privy while Mattie kept peep. For all her mortal diseased and emaciated condition, Marion would insist on cooking up the crack—remarkable, for although Betty Crocker she weren't, Marion could cook crack like a champ, her hands sure and quick—and invariably would manage to toss a rock into the bathtub for her later, solitary recovery. What a gal. May she rest in peace.

As soon as Marion passed away, Mattie invited a young knock-out ingenue (whom he'd been sniffing after for a good year) to move in with him, along with her newly acquired husband (Karen's stammering get); she with a good two-hundred-dollar-per-day dope habit (which Junior already had to meet) and their rent payment doled out on the ladies' back (to Mattie), all right in the middle of Mattie's living room. The two newlyweds hung some bedsheets from the ceiling to simulate walls (for privacy), and that was the last I'd seen of the mess. Though I could hear the screaming through the windows, out on the sidewalk and observe the dumb kid, lugging boosted A/C's and car batteries, like an Egyptian slave while wifey wouldn't allow him entry to the house without any dope, as she put out for Mattie. I had thought that kid's life strange while living with Karen, but this took the cake.

Styling is something many modern bums engage in besides, that is, looking like bums. Such as the night out in Chinatown with Karen (during our period of détente) when I decked out in my newly acquired pimp ensemble. Or, the summer I sported open-backed satin vests from a goodly supply at Trash and Vaudeville antique clothing shop, worn with provocative unisex slacks—my initial undertaking with panache as a bum. One night I attended a tattoo flash exhibit at a West Village gallery clad in a long sleeve gold lamé shirt that looked like something Elvis Presley would wear (25¢ at a Bowery thrift shop). One winter Robin wore tight over-the-knee cordovan boots trimmed in rabbit fur with high Cuban heels and skirts so short you could see her luscious crack. Wanda was good for wild outfits, one day in a black charmeuse flamenco skirt with a half-dozen crinoline petticoats, white ruffled blouse with puffy sleeves, knee-high black leather boots, and a rhinestone-studded tiara. She was a caution. Some of the blints on the stroll turned their pants inside out (pockets flapping) and worked completely topless—that was fast work! (traffic piled up, and rear-end collisions.) Another effective hook was a white or pastel blouse with baby doll sleeves and Peter Pan collar, red or black patent leather Mary Janes (or heels) with turned-down white anklets and a miniskirt to flash a smooth snatch—"Oo daddy! Goin' out?" One cool cat wore pleated peg-leg trousers like from a zoot suit, Tom Jones shirt with balloon sleeves and long pointy collars, Panama hat and bucks, complete with dundrearies—a real blade, sharp as a dagger. Everyone on the needle. Some with tattoos across the forehead. We had style.

Plastic or latex miniskirts with skimpy tops, a bit of flash and high heels never fail to draw horny men like honey. Those girls burn out fast, but when they're hot they're hot; frisky and furry and full of fleas. I can still envision them, lined up on the sidewalk like party favors, stepping into the street as cars slow down, catcalling, "Boodles! Wanna date?" That's all they have is their looks, and those they pander shamelessly.

As cook at the Catholic Worker, I had access to the clothing room and so had my pick of the jumble. There were mucho nice garments to be had, items of good quality and practically brand new as frequently someone would become late and the spouse donate their entire wardrobe to charity. I usually looked like a bum but it was often because of the incongruity of my ensemble as well as the wearing of multiple layers in cold weather. You don't need rags to dress like a bum.

You may wonder where we bums obtain such gear. Well, that's a good question. First of all, you must keep your eyes peeled. There's lots of clothing thrown away in the city. Also, church clothing drives. Charity organizations like the Catholic Worker. Thrift shops like the Salvation Army. And you must be ready to cash in on someone else's spending spree, like with me in Chinatown when Karen had her windfall and was buying like crazy, whatever I brought to the counter. The skirts from the stroll are quick to take advantage of the generous john, will lead him to boutiques and drool over items in the window, shoe stores, gourmet food shops, urging him to splurge on them. Those dolls are city slickers to a T. I have come by nice outfits just by being alert to discarded freebies along my daily way. Especially if you have a spot at which to collect things, amassing a wardrobe. At the

Kenmore Hotel, there was one blighter who collected used clothes ("I'm in the garment business") and would sell or trade the items for cigarettes, beer, joints. There are bums who collect clothes from churches, even from the trash and sell the merchandise at sidewalk bazaars (cheap). Flea markets. Cheapo thrift shops in ghetto areas. I have acquired copious bonny vesture from such sources. And there are secondhand shops like Twice Blessed or Second Time Around for inexpensive previously owned items. The main thing is to always be on the alert when passing such treasures, you can find things you could never shop for. There's nothing like a secondhand shop or a full ashcan for splendid sartorial surprises.

There is a mammoth Salvation Army outlet—an entire building—over on the west side, at 208 Eighth Avenue. I've only been there a couple of times because it was so out of the way from my locus over on the east side, but the unnew depot had everything—it is a department store like Macy's, huge, at least six floors, miles and miles of merchandise, practically anything you want and cheap: men's, women's, and children's apparel, shoes, furniture, appliances, housewares, toys, the works. I once ran into a woman there whom I had once dated, who played the rich widow (or grass widow) role—lived in an expensive tower block near Sutton Place. And she was embarrassed upon meeting me there in the thrift store. Ha, just another dowdy bum scrounging through the discarded chattels of her betters. Now, if that affectress would have been more honest and didn't project the façade of a fastuous dowager, then I wouldn't call her a bum. Alas, it all comes down to attitude, to outlook.

There were also a slew of secondhand shops on Seventh Avenue in the Forties, which wasn't my propinquity but a lot of used goods and clothing to be had, cheap—the Hell's Kitchen vicinage.

There were a couple of times I went for an AIDS test, a double check, a month or so apart for each test. Each time was at a different location. Once I went alone, another time accompanied by a Catholic Worker (Sabra). It was both times very heavy since just testing out connotes some degree of concern. When everyone on the street has the unalterable conviction that, "We're all going to get it." Going back a week later for the results; the dread; the relief. You can understand how AIDS becomes so prevalent. The street lifestyle lends itself to a complete wearing down, a consuming, an abrasion, an attrition of your very human substance; your skin, your hair, your vitality, your organs, your nerves. Days without proper rest, weeks without proper nourishment, hygiene nonexistent in your filth and urine-laminated world. Eating garbage from the street, never cleaning your works, sharing works, sex without condoms. Your body a sponge for germs, your overtaxed immune system has retired.

Suicide was a not unpopular affair amongst the plebeian sectarians of the Allen Street stroll. Prior to experiencing the junkie depression of a full-blown addict, it had been inconceivable for me to fathom the intentional taking of one's own life. However, the street has its subtle way of eventuating its nihilistic gramarye.

My aborted suicide attempt was arranged in the most bizarre fashion I could devise. I had been shooting coke for days, dime shots. My (Kenmore) hotel room, reflecting my condition, was a shambles. I had one twenty-dollar bag of coke left (a gram), more than I could shoot at one time and hope to live. Yet there weren't two shots in the bag. I needed more than half a gram to get off. (It might be worth mentioning here that when I began shooting coke I would derive ten shots from a gram bag—quite an appreciation in a couple of years.) Withal I didn't even consider cooking the remainder, that wouldn't have served. So I decided to ginger it up for a dead cert, shoot the whole bag and do the Dutch. It had to be dramatic for the city news. My big exit statement.

I pulled out my eyebrows. Stripped down. Shaved. Red lipstick. Black patent leather high heel pumps. I bondaged myself with red and black electrical tape around my arms, legs, feet, around the shoes, waist, chest, neck. I hung syringes from my ears like long dangling earrings, still with their bright orange sheaths over the needles. I had electrical tape wrapped around my head, face, eyes, mouth, groin; wrapped up in tape between my fingers, around my hand, wrists, cutting off my circulation. And, finally, I pulled a sheer nylon stocking shot with holes over my head and face. I had positioned a chair, elevated, facing the medicine cabinet mirror and mixed up the shot, a whole twenty of C (about a gram), and drew it up. I then strapped myself into the chair with the electrical tape and picked up the gun. This was it. I had stuck a brief note to the wall next to me, stating: "It's been fun, now it's time to say good-bye." There was a beer cracked and cigarette burning. I could barely move in the chair being so tightly wound in, I looked shattered, I could hardly make a decent shot being so restricted by my bonds. And I reached for a swig of beer that was all slobbering down my whole front, went for the cigarette I couldn't bring to my mouth, only smell the smoke and I looked in the mirror at my doomed facies and said, "I have something to live for—beer and cigarettes." It was enough to save myself. I guess all I needed was a little drama in my life.

The Kenmore Hotel on East Twenty-Third Street, the Hotel from Hell, an inenarrable barrow of badness and misdoing, was a junkie's delight. Twenty-three floors, nearly one thousand rooms and seamy, it was a SRO of predominantly deadbeat welfare recipients, though a fraction were short-term visitants; after all, my first weekend at the Kenmore was paid for as a one-night stand when I was homeless and bouncing around the streets. By the time of my residency at that blackened yellow brick building, the Kenmore had been run-down and neglected and outright vandalized for a duration of time long enough to render the place practically beyond repair, certainly beyond redemption. The building owner, a shifty Vietnamese slumlord, had enough Vietnam refugees working there to keep the operation functioning, that is, filled to capacity and collecting the rents which, evidently, were not applied towards maintenance. It was a sad, seedy, down-at-heel settlement, squalid and dismal, wheezing away what was left of its life under a hazy Paris-green sky streaked with orange that would be pretty in another part of the country but only bespoke of an unhealthy smog from the nearby East River blast furnaces, bumper-to-bumper carbon monoxide, and jets dumping fuel prior to landing at La Guardia airport—the putrid man-made pall that envelopes New York City. And some claim the Kenmore Hotel was one of the gates between the land of the living and the necromancer's realm of darkness (through which the streets of the city twine).

The Kenmore Hotel was an H-shaped building, which allowed for twice as many rooms whose windows faced each other than those (like mine) which faced out towards the street. At one point, early on in my residency, I had a room on the fifteenth floor that faced the interior of the building, that is my window faced a wall of neighboring windows. I was shooting plenty in those days and, being summer, the curtains were often ajar to allow some air and light to flow through. On one occasion, as I plunged a shot home, I heard through my window, plain as day, "There he goes!"

The hotel was a free-for-all. The spade front door guard (a degenerate hotel resident) allowed anyone entry who gave him a dollar or a joint or a soda or a rock or even a cigarette. The front desk, a bulletproof enclosure, was manned by staff who spoke only Vietnamese, or a Caucasian one-armed retiree (lobster shift) who, one and all, were petrified of the resident rabble. Room burglaries and muggings were as common as the mice and roaches which infested that "vast, unbottom'd, boundless pit."[1] Electric, heat, cold and hot water outages were as regular as the rising sun. You could buy any illicit drugs or bootleg whiskey right in the hotel. Crack dealers and prostitutes would solicit continually left, right and center. Stolen merchandise abounded, alcohol, crack and dope flowed freely, life spilled out of the rooms and into the hallways. In fact, there were homeless bums living on the stairwell landings and on the roof. I had once been one such squatter myself, camping out on the Kenmore Hotel roof for a weekend. Hibachis and electric fry pans roasted in the hallways and at dinnertime (around five o'clock p.m.), the fuses kept blowing for a good hour as residents operated their microwaves for which the building's wiring was inadequate. An all-around calamity of slamming doors, shouts and screams, barking dogs, crying cats, shrieking birds, blasting music, amplified guitars, conga drums, blaring televisions, knocking, clanking, grating, horselaughter, wailing babies, breaking glass, gunshots, assaults and parties in equal measure, a cacophony of noise.

There was conceivably more drug dealing in the Kenmore Hotel than in any equal area of Hell's Kitchen, Alphabet City, Washington Heights or Harlem. You could buy children for food stamps, guns, snuff films; there were in-house rackets: shylocks, bookies, card games, numbers; trade food stamps for cash; buy coke, boo, crack, needles and smack. There were lezzies, homos and queens; voodoo and black magic. If it was vice you wanted, you didn't even have to leave the building. Supplicating bawds and dealers knocking on room doors—personalized escort and home contraband service. Pizza and Chinese food delivery (until that was repealed due to continual stickups). It was Xanadu. Walk

---

1 Robert Burns

around the hotel wearing nothing but your underwear, in the most bedraggled condition, freshly dried blood in rivulets down the tracks on your black-and-blue arms and no one batted an eye. And the place was filthy.

The unsupervised pair of Mexican illegals who swept the floors and collected the trash were hopelessly inadequate as well as being regularly pulled into rooms by resident homosexuals and used as punks. There was garbage all over the floors, vermin, elevators were urinals, people defecated in the most unlikely places. The plaster walls were being eroded, breathing moisture, black mold and decay as water from broken and leaking pipes in the walls leeched its way through and exuded a dripping, overwhelming, swampy miasma throughout entire areas of the building (including the rooms) rendering those sections hygrophilous breeding grounds for fetid pathogens most vile. The acoustical tile ceilings in the bathrooms and hallways were practically nonexistent, having been either torn down by ravaging crack fiends or fallen down of their own sodden resignation. The communal baths and toilets on each floor percolated the pong of raw sewage, vomit and mephitic vapors and were littered with empty crack vials and used syringes, discarded lighters and cigarette butts. Hallway floors were sticky with split soda, every corner a dump of candy bar wrappers, crumpled cigarette packs, pizza crusts and potato chip bags. Mice ran freely throughout the hallways and under doors into the rooms, roaches conducted maneuvers over every surface, entire areas of the building were in perpetual darkness due to missing lightbulbs and broken fixtures. The whole pestilent and fungoid gumbo was continually being further defiled by the Vandalic resident maniacs. As are the native Third World aborigines part of nature with the jungle in which they live, likewise were the Kenmore residents an extension of the indigenous vermin which infested that living cloaca.

411

At occasional quiet moments in the hotel, say from five a.m. to nine a.m., it was not unusual to hear the loud crashing of a room door being kicked in by deranged burglars. The elderly and disabled tenants of the hotel were regular victims of stickups and muggings, especially the old bag ladies who lived there in perpetual terror. The elevators were a favorite spot for these assaults. And fear be unto the wary on monthly days when welfare and food stamps and disability checks fructified.

Another favorite pastime of the demented denizens of the Kenmore was to start fires and pull false alarms. It was commonplace to see flames from a burning mattress or wardrobe licking out of windows around which were the ragged, scorched feathers of bygone fires, the hallways filled with smoke. But most annoying were the repeated false alarms pulled in the middle of the night, deafening, strident, clanging tocsins sounding off in the hallways followed by the fire brigade arriving clad cap-a-pie in full battle array with screaming sirens, *Klaxons*, bullhorns, flashing lights, yelling and banging on doors, the works. There was rarely peace and quiet at the Kenmore.

All of this routine run of activity was merely atmosphere for the Kenmore Hotel, accepted and shrugged off by the resident life-forms whose sole purpose in being alive was to get high and party. When those creatures would crash after a few days of continual boosting, nothing short of an atom bomb could rouse them. Therefore, it was "anything goes" for my first few years at the Kenmore, with no diminution in malefaction, that is until I acquired my family of pets and achieved sobriety.

A number of the Kenmore Hotel's residents sold secondhand merchandise on the sidewalk in front of the hotel where there was lively foot traffic as well as the overflow from Baruch College across Twenty-Third Street; setting up peddlar's tables or leaning the goods against a building wall amidst more loitering hotel guests conducting every sort of business from shoe shining to dope dealing to hustling tricks. The most frequent wares offered were (used) mass market paperbacks but small appliances also were common, from toasters to vacuum cleaners. One gal (who was very popular) had a small stand where she hand painted washable tattoos on customers. One day I stopped to inspect a collection of six or eight full-length living-room-wall-size mirrors—thick, ornate and heavy. Any one of those must have weighed a good fifty pounds. Beautiful, antique, upscale items, all in perfect condition. The vendor, with whom I was acquainted, told me he was going to buy a *Blimpie* for his dinner, intimating there was money on the ledger. So I asked him what he did with his unsold stock at day's end, unable to envision him lugging all those mirrors to safety. And he replied, "I break 'em!"

On impecunious days, between my bimonthly welfare payments, eschewing work religiously, my daily requirement of beer and cigarettes were obtained on credit from Jose's bodega on First Street or Hanna's grocery on Twenty-Third Street. Since those necessary purchases would run up a considerable tab over a two-week period, I was restricted to the bare minimum in beer consumption which was a single forty-ounce bottle of Midnight Dragon (malt liquor) that retailed at ninety-nine cents. That five cups of beer I would guzzle on an empty stomach, as fast as humanly possible, in order to attain the maximum effect of the little alcohol contained therein. If my purchase was made at Hanna's, I would sometimes follow up with a fried egg and cheese on white bread sandwich (one dollar), and complete the ritual with a nap up in my snuggery at the Kenmore Hotel (early morning was the only reliable time of quietude there). Occasionally, I would obtain one forty-ounce beer from Jose in the morning and another from Hanna at night. Either of those establishments would allow only a single bottle of beer to be charged per day, not willing to contribute towards drunkenness yet compassionate enough to forestall convulsions.

On days when I'd work at a deli or a coffee shop, my constant foible was augmented by a pint of cheap schnapps and a dime of rough weed, wheedled from the three cannabis wallahs at Madison Square Park for eight possibles. "Eight-dollar man!" the chief would scorn me with derision. I had initiated that practice by soft-soaping them that I resold the bags for ten bucks, thereby realizing a meager two-dollar profit. But that ruse was short-lived, though they tolerated my penurious patronization out of some altruistic prepossession, a logic-defying sentiment in dope dealers.

Frequently, after I took a casual day job for an extended period, I would succumb to the ravening lure of the needle and cop a gram of C, on the path of reckless ruin, only to regret my weakness as soon as it was consummated and carry my distress around the next day like a despondent sluggard, until I had some more wampum in my clutches after work whence I was off for another rum go, to conciliate that ancient Mammon of Unrighteousness, and the thrill of the first shot.

Mine was not such a malcontent mode of being, save for my defiling bouts with cocaine. But the stranglehold on my serenity, my fortitude, my resources, that crack and the gun exerted over my very constitutional existence became a haunting psychoneurotic disorder that allowed me no peace, only ultimate sadness in my subjugation to its evil embrace. It always recurred, like some deviable tertian ague and stood like an eclipse between me and my good nature, a parasite that was sucking my blood. I had become comfortable with my frugal lifestyle and found validation in my perambulations through the city and my avid reading, yet this constancy was ever threatened by the ineluctable wild card of cocaine and my friable, unpredictable resolve against it. And, thus, did I sink into the dismal junkie depression of an addict, for the umpteenth time, never believing I'd at anytime finally pull out, for feeling like this was truly the end.

By the time of my interment in the Kenmore Hotel, I had given up using commercial banks for good, having put the banjax on my credibility long since, and hence had no compunction regarding the kiting (or bouncing) perfectly serviceable bank checks, inscribed with a prior address and, for all intents and purposes, a prior identity. The holiday season abounded with Christmas fervor in full swing; garland-laced streets, shimmering reflections of multicolored lights, merchants as well as consumers were earning and spending with Dionysiac abandon and thus did I exult in the ritual festive esprit. I was only struck by the idea as I passed by a liquor store in whose window was a large signboard proclaiming, "We accept personal checks." It seemed to me they were just asking for it as I spun my devious noological wheels to devise a plan.

Back in my hotel room I employed all my sartorial and tonsorial science to step back in time, creating the wise of a suburban yuppie commuter mid-management clone. In my worsted suit, silk tie, shined shoes, combed and shaved, overcoat over my arm in whose hand clutched a paperback, pen in shirt pocket and ID ready in wallet, I whipped out my checkbook with practiced ease and, amidst (as planned) such mad rush hour hurly-burly you'd think they were giving the stuff away, I signed off on a $75 whiskey purchase for four days running. On day five, store personnel were asking for their $300, a hitch which, sadly, soured the entire hustle. Much of the connived liquor I fenced at Jose's bodega for hard cash. That hoax was an out-and-out swindle which I never felt compelled to square when I caught up on my IOU's before I quit NYC at the conclusion of my ten-year stint as a New York City bum. Confidence man, forger, cracksman, racketeer—as a street gamin one becomes a jack-of-all-hustlers.

My across-the-hall neighbor at the Kenmore Hotel, who occupied the opposing dead-end room from mine, was a hardcase old homosexual who, after my initial couple of rebuffs, stopped hitting on me; though he maintained relations with the brain-damaged kid next door to his room, as well as with one of the Mexican floor sweepers. James, a tall, narrow, distinguished looking old lecher, austere, neatly trimmed white beard and often sporting a Greek sailor's beret, he frequently wore a black tuxedo which he donned for his part-time (lobster shift) cashier slot at Cosmos Diner (at First Avenue and Twenty-Third Street), a gravy job as James collected SSI. I once procured a cashier's position for him at a coffee shop on Park Avenue at which I was employed as a coffee man, packer and all-around feeder. When James showed up, late, for his first (and only) day, I became so embarrassed—I never saw a worse cashier in my life. A total disaster. The boss was still shaking his head as I elbowed my way in to take cash and dispense with the long line of frustrated customers waiting to pay their tabs while James stood by and commented, "I say, you're a crackerjack." But I maintained good relations with James because he was a harmless and amusing old sot and, besides, it never hurts to have a friend close to home keeping a weather eye. I used to sometimes collect bruised fruit from the Korean markets on First

Avenue (gratis) and give bananas to James. And I once visited him in Cabrini Hospital, bringing him a can of beer and a bag of *Fritos*. When I left NYC for Vermont, James gave me his address so I could write. He's still waiting for a letter as far as I know.

One age-encrusted hotel busybody would very slowly reconnoiter the hallways, pushing a broom, all the while listening and cataloging every sound, spending three minutes sweeping outside a curious room, inching closer to the door with Dumbo ears, certain that something fishy was going on as secret door knocks recurred and muffled ID's were conveyed through cupped hands held against the door at all hours of the day and night. That spy was more obvious than the covert traffic. I'd hear the broom outside my room door and call out to the snoop, "I am sweeping, Sweep, Sweep!"

There was one girlie whom I loved to hear lecturing her mentally deficient girlfriends in her fulminating Southern accent (while eating soup from a Chinese white box): "So you get soup (pause) *and* noodles (pause) *plus* chicken (pause) for a dollar, know what I'm sayin'?" Or, "So she sends me down to buy her oatmeal and tells me to get regular, not instant. Now why would she want regular when she could get instant? Know what I'm sayin'?"

There were a couple of dwarfs included in the Kenmore's resident rogues' gallery, which seemed to kind of round out (or bottom out) the overall picture. One character, with sheeny black hair and a leg brace worn beneath his stiff new dungarees (rolled with six-inch cuffs), would frequently pull out and swig from a Drano can, often unable to conceal his mirth from the reaction of passersby. That one sketch alone made me like the joker.

Another homunculus, less fortunate and more conspicuous than his frater, was missing his nose; that appendage having been thoroughly hacked off as (rumor had it) street justice for being a thief and a rat. That balding, gray and wrinkled gnome of Hispanic civism and unkempt was as wretched a specimen of joylessness

417

as ever skulked the infernal regions of the Hotel from Hell. He would lurk about the Kenmore lobby in some sick parody of martyrdom, occasionally wearing either of a couple of prostheses he had which lent a more bizarre aspect than the alien death's head feature *au naturel*.

Harold, of Tom and Harold—Tom being the Kenmore's thirty year old haberdasher (used clothing) and Harold's special friend. Harold, in his late fifties but in good shape with a genial smile, on a pension or SSI; the two had adjoining double-size rooms with a shared bath. Harold also had a prior, alternate special friend, a twenty-year-old Nelly and very out there crack fiend who still came around on occasion. Now, Harold's room was at an inside corner of the building's H configuration while, just around the bend of the hallway was the floor's public lavatory. Keep in mind now that those rooms were located on the fourteenth floor, a long way down if one were to fall from a window. One day I stepped into said lavatory in time to witness the above mentioned crack fiend perched on the open window ledge, just above the urinals (his back to me), and watched in frozen amazement as the dude launched himself into the air in a bionic (doubtless crack-induced) Evel Knievel jump and flew in an arc to land on Harold's open window ledge—a death-defying leap. The cat landed perfectly, foot on the embrasure and hand grasping the upper open sash window and, like a smooth criminal, he was inside Harold's room.

A day later, I was next to Harold's room in the hallway, knocking on Tom's door (to smoke a joint) when I overheard the Nelly speaking to Harold from the hallway next to me—"I know who stole your watch; I can get it back for you, they want five dollars for it." And I just thought to myself that between that guy and Tom, they had poor Harold coming and going. But who was I to interfere in someone else's scam. As much as I felt for Harold,

I wasn't his guardian angel. Such were the relationships at the Kenmore.

Most of the Kenmore Hotel's residents were the dregs, the very sullage of the gutter, obnoxious sleazebags who pushed their trip on everyone else, be it noise, filth or hard looks. In a trash dump of an elevator one time, a vile and grotty negro sneered to the passengers at large, "Look at this shit" (waving his arm at the accumulated trash on the floor), and in the same breath he threw down an empty food wrapper, adding to the pile of garbage. Another time in an elevator, a belligerent black buck started prattling some crap to me which I ignored. He tried again. I continued to ignore him. Then he turned to his nasty girlfriend and lamented, "We spend our lives trying to be nice to the white man and he won't even acknowledge us." I continued to stare straight ahead.

There was a hilding resident mestizo who'd strut around the Kenmore vicinity wearing a feathered headdress, spouting, "White man is stupid!" He'd march right up to someone weak-willed (an old lady) and thrust his scowling face an inch from his victim while giving them the evil eye—a loathly bully. One day as I entered the Kenmore lobby carrying a grocery bag in each arm, the same creepy shitheel called after me, "Thanks for holding the door, Next time I'll kick your ass." I turned towards the scumbag and said, "Why wait?" Therewith the turd marched up to me, at which point I dropped my groceries and punched his ugly face, Pow! Regretfully, that was my only good shot; the bastard was bigger than I and soon had the better of me, but I stood up to the worthless piece of dog meat and took my punches until the Peelers arrived and dragged us both off to lockup. What irked me more than being charged with assault was losing all my groceries.

Violence never pays and I always tried to steer clear of trouble. I've walked away from many a donnybrook on the street and even acted as mediator between adversaries. But sometimes you just have to make a stand, when you've taken all you can take and are pushed against the wall.

I was forever dreaming up new hiding places to stash my cash in my hotel room. Not that I ever had much to stash, but paranoia stalks the drug addict at every turn, a ubication, like a cold breath on the back of your neck. One favorite secret place was behind my room's door lock. This entailed removing the doorknob and deadbolt knob and unscrewing the escutcheon (scratch-plate), thereby exposing the inner door lock mechanism—a good five minute operation. Into this recess I could conceal a couple of folded frogskins. Another hidey-hole I made the mistake of once utilizing was an opening about the circumference of a twenty-five cent piece beneath my room's porcelain sink. There were two of those openings at the rear of the sink, beneath the faucets, and into one of them I slipped a rolled-up Jackson. In attempting to retrieve the double sawbuck, I only succeeded in hopelessly pushing the script beyond redemption, deep into the cavity of the basin. Frantic beyond reason (needing the ointment to go cop), I proceeded to smash the bottom of the bowl to bits with the back of my meat cleaver, finally rescuing the green and rendering my laver a destroyed unusable disaster. It would be months before I was able to persuade the maintenance chief to replace the sink, claiming it had been in that condition since my initial occupancy. Between the smashing of my sink and its successor, a period of time elapsed long enough for whole sunflower seeds accidentally dropped into the drain to sprout (the sink not being in use, hence the seeds collected in the drain's elbow rather than being washed away), and leafy vines came climbing out of the drainpipe one night like some mutant science fiction beanstalk invading the hotel's plumbing during the hours of darkness. They looked so pretty as they grew that I allowed them to remain undisturbed until such time as the sink was replaced. On one occasion, when I ventured out to cop in the middle of the night, figged out in punk drag, with no safe place on my person to secret my loot, I made a slug and packed it—shades of Papillon.

PART FOUR

REBIRTH

The first time the kid spoke to me I was lying flat on my back on a bare greasy mattress at the Kenmore Hotel, languid and sick as a dog, crashing badly from shooting coke and smoking crack for days. Aching in the joints, muscles and ligaments from being frozen in kinky catatonic positions for consecutive forty minute clips during the preceding Walpurgisnacht[1], I had a bad cough, a sore throat, my numbed, bruised arms like bloody pincushions were swollen with trauma; I was shaking with chills, headache pounding, my dirty, stinking room looked as though a bomb had gone off in it and taken out the heat in the process, freezing, in the winter of my soul. I was thoroughly wretched, filled to overflowing with self-pity and worry as I had reached a point where I'd completely lost all control over my situation, my misbegotten, wounding condition seeming beyond my ability with which to cope, turning on some abnormal hinge as if by its own volition. I was the runaway locomotive, the stampeding herd, the berserker run amok. Nothing and no one could save me from certain doom, as I lie there in a half-delirium, gasping for breath, knocking on heaven's door. And from out of that crisis of my world emerged my saving grace, a superior moral fiber, my elemental nature, the best of me, popping up out of the morass in the voice of the kid, a baby voice: ("I love you Davy"). "I turned as at some annunciation."[2] What a soothing and pleasant surprise, dream-like; wishful thinking was it? or deliriousness, yet coming from inside me, audibly, from my lips. My life essence reaching out in a desperate effort to save myself, to save us both. The true split personality. ("You like the good life Davy, you like it clean and nice, you don't have to be sick like that, we can do it together, we can make the nice place just the way we like it, we'll take a nice shower and dress real nice, and we can go get the nice breakfast,

---

1 Nightmare
2 D.H. Lawrence, *Sons and Lovers*

and we'll be the good guy right Davy? We don't have to live the terrible way, see Davy, we can do the right way, that's us.")

And so I allowed myself to be guided by the kid inside me, reduced to puerilism and starting life all over. A second try. Being led by the hand along the right path, isolated by goodness, insulated from bad influence, a growing up and learning though, this time around, the child being father to the man ("Come on Davy, we can get all fix up"), the kid coaxing me along in clear baby voice, leading me, transmuting the warring faction of destructiveness with the sweeter portion of righteousness. And so it began, a reforming of myself, a shunning of the world as I had known it, a dissembling of bad and wrong parts of myself and a new creation in its place. Not a recovery but a revision, a melioration that required a certain alchemy to achieve. And hence, with the kid as companion and guide, I made my new way. And it went in simple baby steps, my new life, the new me. We (me and the kid) cleaned up our act. I started to work again. Still ever the bum, but a good guy now. And it was funny too as the kid always spoke to me aloud which, in the least, drew stares. Walking along the street in clarion soliloquy, and in my new temporary jobs the kid would often exclaim lustily without warning—for instance, the boss at work would tell me to do something and the kid would yell, "Aaghh!" Or would answer, "Ben de bee!" (We created our own neologic language). And although the kid was very vocal and used me as his spokesman, I never once answered the kid; I was mute to his disquisitions. I, as the kid, was a one-sided interlocutor, verbalizing the kid's solecisms; I never tried to palliate the kid's confabulation.

For all outward appearances, the kid's act was a retard act, which left my other primary self withdrawn into my own world and a sort of dementia in its place that I could view from without and enjoy as observing a farce. By allowing the retard-persona of the kid to manifest my outward character, I didn't have to deal with all the everyday hassles from which I wished to extricate myself, while still there, present on the scene (in the background) guiding the kid in my daily endeavors. I was at once set apart from society as I observed and laughed at it. And, moreover, the kid helped me to keep my inner focus in perspective as I didn't need to become involved in the repetitive minutiae of my daily existence which could drain my energy and creative reserves through such requisite demands—the kid became my ongoing escape hatch. Thusly, with the aid of the kid, my last ditch only hope at life, I was saved from myself. But the early days were not without slips.

I ran into Wanda after the implementation of my new persona and she remarked in all seriousness, "Very interesting." All this kid business, with its contingent infantile, regressive split personality might seem pretty absurd, insane in itself one could surmise, as though my new peculiarity were a caveat of my bum endeavor, of its seasoning or ripening, my evolving life space, *la vita nuova*. Well, one couldn't get much more insane than the way I'd been living, a moribund junkie in a land of deceit, subterfuge and duplicity (not unlike straight society), with people dying, vanishing and being chopped up all around me.

Tina, the Chinese dragon lady, one of the neighborhood trulls in our crowd, was found dismembered under the Williamsburg Bridge, her body parts each in a cardboard box amongst the waterfront garbage. This sent a wave of delicious frisson through the current stock of indiscriminate strumpets on the block, which extended for a few days, with the certainty that an authentic madman was on the prowl in the area although, in fact, many of those selfsame slatterns secretly dreamed of just such a fate as they made their nightly sorties into the fuliginous uncertainties of their trade. This abhorrent crime of savagery never received the slightest mention in the newspapers or tabloids; another hushed up atrocity that the not bright police would never solve (save the culprit fell into

427

their laps), so why shake up the working, taxpaying public over a homeless prostitute?

Within or without the mutual harem of our native district, Tina was one sexy tomato. Exotic as only an Oriental can be, she was melt in your mouth-watering cromulent and had that natural Asian submissive serenity which seems to so attract western men as it's not a natural inbred trait of American women. Which is not to say that Tina lacked any of the sly cunning which only a Chinese Circe could marshal with all her ophidian, vespertilian instinct. Tina enjoyed much success in her Cyprian trade on the street and was admired and loathed in equal measure by her cohorts. She was a wanga dream catcher of alpha talent and I was deeply entranced by her bewitching charms with her svelte, long legged, high cheekbone, golden skin, pouty lipped, deep space-eyed promises, in her slinky black sheath (split cheongsam style) and high heels, with that glassy black hair only Asians possess. Pure seduction. The dragon lady. She had a cardboard revetment against my apartment building's sideyard chain-link fence, beneath some shade trees, facing Houston Street, between First and Second Avenues; a roomy barricade, a good five feet in height, cozy as hell in the anthracitic dead of night. Tina's was one of a number of cardboard hootches in which I occasionally enjoyed camping out—back to basics for me as an ad hoc apartment dweller. And, as with all of those heart-robbing street vixens in their fragile bivouacs, Who slept at night?

I had the distinction of sharing Tina's company *à deux* in my First Street balliwick, for the three days (and two nights) preceding her demise, the duration in which the witch never once relinquished her grip on her crack pipe. Even during our excursions out to cop, and our eventual cozying up, that scepter was ever clutched in the siren's claws. Amazing. *Requiescat in pace.*

Or, take another acquaintance of mine, JC, a lesbian who was molested and abused as a youngster by her four older brothers and has been keeping that hurt warm ever since, who commented upon gazing around my First Street apartment when it was the OD lounge, "Normal people don't live like this," to which I replied, "Who said I was normal," at which she countered, "So you're a weirdo," and my riposte, "From the word go." Here was a bull dagger who hated men yet prostituted herself to them in the most intimate ways to earn money for her drugs. She was a dope addict, a coke addict, a crack addict and an alcoholic who lived on the street cozening naive femmes with her sophistry and she was lecturing me on being normal. Each and every one a quiz, a *rara avis*, a clockwork orange with a similar story where insanity *is* the norm. And if the only way I could drag myself out of it was by living with an invisible kid who talked to me then so be it. "Works for me," as one may hear in a twelve-step meeting room where people hold hands and pray.

Wanda was cooling her jets in lockup, having been picked up for sitting in the middle of Allen Street, the four southbound lanes, and cooking crack. Stalled traffic, horns blaring, sidewalk observers forming a circle. Sometimes one intentionally gets arrested, or goes to the hospital or detox, just to take a break, to rest and be warm and fed. I've seen a desperate slag lie down in the middle of Second Avenue until an ambulance came and took her away. I myself have gone to the hospital on an imagined OD in the hopes of being admitted. When you have to finally take a break, the street is no place to do it.

The Bowery detox (detoxification facility) on Third Street between Second and Third Avenues is like checking into a hotel. An entire floor of a huge edifice that takes up half a city block; a multichambered, fully staffed accommodation. There are fifty beds in an enormous L-shaped dormitory room arranged barracks fashion, each bed having its own nightstand with drawers and a lamp, clean pillow, sheets, blankets, all necessary toiletries, towels, pajamas, slippers, bathrobe. There are magazines and paperbacks in plenty, always a full coffee urn, with cookies, and smoking is permitted. Movies twice a day, AA guest speakers daily, three more than adequate hot meals a day, clean toilets, sinks and showers with *Kwell* lotion for scabies and lice. Nurses on duty around the clock, physicians on call, full-time counselors to hear your woes. A five day detox program for alcohol, seven days for drugs. Pit stop to recharge your batteries.

The haunting clientage of largely middle-aged alcoholics and addicts were frequently pretty stove up—seeking a respite from their chronic self-abuse; mixed in with some younger gits in their twenties, enrolled for various reasons from court or shelter mandates to questing pilgrims seeking some illuminating apperception which might, hopefully, give direction to their wayward lives. An overall apathetic bunch, an eddy in the prodigal spate, the fickle fluvial flux of street life.

There was a time during one of my stays at Bowery detox when I was scheduled to be discharged in a couple of days and I still had major trauma in one of my arms, so requested some medicamentation—a little Shiatsu—before I went back to the street since I knew I'd start shooting again. So I complained to the nurses who arranged for me to go to Bellevue Hospital during the late night downtime where I was to be treated in the emergency room; a time of night when inmates from Riker's Island and the Tombs are brought in, shackled and chained like the curly wolves that they are. While in the examination room at the hospital, I espy a cart chock-full of syringes and needles of all size and description. So I filled my pockets and, upon returning to detox, I was searched, busted, and kicked out on my grass onto the sidewalk at four o'clock in the morning, flat broke, in the glacial permafrost of deep winter... "Aarrghh, pea soup!"

Of the half gross of assorted sets of syringes I thieved from the hospital emergency room, a couple of dozen came equipped with detachable needles that I later discerned were intended to be discarded after the solution was drawn into the syringe—their gauge being too large for IV use and their outer surface of a rough finish and the tips not very sharp—those points were never meant to be used for injection. But use them I did, despite the brutal ravaging to my arms and veins they begot. Additionally, those throwaway points were not furnished with screw-on attachments for the barrel as the following scenario illustrates.

The upper (top) portion of a syringe's barrel is equipped with a couple of protrusions (one opposite the other), like a pair of stabilizers, under which one's first and middle fingers support the syringe while the thumb of the same hand depresses the plunger into the barrel, thereby injecting the shot. I was barricaded in my oneiric, candlelit, coal-pit of a kitchen, a sheet hung over the doorway to the living room as an added blackout to the already draped windows—one could never be too careful in shielding spying eyes from observing one's dastardly, illegal, reprehensible acts. Seated naked at my desk on my potty chair and sweating profusely, I was engrossed in attempting to dislodge a clogged needle—one of the bogus points described above—which must have had a massive obstruction stuck in the point, the needle's rough inner surface not helping the situation any. Whatever the logistics, I was determined to not lose that shot.

I turned the syringe with the needle facing upward (towards my face) and, held between both of my hands with a thumb pressing downward against each protrusion of the barrel and the small knuckle of each hand's first finger on either side of the plunger pushing upward, I squeezed with all my might. Something had to give: Twock! The entire needle came flying off the syringe and, like a quarrel from an arbalest, shot completely through my upper lip like some newfangled punk piercing. I was instantly

431

sobered. Less than four inches higher and I would have been blinded. What an eejit. One of my worst fears, which I repeatedly toyed with, was putting the needle through my eye after a shot as I flip-flopped with the sticker, rushing, watching the point twinkle, closer and closer, she loves me, she loves me not, isn't this just fun fun fun... Holy sheet!

Even better than the Bowery was the detox at Beth Israel Hospital, which had a waiting list for admittance, so highly coveted was it. At Beth Israel one was given phenobarbital for alcoholism and Methadone for heroin addiction. You didn't even have to be an addict, just claim that you were and stay high all day, lying around like a reptile sunning itself, your meals delivered to your nice clean bed. There was one kindly nurse who brought *Blimpies* for all the detox patients every Friday night. Rec room with TV and it was coed.

In addition to detox, there is rehabilitation (rehab) for those seriously minded about attaining sobriety and willing to change their lives. Usually, a rehab is a live-in, lockdown situation where the inmates are treated roughly and demeaned. Rehabs fill their victims' clogged, mushy brains with pedagogical indoctrination (brainwashing) designed to not only mold them, but to flush out impure compulsive reside with its rote provincial drills. I've known a rehab inmate who was late for something; they put him in a dress, shaved his head, and had him parade around all day with a mop and bucket. I'd be damned if I'd put up with that.

I attended an outpatient rehab—an overpriced facility of large dimension, comfortably furnished, multiple private counseling rooms, capacious auditorium, kitchen, potted plants, generously staffed and a bit pretentious—Greenwich House on West Twenty-Seventh Street where one toffee-nosed counselor, a deaf-minded self-styled Pygmalion (as phony as a three-dollar bill), would greet us, "Hello, wimps." I told him I didn't appreciate such a salutation. This was the same counselor who, upon my arriving for my hourly one-on-one session, kept me waiting for fifteen minutes only to inform me he'd have to conclude that day's therapy thirty minutes early. So, I asked if I'd be charged for the full hour, at which he snatched up his telephone with a flourish and (with a conspiratorial nod towards me) informed his famulus, "No charge for Mr. Bozo today." Next time I see the crook he berates me with, "You didn't tell me that welfare is paying for your treatment!" So I told him, "Somebody is paying," at which he snorted derisively. Guess who was charged and paid for the swindle. The same one who always pays, the poor working stiff, the taxpayer, the same one who is put remorselessly through the wringer for his entire taxpaying life, squeezed to death to keep the economy greased. Naturally, my enrolling in that rehab program was strictly to qualify for some welfare benefit, some handout. I never put much stock in help programs which, to my observation, don't help much.

It might occur to sane normal people that a reassessment would be in order amongst the bum contingency, a periodic taking stock of one's situation, to revaluate one's priorities, to look anew at one's position in things, that is, his being a bum; a reflection of one's weal and hopes and expectations, if any. And yet, in my experience, there is not ever even a smidgen of anything approaching deep thought, or taking stock, or anything remotely resembling consciousness of one's role as a bum or his place in things, viz., amongst the general bum population. That is because the mentality of the bum, once set, is ossified like concrete and nothing, not conscience or memory, can move it. Thus, for the most part, once a bum, always a bum. There is no rehabilitating the hardcore bum. And I am a case in point.

Near the conclusion of my ten-year stint as a New York City bum, I was diagnosed with sciatica of my left leg, a severe impairment to my walking endurance, debilitating and painful. The sciatica was the first indication that I was getting old, that my body, ever so resilient and sound, was beginning to break down. The sciatica was a decisive factor in my opting to give up the life of a New York City bum, to pack it in and retire from the street, which is no place for the physically challenged. Survival of the fittest is a provisory mandate of the street by which selection is made and the infirm are culled. So, very timely, at nearly fifty years old, did I give up my act on the streets of New York City where, had I persisted, I may very well have joined the legions of faithful (and not so faithful) departed. Ten years hence, I would be a near wreck, a seeming shadow of my former vigorous, frenzied, outgoing self, but that's alright. A fair price to pay for the wild and full and reckless life of a New York City bum. For having lived the dream (nightmare).

I'd always been a hard walker. Ever since I gave up driving, an automobile being a superfluous luxury in New York City and, for me, outrageously expensive, having wrecked four new cars in four years as a drunk (blackout) driver, not to mention the cost of parking and insurance. But I enjoyed walking so much that I'd frequently elect to walk before I'd ride a train or take a taxi. Walking home from work daily for years, prompted by the transit strike of 1980, crossing the 59th Street Bridge,[1] the city to Astoria, an hour and a half of hard Olympian walking. I developed such a joy and appreciation of walking, seeing and experiencing millions of things that a rider misses. I feel that my propensity for walking contributed a confidence and eagerness towards hitting the street to begin with, crack notwithstanding. Certainly, in my opinion, not a vocation for the fainthearted though, in some cases,

1 New York City's busiest bridge, carrying 180,000 vehicles daily

perhaps, just the ticket for a withdrawn or repressed personality to either rise to the occasion or perish. The acid test.

On giving up the life, there were times when I had to choose between one walk or another, conscience or passion, to reach the big decision, to follow my head or my heart. It didn't come all at once, but in cameos. Each time a small revelation yet I didn't fail to recognize each for what it was, its value, its weight. One was my aborted suicide. One was watching me in a mirror wearing a rubberized pig's mask where I was the devil—whispering, beckoning, tempting, cooing—to take that irrevocable step. And, too, the disregarded, doomful fantasies: One was deciding on a stickup where I'd be sure to get caught and given serious time in a penitentiary. One was to intentionally contract AIDS. One was to poke my eye out with an IV needle. One was walking the stroll in drag where I'd be sure to get my ass kicked or killed. Overdoses I'd already lost count of, each time gaining on the big one with my name already on it.

How came I from the clean ordered warmth and security of my youth to this rioting confusion of madness, seeking, grabbing, as I careened and reeled across the monuments of the city; the residuum of my life, both contained and spilling forth across the curbs and frothing along the gutters, both seeing and blind, the blot and blur of years, the insensate iniquities, buried at the crossroads, the four points of the compass, the four winds blowing across the teeming and desolate streets of my heart, my soul; the city of my hope, my dreams, my fortune, New York, my Gehenna, my exile, my destroyer. A sacrifice to all the wasted souls that have gone before me, a martyr, a prophet, Quasimodo in the catbird seat; a shrine upon the catafalque of the zombies.

There came a point when it was no longer side tripping, no more just a game to be played. And with each cognition a verdict, a

435

resolution had to be reached, a turning point, a new path chosen, a line of demarcation where I either stopped or crossed over. And with each waive, phase out, each disclaimer made, marked and remembered, a tear was shed, the jig was up, a page turned on a new chapter. Until the life was left behind lock, stock and barrel. That's how I came to be here today instead of toast. People who say to me now, "I wish I'd known you then," I reply, "No, you wouldn't have wanted to know me then."

Drawn and led by the remote and demented lure of whiskey and crack, its enchantment, seduction, the fabulous and solitary wonder, the street and its evil hunger, the magnificence and heat and color of dancing fetishes draped around the lamplight of the night. A whirling orgy of fantasia wrapped in tight legs, in high heels, ripe kittens and chickens strolling down the avenues of lust and desire, irresistible, insatiable, we are lost, we are found, a constellation of pyrotechnics, bedizened firebrands flaming, burning, hot on fire, frozen in time. A farrago of ardent saltation and singing the bittersweet soul music of the street, like savages in some primitive carnival, flung to this odd pulchritude.

At times though I committed acts that may be construed as abhorrent, I can only say that sometimes when in Rome one must do as the Romans. Withal I make no excuses for my actions, I went where my heart, my passions and my conscience led me and never shirked from what I had to do. For I believe I have given in kind as I have received, and balanced the scales thereby. And mayhap at times I have done wrong and been bad, I like to think I have turned out good in the end.

During my ten-year reign as a bum on the streets of New York City, I have witnessed amongst my peers strange and stranger still types of behavior. From classic textbook cases to the most creative. Acts so severe, I turned away with a shudder. I've witnessed a deranged derelict skin all the flesh from his phallus with a blade, like peeling the casing from a sausage. I've seen a troubled Ishmael wrapped from head to foot in heavy-duty plastic garbage bags in the blistering (90° F) summer sun, and watched the same sort of wretch smear himself about the head, face and chest with fresh human excrement. I've seen an unhinged loser repeatedly smash his forehead and face against a brick wall and watched a young gamine fatally fling herself in front of a speeding subway train. With horrid fascination I watched murder committed from across the street, saw a man's brains beaten out with an iron rod.

Walking through Tribeca one afternoon, I came upon an imbroglio where a ex-motorcyclist had spotted his recently heisted bike and stopped the usurper who had unwittingly purchased it from the thief. A fight ensued whereby the new possessor of the stolen bike beat the brains out of the rightful owner with a tire iron. I observed with incredulity as the victim not only remained standing but continued to attack his foe as his brains and skull were whipped into a frothy mist. That's the power of the mind for you. Or adrenaline. All those dolorous twists and turns of the street which hang like an albatross from the necks of the forsaken and the damned.

I've seen bug behavior that was the direct result of street living and bug acts that were put on as one might wear a suit of armor or an invisibility cloak, a panoply for protection. I never felt the need to play a bug game. But from the initial emergence of the kid, whom I liked so much and who did me such great service, whom I allowed to come and go at will, to sometimes assuming the kid character for lengths of time immeasurable—my personification—I lived an act that was no act, lived a persona that was my true soul, my subconscious rising to the fore to guide, protect and save me, a bug act to rival the best because it was natural. The kid defined me as do hormones their respective host. I not so much re-characterized myself as realigned myself. People who had known me previously, honestly thought I'd gone over the edge. And I was indifferent to their reactions, so absorbed with the kid character as I was, my new carapace. It was the start of a new era in my life that has lasted to date—an epoch reign. Though, with time, the kid has become more homogenous and laid-back. But in the early days the kid was very assertive.

Much of the kid's success was his jocularity. That he endured and held my interest was due to his quick wit and innocence, something I thought I had lost long ago, braindead as I was. One psychiatrist said (of the kid) it was very inventive of me. Truly, something out of my control, is why I was so affected. And grateful—probably why I'm still here. (And so is the kid.)

Living at the time at the Kenmore Hotel on Twenty-Third Street and taking all my meals at Saint Joseph House on First Street, I was not restricted to the soup line but was allowed to eat with the staff, and this extended to three meals per day, all of which I usually took advantage. Thus my daily mealtime walking involved one hundred fifty blocks. On Second Avenue at Fourteenth Street stood Honey Bunch Pet Shop, which I passed six times a day and frequently stopped to gaze through the window at the puppies and kittens, at the kid's excited insistence. "Look Davy, Look at the guy!" Somewhere along the line, for at least a week, there appeared a glass aquarium containing half a dozen of some sort of small rodent, mousey gray in color, long haired, with stubby little tails. There was a whole family—mamma, poppa, and four teeny babies. Adorable, funny, cute as little buttons. It was wintertime. We would stand there (me and the kid) freezing, for a half hour and more until the cold drove us on. The kid fell in love with them, I still didn't know what kind of rat they were. After a few days, one of the babies disappeared, we went into the shop. Found out the baby had been sold, learned they were teddy bear hamsters, I had never seen anything like them, some newly developed breed. A day or two later another baby was sold, the kid became frantic, heartbroken. The family was being torn apart. The kid (he was always just the kid) begged, whimpered and whined for me to buy the remaining survivors. "Please, Davy, can't we have the little babies, look how nice." The kid was, by that point, a continuous, ever-present nonstop rider with me. He wasn't letting me get away. I had to give in, there would have been no peace other-wise. But I was flat broke, wouldn't have any cash for a few days. Back in the store, I met the clerk who was the caretaker of the stock. It turned out he had hamsters himself for pets. Sure, he would hold the family for me for a few days, no deposit necessary. Good as his word, he slapped a SOLD sign on the tank right in front of me.

Already, the kid was lifting me out of the mire. I started to care about the kid's feelings of love. I accepted responsibility, I soon had four new mouths to feed and hearts to appease. I cleaned and prepared my room for our new family members—more caring—meeting my call to duty head-on. I experienced joy and elation over something worthwhile, sentiments long ignored and forgotten. On the New York City streets, especially amongst the bum population where life is cheap, caring and emotional entan-glements like love are dangerous child's play, notions that only left one vulnerable to attack and harm, sort of like wearing gold jewelry. Inadvertently, the kid was drawing me over perhaps the most important threshold which had kept me apart from that which is most worthwhile in life, the commodity of wholesomeness. And the vehicle, the agent, the means by which this all became possible, became necessary, were the hamsters. My little salvations. My redemption. My hopeless, worthless life suddenly had meaning; I had something to pin my faith on. I came to live vicariously through those small, simple creatures. There became a purpose to my days. In caring for my pets, I cared for myself. Their comfort became my comfort. What was likable, good and satisfying for those aboriginal, miniature people was the same for me. They were like little prehistoric missing links. Precious, priceless treasures.

Their welfare became my primary concern. I needed equipment, supplies, appliances, thus I immediately became employed. With the hamsters came the need of money—brass—lots of it.

I brought the babies home from the pet shop, carrying a large paper grocery bag filled with pine shavings, hamster feed, alfalfa and four cardboard bird boxes each containing one member of my new family. By the time I stepped onto the crowded elevator to reach my fourteenth floor hotel room, the individual boxes were vibrating to beat the band. And thus one passenger (a veteran black female resident whom I liked because she was boisterous and funny) asked me what was jumping around in my bag. I told her, "a rattlesnake." And she volleyed back with, "O-o baby, gon' show me yo' rattlesnake?"

At first, to accommodate the hamsters, I took a wooden, three-shelf bookcase I had in my hotel room and flipped it on its back to form a three-compartment unit. Into this housing I placed Woolly in one compartment and Maw and the babies in another. Soon Maw was picking on the babies so I moved the offspring into the third compartment. Then, the two siblings, Dino and Bean, were clashing, so I divided that compartment in half. But soon they were all chewing through the wooden walls, excavating, boring holes at night that sounded like crosscutting wood. The wooden condominium floor became saturated with urine in spite of the pine shavings which covered it. And Dino and Bean kept getting over, under and around their partition and fighting. The jar caps I used for their water kept getting tipped over and fouled with wood shavings. And the screen top to the entire cooperative had to be pulled up and re-thumbtacked into place repeatedly. An absolute mess. I recalled, when I first bought the hamsters, the clerk warned me that I'd have to separate them. I said that I wanted to keep everybody together. He told me, "They don't like to be together." I said, "But..." and he forewarned, "You'll see." And so I quickly realized that I needed four glass aquarium tanks, which could be cleaned, with screen tops that could be secure. With clips to hold the tops down. And water bottles. And food dishes. And merry-go-rounds. All the while, I was having a hard time just affording their daily seed, grain and alfalfa. Thus a full-time job became unavoidable. Nonetheless, it was a gradual process, with juggling my cocaine slips and cementing my absolute devotion to my pets.

Step by loving step, my hamsters led me back to the land of the living, impinging upon me the need to confront the inevitable (drug) Armageddon and urging my final triumph which would prove to be my reviviscence, my reincarnation, my miraculous epiphany. And all my pets had to offer was their pure, irresistible, loving nature. A bargain by any measure.

Plagued by guilt, time after time, I ignored my pets as they clambered up the side of their tanks, furiously begging to be picked up, to be let out, while I was selfishly consumed with smoking crack, or shooting up, or passed out drunk. Only to be tormented by incessant, nagging, haunting remorse after the fact as the broken record of resolutions, vows and promises were sworn for the millionth time, all a portentous precursor to the crowning event which was to be my destiny, *qv* Woolly.

In the sweltry honeymoon days with my new family, before I had procured their glass tanks with individual water bottles, when their water supply was in jar caps placed on the wood shaving-strewn floor of their wooden compartments, I had neglected to check their water level one night whence I passed out drunk. Upon awakening from my besotted stupor, some ten hours later, in the sulfuric heat of my hotel room, it was to discover the water caps tipped over and dry—not even a drop of water for those poor babies. The kid was beside me in a flummox, drubbing me with his ire, stentoriously berating me aloud, as though I were Norman Bates being scolded by his self-same mother (in the motion picture, *Psycho*).

441

One time, right after I had injected a shot of C, I picked up Dino, with rillets of blood running down my arm and, as I cradled that cuddly baby, he attempted to lick the tainted blood and I was horror-stricken that such a precious little sweetheart might inadvertently ingest such a baneful nostrum and I knew, with all certitude, that my *modus operandi* could not go on.

My southern exposed room on the fourteenth floor of the Kenmore Hotel was over one hundred degrees Fahrenheit on sunny summer days, the metal doorframes and porcelain sink were hot to the touch. Until I saved enough money for an air conditioner, I would walk over to Diamond Ice Company on West Sixteenth Street every afternoon after work and buy a chunk of dry ice that I'd distribute between the glass hamster tanks' walls to chill the glass. Finally, I took a job as a griddle man at a busy breakfast spot near the (original) World Trade Centers, the highest paying cash job I could find in a hurry.

Having to be at work at four-thirty in the morning to cook home fries in order to serve at five a.m., working the merciless griddle through a torturous breakfast—I had smoke coming out of my elbows. I had to arise at three a.m., feed the hamsters, catch the one running around the room all night (I called it happy hour), in and out of the bath where I was invariably sick, waking up still drunk; then out and down into the subway tunnels to wait forty-five minutes for a connection at Union Square station, a human icicle in the dead of winter; with the high-volume loudspeakers blaring and echoing in the cavernous twelve-track station, breaking my eardrums, some foreigner who couldn't even spic English telling me to "Stand behind the line," over and over and over and over. I was a mental case by the time the train came each morning. Arrive at work where the all-night porter forgot to boil the potatoes (for home fries), or peel the potatoes, or let the water boil away and the potatoes (in the dry pot) were actually on flaming fire. And there were the invariable early birds (ordering a bacon and egg roll) who interfered with my having a smooth setup. Stress from the word go. Exactly what I became a bum to avoid. Is there no justice in life?

In addition to an air conditioner (for our hotel room), we needed space heaters for total climate control, a mini-refrigerator for the hamsters' perishable foodstuffs, all of which served me as well. Never would I have worked for and purchased such extravagant luxuries for myself, a bum.

It was with considerable excitement that I ventured forth to procure a small refrigerator on Fourteenth Street, west of Union Square, where appliance and electronic stores are legion, all competing to deal, their showcase windows crammed with bargains. I had fifty dollars to spend, plus a fin left over for cab fare back to the hotel with my burden. In the emporium, whose aisles and walls were stacked to the ceiling with merchandise, I was soon accosted by a slick salesman who directed me to the exact item of my desire, cheap, next to which were piled most appropriate microwave ovens. The combined price of both refrigerator and microwave came to a paltry fifteen chips over my bankroll, thus I appealed to the salesman: I must have both items and all I have is fifty dollars; I simply couldn't take one without the other. Without missing a beat, the agent pushed a box each of refrigerator and microwave towards me as he held out his hand for the green. Those places wanted to deal, where money talks and nobody walks. I love New York. Back in my sanctuary, ecstatic over my new acquisitions, oven piggyback on the cooler, they fit perfectly snug between the foot of the bed and a three-drawer chest upon which rested a customized piece of painted plywood, atop which stood the four twenty-gallon hamster tanks. The refrigerator and oven upgraded my lifestyle considerably. Sobriety has manifold rewards.

443

The air conditioner came a bit more dear than the refrigerator and microwave. I had been given a large window unit by my canary-breeding friend Annie which, upon lugging the monster up to my fourteenth floor habitation, didn't work. In the end, I was able (after two weeks of slaving and scrimping) to acquire a perfect streamlined window air conditioner from an appliance outlet on First Avenue for $400 hard-won folding green. Unhappy at first with the performance, as the device did not lower the humidity enough to meet my desideration, I returned and exchanged the unit for a replacement, much to the dealer's chagrin. By then I thought I had it made but, as every parent discovers, the expenses kept mounting. I was becoming quite the sophisticated bum.

The hamsters' eventual individual housing and recreational installations kept growing by increments, regularly being replaced for more elaborate equipment, worked for, paid for. Ten-gallon tanks were replaced with twenty-gallon tanks. Maw eventually would birth ten more babies (I couldn't deny Woolly), all of whom I kept and so added ten more tanks and setups, costing hundreds of mint leaves and inestimable toil. Expensive tubular shelving to accommodate the ever-increasing space required by all that mare's nest in my eleven-by-seven-foot hotel room which soon took on the aspect of a pet shop.

I paneled the room's walls with cedar shingles to provide my little darlings a natural rustic element against which to rub and chew-on when they were let out to run loose. This lent the atmosphere of a mountain cabin. I added not a few potted plants for guess who to chew and dig in. It took me about a year to create a hamster heaven on earth and, in so doing, made a heaven for myself as well; a hopeless addict and homeless bum who could never go back to my profession, a dark horse berated by a family who long ago lost faith, a walking risk and hazard, manic-depressive, outcast, misanthrope, criminal. Yet, for all intents and purposes, I was sober, was employed full-time, had made some friends, was

back on speaking terms with my family, was undergoing psycho-
therapy, had a permanent residence. But it was a house of cards,
mine, the tiniest spark sending it all to kingdom come. Only
thing was to persevere and let the anodyne of time strengthen
from within.

When I first acquired the hamsters, I invited Wanda over to
inspect my latest fancy. This is telling of how I valued Wanda's
opinion and approval. Well, she really liked them. Examined them
closely. Insisted on feeding them. Commented appreciatively. I
was pleased with Wanda's grave respect over the serious responsibility with which I'd burdened myself. Good ole Wanda. I wish
I could put her in a tank and keep her as a pet. But, alas, Wanda
would never be caged. Yet, forever has Wanda been captured in
my heart. Or, do I have that captured bit backwards?

There was so much trouble to be had at the Kenmore Hotel, it
was as though a shadow of doom tainted the structure and each
inhabitant had his own personal black cloud above his head that
accompanied him around. The value of life was naught. The
necessity of standing one's ground, posturing, and not backing
down was a tiring reality that, like prison, if allowed to relax only
once was to invite a watershed of abuse to follow, like the bird
in a crowded cage that all the others pick on until it is devoid of
feathers and covered in bleeding sores.

I had more than my share of fistfights and trouble over the
years at the Kenmore. One time in particular stands out because
it involved the hamsters and gives weight to the fact that once
you have something dear that you cherish, it becomes a liability, a
vulnerability by which your enemies hold leverage. I had already,
by that time, become votary to the hamsters, they were my oracle,
my genius loci.

The skeevy little spic who sold nickel caps of crack on the seventeenth floor front stairwell landing was only a worker for Slim, a tall lean scarred spade from Lenox Avenue, and the skeeve comes knocking at my door early one evening, like a *Fuller Brush* salesman peddling his wares, and I spent my last ten frogskins for two caps even though I was already drinking gin to crash. The little turd sold me dummies. Like, how could he hope to get away with such a gag, we both lived in the same building and were acquainted through the trade.

I kept drinking while I made ready. I donned my steel toe work shoes, tight jeans with a wide belt into which was tucked the meat cleaver in the back and a pointy ten-inch curved blade boning knife (very sleek and sharp) in the front. No shirt. I taped each of my hands tightly across the knuckles and wound around my palms with red electrical tape, tied my hair back, all the while doing a slow burn. I finished my bottle, smoked a cigarette, and went out hunting the skinny little rat, the ebullition of my wrath about to spill over. On the crowded elevator up to the skank's floor, everyone took one glance at me and kept staring straight ahead. A cute little frail sister, Sandra, kept glancing down at my hands, wound red and tight like a boxer's. I kept my gaze down, shaking my head in resignation. This was bad business.

When I found the worthless piece of dogmeat standing in his spot on the landing—as scuzzy, foul-breathed, shifty-eyed a tatterdemalion as ever was scraped off the sole of a whore's boot—I picked him up off the floor by his neck, held him against a wall with my left hand under his chin while, with the flat side of the cleaver in my right hand, I kept smacking his forehead saying, "Lie down," with each smack. Once he was on his back, I pulled the boning knife out with my left hand and pricked his Adam's apple with the tip, enough to draw blood. "Gimme my money." His eyes were wide with panic as he sputtered, "I don't have any money." I order him to empty his pockets which he turns inside out, there's only two or three bucks. (He probably already smoked up my stolen dime.) And here comes Slim—towery, spidery, rattle-boned dagger of a devil—bounding down the stairs and he yells, "How much he owe you!" and I shift the curved and glinting blade towards Slim, still bent over dogmeat with the cleaver, and I answer (pointing with the tip of the knife), "Ten bucks!" Slim pulls a thick bankroll from his pocket, peels off a Hamilton, reaches it out towards me and I lean over and snatch it. Dog/rat is still on his back between my spread legs, sensibly not moving a muscle, everyone's heart beating a drumfire. With one smooth motion I'm gone down the stairwell, vanished like a magic trick.

Back at my oasis, it wasn't long before an emissary arrived from the enemy camp. I knew the messenger, he was neutral, someone I could believe as far as that went. Had I, in my blind fury, thought I could commit this act of retribution, delict of passion, madcap heroics, with all I had to lose, against mongoloids who have absolutely nothing, and resume my good life as though awakening from a bad dream? They knew about the hamsters. It was described to me exactly how the pure hearts would be nailed to the wall... I'd destroy my babies myself before allowing them to befall unto such a heinous, blackhearted fate. Heaven forefend. There had to be a better way out.

I knew who controlled all the crack action in the hotel, old Nebuchadnezzar up on the top floor. I divined that he would have enough horse sense, if not sobriety, to desire an equitable resolution to this minatory incident. I ran up to his inner sanctum, unarmed, presented the facts from my end and, as Mr. Big is digesting the absurdity of just how quickly events can escalate, suddenly here is Slim, yelling out in the hallway, the door is opened and Slim has worked himself into a frenzy and is swinging a baseball bat around and demanding his ten smackers. It could have been ten thousand bananas or ten cents. The issue was who would dominate the other. Big man doesn't need to tell me that ten berries is a small price to pay to resolve this nightmare. Funny how it was whitey (me) who had to knuckle under. Such drama manufactured by us congeners and yet this was my home, such as it was, and I would not run come hell or high water. I asked for an hour's time which was granted though, with Slim in his current state, I thought I might only have half that time. Naturally I had smoked the ten spot before I even returned to my room, what now seems ages ago. With my hamsters' lives on the line, I made haste to Saint Joe's. I arrived there as they were just ending mass in the dining room. I took that as a good sign. Once mass broke up I corralled a likely couple, two resident volunteers soon to be married, and laid out the whole sordid tale. A couple of fins were excavated from the house treasury and I was rushing back to the Kenmore, chanting a paternoster along the way. Well, miraculously, that incident worked out. I repaid the ten pieces of money two times over but continued with my slips until the fateful day I laid down the drugs and booze forever with the everlasting manifestation of Woolly. And the skeevy little beat artist got away with his rip, though I don't know what Slim did to him, probably nothing of consequence. Accursed drug world where a life is worth less than a cap.

The seizing of the Kenmore Hotel by the US Marshals came about as a big shock to the building's residents. One fine day, like a thunderbolt, there they were, a group of about fifty armed commandos swooping down upon the hotel's inhabitants like a SWAT team. Room to room, knock knock on the door, "Open up, US Marshals, We're seizing the building." Oh, they were in their element, loving every minute of their G-man act—gung ho Geronimo morons.

There had been one too many murders, plus so much hanky-panky and skullduggery going on in the Kenmore for so long that someone somewhere finally decided to do something about it. But the underlying impetus of such action was urban renewal, part of the city's efforts to clean up and revitalize blighted areas of the metropolis. The storm troopers entered my room, I was clad only in underpants. They asked for ID. I complied. Over two hundred guests were arrested and carted off in paddy wagons—no ID, outstanding warrants, contraband visible. It was the city's most prominent pinch of the year—cleaned out that viper's nest.

It didn't take long for things to quiet down at the Kenmore bughouse. Meddlesome guests were busy discussing the astonishing developments and reflecting on the hotel's cliometric desecration by heterodox rites and mystic idolatry, those *non compos mentis* boo-birds conveniently overlooking some key lacuna when all they had to do was glance in the mirror, for the entire hotel, save a few isolated exceptions, was a sinkhole of abominable excesses, lechery and dark crimes such as would have made Arminius blanch.

There was at the Kenmore Hotel an exquisite specimen of ergogenic carnality in the gynic incarnation of one Cheri, affectionately known as Cherry, who was the one-time girlfriend of Kenmore crack dealer supremo, Carlos (also, artificer of the hotel lobby murals), and was a congenital virtuoso of the skin flute and had gone down on half the dudes in the building (numbering in the hundreds), of whom the most unstable were at her beck and call. Thus was Cherry not one to be toyed with. At one point, Cherry moved in with a cross-dresser down the hallway from my room and hence became my neighbor. One night Cherry was having a witches' Sabbath which spilled out into the hallway that went on until I came out of my room and dived into the *tintamarre*, hurling invectives at Cherry who was a monomaniac in such moments. The following morning, five a.m., as I padded out of my crib to work, there, sitting in the middle of the hall directly in my path was a homemade fetish, fresh and throbbing—a tiny urn with a twist of raffia and some hexalogical etchings on it which, not putting much stock in mumbo jumbo, nonetheless could be a precursor of things to come, a straw in the wind, no less deadly than Lucrezia's poison vial. Thus did I detour to the freak's room, awaken the pair, and apologize to Cheri for any misunderstanding. Better safe than sorry.

Before long, some mysterious city agency took charge of the Kenmore and proceeded to renovate the building. The marshals remained in place throughout. Due to the mass arrests and succeeding exodus of many of the resident lowlifes, the hotel was vastly vacant as a result. The new administration moved everyone from the west side of the building over to the east side (where was located my room) and began interior demolition. Even though it would be luxurious accommodations when they were through, I knew I had to get out. My nerves were shot. The mountains beckoned. I had my fill of the city.

Until the seizing of the Kenmore Hotel by US Marshals and my subsequent acquisition of my room's adjoining bathroom for my private use (requiring a doctor's note), the use of toilet facilities required some ingenuity. One certainly didn't want to go near the communal facilities on each floor, servicing over forty residents each, what with the intentional despoiling, vandalism, drug usage and crappy slag all combining to render those regions as reeking and unsanitary as a cesspit. There should have been a warning posted over each lavatory entrance: Enter at your own risk. Therefore, my daily GI's were performed in the privacy of my own room, my temple, using plastic bags procured from rolls of the same in the produce section of the local supermarket, and disposed of in the hallway refuse chute. Neat, simple and clean. Hey, you do what you gotta do.

When showering (prior to my private full bath), I would place all my valuables (money, ID, dope, keys) into a *Ziploc* baggie and bring this fund into the shower with me—always with one eye on the compartment door, soap in my eyes and all, for fear of the stickup man preying on an easy target. As it so happened, when I was using one such shower (of my preference) on a floor designated largely for females (fairly clean), some chick's goony boyfriend came pounding on the bath compartment door demanding my immediate evacuation therefrom. I had no choice but to conclude my ablutions forthwith or risk a bashing. When I could, I showered at the gym. During protracted coke runs, showers weren't even on the itinerary. The only other alternative was to rely on shelters which allowed showers for the bums, like Holy Name Society on Bleeker Street. In the often hectic, drug-oriented lifestyle of the street, such inconveniences were accepted as par for the course, no more objectionable than walking to a soup kitchen for a meal. After all, the bum's most copious asset is time, all the time in the world to devote to the basic, humdrum pleasures of simply living.

My first serious attempt at creative writing (my first novella), *Wolf Pack*, was written in the Kenmore Hotel, in my little cubby hole surrounded by a dozen hamster tanks, my mini haven retreat in the midst of mayhem island. I was focused intently on putting that book together to use as a Christmas gift for my family and friends, but mainly for my Dad who was about to "shuffle off this mortal coil."[1] This would surely be Dad's last Christmas and I wanted to leave him with a fond memory of his notional son.

The story, about a pack of wolves, was based upon the antics of my family of hamsters and, besides being my first major work of fiction, was a rush job to boot. I was smoking (pot) and drinking (beer) aplenty at that time and could not have persevered with the writing project if I continued with such a sideline. And so I quit cold turkey, in order to meet my writing deadline, which was an added stressor to the project, going through the shakes on top of maintaining a handle on the writing.

I was working as a feeder at Jasmin Coffee Shop at the time (Lexington Avenue in Curry Hill)[2] and so would arise at three a.m. and write for two hours before heading out to work. When I brought the finished product into the job to show everyone, they admitted that they'd all thought it had been bunkum and were quite proud of their very own coffee man who really wrote a book.

I had bought a small decorative notebook to copy the final draft into and couldn't print out the written characters consistently, day after day, unless I was cold sober. Using some caseworker's desk in the hotel during the early morning, hunched over the work, diligently printing page after page (of the finished version) was a grueling ordeal, but achieved at last. That was tough going, being on the wagon and all.

---

1 Shakespeare
2 Indian restaurants, 20th to 29th Streets

I had the whole notebook copied and bound, about a dozen finished books, at a stationery store right across from the Kenmore Hotel. Those were the days (1980s and 90s) when independent stationery stores were prevalent and one could obtain personalized service, especially if they knew you as a loyal customer. Those little stationery stores (packed to the rafters with merchandise) were a precious aspect of times past that I sorely miss, that will never be replaced by all the *Staples* and *Kinkos* in the world. Working on *Wolf Pack* is just another fond memory of my years on the street, many of which yielded productivity from what may have seemed utter chaos.

While residing at the Kenmore Hotel, up on the troublous fourteenth floor, I happened along my hallway one day to observe a clutch of loony yo-yos surrounding a small garter snake on the floor, too terrified and superstitious to touch it. A select segment of that population dabbled in the black art, so I told them, "Stand back, That's a rattlesnake!" and, by the cross, they all flattened against the wall as though it were a proverbial incarnate juju sent to hex their accursed and sinful lives. I then proceeded to pick the poor creature up and carried it to my room as the spectators looked on transfixed. I placed the snake in a spare ten-gallon aquarium tank and pelted over to *Petland* for some crickets. But, alas, I don't think the little serpent's mouth could accommodate even the smallest of the insects, plus I needed to provide a more woodsy environment and so I set up a twenty-gallon long tank like a forest glen with earth, plants, moss, rock and a small (baked clay) pond. Back to *Petland* to purchase six of the smallest tetras I could find, and those I returned to the snake's pond. Well, you should have seen that guy gobble down those fish, catching them on the fin, even gulping the couple that managed to jump out of the water (poor things), dirt and all. I continued thereafter to buy a half dozen of the fish daily for my snake, naming him Juika Bloth after the protagonist's pet eagle in a novel I was reading at the time, entitled *Raptor*. It wasn't long before I was choosing small minnows for Juika Bloth and, soon, larger minnows when, by then end of only a month, that snake had doubled in both length and girth, devouring all those fish like a beast. He (a male) was beautiful. By then, Juika Bloth could handle crickets easily and when he had grown to almost the length of the tank and the dog days of summer were on the wane it was time to turn him loose so he could find a hibernation hole.

Over to the lovely, contained, Edenic garden of Church of the Transfiguration on East Twenty-Ninth Street I brought my gorgeous pet, in the Eos of our divergence, setting him free in that extensive paradise, near the central fountain, along with fifty crickets to insure he'd find a square meal. That very same afternoon, during my lunch break from Bagel Maven, I padded back to the churchyard and, lo and behold, there was Juika Bloth slithering along the garden border, fearless (bless him), as I bent over and stroked his back while he lay still. Oh dear, I prayed he'd be alright. For the following week, everyday, at five o'clock in the morning, on my way to work, I'd creep into the church garden and release twenty to thirty crickets (purchased the day before) in the twilight of daybreak, hoping some early rising cleric didn't observe me through the windows of the rectory which overlooked the scene of my subversive spookery. On the following Saturday, I visited that peaceful Elysium and asked a priest there if I could contribute my labor at weeding the pleasance and mentioned that I'd seen a garter snake therein and how snakes were good for the garden (worried that some gardener might hurt the precious critter), while the priest echoed my sentiment, nodding, repeating,

"Snakes are good for the garden," and so my fears were allayed. And I like to fancy that sinuous serpent slithering through the Garden of Eden in all his splendrous seduction—*cherchez la femme*.

An afterword on the crickets. I kept Juika Bloth's tank set up in my room as a sort of vivarium because it looked so nice, where there remained four live crickets within which I fancied and took care to feed—raw ground beef, raw potatoes, raw apple, cornbread—and enjoyed their cricking through the night. (James across the hall inquired, "Are there crickets in your room?") Yet the little orchestra multiplied like mad and by mid-winter the tank was so packed with hundreds of the insects, they even covered the inside of the screen top (upside down) and the tank had begun to stink, bad. (I had the hamsters' wellbeing to consider.) After consulting with a friend in a pet shop, I determined the most humane (!) method of disposing of those lovely creatures was by lowering the temperature and thus I left the tank outdoors in the harsh winter elements and pray those tiny crickets lost consciousness before expiring. Little good ever seems to come from man's interference with nature.

Even with the hamsters to love and care for, and with the kid babysitting, I continued using cocaine. Its foothold was too strong, its root system too deep. I had tried almost every means ever invented in order to desist, the latest being acupuncture, but I was a hopeless case. Probably, I didn't want to stop. And yet it happened. Even as I write, it's been a lifetime (20 years) since I've touched hard drugs or hard liquor. Still—I never did it on my own, couldn't have ever kicked, the drug was stronger than me, I just couldn't resist. So, the only explanation is just a circumstance. Woolly was there and looking at me. I was losing the shot, kept missing, the needle was clogged, blood clotting in the barrel, a desperate moment. I was in bad shape...

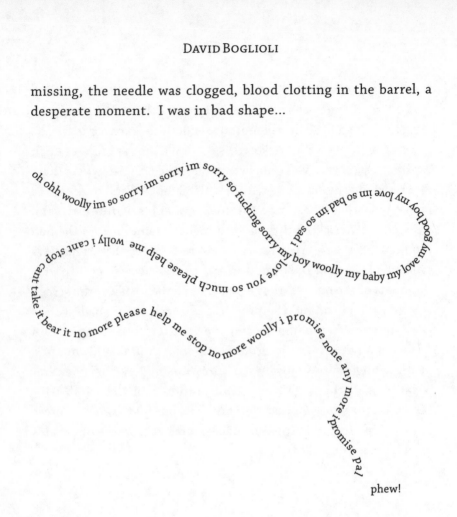

phew!

The needle is on the floor, or somewhere; I'm exhausted. Woolly is still, through all of this, sitting up, looking at me. I'm forgiven. It's over. All over. No more, Woolly, I promise. What a relief.

What happened to me is something that can't be explained, but just is. And from that moment on, I accepted Woolly as my spirit-helper, my guiding light; shining on like the light of eternity.[1]

---

1 Earl Murray, *High Freedom*, paraphrase

I pick up Woolly and hold him, kiss him, he is so beautiful, so nice, so good. And he has forgiven me this one last transgression. He is all mine. He believes me when I say no more. He, Woolly, is better than anything. Much more than I deserve. I could never be as good or as beautiful as Woolly. But I can have him, hold him, love and kiss him. And somehow be worthy if I just only continue not to pick up. And, many moons later, I still haven't touched hard drugs or hard liquor because I still have a hamster, like I promised. *Dei gratia*. And I always remember Woolly—best at hide and seek tag, who came when I called him, king of all hamster antics. Woolly's picture is up, I pray to him, for his spirit and soul, everyday, and he is with me still. Amazing.

Although, there are, no doubt, stranger tales in the city—this is my story and it is true, really happened to me. And, one day, when I die it won't be from an OD shot. And I have Woolly to thank, I can never take credit because I still shoot up in my dreams and it is always a nightmare, just like it was always a nightmare in real time, in real space, like that last time, and I had to put poor Woolly, good beautiful Woolly through it to bear witness to just how bad, what a nightmare it is, was, and always will be, the life of a junkie is no life but a living nightmare.

The kid was nowhere to be found at times of regression, not that he was sought, or even missed, so consumed as I was from the instant of decision through the lengthy, grueling process of using. The kid knew when a battle was lost. Wouldn't speak to me. Though he wasn't above scolding me after the fact. Senseless though it was.

I was wending my way to breakfast at Saint Joe's, down Second Avenue at seven a.m., a scorching Saturday in July, temperature prodding 90° F and climbing, nighttime rats still prowling, when I saw Polly (a fledgling), she was winking at death. It was love at first sight. Covered with down and only a few pinfeathers, standing amidst a pile of garbage, she was pitiful. And adorable. House sparrows—very few reach adulthood, I didn't know the statistics then, yet intuitively my soul felt that precious life to be mine for the saving. I was overwrought with compassion. Having been softened up by the kid and the hamsters, my heart was ripe for falling in love.

It was touch and go to keep Polly alive. My friend Annie (who raises canaries) was an enormous help. Also, Saint Mark's Veterinary Hospital was indispensible. I was working at the time pumping coffee in a bagel shop and brought Polly into work on Monday so I could feed her every two hours. The boss nearly threw me and the bird out. I took the next two days off. Hand-feeding Polly different baby bird foods Annie gave me, dripping Pedialyte down her throat. Bringing her three times to the vet for inoculations and vitamin booster, Polly weighed less than ten grams.

It took Polly a good year to fill out in her plumage, she was the runt of the brood, because there were originally two sparrows which I rescued (kidnapped), one of which flew out of my window inside of a few days, light years more advanced in development over Polly was her brother. It also took Polly around four months to stabilize her diet. So finicky. It took six months before Polly would come out of her aviary and a year before she would land on me. Slow to warm up to things but, once decided upon, Polly was insistent on having her way which, overall, made it easy to please her: Polly always had to come first. For instance, when I would come home each day from work, the first thing I had to do was open the door to Polly's aviary, then I could go about my business. If I did one other thing first, let me tell you, I didn't hear the end of it for the rest of the night. Also, if I wanted Polly to land on me, all I had to do was pick up a hamster and she was on me like glue. Beautiful.

Polly also often required my undivided attention; if I was talking on the telephone Polly would complain incessantly for being ignored, and if I went into the bathroom (my smoking room) she'd cry until I came out again. Years later, after we became inseparable, Polly would hop across the book I was reading while I was lying in bed and she would turn (or attempt to turn) the pages with her beak. My little helper. Always with me, wherever I was in the house. Also, after Polly had the run of the house, she'd wake me up in the mornings by landing on my face and pulling hairs out of my nose until I arose. Very smart girl. And determined. And pretty too in her variegated complexion of ochre, sepia and umber. Polly was also my watchdog. If I thought I heard a noise, I only had to look over at Polly to see by her reaction if anything was amiss. And each day she must have practiced new flying techniques for, when I arrived home from work, Polly would show off her latest flying acrobatics which would involve loop the loops, wingovers, and twirling around branches by her feet. What a wonderful girl.

Years later, in our own house, Polly would talk to me constantly, keep me company while cooking in the kitchen and take baths on the kitchen counter like a duck. Always had to sample whatever I was eating: macaroni, fried fish, mayonnaise, cold cuts, eggs, hamburger (when I was omnivorous), white bread, corn bread, polenta... Pancakes were Polly's favorite: as soon as she saw me take out the mixing bowl in the morning, Polly was zooming round and round the house like a rocket, swooping through the kitchen and hopping across the work counter, chirping plaintively, an impatient customer. And Polly didn't want me to go out, would start to cry as soon as I put on my coat. Very proprietary. And jealous! I couldn't so much as look out the window at other birds (at the feeders) without Polly chirping on my shoulder. What a great kid. Pure devotion.

I had forgotten what it was like to know unbridled love, love encouraged, boundless love. Before life with Polly and the hamsters, my love had been like a fire smothered and scattered to the winds. I had forgotten how to love. I was loveless. It was the kid and my pets who awakened that long dormant emotion, long forgotten sense now suddenly was back. Thanks to my sweethearts.

A few words about Saint Mark's Veterinary Hospital on Ninth Street between First and Second Avenues, and of Dr. Sally Haddock, founder and proprietress of that noble establishment. Simply put, the vets at Saint Mark's treated and saved the lives of numerous pets of mine, not least of whom were Woolly and Polly, and more than a few hamsters. They have an excellent avian department and treat a full line of exotics, including reptiles. They have performed surgeries on my hamsters, boarded Polly, made house calls, and extended credit (against their policy) when I was in dire straits. And sent compassionate sympathy cards with handwritten notes when any of my darlings have crossed over. All in all, some of the nicest most competent doctors I would ever want to entrust the care of my precious babies to. I don't know where I would have been without them. And while I'm at it, I must give honorable mention to Annie, NYC licensed breeder of canaries who, despite being afflicted with a debilitating disease, gave tirelessly of both goods and advice in nursing Polly during our crucial first days and weeks together. My heartfelt thanks to those special people who have helped me with my pets. And, finally, in remembrance of Michael (RIP), founder and proprietor of 33rd and Bird, who gave personalized attention to Polly when she was a baby. Documented proof that animal lovers will help even a bum when the welfare of his pet is at stake.

During the first week that Polly was living in a spare glass aquarium tank, I constructed an aviary in our seven-by-eleven foot hotel room, a nine-foot long by four-foot by four-foot wood frame, panel floor, mesh enclosure, held up against the ceiling by all but an enchanted spell. The room was already packed with a dozen twenty-gallon glass aquarium tanks (I had twelve hamsters by then) and with a birdcage taking up half the ceiling, the room resembled a crowded pet shop. I bought rare and costly Mexican manzanita branches for Polly to perch on, having to amortize them weekly on layaway was how I afforded them. At the same time, I was engaged in desperate battle against the hotel's mouse and roach infestations which were attracted to my room by all the pet food. And trouble kept percolating outside my room as the Kenmore's bedlam and racket persisted (I was sober by then) and the noise affecting me was also affecting Polly and I promised her I would move us out, that we'd head for the hills. "We'll go up to the mountains Polly, I promise."

Meanwhile, three, four, five false fire alarms per night continued. Me and Polly were a nervous wreck. I made arrangements with someone I knew up in Vermont and started packing. This was no small move. With twelve hamsters, each in their own tank, and a bird, I couldn't just hop on a bus. I had to set up transportation—my brother-in-law again (man of mettle), driving up north during a spring blizzard in an overstuffed station wagon. I hated to desert my beautiful hotel room—seemed I'd just finished fixing it up but its days were numbered anyway what with the hotel's renovation running full tilt, plus my nerves were shot and my poor bird was becoming neurotic as well, so off we went.

461

I think I would be in that hotel room to this day if it weren't for Polly. For that, I owe a lot to my pets; not only attaining sobriety (an impossible *fait accompli* that the best experts couldn't achieve), but also for escaping from the City That Never Sleeps (nor lets you sleep). And I didn't know then that Polly would be mine for eleven halcyon years—a lifetime.

For many years at the Kenmore Hotel I had a preoccupation with death. This was a combination of my drug-induced high blood pressure that kept me speeding around for days, dehydrated, no rest, psychotic... And of the constant labored breathing, panting with the least exertion, resultant from my nonstop smoking. It had my attention all right. I was less worried than resigned—this was the bed I had made for myself and I abidingly lay in it. I did, however, take precautions with my pets. I found a wildlife rescue couple who would care for Polly and the hamsters in the event of my demise. And I arranged my hotel room with weeks worth of food and water for any hamster left out of its tank; with always tons of food and full water bottles in their homes at all times. This was an obsession. It seemed, at times, I was just waiting for the heavy doors to close, expectantly, surprised when each new day found me still alive and kicking. So many people around me were dropping like flies—the high cost of street life. I can attribute my survival to any number of singularities but, in the end, I think it just came down to luck. I was lucky alright. *Om mani padme hum!*

I was so much an integral part of the city by then, a hard-bitten, decade-old campaigner of the streets, a part of its very substance, not only of its makeup but of its continual erosion, its constant flux, being ground to a powder, to be replaced with fresh steel, fresh paint, fresh pollution—its inexhaustible mimetism. As much as I longed to continue, to endure, my time, my usefulness had come to an end, I could feel it in my bones, my flesh, see it in my mirrored reflection. It was time to put me out to pasture, to crop green grass and to savor sunsets and sunrises, to listen to the grass grow and the march of time, and to write memoirs as a pensioner and a come-outer. If only I could find a way out of this mantrap of a city, this mire of my own device, this truth for which I once so hungered, the bizarrities which had once so baited me, from which (with the virtue of my new resolve) I needed to extricate myself.

With the advent of the kid and, ultimately, with the addition of the hamsters and Polly, I consolidated my world, condensed my life into what evolved as my vocation as an anchorite. With rapid strides did I shed my associations with and interests in my surrounding environment (which had diminished to a relict), withdrawing into a self-contained sphere of solitude. All of my prior pinko philosophy seemed to suddenly crystalize whereby the surrounding congestion of the city, once so stimulating, became an intolerable distraction and annoyance and my need to conflate my prunes and prisms and to isolate myself became paramount. Thus did germinate the seed which would blossom some few years hence that led me and my menagerie out of New York City and up to the sylvan wilds of Vermont, where I would commune with nature and devote myself to my pets, and just living, as unaffected by external influences as was practicable. That would be my hermitage, my dharmic purpose, my astral role at last.

My clearest memory of desiring an escape to the mountains from New York City traces back to my days at Bagel Maven and Goody, the beefy blond German waitress, always buzzing on Blue Nun or Almaden, who received German supermarket rags in the

463

mail from her mom, and would tear-out pictures of animals for me, which I plastered on the wall surrounding my coffee urn; whom all the cool people (female cashiers) liked. Though she resided in the city (big pad on West Fourteenth Street), Goody weekended with hubby and friends at their mountain retreat in Vermont, where the chipmunks hid acorns in Goody's shoes and they had huge barbeques and Goody remained drunk. The offhand manner of which she seemed unaware, downplaying her good fortune as though it were normal, everyday life. And I envied her aesthetic prosperity enough that I determined, then and there, to begin saving for my eventual move up to Vermont, having had my fill by then of all the city's negativity (such as noise) from which I could find no escape. I saw, through Goody, that such a getaway was plausible.

I couldn't ask for more agreeable companionship than to have a cute little hamster running around the room all through the night, like a cuddly miniature toy come to life, adorable, funny and sweet. Not to be outdone, here comes a dicky sparrow plummeting out of thin air, insistent on having her fair share of attention. Absolutely gorgeous in all her tiny perfection, Polly is the quintessential ideal best friend, bonding, devoted, and ubiquitous.

Peerlessly suited to my solitary lifestyle, with their pure and guileless hearts, I couldn't get by without my pets. Whoever would have thought that a little hamster or a tiny bird could have such depth; having gained from two pint-size creatures what the balance of my life (family, friends, profession) failed to furnish—true love and devotion and honesty—the only commodities worth living for. And to this day they guide me and by this pencraft I dower them immortality. And I am a bum forever so I can devote myself to my pets, their well-being, twenty-four/seven, and never have to go back to a world, a life, that drives me to drink and drug myself to death.

These remembrances, though drafted in the field, do not do justice to the street, cannot remember how bad it was, the despair, the suffusing depression of the spirit, the soul. Hopelessness, embossed wanderings, hunger and fear—it was rough at the best of times, and time on the street proper was near impossible, especially during the fierce New York winters—roving around the teeming streets always broke, bypassing mouthwatering eateries crowded with patrons, Tantalus dying for a hot or cold drink, a nice fresh bagel, a slice of pizza, a plate of eggs, not even a cigarette or a hope of a handout, weary and nowhere to stop for a rest—haunted with the harbinger that you're hunted—these are the uninter-pretable, unconveyable haranguers of the street forever etched on my memory. At no time allow the romance of this adventure to mask the menace, the blood-and-guts suffering and danger that the street hurls at one like whitewater. In such wise is my jeremiad. It takes heart and fortitude (and not a small amount of luck) or thou art lost.

And yet, if one can but overcome the main obstacle of the street—that being homeless—say, by securing a hotel room, there is much to be said for being a bum. For the rhapsodic indepen-dence of leisure and the slowing down from the man-killing pace of urban competition. The daily choice of working or not, of lying in bed or spending the day in the library. Of devoting half the day to cooking or going to a soup kitchen. Of peregrinating the endless pathways and detours of wonder and entertainment and education that are the city, or relaxing in the park and watching the birds and squirrels, or going swimming or exercising at a gym, or visiting the endless galleries and cultural exhibits at hand, taking a course or a class, or playing a game of chess or mah jongg at the commons. Going shopping at the *Salvation Army* or the Catholic Worker, visiting the zoo or bicycling in Central Park. You can sing in the subway or draw in Washington Square Park or work on a craft in your room or drink or go to a meeting. Spend time gazing at antiques along Madison Avenue or in curio shops off Canal Street or used bookstores on University Place and the Strand on Broadway for out-of-print books—23 miles of books, or variety stores like the Pushcart on lower Broadway. All these and more are your daily choices as a freewheeling bum in New York City where the distillates of the world are only a subway ride away. I often stopped in pet shops to look at the tropical fish. Many *Petlands* are well stocked, the branch on Nassau Street copious with diverse aquatic flora; and there's an extensive aquarium on Fifty-Ninth street near First Avenue; and the Greater New York Aquarium on Twenty-Third Street between First and Second Avenues for saltwater fish. For avian enjoyment there is 33rd and Bird on Thirty-Third Street near Park Avenue or the Urban Bird on West Broadway in Tribeca where you are encouraged to feed the baby parrots. I also enjoyed browsing lingerie shops, I knew them all in midtown and lower Manhattan.

I love being a bum and wouldn't have any other life. I'm not sorry for the years I spent at a career for they were fructuous. But I am my own man now and answer to no one. Not that I am without hardship or worry, nor can I exist for long without supplementing my income, although poverty holds no terror for me. I have learned to do with less. And I can walk away from a job in the blink of an eye if something bugs me. I am more independent than I have ever been and go where my heart leads me. Especially now, as I approach my golden years. I'm not concerned with pleasing others. I am a recluse. I enjoy nature and wildlife and do what I can to encourage their prosperity. I have my pets. As a human being I feel very little solidarity with my own kind.

I abjure most of what modern civilization and technology have to offer and am happy being an outcast. I am the apotheosis of the consummate bum. And, thanks to Woolly and Polly, my heart sings.

Immediately prior to leaving New York City for the weald and wold of Vermont, I paid all of my outstanding bills, both current and ancient, whose grand total was considerable in light of my marginal circumstances. I was collecting welfare right up to my very last day in the Big Apple. Having been fired from my yearlong job at Bagel Maven by the boss' wife (for fighting with a coworker right on the serving line), I had only sporadic employment for some months. I had been working as a sandwich and griddle man in a Second Avenue deli, near the police academy, serving a clientele of cadets who were forever stealing, then making light of the fact when caught. None of the civilian neighborhood traffic would patronize the store as long as the cadets were in evidence (an indication of public sentiment).

My life savings, for my move to Vermont, had been devoured by an ex-spouse who never worked a day in her life, hounding me to pay medical costs and child support for a thirty-year-old bum still sponging off Mom. Unreal. My local debts included a forty-dollar bill at the hardware store across from the Kenmore, and a seventy-dollar tab with Hanna who, after a week of fretful worry that I'd bilk her (aware that I was leaving town), was so relieved (and surprised) when I paid in full, that she gifted me with a six-pack of beer for the road. Both Hanna and her goodman had long addressed me as Tattoo. "Tattoo, take one packet Budweiser for your trip." I even paid Jose who I think was, weekly, ready to write-off those local beer and cigarette tabs so many bums copped out on. I wanted to exit New York City with a clear conscience so I paid off a midtown liquor store for a pint of gin, a tab that was five years old, astounding the clerk who had trusted me so that he called up to the owner with the news. I never, however, managed to track down Berto, an old waiter to whom I owed twenty dollars, an onus I carry on my conscience to this day. "Sorry, Berto." I also was forced, by exiguousness, to postpone payment to Saint Mark's Veterinary Hospital on an outstanding bill of one hundred dollars which, ever grateful for their lifesaving service and trust, I finally made good on one year hence, mailing a check for the full amount to Dr. Sally from Vermont. All those IOU's of which I had been levant and on which I could have easily reneged though, with the kid ever beside me, I left New York City with a clean slate.

There was an affable old hombre of my acquaintance, a retired junkie and friend of Wanda's, who would visit the Allen Street stroll once in a blue moon, who related to me the tale of how he became a dope fiend. The gist of it was that, when he was a kid in the ghetto, he would gaze in awe and admiration at the needle tracks on the arms of the older coves (his role models) and say, "Wow!"

Another confidante and companion from the stroll, a ravishing black meretrix, explained to me the roots of her consistently smart splendor. She told me that when she was a little girl of the slums, she'd gaze in envy at the alluring prostitutes (naive of what they were) who were always so chic and attractive in their fashionable façade and tell herself that one day she would look like that.

Two prime examples of how a beguiling, seductive veneer can impress itself upon an impoverished youthful innocence as a one-way primrose garden path through sunshine. But the moral of these tales (if there is one) is that neither of those persons are dissatisfied nor regretful with their choice, their calling and its consequences. Both of those files, one junkie, one whore, accept the drawbacks of their walk in life and each has found peace of mind therein. So, not all easy one-way tickets lead to hell. There is redemption to be had at the bottom of the snake pit. And I, for another, have come through the fire, the bad, pernicious street as a bum and I have no complaints, no regrets. *Ad astra per aspera.* I like to think that I never intentionally hurt anyone (who didn't deserve it) other than myself and if I had to do it over again, fain, I would jump at the chance.

There is no one more in tune with the street, with its nuances than a street person, a tramp. The bums of the street—hustlers, druggies and various grifters—are the very meat of the street, they define and embody it. And I can avouch, from experience, that it is something worth knowing, one of life's truths—being streetwise. Not to put a dollar value on it, for what is the value of knowledge? It's priceless.

At the same continuum there is a growing *vox populi* as well as governmental response to the homeless (and to the lower class in general) that, even as I write, gravitates towards demolition of skid row residences (such as flophouses and SRO's) and the forging of urban renewal projects geared to attract a gentrified (yuppie) context, thereby driving the transients back underground.

The war against the homeless (domiciled citizens versus outlaw citizens) stems largely from the willful violation of behavioral norms of public space by the homeless, and the "broken window" theory whereby blatant acts of impropriety are a signal to criminals that an area is unregulated and to domiciled citizens that an area is unsafe. Big Brother (government employee unions, Congress, the rich) would homogenize America into a cloned society, regulated by sumptuary laws and the paramilitary so that the fragmented distinctions which always defined America are lost to history.[1] "If

---

1 Leonard C. Feldman, *Citizens Without Shelter*, paraphrase

current trends continue, the city will turn into a place that caters primarily to the middle and upper classes, and as a showcase for visitors. The poor, the homeless, the immigrants will either join the middle class or move elsewhere, for the infrastructure that the poor need to survive—cheap restaurants and grocery stores, low rents, inexpensive clothing stores—will diminish. And yet, the city needs the working poor who perform work that is necessary, but that no one else wants to do."[1] Irrespective of this reality, American middle class citizens will not permit immigrants or homeless to achieve parity with bona fide middle class Americans. Where will the poor and the homeless of tomorrow surface? Wherefore the value of a lost culture complex?

Although my closest friends on the street were whores, and that I enjoyed many personable liaisons with sexy sirens, I was never a paying customer. Most prostitutes despise their johns and once a fee changes hands, a business proposition engaged, the mack is reduced to an insignificant turd at the mercy of the controlling harlot. My approach was social and to offer my saucy friends drugs, by which to satisfy their primary desire, which was our truck. What followed, by way of mutual pleasure or reward, was a logical sequence or by-product which anyone in any walk of life might enjoy from a date that progressed from whatever investments the host and guest each might employ (say, an entertainment shared or dinner). My design was sincere, my efforts in earnest, and I was never stingy with the drugs. And occasionally I would get lucky. After all, we were all out for a good time, given the right situation. Moreover, my guest's pleasure was my primary concern. However, in dealing sex with a slattern, one is

---

1 William B. Helmreich, *The New York Nobody Knows*, paraphrase

often dealing with their sickness and many harlots are reluctant to expose that disease to their friends (whether mental or corporal). Similarly, I often was loath to deal with the illness of my friends—that was their own private cross of which I was renitent to share. Exceptions non obstante. Nonetheless, I would brook no calumny against those full-blooded, brave-souled daughters of the street.

I say I was never a paying customer with the whores but there was one exception. Doris (or Dee) was a drab of long acquaintance—dirty-blond hair, short skirt and heels—who ran with my immediate circle of friends, as fun-loving and foxy as they come, whom I liked and enjoyed being around. Somehow, she corralled me one night and begged me for a trick (score) and, hence, we made an assignation for the entire evening for $50, for which she thanked me wholeheartedly from the outset. Before snuggling into bed, I rolled up the pay and wedged it behind the doorknob of my pad and instructed Dee that she could take it upon exiting in the morning. Well, all I will say is, that girl threw one of the best lays on me that I will remember for the rest of my life—gave me every nickel's worth—besides seeming to take carnal delight in the sin herself (which I took as an added bonus). I smile with quiet pleasure even in the retelling. Doris had every addiction (heroin, crack, etc.) and a boyfriend who beat her and no fixed residence, but she was fain and prone for the long haul and kept her head above water and never missed an opportunity for a good time. I love them all.

There were many conspicuous and zany denizens on the streets of the East Village whose presence was so common as to seem to be part of the landscape, veritable fixtures in the scenery. Noteworthy of these were one cool cat who had a pushcart type of

471

percussion ensemble complete with homemade drums and traps. He would beat on the cart's built-in, hollow, wooden tom-toms with mallets for up to ten minutes a go, all the while keeping the rhythm by pumping his knees. He always had a crowd. The guy was out of sight. Once, while watching him play, I picked up a sweet little Oriental bird from the audience who accompanied me home for the night. She had breast implants (some of the finest knockers I ever saw) of which she was inordinately proud. All it cost me was a barbeque chicken take-out with extra sauce. It turned out she was a gamine who wanted to remain in my apartment the next day while I went to work. I declined the offer and turned her out in the morning whence she dunned me for a fin for coffee. I kicked myself in the part that goes over the fence last as I searched for her high and low everyday for a week, to no avail. I can be real jerk sometimes.

A common sight was a scraggy rubbish collector who pedalled around the sidewalks on a bicycle equipped with multiple wire baskets and on whose handlebars were a string of bells that he'd jangle to alert pedestrians to move out of his way as he wobbled by. He sported a long white beard and had long white hair (an up-to-date animate Rip van Winkle) and his velocipede was copiously festooned with flags and shiny reflective objects. His baskets were often filled with the oddest virtu and junk imaginable, *objets trouves*.

Another unique street performer was a Jack with a custom carved, three-string electric guitar whose battery-powered amplifier was in his guitar case. He would play the same riff over and over everyplace you'd see him, singing, "I'm just one of the people!" Often, in the evenings, playing for the crowd outside CBGB's[1] (Country, Bluegrass & Blues) on Third Avenue, where I once met

---

1 Punk rock's New York headquarters (circa 1975)

and spoke with the chappie's son who surprised me when he told me, "That's my father."

And there was Twiggy, a tall, slender, long-haired transvestite who was forever selling either crack or dope, dressed like bizarro, face always with makeup, consuming all his profits. He lived for awhile on the Allen Street stroll. He was one funny cat.

One dude had a self-amplified keyboard (like a portable clavichord) that hung from around his neck and he'd play this instrument while he sang, "Invisible man, that's what I am, Invisible man, Invisible man." The guy was *sui generis*.

And there were a few other worthless rigs who were a lot less exciting yet, nonetheless, equally visible. One pair were a slovenly Indian couple (South American), the bloke perpetually passed out drunk on the sidewalk while the fat squaw begged from passersby, "Spare some change for a couple of Indians?"

Another couple were a garrulous black biddy, Jude, with dugs like watermelons, and her laconic, tangle haired and bearded Caucasian swain who would sit on the sidewalk, propped against a building, with a cup out, while Jude passed the beer bottle. The vagrant sot wouldn't even ask for donations yet people would toss coins into his cup. Amazing. Jude was proficient at ingratiating herself with the staff at the Catholic Worker, visceral makebate though she was, where she collected enough food to feed both herself and her beau. I was present at Saint Joe's one evening, having dinner, when Jude threw a plate of food into a fellow kafir's face and all the staff did was tell Jude to calm down, to sit down and eat. Didn't even throw her out. I'd never get away with a stunt like that.

Finally, I'm including mention of a couple of acts which haunted Times Square because they recall my bum roots when I first started with crack in Hell's Kitchen and the Normandi Hotel as I'd often roam the Times Square district, learning the ropes, so to speak, on location. One character spoke to his sidewalk audience as he did a soft-shoe while he juggled four balls, all the while taking his derby hat off and on and simultaneously bowing down to retrieve coins from the sidewalk. He was tricked out in a loud, oversize plaid blazer, immense bow tie, baggy, pleated, cuffed trousers, and round-toe oxfords. An alky of the old school, still standing, still carrying the oriflamme. I gave him my last change.

And lastly there was a pair of roving black teens who played a percussion kit of assorted empty, inverted, plastic five-gallon buckets, a steel automobile tire rim, a metal box fan housing, and what appeared to be a toaster oven, squatting amidst this percussive hodgepodge beating with claves in a contrapuntal psychic trance and frenzy, sweating feverishly, looking for all the world like a couple of mad Tasmanian devils or New Wave druids on crack. They were set up in the small triangular desert island (Longacre Square) between Forty-Second and Forty-Third Street where Broadway and Seventh Avenue approach a merger, forming a triune, as they crisscross just north of Times Square, circumscribed on all sides by clamorous bumper to bumper traffic, the sound of the beat carrying a good quarter mile through the congested din, touching a primal chord in every vicinal soul, drawing forth all animal life (birds, bugs and fish) as like Congolese drums attract nature with their rhythm, the call of the wild. Surrounded by a tightly packed crowd of spell-struck infatuates, the duo raked in big bucks for their efforts; even I gave a dollar. A couple of the new breed, an irrepressible tide, the molten current, the Zeitgeist of dissident urban America.

All these people—be they street musicians, merry-andrews, trash scavengers, prostitutes, dope dealers, transient kitchen workers, welfare recipients, disabled, dispossessed, alcoholic, schizophrenic—they are all my people. Many are on the street by circumstance and some, like myself, by choice. And though I may have been a child of fortune, I share an attitude, an outlook

474

with most bums, as with most recreants, of a rejection of all the hypocrisy of our wasteful, arrogant society, of the class system, science, technology, and Gresham's law; gone with all my elegiac sentiments for a lost innocence, lost faith, lost belief in the nice policeman on the corner, of a merciful God, an egalitarian America. And yet, like it or not, I hew to this system, I live off it, I am one of its participants as well as a victim. I don't offer any conclusions, only my story as a representative of this coeval urban phenomenon, the eponymic New York City bum.

I asseverate a critical philippic at America yet, in the same breath, I'm glad to be American. I just call it as I see it, I call a spade a spade. I am a paradox, a creation, a creature of America, and I see America as a paradox, a creature of its own creation— still the land of plenty where even bums can live like kings. New York City is the greatest city on earth and I am proud to have lived as a bum on its streets, in its bowels, and to pay tribute in these pages. But I've grown and am grateful and fortunate to have reft the evils of urban life for more natural horizons. Though the streets and mice and sparrows of the city beckon me to revisit, and the wonder and allure and smut that I left behind.

I hated the street yet I loved it. It is so raw, present, ready. And in the end I couldn't keep up. Gave my all. No complaints. Happy to have gotten out alive. To tell my story. For the good it can do, your enjoyment, enlightenment. A champion for the bums.

And thus we come to the denouement of my tale, the omega point. I hope it has been a satisfactory read.

I am the mouse and the sparrow of the city. Running in the gutter and flying above. I enjoy the most putrid of viands yet wash myself clean each day in the fountain. I am every man, whose hopeful fate is in the hands of Our Lady.

finis

GLOSSARY

9/11 World Trade Center attack
abase to lower
abatis deadly obstacle
Abbevillian lower Paleolithic
abject spiritless, hopeless
abjur renounce
ablution bathing
à bon chat, bon rat for a good cat, a good rat
aboriginal native
abrogate annul, nullify
Abraham's bosom heaven
a cappella vocals without instruments
Aceldama blood money for betrayal
acme summit, apex
acrimonious caustic, rancorous
actinic visible radiant energy
acumen discernment
ad astra per aspera to the stars by hard ways
à deux two intimate people
ad hoc improvised
adjuration earnest urging
ad nauseam sickening degree
ad rem relevantly
adumbrate obscure, overshadow
adumbrative foreshadow, suggestive
advertence heedfulness
adytum sanctum
aegis protection
affaire liaison
afreet evil jinni
agglomerate clustered together but not coherent
agoraphobia fear of open or public spaces
aigrette spray of feathers or gems
à la mode fashionable, stylish
Alanon support group for AA
alarums and excursions clamor, excitement

albedo light
alchemy mysterious transmuting
alembic that which refines or transmutes
alentours precincts, environs
alluvial detrital deposits by running water
Almaden white wine
Alphabet City Avenues A, B, C, D in NYC
alsatia criminal purlieu or sanctuary
altruism welfare for others
amah Asian female servant
amanuensis secretary
amaranthine undying
amative amorous
ambient encompassing
ambit sphere of action
amerce punish
amorphous shapeless
amortize to pay off gradually
amphibolous ambiguous or equivocal
anachronism error in chronology
anarchy disorder
anathema curse
anatomize dissect, analyze
anchorite recluse
anfractuous torturous, winding
anima feminine part of male
animus masculine part of the female personality
anodyne palliative
anomy personal uncertainty
Anschauung attitude
antebellum pre-civil war
antediluvian primitive
anthracite black
antipode opposite, contrary
antonymic opposite meaning, i.e., bad is good
à outrance unsparingly
aphelion point farthest from sun

apocryphal fictitious

apogee highest or farthest point

Apollyon Satan

apostasy abandonment of previous loyalty

apotheosis quintessence

approbation commendation, praise

appropinquate approach emphatically

aquavit gin

arab vagrant

Ararat cradle of civilization

arbalest crossbow

arcana mysterious knowledge

archaic old

archetype inherited symbolic image

archipelago group of islands

argence whiteness

argonaut adventurer

argosy rich supply

argot dialect

Argus-eyed observant, vigilant

Armageddon final battle between good and evil

Arminius preached salvation for all

arrant extreme

arrogate ascribe without justification

art deco geometric and zigzag characteristics

artifice trick, stratagem

Ashcan school of painting that depicts realistic city life

asperse villify, malign

aspic clear savory jelly

asseverate affirm, declare

assiduous unremitting application

Astoria suburb of New York City

atavistic a throwback

ataxis incoordination

atelier workshop

atrophic wasting away

au courant fashionable

au fait up to date

Augean stable filth and corruption

augur omen

aura personal atmosphere

Automat 3 Ave. at 42nd St. (closed)

avant-garde new concepts

avatar embodiment of philosophy in human form

aviary large birdcage

AZT AIDS treatment

babu bossman

Babylonian sensual pleasure

Bacchus God of wine

backhand cutting offense

bagatelle game, trifle

Balducci's high-end deli and market

banana currency, banknote

bandog watchdog

bane poison

banjax ruin, smash

barista coffee server

barn burner arousing excitement

Barney's better conservative clothier

baroque grotesque, extravagant, flamboyant

barrack scoff

barrio Spanish-speaking ghetto

barrow mound

bar sinister of illegitimate birth

basal fundamental

basuco freebase cocaine, crack

batik hand-printed fabric

beam up crack smoking

beano currency, banknote

beard the lion tease, defy

beau boyfriend

beau geste a noble act

beau ideal ideal beauty

Bedouin Arab

Beelzebub devil

Belial devil

bellwether leader

ben greenhorn

benedict newly married man

benison blessing

benny $100 bill

478

Bernard Goetz subway folk hero, shot his assailants

berries currency, banknote

bête noire detestable person

bêtise stupidity

B-girl bar entertainer

bias tendency, bent

bibelot trinket

Big Brother power of the state, per George Orwell

big house prison

bijou prized jewel

bilious peevish

bimmy stick needle-tipped pole

bird dog pimp

birl swirl

bivouac temporary encampment

bizzy policeman

Black Hand Mafia

blackleg swindler

Black Maria paddy wagon

blast puff of crack

blind alley mistaken course or direction

blind tiger unlicensed liquor store

blint girl, slut

Blue Nun white wine

blunt currency, banknote

bobo one hundred dollars

bocci Italian bowling

bodega Hispanic grocery store

body politic national population

boffin scientific expert

bon ton fashionable style

bone crusher septicemia, blood poisoning

boo marijuana

boo-bird jeerer

boodle swag, money

boosting IV injecting

booty plunder

boo-yah very good

Borgian characterized by intrigue

boscage thicket of shrubbery

Boston marriage lesbian relationship

botanica herb and charm shop

bougie candle

boulangerie bakery

bourne destination, goal

brass currency, banknote

Brave New World dystopian world by Aldous Huxley

bricks projects

bricks and clicks career, occupation

bromide a bore

brume mist, fog

brummagem tawdry, spurious

bucks round-toed oxfords made from buckskin

bug juice generic Koolaid

bull dagger butch dyke

bunco con game

bundu uninhabited wild region

bunker mentality chauvinistic

bupkes kaput, nothing

burning bush God incarnate

busker street musician

busman's holiday vacation spent doing what you do for a living

Bustello Latin coffee

buttermilk sky lowering cloudscape

byzantine devious

C cocaine (coke)

cabalist mysterious, esoteric

cabbage currency, banknote

cacodemon demon

cacoethes mania

cadenza pre-end flourish

caird tramp, gypsy

cairn memorial, landmark

caitiff wretched person

calaboose jail

calcify harden, inflexible

Caliban savage, deformed slave

caliginous dark, misty

callet prostitute

callidity skill

callipygous shapely buttocks

callow inexperienced, immature
calumet peace offering
calumny harmful misrepresentation
calyx outer whorl of a flower
Camelot idyllic happiness
campy affected, effeminate
canalize direct into a channel
canapé bite-size cold hors d'oeuvre
canard fabricated report
canescent hoary
canton section, division
cap small container of crack
cap-a-pie head to toe
Captain Nemo submarine captain
captious critical
carapace protective shell
card-carrying authentic
carp complain
carrot advantage
carry coals to Newcastle something superfluous
carte blanche full discretionary power
caryatid bent female figure
Cassandra one who predicts misfortune
casuistry rationalization
casus belli reason for going to war
cat's paw dupe, tool
catafalque coffin stand
catalyze to bring about
catamite boy kept by a pederast
catatonic stupor, rigidity
Catch-22 situation with no solution
catechize question
cathartic spiritually renewing
cathexis mental or emotional energy
catholicity liberality of views
catholicon panacea
caveat modifying explanation
CBGB country, bluegrass, and blues
celerity quick movement
cenotaph memorial
Cerberus three-headed dog
Challenger Deep deepest point on earth

chanteuse ornament
chapeau cap
charmeuse fine crepe
charnel crypt
Chatham Square confluence of Canal St. & Bowery (Pell, Mott & Doyers St.)
chatoyance undulating white light
chattel tangible property
chawbacon hick
chemism chemical affinity
cheongsam sheath with slit
cherchez la femme "look for the woman"
chevre goat cheese
chiaroscuro contrasting light and shade
chicane obstacle, switchback
Chicano Mexican
chichi chic
Chico renowned graffiti artist
chiffonier highboy
Child of Ham forsaken prodigy of Noah's son
chimera illusion
chippie mild desire for dope
chips currency
chitin hard outer coating
chloral knockout drops
chops mouth
choses personal personal property
chrysalis protective covering
chthonic infernal
chuck endearment
Cimmerian gloomy
circadian twenty-four-hour cycle
Circe witch
circumjacency surrounding area
Cisco cheap wine
city gin tap water
clabbered curdled
clairvoyance divination, ESP
clamant clamorous, urgent
clarion loud & clear
clay mankind
cliometric applied historical methods

480

cloaca sewer

clobber clothes

clockwork orange oddball

clou major interest

C-note one hundred dollars

cobber buddy

Coca-Cola cocaine

coelacanth prehistoric fish

coeval contemporary

cognitive dissonance psychological conflict

coif hairdo

cold-cop buy drugs from strangers

collective bargaining employer-labor union negotiations

colligate group together

collocate side-by-side

colubrine snake-like

come-outer withdrawal from Establishment

compradore intermediary

concatenate link together

concupiscent sexual desire

condign deserved

confabulation conference

conflate fuse, blend

congeners of similar nature

congeries aggregation, collection

Con Safos farewell

conscription compulsory enrollment

conspiracy group of ravens

Continental breakfast toast and coffee

contrapuntal counterpoint

contumacious rebellious

contumely harsh treatment

conurbation urban aggregation

cop to purchase drugs

corner private, secret, or remote place

corporal bodily

corps d'elite best people in a category

corsair pirate

coruscate sparkle

corvine crow-like

costermonger hawker of fruit and vegetables

cote shed or coop

cot-shelter lean-to or tent

covey group of grouses

cowrie currency, banknote

coxcombry foppery

crack smokable cocaine concentrate

crack house where crack is sold and used

cracksman safecracker

crack smile slash to the cheek by razor or knife

credo creed

crepehanging funebrial, saturnine

crescent young, increasing

crib room for prostitution

cri de coeur cry from the heart

crocodile tears false tears

cromlech obelisk, monolith

cromulent fine, acceptable

cruciation suffering

cub apprentice

cuddy small room or shelter

CUNY City University of New York

cupboard lover summer soldier

curate's egg with good and bad qualities

cutesy-poo impertinent

CV résumé

cynosure focus of attention

Cyprian prostitute

D heroin (dope)

Dantean hellish quality

dark horse unlikely to succeed

dead ass tedious, wearisome

dead game cocksure

decant pour from one vessel to another

decoupage shellacked paper cutouts

defalcate embezzlement

defeasance defeat

deglutition swallowing

Dei gratia thank God

dekko espy, glimpse

delectation enjoyment, delight

deleterious harmful

deliquesce dissolve, melt

delphic ambiguous, obscure

delta floodplain

demesne region, realm

demimondaine semi-respectable woman

demo crack-pipe

demographic characteristic of a population

denizen inhabitant

depredate plunder, ravage

deracinate uproot

de rigueur proper

dernier cri newest fashion

dervish whirling dance

descry discover, reveal

deshabille negligee

desideration desire

desideratum something desired as essential

destinate ordane, necessitate

desuetude disuse

détente friendship

devoir responsibility, duty

devolution retrograde evolution

dharmic divine law

diablerie black magic

diapason burst of sound

diaphanous insubstantial

diasporic settlement far from homeland

diatribe prolonged discourse

dichotomy duality

didactic instructive

dilettante artiste

Dionysiac frenzied

diorama life-like exhibit

dip pickpocket

dip snuff

direption depredation

dirty dancer $100 bill

disambiguation single meaning

discursion excursion, sidetrack

disprize scorn, undervalue

disquisition discourse

distaff female

diurnal daily

dodge hustle

dog days inactivity, stagnation

Dogberry policeman

doggerel trivial

dolce far niente carefree idleness

dollie (female) general population

dolorous miserable

dome world crack world

domino masquerade

doobie marijuana cigarette

doojee heroin

doppelganger dual nature

do-re-mi currency, banknote

doss sleep, bed

dowager dignified elderly woman

doyenne uniquely skilled per long experience

drag queen female impersonator

drag transvestite (in drag)

drift group of swine

drop a brick boo-boo

dropsy edema

druid wizard

duchy special domain

dudgeon indignation

dun demand payment

dundrearies flowing sideburns

duplicitous deceptive

Dutch suicide

dyscrasia abnormal blood

dysphoria unwell or unhappy

Ebola fatal virus

ebullition violent outburst

éclat brilliance

eejit idiot

effable definable

effluvium waste

effulgence brilliance

egalitarianism equality

Egeria female consort

egg cream milk, chocolate syrup, and selzer

egg in my beer good things in life

egghead intellectual

eggplant Negro

egregious flagrant, conspicuous

Egyptian darkness very dark

eidetic vivid recall of visual image

eidolon phantom

eight ball 3½ grams, ⅛ ounce

élan enthusiasm

élan vital vital force

eldritch eerie, weird

elegiac sorrowful

elide curtail, abridge

Elysian fields blissful, delightful

Elysium paradise

emboss exhaustion from being hunted

emeritus retired

emolument compensation

empyrean heavenly

endemic native

enfants terribles unorthodox, innovative

enfin in conclusion

enfranchise to set free

English breakfast eggs, sausages, etc.

ennui boredom

entre nous confidential

entrepôt intermediary trade center

entropic disorganization, chaos

entropy chaos

Eos goddess of dawn

ephemeral transient

epicene effeminate, intersexual

epiphany illuminating realization

eponymic name root

equivocal obscure

Erebus darkness

erogenic erotic

eschew shun

esoteric confidential, private

esprit vivacious cleverness

estaminet small café

ethnocentrism ethnic conceit

etiology origin

euchre cheat, trick

euthanize mercy killing

evanescent transient

Evel Knievel motorcycle stunt driver

eversion turning inside out

evincible revealing

evulgate divulge

excreta feces

execrate denounce

exegesis explanation

exigent demanding

exsiccate dry out

extemporize improvise

extirpate exterminate

extrusion to force or press out

faccia brutto face of a brute

facies general appearance

factotum servant

faience opaque glaze

fail-safe problem free

fain willing, inclined

fain and prone willing -hearted and well-disposed

fairing gift, present

fait accompli something accomplished

fakir impostor

falcate hooked

famulus private secretary

fane temple, shrine

fanfaronade bluster

fantod fit, fidgets

FAO Schwartz famous toy store

fastuous arrogant

Faustian without regard for future cost

faute de mieux for lack of anything better

favella hobo jungle

fawn grayish-brown

fealty fidelity, loyalty

febrile feverish

feculent foul, fecal

fecund fertile

feeder coffee man

feet of clay unsuspected weakness

femme fatale seductive woman

feng shui divine completeness

ferly wonder

fetch alter ego, doppelganger

fetches desolate land

feticide abortion

fetid malodorous

fiches rows of images

fiduciary trust, confidence

fifth column double agent

fig dress, array

file shrewd or crafty person

fille de joie prostitute

fin five dollars

finis end, conclusion

five-0 police

Five Points confluence of Baxter, Moscow & Worth St. (Paradise Sq., Little Water St. extinct)

flagitious villainous

flapper liberated woman

flash tattoo designs

flash house premises for underground activity

flat-ass penniless, broke

fledgling young bird

fleer scoff, sneer

flews sagging skin on lips

flocculate loosely aggregated particles

flower power (1960s) hippie movement

fluvial flowing

fly doorway

fly flash clothing

foliated layered

folie à deux double madness

forsooth in truth

fougasse flat Italian yeast bread

four-flush bluff

foursquare bold, direct

Fourth Estate public press

fractal irregular shape

frangipane almond cake

fresco painting on wet plaster

Freudian erotic

frisson thrill

frogskin paper money, currency

Front Porch power resort, viz. Raffles Hotel

frou-frou showy adornment

fructify bear fruit

fructuous fruitful

fruitcake homosexual

fulguration flashing like lightning

fuliginous murky

fulminate denunciate

fulsome offensive

funebrious funeral

fungible interchangeable

fungoid fungal

funicular simultaneous ascending & descending

fustian high-flown

gaggle group of ducks

gamin male street urchin

gamine female street urchin

ganef thief

garde-manger cold food specialization

Gehenna hell

gelid ice-cold

gelt currency, banknote

geneva gin

genius loci pervading spirit

gentrify renewal to oblige the affluent

gentry aristocracy

Gen-X born again

Geronimo fierce Indian warrior

gestalt integrated phenomenon not derivable by summation of its parts

gestaltist stresses uniform behavior

get off the dime get away, quit, vacate

Gethsemane agony, suffering

GI gastrointestinal

gimmix hypodermic syringe

ginchy oversexed

girandole pendant earring

girn snarl

girt equip, prepare for action

git foolish person

gizzard throat

glabrous bald

glaucous frosted

GLBTQ gay, lesbian, bisexual, transgender, queer lives

gleed glowing coal

glim sight

gloam twilight

G-man government man

GM garde-manger

Gnostic emancipation from evil comes from esoteric knowledge of spiritual truths

gob mouth

godown warehouse

god's penny wages, pay

gook Asian

Gordian knot intricate problem

gossamery insubstantial, delicate

Gott God

gouache opaque

gramarye sorcery

gramineous grassy

Grant fifty dollars

Grapevine transexual club

grass widow discarded mistress

graveolent rank, repulsive

greaser Hispanic, Mexican

green currency, banknote

green-eye envy

Gresham's law inferior objects drive out superior ones

gris-gris amulet or incantation

grotty filthy, gross

guinea stinker Italian cigar

gullet throat

gulosity greediness

gun hypodermic syringe

gunboat diplomacy diplomacy backed by military force

gunsel gunman

gustable tasteful

Guy Fawkes British terrorist

gynic female

Hades Hell

hakata seeds, dice, shells

halcyon happy, golden

halitosis bad breath

Hamilton ten dollars

Hannibal, Missouri home of Huckleberry Finn

Happy Hooligan tramp cartoon figure

harangue lecture

harbinger precursor

harlequin clown

harpy part woman, part bird

harridan shrew

haute cuisine classical cuisine

hawkshaw detective

head fellatio

head toilet

Heathcliff deformed child

heavy doors heaven

hebdomadal weekly

Hecate Goddess of night

hegemony domination

Hell's kitchen Hispanic ghetto

helotry slavery

heretic unorthodox

hermaphrodite transexual

hermetic recondite, solitary

hermitage hideaway

heteroclite deviant

heterodox unconventional, unorthodox

hew adhere

hex evil spell

Hiawatha Indian hero

hibernal arctic

hiatus interruption in time

hie hasten

hieratic stylized cursive writing

hierodule prostitute, slave

hierophant advocate

hilding base, contemptible

hinky jittery, suspicious

hinterland outskirts, borderland

Hip City author's street tag

histrionics acting

hoary ancient

Hobson's choice apparent free choice when in fact there is no alternative

holistic nature is an interacting whole

holland heavily sized cloth

Holmesian detective-like

holy grail significant goal/object

Homeric heroic

hominal bipedal primate

homunculus midget

hood hoodlum

hoosgow jail

hophead speed freak

hoser con man

Hotel from Hell tabloid moniker for Kenmore Hotel

hot pillow premises for sexual liaisons

houri voluptuous woman

hoyden saucy girl

Hoyle author of rules for games

hundo one hundred dollars

Hydra many-headed monster

Hygeia Goddess of health

hygrophilous growing in moist places

hyperbole exaggeration

hyperborean arctic

ice kill

iced secured

icon symbol, idol

iconoclasm anti-Establishment

ictus recurring beat

id psychological desires

idée fixe obsession

ideogram pictorial symbol

idiocratic eccentric

idiot savant narrow-mindedness

ignis fatuus deceptive goal or hope

ignominious dishonorable

ilk kind, sort

illicit unlawful

imbrication overlapping pattern

imbroglio violent altercation

imbruement influence, stain

immolate sacrifice, destroy

immutable unalterable

impecunious penniless

imperialism territorial acquisition

impinge have an effect

implacable unable to be changed

importunate troublesome

inamorata amour

incarnadine red

inchoative formative

in clover prosperous

incunabulum historical art of industry

Indic relating to India

indigenous nature

indign undeserving, unworthy

indomitable unconquerable

indurate morally hardened

induration hardness

ineluctable inevitable

inenarrable indescribable

infernal hellish, diabolical

inflorescence budding floral clusters

infrastructure framework of a system

ingénue naive girl

ingrate ungrateful person

inimical hostile

iniquitous wicked

in loco parentis daycare

inordinate excessive

insipid tasteless, flat

interface boundary

interlocutor conversationalist

interment burial

internecine mutually destructive

in the teeth in defiance of

intrinsic essential nature

invidious obnoxious

ipsissima verba quoted language

irenic peace, moderation, conciliation

irredenta foreign element in USA

irrefragable impossible to break, refute or alter

Ishmael outcast

isinglass pure gelatine

Isis Egyptian goddess

Iwo Jima Pacific island battlefield

jack currency, banknote

jackleg unscrupulous character

jack-o-lantern deceptive goal or hope

jack-roller thief, mugger

Jackson twenty-dollar bill

jaded exhausted

Janus-faced two-faced, duplicitous

japan high gloss

jarvey cab driver

jasper bloke, fellow, dude

jaundice envy, distaste, hostility

jay dupe, victim

je ne sais quoi hard to describe

jehu cab driver

jejune dull

jellyfish wimp

jeremiad lamentation

Jesuitical intriguing

jeunesse dorée wealthy and fashionable youth

jigaboo negro

Jim Jones psychotic evangelist

jitney unlicensed taxicab

Job's comforter one who depresses while seemingly giving solace

jocose merry, humorous

joie de vivre enjoyment of life

jones full blown habit

Judas traitor

juggernaut inexorable force

juju fetish, charm

juke cheat, deceive

juvenescence youthful

kafir Negro

Kafkaesque bizarre

kale currency, banknote

kampong third world hamlet

karma destiny

Katharine Gibbs founder of elite secretarial college

katzenjammer discordant clamor

ken know, view

kibble pelleted animal food

kicks shoes

kip bed, sleep

kismet fate

kite rubber bank check

kith familiar relative

Klaxon electric horn

kleptocracy government at expense of governed

knavish dishonest

knee-jerk reaction

knife-edge uncertainty, danger, risk

Kojak TV detective

koolokamba gorilla

kowtow obsequious deference, fawn

kraal enclosure

laches negligence

lacuna missing part

lagniappe gratuitous gift

laissez-faire non-governmental interference

laissez-passer permit to pass

lambent flickering

lamia vampire

large $1,000

latrate bark like a dog

laver washbowl

la vita nuova my new life

Lazarus beggar

leal true, loyal

leash group of foxes

Lebensraum space for life

lection liturgical reading

legume edible dried seed or pod

leman sweetheart, mistress

lesion abnormal change of organ

Lethean waters causing amnesia
lettuce leaves currency, banknote
levant in default of debt
Leviathan huge, insatiable
licentious indiscriminate sexuality
lime rickey lime soda & cherry syrup
liminal transitional
lineal hereditary
locus location, site
Loesida lower east sider
lolly currency, banknote
lorn desolate, forsaken
Lorne Campbell founder of Hell's Angels
Lot's wife turned into a pillar of salt upon looking back at Sodom
lousy replete, rich
lucre currency
Lucrezia witch
lucy loose cigarette
lugs superior airs, affectations
Ma Barker gang leader
mac john
macaronic vernacular
mack daddy pimp
maculate splotched
magdalene reformed prostitute
maggot fantastic idea
Magian magical
magic bullet curative, therapeutic
magma sediment, dregs
magpie acquisition
makebate contentious, quarrelsome
makeless peerless, matchless
maladroit awkward, inept
malaise ill being
mal à propos inappropriate
malediction curse, execration
malefaction crime
maleficence evil
malinger pretend illness
malison curse, damnation
malt powdered germinated barley
Malthusian birth control

malversation corrupt administration
mammered muttered, stuttered
Mammon debasing wealth
mandamus court-issued writ
mandarin highbrow
maniple long narrow strip of silk
manqué frustrated aspirations
manumit release from slavery
manzanita twisting hardwood
marabout Muslim dervish
march region, zone
marmelized thrashed, beat up
Mary Jane marijuana
Mary Janes round-toed flat slippers
Masonite compressed sawdust and glue
masque masquerade
Matins and Lauds midnight/3:00 a.m.
matutinal morning, early
maudlin weakly sentimental
maverick renegade
maya illusion
mayhem damage, violence
mazuma banknote, currency
meat-and-potatoes essential, vital
medicament applied therapy
meed reward
meet fitting, expedient
meliorate improve
memento mori death's head
mentation mental activity
mephitic foul smelling
Mercury god of travel
meretricious tawdry, gaudy
meretrix prostitute
merry-Andrew clown
merry-go-round hamster wheel
mesmeric mesmerizing
mestizo half-breed
metamorphosis striking alteration
metaphysics philosophy
metathesis change of condition
Methuselah ancient
mezzanine building's mid-story

Mickey Finn chloral hydrate

micturition urination

Midas golden

mimesis imitation

mimetism imitative, mimicry

minatory threatening

mint leaves banknote, currency

minx wanton woman

misanthrope manhater

mise-en-place everything in place

mise-en-scene environment, milieu

MIT Massachusetts Institute of Technology

mitt hand

modiste dressmaker & milliner

modus operandi method of procedure

modus vivendi way of life

moiety half

moira fate

mojo magic charm

moll prostitute

mommy track reduced work hours

money shot one hundred dollars

monkey drug habit

monkey grease currency

monomaniac fixation on a single idea

monstrance vessel of consecrated host

monticulous mountainous

moor expanse of open land

mopus currency, banknote

mordant caustic

mordent tonal alteration

moribund approaching death

motile mobile

motley incongruous elements

moxie courage, determination

Mr. Charlie white man

Mr. D. the devil

Mrs. Grundy prudish

mudger opposition

mufti ordinary dress

mulct swindle

muliebral femininity

mullah educated Muslim

murid comprising mice and rats

Museum Mile 5 Ave. from 82 St. to 104 St., NYC

mutable inconstant

nadir lowest point

naiad river nymph

naif naive person

narthex church portico or vestibule

nascent beginning, new

nates buttocks

Nautilus fictitious submarine

neatherd cowherd

Nebuchadnezzar Babylonian king

necrolith tomb

needful banknote, currency

Nelly effeminate homosexual

neologic meaningless language coined by a psychotic

neophyte novice, beginner

nescient ignorant

New Age modern, contemporary

New Jack black hipster

New Wave outrageous, unconventional

New York minute flash, instant

nexus center, focus

nidus nest, locale

nigger obnoxious bully

nigh nearly, almost

nihilistic existence is senseless

9/11 World Trade Center attack

Nirvana heaven

nisus endeavor

nobble swindle, cheat

nobby smart, chic

noble savage uncorrupted non-European

noetic of the intellect

noir shadowy, sleazy

nonce the time being

non compos mentis not of sound mind

non obstante notwithstanding

nonpolemic noncontroversial

noodle head, noggin

noological mental

Norman Rockwell illustrator of Americana

nostrum panacea, remedy

noumenon senseless thought

nouvelle cuisine modern cuisine

nugacious trifling, nugatory

nugatory inconsequential

nuggett $100 bill

number score for a sexual hustle

numen spiritual force

nunchakus two hardwood sticks connected by a short rope or chain

obfuscate darken

objets trouvés junk held to have value

oblation worship, devotion

obliquity deviation from morality

obloquy condemnation

obstreperous unruly, clamorous

obtrude intrude

Occident western

odyssey long wandering quest

ointment currency, banknote

oligarchy corrupt selfish government

olla podrida hodgepodge

omega end

om mani padme hum "Thanks be to God"

omnium gatherum conglomeration

omnivorous animal & vegeable diet

oneiric dreamy

onomatopoeia vocalization of animal sound

on the block engaged in prostitution

on the lam escape

ontology existential theology

onus burden, obligation

ooftish banknote, currency

ophidian snake-like

opprobrium disgrace

oppugnant caustic, acrid

oracle sacred medium

orchestra group of crickets

Oreo Negro with white affectations

oriflamme banner

orison prayer

Orwellian dystopian world of *1984*

ossify harden

ossuary grave

ostensible apparent

ouma elderly woman

ovine relating to sheep

oxymoron combination of incongruous words

Oz mythical land

Pago Pago South Sea island

pail group of wasps

paladin champion

palaver idle talk

palimpsest diverse subsurface layers

palladium safeguard

palliate soothing

palliative comforter, balm

pallid dull

palooka incompetent boxer

pan all of a group

panacea cure-all

panache flamboyance

Pandora's box source of troubles

panoply protective covering

pansexual divergent sexuality

paphian prostitute

Papillon prisoner who hid cash in his rectum

parable moral or religious example

paradiddle alternating successive drumbeats

paradigm pattern, archetype

paraphilia unusual sexuality

parce que because, forasmuch

pareve without animal products

Paris green toxic yellowish green

parity equality

parlance idiom, dialect

parse minute examination

parterre ornamental garden

Parthian shot fired in retreat

parturient giving birth

parvenu nouveau autocrat

passementerie ornamental trimming

pastiche potpourri

paté cooked forcemeat

pater father

paternoster repetitious prayer

pathogen causing disease

pathos sympathetic pity

patina superficial exterior

patisserie pastry shop

patrimony heritage

patulous spreading from center

pawky canny, shrewd

pdq pretty damn quick

peccancy crime, fault, sin

peccant faulty, sin

pedagogue education

pede claudo slowly but surely

Pedialyte electrolyte supplement

Peeler policeman

pejorative deprecatory

pelf banknote, currency

penetralia innermost part

pentimento reappearance of something obscured

penumbrae fringe of illumination

penury poverty

perambulation walking

percolate penetrate, seep

per diem daily

perdu soldier on hazardous duty

peregrinate walk

peremptory haughty, final

peripatetic itinerant pedestrian

permutation transformation, rearrangement

perron outdoor stairway with platform at top

persiflage frivolous raillery

pertinacious obstinate

pestilent deadly

pettifogger quibble, carp

phantasmagoria shifting succession of things seen and imagined

pharisaical hypocritical

pharisean sanctimonious

philanthropy promotion of goodwill

philistine hostile to culture & arts

philippic tirade

philosopher's stone key to success

philtre love potion

phlebotomy drawing blood

Phoenix bird resurrected from its own ashes

piano ranges and ovens

picaresque roguish

picayune paltry, petty

piece handgun

pièce montée centerpiece

pied-à-terre second lodging

Pierre exclusive hotel in NYC

pig police

pig in a poke something whose value is obscured

pilca space between thumb & finger

pinch arrest, apprehend

pink-collar jobs held by women

pinko advanced liberal views

pis aller last resource or device

placa memorial

planchette device for paranormal writing

plaudit applause, approval

plebian common

pledget absorbent compress

plenipotent full power

plexiform interwoven combination of parts

plinth base

plutocracy government by the wealthy

pneumatic air driven

po-face hypocritically solemn

pogrom organized massacre

point needle for a hypodermic syringe

polemic refutation of another's principles

politesse decorousness

poltergeist mischievous ghost

poltroon coward
polyglot multilingual
polymorphous various characters & styles
pong offensive odor
pork barrel slush fund illicit government appropriations
portamenti gliding sounds
possible currency, banknote
posslq persons of the opposite sex sharing living quarters
postprandial after dinner
posy artificial sentiment
potation alcoholic drink
pottage thick soup
power elite rich and powerful, superclass
prana essence, life force
praxis action, practice
preciosity fastidious refinement
prehominid extinct primates
prelapsarian innocent, arcadian
premonitory forewarning
prescient foresight
prestidigitator sleight of hand
prevenient anticipatory, antecedent
priest hole hidey-hole
prima facie apparent
Prime Six a.m.
primogeniture rights of inheritance
primordial primary, primeval
Prince Albert dandy or invert
procacious brazen, bold
Procrustean conformity by arbitrary means
prodigal luxuriant
prodigy extraordinary, omen
profligate dissolute, extravagant
prognosticate predict, foretell
Promethean daringly original
promulgate declare
propinquity proximity
propitiate appease, pacify
proscriptive condemned
proselytize convert to new faith

prosthesis artificial body part
prosy commonplace
protean versatile, diverse
protohuman early hominid
provenient origin, source
provisory conditional
prunes and prisms airs and graces
prurient sexual arousal
psychotomimetic behavioral affectation
PTSD post traumatic stress disorder
pudicity solicitousness, modesty
puerile juvenile
puerilism childish behavior
puissance power, strength
pulchritude beauty, physical comeliness
pullulate swarm, teem
puncheon rough timber
punk homosexual partner
purl gentle movement
purlieu neighborhood, environs
purulent discharging pus
pusillanimous timid, cowardly
putative assumed, accepted
pyemia pus-filled abscess
Pygmalion alchemist
Pyrrhic achieved at excessive cost
Quan Yin Goddess of compassion
quarrel bolt for crossbow
Quasimodo deformed beggar
quean prostitute
queen drag queen
querent inquiry
quiddative clannish, select
quintessence essence
quixotic capricious, unpredictable
quiz eccentric person
quod jail
quondam former, erstwhile
quotidian everyday, commonplace
qv (quod vide) which see
rachitic rickety
raffia plant fiber strand
railroad flat rooms in a line

raison d'être reason for being
ramada open-sided shelter
ramate branching
ramose having branches
rapine pillage, plunder
rapparee plunderer, vagabond
rapprochement cordial relations
rara avis rare bird
Rasputin manipulator, deceiver, mystic
rataplan repetitive beat
ravening plunder
readhead $100 bill
reagent causing chemical reaction
rebarbative repellent
recreant unfaithful to duty or allegiance
recontre confrontation
recrudescence renewal
rectory priest's residence
recusant nonconformity
redd clean up
redoubt dwelling
redound reflect
redress remedy
reeve local official
refection food and drink, repast
refluent flowing back
reft tear away
regolith residual material
reification confirm as real
reindue don, put on
relict remnant
remissible forgivable
remonstrate expostulate in opposition
remuneration pay
renaissance revival, rebirth
renitent reluctant
renunciate ascetic self-denial
repatriate restore allegiance to
repin dejection
replevy take or get back
requiescat in pace rest in peace
res publica state or commonwealth
reticular network, net

revanche revenge, recover
revenant reincarnate being
revetment barricade shelter
rialto theater district
riff musical improvisation
rill runnel
ringer impostor, fake
RIP rest in peace
risible laughable
Robert Moses NYC parks & highways commissioner
rock crack
rodomontade bragging speech
Romper Room kiddie TV show
roseate optimistic, favorable
Rosetta stone clue to understanding
Rotarian service club member
roue libertine, rake
rough trade rugged male homosexual
rozzer police
Rubicon determining threshold
rubric category, name
ruca girlfriend
ruche trimming material
rum dangerous
rune mystery, magic
Ruritanian romantic situation
ruth compassion
sacré bleu surprise, expletive
salacious lustful
salacity lustfulness
salamander broiler
saltatory jumping around
salubrious healthful
samsara infinite misery, karma
sanguine confident, optimistic
sandhog tunnel laborer
sans without
sapience sagacity, wisdom
Saracen arab
sartorial related to clothes
satrap ruler
saturnine surly, sullen

saurian crocodiles, lizards

savant expert

savarin yeast coffee cake

sawbuck ten dollars

scag heroin

scatology degeneracy

schism division, separation

schlemiel chump

schlock duffer, dunce

schmaltz rendered chicken fat with onions

sciatica damaged sciatic nerve

Scotch twilight murkiness

Scotty crack

scrofulous sick looking

scrumble overlay of one coat upon another, which is then etched to the undercoat

scry fortune telling

scurrilous vulgar, evil

sectarian group member

sedulous diligent

septic putrefaction

sepulchral funeral

sequacious tractable, subservient

seraphic celestial

sere dried, withered

serendipity finding agreeable things not sought

shadow work scavenging

shamus police officer

Shangri-la utopia, paradise

shank's mare walking

shebeen after-hours bar

sheila girl

shekel banknote, currency

shemozzle mess, jumble

shent ruin, destroy

shero woman hero

Shiatsu acupressure

shibboleth platitude, cliché

Shiite Muslim

shill decoy

shine liking, fancy

shirtwaist ladies' male-type blouse

shirty angry

shivaree ruckus

shooting gallery premises for IV use

shot IV injection

shpilkes agitation, impatience

shtarker tough guy

sibyl prophetess

siege mentality defensive, fearful

Sikh classless society of India

simoleon currency, banknote

simon-pure pretentiously pure

sine qua non indispensably essential

SIS Secret Intelligence Service

Sisyphean endless repetition

situs site of origin

skell scamp

ski bum ski season outlander

skin flute penis

skint flat broke

skulk group of foxes

slag prostitute

slattern prostitute

slither group of snakes

sloe livid

slub kink

slug suppository

smack heroin

smalto enamel used in mosaic work

smite strike sharply and heavily

sociopath antisocial

sock in restrict from flying

Socratic systematic doubt and questioning

Sodom city of wickedness

sodomy oral, anal, bestial sex

soffit underside of stairway

soft-shoe tap dance without taps

soft-soap cajole

SoHo South of Houston (Street)

soigné sleek, well-groomed

SOL shit out of luck

solecism breach of etiquette

soliloquy talk to self

solus alone

sonance sound

sonsy buxom

sophistic plausible but fallacious

sophistry deceptive reasoning

soteriological salvation through Jesus Christ

souk market stall

spanger spare change beggar

spavined decrepit, old

speak spaghet speakeasy spaghetti

specious showy

spectral ghostly

speedball cocaine and heroin mixed

spelunk explore caves

spic Hispanic

Spithead British naval base

splenetic malevolent, spiteful

spondulicks currency, banknote

spread the toils enmesh, entangle

spurious false, fake

squeeze intravenous injection

SSDI Social Security Disability Insurance

SSI Social Security Insurance

stasis stagnation

STD sexually transmitted disease

stela commemoration

stentorious loud

stilly still, quiet

stochastic random

straw front false appearance

straw in the wind precursor

strident harsh, insistent, discordant

stroll prostitute's soliciting promenade

stroppy touchy, belligerent

Stygian extremely dark

Styx river of death

sub rosa private, secretive

subaltern subordinate

success fou extraordinary success

succubus female demon

sufflate inflate

Sufi Muslim mystic

sugar banknote, currency

sugar bush sugar or rock maple forest

sui generis unique, peculiar

sullage refuse, sewage

sumptuary regulations on pleasure

sundowner hobo, tramp

supercede obsolete, replace

superego conscience, morality

surety assurance, guarantee

surreal fantastic

susurrant rustling, whispering

suum cuique to each his own

swag profits, spoils

swami seer, pundit

SWAT special weapons and tactics

sweltry muggy

sybarite voluptuary, sensualist

sybil prophetess

sylvan woods, forest

sylvatic animalistic

symbiotic intimate association

syncopal restricted blood flow to brain

synechdochical a part is put for the whole, or the whole for a part

tabla drum

tableau vivant living picture

tacquería taco and burrito café

Tai Chi meditative movements

tallow fat, paraffin, & beeswax

Tammany Society political organization

Tantalus condemned to starve amidst bounty

tare undesirable element

Tasmanian devil savage marsupial

tatterdemalion ragged, disreputable

tchotchkes trinket, knickknack

telluric terrestrial

telos goal

temerarious daring, rash

tenebrous dark, murky, obscure

tensity tenseness

teratoid deviant

tergiversation desertion of faith

terra incognita unknown territory

tertian ague malaria
tessellated checkered
tetra small tropical fish
Teutonic Germanic
thanatology study of death
thespian acting
Third Estate the common people
third eye ESP
three-alarm very strong
threnody elegy
tie-dyed eclectic, multi-faceted
tin rocks coinage
tintamarre din, clamor
titrate adjust
tocsin alarm bell
toffee-nosed snobbish
toft settlement
ton vogue, fashion
tonsorial grooming
tootie currency, banknote
too-too extreme
tout de suite pronto
tower block apartment building
trace footprint
traduce betray
tranche de vie slice of life
transexual gender reassignment
transmogrify disturbing transformation
transvestite cross-dresser
trepan entrap, lure
très chic well turned-out
trey bag three-dollar dope bag
trey bag hooker $3 trick hooker
Tribeca triangle below Canal Street
trig prim
trimmer thieving prostitute
tristful melancholy
tromp l'oeil illusion, deception
trope cliché
tropistic reflex, propensity
truck mutuality
trucks homosexual rendezvous
truculent cruel, savage

trull prostitute
tucker food
tureen earthenware casserole
turpitude depravity
twelfth-step assist recovering alcoholics
twelve steps AA recovery program
twig notice, observe
tyro amateur, novice
ubication location, place
ubiquitous widespread
ubiquity omnipresence
ultima Thule arctic region
ululate howl, wail
umbra dark, shadowed
unctuous ingratiating
upas harmful area
uptown Cadillacs sneakers
uroborous self-devouring snake
USFDA United States Food & Drug Administration
usquebaugh whiskey
uxorial wife-like
vade mecum manual, guidebook
valediction farewell
Valhalla heaven
vamp seductress
Vandalic destructive
vapid lacking tang
vaward forefront
velleity lowest degree of volition
velocipede bicycle
ventre à terre at great speed
veracious truthful, honest
veridic truthful, genuine
verjuice acid disposition
vespertilian bat-like
Vesuvius volcano near Pompeii
viand food
vic victim
vicar administrative agent
vicarious substitutionary
vicinage vicinity
vicinal local

Glossary

vicissitude mutability
vieux jeu old-fashioned
vindaloo curried Indian dish
virtu objets d'art
virulent malignant
viscereal unreasoning
vitiate debase, impair
vitrine glass showcase
vivarium terrarium
vivify animate, quicken
voracious ravenous
votary devotee
vox populi popular sentiment
vulpine crafty, foxy
waddie cowboy
waffle equivocate, vacillate
wallah specialist
wanga occult
WASP White Anglo-Saxon Protestant
waxy temper, rage
weal well-being
weald forest
weather eye shrewd watchfulness
weed marijuana
weft web, fabric
welkin heaven
whelp birth
wherewithal currency, banknote
whiffet jerkwater youngster
whip and spur hasten

whip-out currency, banknote
whist silent, quiet
white-bread Caucasian
white-bready white middle-class style
whited sepulcher hypocrite
wight creature
wit intelligence
witches' Sabbath black mass
wog Arab
wold region
wolf's tail radiate, scatter
works hypodermic syringe
wriggle group of worms
wuss homosexual
Xanadu idyll
xeno foreign, strange
xenophile foreign attraction
yap mouth
yard one hundred dollars
yardbird inept rookie
yegg thief, crook
yeoman's service aid
Yid Jew
yohimbine challenge simulated PTSD
yuppie young urban professional
Zeitgeist cultural climate
zither stringed instrument
zodiacal light diffuse glow
zoic animalistic

THE FOLLOWING IS A SAMPLE FROM *DETOUR*, A REAL-LIFE NOVEL
BY THE AUTHOR OF *NEW YORK CITY BUM*.

The first week of August in the high elevations of the Green Mountains carries the early bite of Autumn; the alpine air so clean and clear with a hint of foliage and mulch and pine resin and freshly cut timber and, perhaps, the season's first waft of woodsmoke. It's chilly yet, at nine o'clock in the morning though sunny, the luminous solar radiance hasn't yet warmed the day's monticulous weather but there's a seasonal, woodsy essence that evokes the better part of all that I love about Vermont. As I ready myself for my bimonthly voyage into town, a joyless yet necessary excursion to resupply my hermitage, deep in the forest of Deerfield Valley, where I've secluded myself for the past ten years, I reflect that if I could have my groceries and laundry and books delivered, I'd never leave my house. I find my trips into civilization as of late increasingly more depressing with the growing conviction that nothing outside my home (save wildlife) will improve my life.

My driver, Priscilla, is late today, a dear and venerable white-haired widow, one of two such whom I employ to taxi me around. Priscilla is my usual shopping chauffeur while Annie is my ride for doctor visits. Two sweet old ladies supplementing their long days (and their income) with companionable service.

While I scan the view from my front-room windows, I search for Crazy George in my panoptic vista, spying every hidey-hole where he'd likely be lurking, motionless, in his creepy modus vivendi, making sure that he's not out there prowling around the driveway, so's I can bring out the trash while I await my car service. The coast looks clear, everything is still and quiet out-side, only a little sporadic bird activity at the feeders; latecomers after the early morning rush. It's ten after nine already, Priscilla is rarely this late; I decide to make the trash run up the driveway to the *Dumpster*.

I pull out the black thirty-gallon plastic bag from my wooden barrel in the kitchen and double knot it. I'm dressed in sweatshirt, jeans and sneakers; my usual traveling togs. I unlatch the three deadbolts on the inside of my front door, a New York precaution out of place in northern New England, but necessary; security measures that include padlocks, police lock, guns and knives ever since Crazy George declared war on me a few years ago. I live this way, ever vigilant because I'm not self-deluding and do not underestimate my adversary. I have weapons scattered through-out my home, within easy reach wherever I might be at any given moment, aware of George's capabilities, from a crashing frontal assault to a silent cat burglary through a locked window.

I almost shot the bastard last night after he dumped a dozen six-foot pot plants (root ball and all) on my front porch in the dark. I trod on them when I stepped out to place food for my itinerant fox and racoons on the deck, flinging the plants out into the driveway, then phoning the landlord to report the malicious prank. Soon enough, here came Crazy George gathering up the plants from in front of my house, ranting and raving that he'd kill me, burn down my house and so forth, so that I stepped out onto my deck, gun in hand, but George had by then retreated back to the infernal regions from whence he'd come. This was an ongoing scenario for the past couple of years following the housebreak (Crazy George's sick terrorist fetish) while I was out, and his placing a cat in the room with my bird and hamster. Ever since that cowardly act, I knew with all certitude that I'd have to kill the perilous bad boy. My only folly was in thinking that I could get away with the murder; if only I'd wait for George to come at me (which I knew was inevitable) I could shoot him in self-defense. Little did I then know that Vermont doesn't work that way.

Nevertheless, I purchased a deathful Ruger .357 magnum snub-nose revolver, capped with steel jacketed hollow points. No expense was spared for Crazy George. I wanted the best of everything for the would-be assassin of my babies. Never, thereafter, did I leave my home without that safeguard—to feed the birds, to shovel snow, to collect the mail, to take out the trash. I knew my enemy well and would never be caught unarmed, for surprise was Crazy George's MO. "The only one who can teach you anything is the enemy,"[1] and when I brought Crazy George to school it would be the last lesson he ever learned. Nobody, save my good friend Christen, knew I packed a gat. That was my big surprise, my ace in the hole, my secret weapon. And when that heater came out, it was coming out hot, blazing, spewing death.

I stepped out of my front door with the bag of trash slung over my shoulder and took a swift glance around—all clear. I stepped down onto the gravel drive and turned right as I began my trudge up the incline to the *Dumpster*, walking the gauntlet between the quartet of bungalows, two by two, of which mine was the first on my side. As I progressed beyond my own house and was between it and my neighbor Jill's (so that my retreat was cut off by a full house-length), out from between the opposite two bungalows stepped George, lip curled in a sneer, axe handle resting on his shoulder in a two-fisted grip. He had me cold and his smirk showed that he knew it. Hell, he'd planned it. How long—hours—had he hidden in the tall vegetation out there, like a Red Indian, knowing it was my shopping day and that sooner or later I'd come out of my camp.

I groaned inwardly, knowing that this was it, the big show-down had arrived at last. As much as I wanted to kill George, I didn't want to upset the pastoral routine of my life. Whether or not I'd go down or go free for the crime, there would still be

---

1 Orson Scott Card, *Ender's Game*

a hullabaloo—fuzz responding, screaming neighbors, George's friends... Nonetheless, I was resigned. That rotten piece of dog meat would never let up, I'd never have any peace as long as Crazy George was left standing.

I continued on up the driveway towards the Dumpster as George began running his mouth, following me.

"I want you out of that house, I'm giving you four days—You hear me?"

By then I had reached the *Dumpster*. I opened the lid and tossed in my bag of trash.

"I hear you," I replied, "Live and let live, George."

And he was abreast of me; axe handle at the ready.

"Let's get this over," challenged my opponent.

Out of my pocket came the hot rod, as if of its own volition, and pointed at George—an accusing finger—no more than two feet from me. I could have reached out and touched him.

"Go on, use your gun," blustered George with a snarl, confident and imperious.

And the steel-trap rosco roared, Kraakoww!, spitting fire, point blank in the chest, the explosion resounding along the driveway— one slug plowing into George's left lung, through his black heart, and out the other side. He fell backward, arms spread-out—a cruciform—eyes wide in astonishment, mouth open in a rictal grimace. Dead before he hit the ground.

Jill, across the driveway, was screaming in her house; two of George's girlfriends (mommy and missy) came charging down the spiral stairs from the Big House at the top of the drive, mommy crying, "Georgie! Georgie!" followed by the landlord who was addressing me as he ran towards us.

"What did you do? Give me the gun!"

And I said to them, "Who's crazy now?" as I walked down the driveway towards my house, thinking that if Kenny (the landlord) ever got ahold of the shooter, he might have plugged me with it—they all worshiped big, bad George. By then, the three were crowded around the body, as I slipped under my roof and closed the door. I placed my iron on the counter, *sans peur et sans reproche* (without fear and without reproach), and picked up the telephone, dialing my friend Chrissy, to have her come and rescue my pets, as the fuzz were surely on their way. While Priscilla still hadn't showed. Won't she be surprised.

ONE DECADE PRIOR TO THAT FATAL CLIMAX AND I AM LEAVING NEW YORK CITY FOR GOOD.

One not insignificant factor that played a role in my deciding on my move to Vermont—my retirement, that included almost ten hamsters (in individual tanks), and a bird (used to living in an aviary)—a move from an established financial, residential and support complex, to a remote hermitage, with no financial structure, cut off from civilization as I had known it, whose demographics to enable one such as myself were nonexistent. A move into a region that required a reliable income, personal transportation (a car), and a residence that ensured privacy and peace and quiet... a long list of needs of which I was in no condition to provide for myself and my family.

The necessary help to enable me to take such a huge gamble, that included my being broke, was readily promised by Kenny, whose situation contained all that I needed to survive and establish myself. The prime drawback of relying on Kenny to come through on his offer was his deep-rooted history of lying, and of changing his bipolar sentiments midstream. And, not to be disregarded, was Kenny's shaky crowd of sycophants, whose negative influence and parasitic tendencies made any move to within a mile of Kenny a poor investment.

However, in my many phone conversations with Kenny during the seminal formation of my deliberations on the feasibility of such a relocation, the following criteria came to light. Kenny's ma had passed away, leaving Kenny without the reliance and support (and companionship) on which he always depended. All Kenny's friends—the crowd of hanger's-on (all dopers, half Kenny's age)—had dispersed, leaving Kenny stranded. Kenny, for whom socializing was the spice of life, as well as the connections that kept Kenny plugged-in to the valley's fluctuating markets, economy, and events, had collapsed. He was so-o lonely, he could squeeze a teardrop from a stone. He had a steady guest registration that required maintenance (cleaning, clerical work, such as letter writing), and he needed a friend, a live-in companion and valet, who could cook. For this Kenny was willing to pay.

In reply to my financial requirements that, minimally, included $35 per week for cigarettes, food for myself, (and beer), Kenny guaranteed me enough work whose remuneration would more than meet my rock-bottom needs. I could sign-up for welfare. And he had a pot-grow operation, run by a new young kid named Damon, who was also a cook, and they had a small farm for produce. The kid was good, Vatican-educated in Rome, but he wasn't live-in. I would like him. They could use some help with the (pot) farming, they made pizza, there was a pond. And I could have my own house, one of four bungalows. He would make me an outdoor aviary for Polly, from netting. When could I come?

The hope of my life for myself and my family. Could it really be so easy? Dropping right in my lap, so timely? I knew exactly what work Kenny was talking about, and I was a natural. Little jobs I had done for Kenny in the past. I made up my mind. We were coming. As soon as spring blossomed.

Damon hated me before I arrived. Damon (a legend in his own eyes) did not want to share Kenny; he wanted all that Kenny had to offer, wanted Kenny totally dependent on himself. When Kenny told Damon he was giving me one of the bungalows, Damon had a conniption. He, Damon, would take the bungalow, would pay Kenny rent, would be on location to oversee the pot-grow, the pizza operation, he could make beer. Was Kenny crazy? Let me (I) have one of the rooms in the Big House. Anything I could do for Kenny, Damon could do better, save cleaning. Damon was not a cleaner.

I pinned Damon for the con man that he was the minute I laid eyes on him. I took in the whole game at a glance—how Damon had beautiful, good-hearted Kenny wrapped around his crooked little finger. And Damon, no dunce, intuited that I saw through his scam, and hence hated me the more for my perception. He, Damon, would easily undermine me, and show Kenny how worthless I was. This was the opening play when I arrived at Kenny's, waiting for me in the wings, out of sight, biding his time, until he could make his grand entrance. For everything was planned with Damon, the maestro of, what he coined as, Grandma's Gardens.

Now, I was twice Damon's age; he had a long way to go to catch up to me. And, what Damon stubbornly overlooked was that Kenny and I went back 40 years together; knew each other like a book. Kenny was well acquainted with my value; as in, I once wrote Kenny a letter to a judge and got Kenny off the hook for $40,000 in alimony arrears. I wrote a letter to an insurance company for a guest at Kenny's, who had taken out a vacation policy. I told how due to an injury (doctor bill for visit included), the policy holder missed out on all the activities she'd planned on. Horseback riding, swimming, hiking, et cetera. She asked for a refund on the cost of her airline ticket (over $1,000) round trip from Austria. She collected. I had written promotional pamphlets for Kenny, advertising copy, done investigative research for Kenny in the past. My grasp of what Kenny needed to keep his rental operation afloat was beyond the ken of a 20-year-old foreigner. So, I wasn't the least bit concerned over Damon's opinions; my nonchalance only serving to fuel Damon's impotence.

D amon had arrived at Kenny's from New York City, with a couple of housemates, at a time when Kenny was open to a new venture. Kenny's ma was still getting around on her own then, which allowed Kenny undistracted focus on that which he always sought—someone smarter than himself who could be of profit to Kenny. One who could easily trick Kenny if that one was a ready con man, being in the right place at the right time, and savvy enough to seize the opportunity Kenny offered. That is, providing anything necessary for some new undertaking that would benefit Kenny.

Thus, a marijuana operation could be installed at Kenny's; cultivated and harvested to yield the best pot, that was worth thousands—easily selling Kenny a bill of goods. An operation over which Kenny essentially had no knowledge, no control and, thus, could be easily fleeced. And so, Kenny turned over an entire bungalow to the three. The pot could be concealed within the house, while the trio's presence could be explained to Ma with the outdoor cultivation of a huge garden—Grandma's Garden. Damon steadily took control.

Moreover, Damon could cook, and easily talked Kenny into supporting a new restaurant, which Damon would run. This is exactly how Kenny gets roped in. By offering Kenny a return for, and the position of front man, of two enterprises that appealed to Kenny. Kenny supplying the property and the building, and willingly providing seed money (however exorbitant), the work and know-how would come from the three, and they would all reap the rewards. And so, trustingly, eager Kenny launches a new business about which he knows nothing. Another member of this trio was Chuck. And, Chuck was pot savvy. He rigged an override on their house's fuse box, to overload the house's electric capacity, to power the grow lights, and wound up burning Kenny's house down to the ground.

The upside of that debacle: the house was insured, enabling Kenny to rebuild a two-story replacement house, entirely wrapped in glass, upper and lower decks, double spiral staircase, full basement (that became the new pot grow room), and a flat roof—a castle in the sky. A house that would acquire the designation of Holiday Inn.

Guilt-ridden, Chuck forever after belonged to Kenny, doing much of the construction on the Holiday Inn, maintaining the garden plot (a showcase garden), that was the cover for the pot operation. Acquiring, in the end, the status of a deity (so pleased was Kenny with the outcome of the fire); Chuck's reward, being allowed to move into the ground floor of the Holiday Inn, much to Damon's frustration and envy. And the establishment of a rift between the two ex-friends.

––––––––––––

My arrival at Kenny's, Vermont, USA, following a ten-hour battle through a springtime blizzard, was a step through the looking glass, into a dreamy land of white. Snow was piled shoulder-high and still falling in the quiet night; having travelled through a timeless white tunnel to find this outpost in the sylvan wilds of the Green Mountains.

Our destination stood at the top of a steep hill, yellow light wavering through a veil of white. The Big House was a crazy Vermont architecture of weird angles, glass, cantilevering decks, and spiral staircase. With Kenny standing atop the stairs in the snow, his two black Labradors flanking him, all smiles on his Mickey Rooney face. And the dogs are upon us, sniffing and prancing, as we step from the car; and then Kenny is there, our arms engulfing each other as the dogs join in, jumping and barking. And we are stepping through the sliding glass doors atop the keep, into a warm and rustic mountain lodge interior—cathedral ceiling, glass wall, hanging hemp macramé, glass bottles of colored herb oil, pine and cedar planking, wood stove cranking; and Kenny is passing a joint on a hemostat, grinning, and I'm also smiling in awe as I take it all in, butcher block, and hanging barnboard cabinets over a floating island breakfast nook, thick shag carpet, an Indian print couch, with a huge, black, cast-iron stove, complete with griddle... Yeah!

And the hamster tanks are set around, with poor brave Polly in her tiny brass cage; I open the door of her captivity and she is out in a flash, clutching Kenny's breast, and I'm as dumbfounded as Kenny is pleased that Polly went, for the first time, near anyone else but me. And we are all laughing, Frank and Kenny haven't seen each other in a long time unremembered, everyone talking at once; "Did you do all this?" "Wait till you see this," while I'm cracking a beer, and Polly won't leave me; and Ethelyn has come upstairs and has a hamster in her shirt pocket, laughing. And it looked, at that new moment like it could truly work out; a future for us all seemed promising.

For all its yearlong accommodation to tourism—its very economic dependence—especially to winter sport, Wilmington, Vermont, in the heart of Deerfield Valley, has resisted modernization admirably. No billboards, no neon lights, no Pizza Hut or Burger King. And no super highway between Wilmington town and

Mount Snow where, in the heart of ski season, Route 9 resembles the Long Island Expressway at rush hour.

Much of the Deerfield Valley area remains as it was over fifty years ago, when I first fell in love with Vermont; remarkably resilient to updating in the face of today's information age, jet age, convenience age. And praise be, for that is much of its charm. Dirt roads, thick forest, dairy barns, and general stores all together lend Deerfield Valley a natural step back in time, one of the few remaining time warps in our vanishing America the Beautiful. Crisp clean air, brooks and lakes, deciduous woods where wildlife still flourishes. Horse farms, maple sugaring.

God, how I love this place.

Higley Hill, a twisting ten-mile dirt road with branching cowpaths, isolated hay and horse pasture, a tunnel through sugar bush and deep pineland. This was Kenny's world, the Promised Land, where he put down his roots and constructed his kingdom. Of infamous repute, a flatland émigré of 50 year standing, Kenny knew everyone in the valley.

Kenny's ambition was always to be landlord to party people, ski bums, vacationers. This grew out of Kenny's avid skiing, and his experience, first-hand, of the dismal accommodations offered to ski bums. One of Vermont's better examples of the inconsistencies life holds, is the hatred, by Vermonters, of tourists (of which ski bums top the list), and the economic dependence on tourism that Vermonters rely on. Such discord is manifest in the treatment of outlanders, by Vermonters, that seems to feed on itself, engendering one of the largest winter sport areas in the world, while accommodations for enthusiasts continue to decline, having hit rock bottom some fifty years ago.

From such sepulchral bed and board lodgings, blossomed Kenny's birth as a landlord, once he acquired his first plot of land in the Mount Snow area in the baby booming age of the 1950s. Ten years later, and the drug explosion—flower power—which embodied Kenny's dream of free love—the avatar of the hippie. Drugs and communal living were to spell Kenny's doom, and the beginning of his selling off, piece by piece, his buildings and land that had been the growth period of Kenny's development.

What remained of Kenny's holdings have been allowed to deteriorate and suffer abuse by the very tenants who have paid back Kenny's lenience and kindness in the most horrid fashion—stealing, defiling and skipping out on the rent—crapping on the goodness with which Kenny had endowed them. Paying back Kenny's good faith by back-stabbing him.

Such treatment, over the years, including financial backers who have revanched on Kenny, have all left Kenny bitter and broke. Hence his deep involvement, his escape, into drugs. Drugs allowed Kenny a Lethean respite from his woes, while elevating him in the hierarchy of the drug world. As a drug provider (or king), Kenny reaped the rewards he always strove for. And although he would forever remain on the outside looking in, Kenny was easily placated with adoration and kudos, however false or feigned.

And thus we find Kenny at the time of my arrival in Vermont, as relevant in time and place to this tale (1996).

Kenny's orthodox Irish parents, of East Meadow, Long Island, were largely responsible for Kenny's ability to build the empire for which he is given credit. Kenny's da, union bigshot on the

Brooklyn docks, during the period prior to container shipping, allowed him enormous opportunity in cargo theft, graft, including payroll manipulation which, together, provided extensive connections within the construction unions, that trickled down to Kenny in stolen building materials, heavy equipment such as bulldozer and backhoe, and building experts, from swimming pool engineers to union masonry crews.

Kenny's ma, twenty-year veteran of Bell Telephone, financed Kenny's projects and paid the taxes on all Kenny's properties. She kept the books. After the demise of Ma and Da, Kenny was not up to the task of managing and maintaining his properties. This was the chink in Kenny's armor, his Achilles heel.

As long as Ma was alive, Kenny's taxes were paid and his dynasty remained intact. On his own, Kenny's trusting heart and ignorance left him quarry to every double-dealer and every sexy siren. And last but not least, was Kenny's avarice, which would lead him down roads of debt from which there was no way back, no extrication.

Of prime importance at Kenny's was the dope operation, that mainly included pot: an entire basement of a house, George's apartment, a couple of flat roofs, and the outdoor farm (mixed in with corn), and scattered in the woods—wherever sunlight reached, there were pot plants in tubs. Well over two thousand plants; some of the best dope you ever smoked, selling for $400 per ounce. The valley's smokers beat a path to Kenny's and George's for the dope. More than they could grow; they would buy pot to resell. Cocaine a big seller. Pills, Valium. And they sold to virtually anybody—high school kids. It's a miracle they were never busted. Everybody knew (the big secret). A veritable procession of vehicles, in and out, 24/7, copping dope. Kenny and George's dream come true. Not to mention, they were all continuously stoned, stoned out of their minds.

The pot-grow operation was very labor intensive. Due to space limitations, plants (from seedlings and clones, on up) had to be re-potted continuously—as they grew, into larger pots, and moved into appropriate areas based on size. Mixing the potting soil by fifty-pound bags (Pro-mix) with pearlite, vermiculite, dried blood, bone meal. Adding plant food, testing pH... A mess of dirt indoors. The watering system, yards and yards of hose on an adjustable wand; every day, the evaporation rate enormous due to the super-hot grow lights (at $150 each), connected to their own timer. Walls and ceilings covered in reflective Mylar panels—it looked like another world—oscillating fans blowing across the plants to hamper mold. Continual battles against spider mites, spraying under the leaves, rinsing those monsters, plants weighing 50 pounds in their wet pots. Trying anything such as ladybugs, by the hundred, watching the spider mites devour your best plants. Nursing the babies. Keeping up with pruning, sweeping and cleaning up. They needed help. It was a full-time job.

They were always trying to get me involved. Pestering me to turn over a portion of my house, my basement, the attic to grow pot. Bugging me to quit my dishwashing job at Dot's Diner and work for them with the pot. Promising me $10 per hour (on which they reneged). Neither Kenny or George had the patience to water so many plants every day. To cut and plant clones. To spray for mites. To clean up, to repot. I finally acquiesced and was hired. I kept track of the clones to develop the best strains, labeling each plant and entering them in a notebook, following their progress. But George was always swiping the best buds before they were ready, drying them in the microwave, to smoke, smoke, smoke up all the profits.

Finally, Kenny took George off the farming program. George was banned from the grow rooms. And when my bills started coming in for my labor, George hit the ceiling. George was so high-strung that, when I made a joke about requiring payment for running to Agway to purchase Quik-Gro for the clones, noting that the last time I did George a favor it ended up costing me $50, George hauled off and punched me in the mouth (drawing blood), convinced I was laughing at him... That was the end for me with the pot plants, and from associating with George. I repossessed my drums—I had been teaching George how to play. And thus was the beginning of George waging covert warfare against me and mine, a harassment campaign that would last for seven years, escalating, climaxing with my finally killing George after he tried to kill my pets. I went to Kenny, the police, year after year... nobody wanted to get involved, to help me, to go against Crazy George. To lean on the law.

But they were all quick to point the finger after the fact. After I dealt with George in the only way he understood, he demanded. For, "when the final showdown came to pass, a lawbook was no good."[1]

G eorge was a genuine nut case, but he played it up also, pretending to be (and becoming) crazier than he truly was. I saw through this, and hence George held little real terror for me. Not that he wasn't crazy; just that I saw his crazy act for what it was—an act. George had the confounded heart of a bully, a coward.

George had to keep people afraid of him. That was his edge. To be unpredictable and, thereby, scary. Kenny fed right into this and, once George saw that he had hooked Kenny, he kept the act cranked up, while poor Kenny believed he had a genuine wacko

---

1 "The Man Who Shot Liberty Valance," song by Burt Bacharach, Hal David

on his hands. Thus, George made a bigger and bigger fool of himself. Shadow boxing, twirling nunchakus. Somewhere along the line, George became wise to my second-sight and that made me a liability. But I didn't care; I was always confident that I would deal with George when the time came.

George had a history in the valley. George used to live with his older brother, a millionaire with a huge house on a prize plot, off Higley Hill. Something went sour, and George shot an arrow at his bro, which hit a glass door that deflected the lethal shot. George's next move was arson, burning brother's house to the ground—whose remains are somewhat of a testament to George's capabilities. Brother moved to California. Since that incident, decades ago, George lived as a kind of homeless person, inhabiting a deserted shack in the woods, with no facilities of any kind, working intermittently as a logger (which paid cash), or splitting firewood, or anything that would keep him isolated in the woods. For all that though, George knew everyone in the valley, was attractive to women, and was considered a good ol' boy by the loose circle of valley natives, all dopers. It was with such a resumé that George blew into Kenny's and, intuiting the opportunities (such as dope) leeched onto Kenny and, in the same breath, George leeched onto me as well; seeing me as helpful to George's covert agenda. From day one, I was "Davy, my smokin' buddy, yuk yuk." Talking me into drum lessons (against my will); as I was not desirous of teaching drumming to one who would never practice. I gave in for Kenny's sake, always pouring oil on the choppy waters, sensitive to alienating any of Kenny's friends. But I saw George as trouble from the get-go—one of my more reliable attributes, being able to read people, unerringly. Such was the scene when I arrived at Kenny's in 1996.

The bonds that drew Kenny and George together were firstly, illiteracy. Kenny could barely read or write (his biggest hang-up); Kenny could never relax and be comfortable unless his company was as dumb as himself. George spoke like a punch-drunk palooka, extra heavy for Kenny's sake.

Next, was Kenny's obsession with women's breasts. A voyeur (as he was too hung up to perform), Kenny surrounded himself with busty females, watched the Playboy channel, and boasted beyond belief of his sexual prowess, questioning others of their sexual exploits. Non-stop. George went right along with this fanfaronade, reacting in awe at Kenny's hyperbole, offering juicy stories of his own. And always ready to start Kenny up. "Hey, lookit the tits on her."

Dope was as important as breathing—the vanity that demanded everyone's respect and admiration. Everyone, that is, but me. George would focus his life on dope, a topic of which he never tired, telling Kenny how much money they could make.

Next, but not least, was money, money, money. And all the dumb flash junk money could buy. A house trailer, new, that just sat there. A vintage white Caddy (a lemon) that just sat there, for all the continual engine repairs. Useless kitchen gadgets; eating out; lawn mowers; snow blowers. Unhappy unless he was buying something new. A new car. A boat that he never used. Whatever someone else had, Kenny also needed. George encouraged these spending sprees. And finally, theft.

Anything was better if it was stolen. Daybreak cruises around diners to swipe CO_2 canisters, used in the grow room to increase the percentage of carbon dioxide in the air. George would make nighttime runs with the van to swipe building supplies from job sites (spotted by Kenny). Rubberized rolls of roofing, new toilets, sinks, glass, floor and wall tiles and their cement, by the five-gallon tubs. A tile-cutting tool. A slate-topped billiard table. A few cars. These were stolen during my last residency at Kenny's. They were kleptomaniacs. I was sick over this activity. When they saw that I didn't approve, they'd try to hide it. Same with the coke and pills; like they could really hide what they were doing right under my nose. This became a point of contention. But George was in for a penny, and for a pound. He would support Kenny in any lunacy. And thus were Kenny and George bonded, Kenny finding the companion he always longed for; George having stepped in shit[1] when he found Kenny.

Dot's Diner, Mount Snow, Vermont, my dishwashing job, two days before Christmas, 1996, and I am kicked out of Kenny's den of thieves. Driving around in a snowstorm, four feet of snow, bird and hamster and all my chattels. We moved into Dot and (hubby) Timmy's basement, so as not to leave them flat during the busiest week of the year. Digging my buried car out the next day, still snowing, vowing to return to New York where one can live on welfare. A desolate time, my only concern being for my pets; and I received my first SSDI check in the mail, $24,000.

I went straight back to Kenny's, where money talks, and offered to take over one of his trashed and abused camps (and replace Damon), making an offer he couldn't refuse. A fortuitous bad time for Kenny; all his winter tenants had moved out en masse, he had no wheels, no money, and along came myself, pulling hundred dollar bills out of my pocket like Kleenex. And that's how I purchased my house. I hired George (who couldn't even sweep a floor), paying him ten dollars per hour, while I went out and worked for half that, just to have someone working on my new house. Buying food and smoke for the two (Kenny and George) who didn't have a pot to piss in.

I gutted the place. Created one huge aviary, knocking down walls and ceiling, installing post and beam—freshly felled. I bought a barn, whose walls I removed and covered the whole interior of

---

1 good fortune

my house with barnboard. Tables and bed were whole trees, bark on, everything rough and raw. Huge glass windows, wood stove, new appliances. I spent $20,000 on fix-up, then SEVCA[1] came in to weatherize.

I purchased antique lamps, chairs, Persian carpet, lace curtains, macramé, afghans. Built-in desk, an entire sheet of plywood, shelving, wall maps. With branching tree-tops in every corner, whose canopy was vault-like; along with Manzanita branches jutting from the walls for Polly to perch on. Polly's open 6' × 4' wood frame with wood flooring hung from the ceiling at the foot of my bed— Polly's inviolable territory—beneath which was the hamster tank, atop massive tree trunks. Dirt box, wood ramps, merry-go-rounds throughout the room; heavy cardboard tubing, piles of soft fabric, cordwood, and potted plants—all hamster delights.

I created a palace that, ten years later, Kenny wanted back. "I can get $1,000 a month for this place." A pipe dream, since Kenny had signed away that house to me with an ironclad (section 8) homebuyer's contract. State sanctioned. Unbreakable. That's really what led to the shooting. George vowed to run me out for Kenny, ("I'll get rid of 'im for ya") but only orchestrated his own death. The price to evict me and bite the hand that fed them.

---

1 Southeastern Vermont Community Action

AUTHOR PROFILE

David Boglioli was born in Brooklyn, New York. He attended Outward Bound School, Rider College, and the Culinary Institute of New York. He is the author of the cookbook, *Canapés That Work*, the novella, *Wolf Pack*, and *Detour*, a real-life novel. He has been a professional drummer and a professional chef. He resides with his pets in New York City and Vermont.